Moral Pani

INTERSECTIONS

TRANSDISCIPLINARY PERSPECTIVES ON GENDERS AND SEXUALITIES
General Editors: Michael Kimmel and Suzanna Walters

Moral Panics, Sex Panics

Fear and the Fight over Sexual Rights

Edited by Gilbert Herdt

NEW YORK UNIVERSITY PRESS
New York and London

ITHACA COLLEGE LIBRARY

HQ
76.8
.U6
M67
2009

478838

NEW YORK UNIVERSITY PRESS
New York and London
www.nyupress.org

© 2009 by New York University
All rights reserved

Library of Congress Cataloging-in-Publication Data

Moral panics, sex panics : fear and the fight over sexual rights /
edited by Gilbert Herdt.
p. cm. — (Intersections: transdisciplinary
perspectives on genders and sexualities)
Includes bibliographical references and index.
ISBN-13: 978–0–8147–3722–4 (cl : alk. paper)
ISBN-10: 0–8147–3722–6 (cl : alk. paper)
ISBN-13: 978–0–8147–3723–1 (pb : alk. paper)
ISBN-10: 0–8147–3723–4 (pb : alk. paper)
1. Gay rights—United States—History. 2. Gender identity—
United States—History. 3. Sexual minorities—United States—History.
4. Ethical absolutism—History. I. Herdt, Gilbert H., 1949–
HQ76.8.U6   M67 2009
306.760973—dc22   2009000174

New York University Press books are printed on acid-free paper, and their
binding materials are chosen for strength and durability. We strive to use
environmentally responsible suppliers and materials to the greatest extent
possible in publishing our books.

Manufactured in the United States of America
c 10 9 8 7 6 5 4 3 2 1
p 10 9 8 7 6 5 4 3 2 1

This book is dedicated to five very special people—my oldest and closest friends from the 1970s to the 90s, whose love has enriched me and changed my life. I offer this work as a token of my respect and love for the many years of the shared project called friendship.

Erick Davis

Jeffrey Weiss

Theo Sandfort

Mirjam Schieveld

Theo van der Meer

Contents

Acknowledgments

This book is the product of some highly impressive presentations and subsequent conversations resulting from the major international conference Sexual Rights and Moral Panics, organized by the National Sexuality Resource Center and the Department of Sexuality Studies at San Francisco State University in June 2005. The conference attracted more than 300 people from thirty-some countries and provided the context for the fifth biannual meetings of the International Association for the Study of Sexuality Society and Culture (IASSCS), an organization that I am proud to have helped found more than a decade ago. Through the great support of the New York Ford Foundation, the conference was a success and spurred me on to produce this book, among the other useful products, informal and formal, that were to follow over the next three years.

I did serve as official chair of the Sexual Rights and Moral Panics conference, but the real work and genius behind it came from Dr. Niels Teunis, then an assistant professor at SFSU, the secretary-treasurer of the IASSCS, a collaborator, and also my long-term partner. He was invaluable in handling conference panics of our own. In a conference about moral panics, no one imagined the sudden and very strange potential disaster of having international conference participants come down with the chicken pox! That is what happened on the second day of the proceedings amid the more than 300 participants. Niels and the SFSU student health physician, through the provision of inoculations and not a small amount of panic containment, skillfully handled what was potentially a dreadful situation. With poise and calm, Niels handled the audience reactions and enabled the conference to go on without a hitch. I am forever indebted to him for this leadership and his great stewardship of the conference.

Additionally, I would like to thank Jennifer Feeney for her magnificent logistical support of the conference. Mona Sagapouletele and Ruslan Valeev, respectively, worked hard to resource and support the project and I am grateful to them. I am especially grateful to Sarah Miller for her important support in the completion of the final stage of this book.

I am very grateful to Barbara Klugman and the Ford Foundation in New York for their support of the conference and for continuing support of the NSRC, all of which has made this unique book possible.

I would also like to thank the Rockefeller Foundation for the 2006 residential fellowship at Villa Serbelloni in Bellagio, Italy, which made the completion of my own contributions to this book possible. The graciousness and help of the staff at Villa Serbelloni made my time there productive and dreamlike.

Last, this book is dedicated to five old and dear friends from the United States and Holland: Dr. Erick Davis, my oldest friend; Dr. Jeff Weiss, an old friend from both coasts; Mirjam Schieveld, Esq., my collaborator and friend from Holland; Dr. Theo Sandfort, a long-time Dutch friend transplanted to New York; and Dr. Theo van der Meer, a dear old friend and colleague from Amsterdam. I know that they will appreciate the passion and importance of this book, even if they might not agree with all of its content. I offer it with affection.

—Gilbert Herdt
San Francisco, California, July 2008

Introduction

Moral Panics, Sexual Rights, and Cultural Anger

Gilbert Herdt

Moral panics are the natural disasters of human society, and, like tsuna-mis and hurricanes, they not only present a crisis for stable social order but also contain much that threatens the well-being of individuals and communities.[1] The social context of moral panics, the sense in which in-dividuals and groups are perceived to pose a threat, the political invention and mobilization of this risk in the media and imagination, and whether these panics are spontaneous or socially generated, have long been de-bated. Such panics and great fears can be short or long term. However, the more serious they are and the longer they endure, the greater the like-lihood that societies will deal with them through the production of the reactive mechanisms of surveillance, regulation, discipline, and punish-ment. When sexualized, moral panics appear to "have much in common with the religious disputes of earlier centuries."[2] Today, however, the cohe-sion and linkage of successive panics as part of a general process of cul-tural anger employed to massage fear suggests the need for a new way of thinking about and analyzing these human disasters.

Sexual crises are known from such historically disparate phenomena as the fear of the masturbation "epidemic" that haunted the 18th and 19th centuries, moral crusades against abortion and unwed teenage mothers, antipornography campaigns, efforts to criminalize prostitution through attacks on the trafficking of women, and panics surrounding homosexual-ity and HIV in the 20th century. What marks each of these cultural hap-penings as "panics" is the level to which the societal and personal expres-sions are out of proportion with the threat posed by the so-called "folk devils" (e.g., masturbating children, unwed mothers) and evil-doers (e.g., homosexuals) groups. In the worst cases, the rights of these persons are qualified or revoked, undermining citizenship and threatening democracy. By citizenship, I mean the full rights, entitlements, and opportunity structures that support household security[3] and well-being ("life, liberty, and the pursuit of happiness") in the public domain as well as in the private lives of individuals. As the studies in this book reveal, cultural reactions of such an extreme kind are not rare; in fact, they seem to be growing more frequent. These panics provoke a cultural anger in the service of moral regulation[4] that targets the vulnerable in societies, compelling the contributing authors in this book to examine how panics provoke new techniques for governing others or for governing the self in the effort to strengthen well-being and social rights.

One of the contentions of this introduction is that moral panics in the United States are also becoming increasingly sexualized–for cultural and political purposes, in part through the Internet.[5] Examples range from panics having to do with gays in the Boy Scouts, fears of STDs, Janet Jackson's bra "malfunction" on television, and fears of oversexed women teachers in the classroom. For example, sociologist Janice Irvine reveals how, in the context of official U.S. government abstinence-only sex education, high school teachers are barred from discussing condoms, homosexuality, and other issues or they can be fired:[6] that is the power of a moral sexual panic that becomes institutionalized over time. As François Girard (2004) has noted, much of this sexual content is antiwoman and antigay. Longer term, the impetus for the sexual preoccupation "within the triangle of class, race, and nationality"[7] involves both the saturation and commercialization of sex in the United States and elsewhere, as well as the rise of neoconservatives and religious fundamentalism that is associated with sexual panics and moral politics. Some current observers believe that moral panics are becoming increasingly frequent and more prominent,[8] especially in the media. As argued below, the cultural politics surrounding homosexuality in countries such as the United States have been infused repeatedly with moral panics and anger, reflecting state economic and social failure[9] that taps into the fears, anxieties, and fantasies of a broad range of people. Some argue that these panics are explicitly used to achieve political hegemony.[10] Sex education has been systematically destabilized in the United States through moral panics.

Sexual panics in advanced welfare capitalism evoke strange, lurid, and disgusting images that merge media and popular reactions "below the surface of civil society,"[11] targeting individuals and groups in ways that produce coherent and incoherent ideological platforms and political strategies. The conscious and unconscious resonances of this process,[12] while unknown, are necessary in understanding the emergence of theoretical formulations of moral panics since the time of the seminal 1972 work of Stanley Cohen, who coined the idea of moral panics. Panics produce state and nonstate stigma, ostracism, and social exclusion—the opposite of what liberalism or neoliberalism has envisioned.[13] Sexual panics, when effective, are liminal and generate images of the monstrous. In media representations, especially,[14] sexual panics may generate the creation of monstrous enemies—sexual scapegoats. This "othering" dehumanizes and strips individuals and whole communities of sexual and reproductive rights, exposing fault lines of structural violence (e.g., racism, poverty, homophobia, etc.).[15] Of course, not all of these events are significant or efficacious. The pattern in these reactions and counterreactions hinge repeatedly on questions of normative sexual citizenship, reproductive accommodation and assimilation, or sexual orientation and gender resistance and defiance. This book examines these themes through the description and analysis of the intersection of moral panics and sexual rights globally but with particular reference to American hegemony at home and abroad.

Defining Panics

While a variety of historical and cultural studies previously examined fears, anxieties, and happenings such as witchcraft accusations and confessions, none of them did so systematically through the concept of moral panic. That awaited the 1972 work of British sociologist Stanley Cohen in his book *Folk Devils and Moral Panics*. Cohen argues that "societies appear to be subject, every now and then, to periods of moral panic. A condition, episode, person, or group of persons emerges to become defined as a threat to societal values and interests."[16] Cohen's study was an effort to understand youth subcultures, delinquency, and police control, and he strongly suggested that media were responsible for panics. Cohen's work did not explicitly concern sexuality, though sexuality was later linked to it in the critiques of Cohen's work by Jeffrey Weeks (1981), Gayle Rubin (1984), and Simon Watney (1987). Cohen's concepts have been critiqued in detail by British academics, including Charles Critcher[17] who looked at the media's role in causing panics; by Watney[18] who studied pornography, AIDS, and sexuality; and by Stuart Hall and his colleagues (1978), who theoretically explored the role of hegemony and police control in the forces that create panics. Angela McRobbie and Sarah Thornton (1995), as noted below, provide significant clarification of the limitations of the concept: that it has often been employed more as a label, thus impeding analysis. In this book we are especially concerned with clarifying the conditions under which moral panics are created at certain times and places and not at others; why certain audiences are more susceptible to the lure of moral panics in the media and others are not; and who gains or benefits from these panics and who is harmed. In other words, we wish to explore the limitations of the ideas in history and culture.

Thirty years after his first book, Cohen[19] reflected that his work "belongs to the distinctive voice of the late Sixties," because it explored anxieties about youth deviance, delinquency, and drugs. Cohen did comment on sexual child abuse scandals and terrible mob reactions to sexual predators in England, but otherwise, sexuality still was not a focus.

Here we need a sharper and somewhat more refined vocabulary to distinguish the social forms to be discussed in this book. Among these, I wish to contrast the following:

1) Moral shock. Moral shock is defined as a socially significant incident or threat that galvanizes public outrage[20] and that is commonly associated with "the idiom of disgust." As an example, Janice Irvine points to the Christian Right using outrage in opposing gay school reform, as in the controversies surrounding gay-straight alliances in high schools.[21]

2) Great fear. This is a term used by John Gagnon (2005) that has some of the connotations of moral shock but is extended over longer periods of time and is at a heightened level of anxiety and worry. Great fear can take either a sexual or nonsexual focus. As with the great fear of masturbation in the 18th and 19th centuries,[22] there were decades of worry that led to a subsequent "panic" without any necessary social changes to the state apparatus. Nevertheless, great fears can alter—even overhaul—and impact our cultural meaning systems and scripts, as we shall see.

3) Moral campaigns. Whether focused on sexual matters such as "purity" or sex education, temperance, or women's emancipation, moral campaigns are defined by strong moral and ethical sentiments and ideologies necessary for changing the way values are organized. Moral campaigns try to implement organizational transformation but though entirely through nonstate mechanisms.[23] Joseph Gusfield (1986) has similarly written of "symbolic crusades" in arenas such as the temperance movement, exploring how social class, domination, conflict, mobility, and reform all

conditioned reactions to moral campaigns as they destabilized public status. It is notable that many examples of anti-sex education fundamentalist efforts described by Irvine (2002) create rhetoric, volatile emotional climates, and mobilize broad constituencies through nonstate means that have broader purposes and hidden agendas[24] going far beyond the particular moral values exploited at the time.

4) Moral panics. Moral panics are large social events occurring in troubled times when a serious threat by evil-doers incites societal reaction: Cohen[25] has responded to criticism that the term "panic" suggests the connotation of "being out of control," which is unfortunate because these panics have a social shape. Sexual panics seem to be increasingly media orchestrated and purposeful or planned, which belies the irrationality implied by the term "panic," until it is realized that panics can be culturally staged. There is a difference in the directionality of these panics. For example, as noted below, it is useful to contrast the historical construct of the Cargo cult, in which the outcome is apocryphal and focused on agents outside of society, with the moral panic that identifies or represents fears of devils within our own midst.

5) Sexual panics. Sexual panics, as employed in this chapter, are a form or subspecies of moral panic. But, in the specifically modern transformation of these large social events we find a peculiar dimension that may be characterized as totalizing sexual events (what Thompson [1998] calls "all pervasive"). The Wilde and Clinton trials, noted below, began in scandal and ended in spectacle, and they belong to this genre. Through state and nonstate mechanisms that impinge on institutions and communities, people become totally overwhelmed by and defined through the meanings and rhetoric of sexual threats and fears. In this view, the sexual "folk devil"–the sexual other, whether oversexed, or undersexed[26]—is stripped of rights, and the cultural imagination becomes obsessed with anxieties about what this evil sexuality will do to warp society and future generations.

6) Cultural Anger. A central weakness of the concept of moral panic in the contextual study has always been its weakness in providing what Watney[27] calls an "overhead narrative," or the way one panic gives way to another and "one anxiety is displaced across different panics." It is this general process that I refer to as cultural anger—the marshalling of intense emotion across diffuse domains and arenas of action to unite disparate individuals and groups in political pursuit of a common enemy or sexual scapegoat. Remarkably, people compelled to vote out of cultural anger

seemingly act against their own socioeconomic interests—an enigma to which we shall return (see chapter 7).

Following Cohen's work there have been several comprehensive social and historical reviews explicitly focused on moral panics.[28] Erich Goode and Nachman Ben-Yehuda employed numerous examples of sexual panics, such as diffusion of sexual psychopath laws from the 1930s to the 50s (as noted by Sutherland in his classic study[29]), the "Boys of Boise" sexual perversion scandal, and antipornography and antiabortion fears (which became larger panics in the 1960s and 70s). The processes of moral panic Goode and Ben-Yehuda noted include heightened concern in a society, increased large-scale hostility, consensus that the problem is "real, serious, and caused by the wrongdoing group," a sense of disproportionality (the problem blown way out of proportion to its accurate appraisal), and volatility (being subject to extreme periods of intensification or lapse possibly resulting in institutional or routine measures that often affect state apparatus via institutional, legislative, and courtroom mechanisms).[30] The sociological framework of these case studies was typically incidental to the larger "social construction of deviance" perspective that informed social constructionism.[31] Thompson (1998) identifies contemporary sources of moral panics and concludes that panics are succeeding each other more rapidly, becoming more comprehensive or totalizing, and perhaps even constituting a "permanent" state of society. The latter is an oxymoron, according to Cohen.[32] This recent work has led to the important idea that the moral panic is not "an isolated phenomenon but a connective strategy"[33] for moral campaigns and the cultural politics and hegemony of civil society in late 20th- and early 21st-century social life.

Subsequently, a variety of social histories of sex panics, generally ushered in by the seminal work of Gayle Rubin (1984), opened up the notion of moral panic in American studies.[34] Rubin viewed a "moral panic" as a crusade that has been incited against a sexual community or deviant sexual practice. Her famous chart ("The Sex Hierarchy: Charmed Circle Versus the Outer Limits," 153) demonstrates a "charmed circle" of social hierarchy in which the sexual "normals" and the "scapegoats" are at the mercy of panics because their sexualities are "evil" compared to "traditional" hetero-normative standards. Others have followed in this line of analysis, and social histories of actual sex panics[35] have found their way into the literature. For example, Fred Fejes (2000) examines the first murder and sex panic in postwar Miami and links mass media panic to the marginalization of homosexuality during the Cold War.

The point is that these studies examined "great fears, both sexual and non-sexual, [that] have swept through many cultures,"[36] while "sexual panics" was not the center of this valuable line of work. Moreover, as Gagnon (2004) has narrated so brilliantly in retrospect, earlier researchers were generally more optimistic about progress in politics and sexual culture than has been borne out in fact.

As these ideas and the critique of moral panics as representational forces suggest, panics are not "an isolated phenomenon but a connective strategy"[37] for the ways in which cultural elites can dominate media and discourse in civil society. Through moral panics, the tug-of-war between state and nonstate and between political, religious, and social coalitions and civil society are reproduced, and these struggles are most recently concerned with issues of rights.

Historicizing Moral Panics

Perhaps the oldest and most famous of all moral panics was the trial of Socrates in ancient Athens. In the view of I. F. Stone, this historic panic was caused by the fear of moral pollution among the students and followers of Socrates, whose political views challenged democracy in the Greek city-state. Socrates dared to suggest that a wise monarch would rule better than a democrat, which provoked a storm of outrage—as well as the reaction (ultimately successful) of silencing him.[38] Socrates responded to his opponents that "He who is now taking away our freedom of speech is also destroying the customs of democracy as surely as if he were gouging out the eyes or cutting out the tongue."[39] Through his suicide—aimed at marking the importance of his ethical stance—Socrates may be claimed as the first of many victims of moral panics in Western civilization. The apocryphal characteristics of this story also suggest the cosmic potential for moral panics to turn political fear into a broader cultural anger that seeks scapegoats.

Moral panics are processes of representing and demonizing scapegoats in popular culture and media, commonly identified with the dread of "folk devils," or subalterns, undermining cherished sociality and morality. But who or what do the panics scapegoat and why? Historians have demonstrated in key cases such as the great fear of masturbation in the 18th and 19th centuries that the panic focused on younger males and provided a powerful mechanism for evading or redirecting unwanted emotions and experiences (such as anger or shame) ultimately concerned with larger patterns of dreaded social failure. Hunt speculates that the deep and persistent anxieties associated with Britain's ability to govern and sustain its empire led to the masturbation panic in that country.[40] Countless children were shackled and mistreated at the hands of parents, teachers, and doctors whose actions, by today's standards, would be child abuse. It seems likely that it was cultural anger that mobilized the 19th-century imagination of masturbation to feed the growing crisis of masculinity and social antagonism surrounding the ebb of British power.[41]

Historically, moral panics such as these have been fired in part by the now famous folk language of a "slippery slope" of moral decay. Once moral "weakness" or temptation is given in to, masturbation leads to homosexuality or degeneracy for boys, or masturbation leads to loss of virginity, lesbianism, prostitution, or nymphomania for girls. As historian Alan Hunt notes, the public had long feared that "the slippery slope is not only a private fate, but also a social disaster; masturbation leads downwards to the theatre, ballroom, public house, bad company, and everlasting ruin."[42]

The Dutch historian, Theo van der Meer (1994) has delineated the "slippery slope" that surrounded the rise of the scourge of "sodomy" in 18th-century Holland. The notion of the slippery slope initiated a moral panic and fear that Catholics had introduced the "sin of sodomy" into Holland in the early modern period, with boys as young as eleven, and older men too, arrested for acts of sodomy. The public came to fear this as a widespread secret network—a remarkable new imaginal (that is, a socially imagined form of conduct and action in the society). As the sexual fear grew, the sodomites were rounded up and executed—first in secret and then in public—as a lesson to people not to fall prey to moral depravity lest they, too, slide down. Eventually the slippery slope preoccupied myriad areas of post-Reformation Dutch thinking about the need to stay busy, be productive, be morally upstanding, and be sexuality sanitary.

Indeed, this provides an exquisite example of panic made into state policy through the Dutch approach to the "cordon sanitare" on which is based the famed "red light" district of Amsterdam and other cities. This state policy was a new cultural mechanism for regulating prostitution and thus solidifying the boundary between the "chosen" and the "fallen." Examples such as these support Foucault's (1980) idea that internalized norms for morally acceptable male gender roles and intimate sexual relationships advanced a new regime of self governance and discipline in the modern period. Even today, gay bashers in Holland are prone to offer the slippery slope argument in defense of their acts of violence against homosexuals with whom they had consensual sex, often for payment.[43]

It is fascinating to see, three hundred years later in the United States, the same notion of a slippery slope,[44] of sexual conservatives' fearful warnings of the risk to heterosexuals by online purveyors of sexual panics. Through this ancient folk model, contemporary moralizers still argue that if marriage is legalized for gay men and lesbians, Americans will want incest, bestiality, and other horrors legalized.[45]

The great fear surrounding gay and lesbian marriage is likely to be with us for a long time (see chapter 5). But not all moral panics are so long lived. In the early 1980s there was a moment in Atlanta, Georgia, when it was so feared that mosquitoes could spread HIV disease that people stayed in doors, avoided going to work, or school, and so on. After a couple of days the panic fizzled. Muggings fanned media fears and sensational outrage associated with police brutality in England; these lasted for quite a while and initiated the original notion of moral panic.[46] Satanic ritual abuse of children beginning in 1980 in the United States and Western Europe became a widespread but short-lived moral panic that ultimately proved to be groundless.[47]

Panics may also have the ultimate effect of displacing responsibility for security and well-being from the self and community to real or imagined others on the margins of society. Consider, for example, the infamous moral panic of homosexual predation that came to be known as the "Boys of Boise" scandal at the height of the Cold War. The scandal became an instant national sensation in the United States, featured on the cover of the *New York Times Magazine*.[48] Subsequent analysis revealed that the charges against "humble and powerless victims" were largely contrived and blown out of proportion—and even politically inspired.[49] The Boise homosexual panic was one of many such panics of the 1950s that secured a new chain of folk devils or demons from the 1930s to the 1950s, beginning with the Catholics and on to the Jews, "Commies," and "Homos."[50] Some people do stand up against panics and speak out against the victimization of innocents or uphold the juridical principle that one is innocent until proven guilty.[51] However, when sex panics and moral campaigns to demonize categories of people are implemented "with the full force of the law,"[52] compassion is hard to come by. For example, when there were widespread calls at the beginning of the AIDS pandemic for "mass quarantining of people," few spoke out in protest.[53] Gary Dowsett chronicles this insidious story in the United States and Australia in chapter 4.

Do people speak out against the violations of rights and citizenship, especially at the beginning of a moral panic? Sometimes yes, and sometimes, when fears are heightened, as with parents who feel "weird" if they defend sex education against its fanatical enemies,[54] the answer is "no." There were few defenders in Boise, and the innocence of the alleged perpetrators was entirely beside the point. As one local farmer remarked, it did not matter if the homosexuals had actually sexually violated the boys or not, "they should be run out of the state" anyway.[55] The sexual sanitation provided by moral panics, the ability of the police or other agents to undertake a "cleansing" of the social body to rid it of miscreants in what Cathy Cohen (1999) has referred to as the "politics of deviancy," is all too painful to observe. Such cases also reveal the generalized crisis associated masculinity and gender roles in the early Cold War period,[56] which Enloe (1993) has referred to as the "militarization of masculinity" in the post–Cold War period. It was legitimately asked not only if homosexuals would corrupt normal men but also whether they lacked "the sort of manly qualities presumed to be needed to wield a gun."[57]

As Judith Levine argues in a controversial book about young people's sexuality and the fear and misrepresentation surrounding the pedophile panic (the book itself created a minor moral panic), that contemporary moral panics sexualize the scapegoats as sexual "monsters" and "predators," whether in the neighborhood, the nuclear family, or now on the Internet.[58] These sexual panics dehumanize the alleged perpetrators, some of whom are innocent bystanders, stripping them of rights and destroying their lives, while at the same time leaving children more vulnerable than ever.[59] It is extraordinary that Hunt's 1998 historical study of school masters and teachers enforcing mechanisms for the control of masturbation in the 19th century reaches the same conclusion: the panic worsened the condition of children while it did nothing to alleviate the fears and anxieties of their parents. Likewise, the threat of the pedophiles (via the Internet) is as great as ever,[60] the prior panics not having secured new mechanisms of protection for individuals or communities and posing the great probability of future panics targeting the same scapegoats.

The link among religion, antisexual and sex-negative attitudes, and moral panics in the modern period is well known.[61] America's Puritan background surely provides support for chronic cycles of purity, hygiene, and Christian reactions to premarital sex, homosexuality, masturbation, and a variety of related fears and anxieties.[62] In the later 20th century these religious and moral campaigns have targeted vulnerable populations.[63]

They have gradually increased both in frequency and number throughout the period following the ascendancy of Reagan and neo-Conservatism.[64] Lessons from the struggle for reproductive rights are also germane. As Joffe's work on reproductive rights has made clear from the beginning, Americans regarded birth control as "immoral" because it made possible nonprocreative sex between married persons.[65] Subsequent changes in the law over the past decade have made abortions increasingly inaccessible to women, especially the poor.[66] Since then, media and electoral campaigns in response to moral panics waged against reproductive rights led to the policy dilemma that the rights could be preserved, but only if the movement became more conservative itself.[67] These transformations are examined by DiMauro and Joffe in chapter 2, but it is useful to note that they are not unique to the United States. Correa and Parker (2004) have shown that new religious fundamentalism is a backlash to cultural change and theocracy in Islamic countries and Pentecostal and radical fringes of the Catholic Church in the South.

Moral panics thus compress social, political, media, and psychological fears and anxieties, whether real or culturally imagined (often a combination of both) and solidify the boundaries between victim and victimizer, safety and danger, based on the widespread notion that folk devils are inside one's own group. When the political reaction and will are great enough, as in "longer-lasting panics," new institutional or organizational mechanisms are created to deal with the threats.[68] The targeted "undesirables" are chased out or scapegoated, new controls are implemented to regulate these populations, yet future panics ensue. It may be argued that these spectacles actually weaken the social fabric, though they may strengthen the hand of elites, at least temporarily.

Anthropologists have long studied a phenomenon in tribal societies at the time of first contact, conquest, and colonization by Western colonial powers that bears a family resemblance to moral panics but takes a different cultural form: the Cargo Cult, or Millenarian Movement. For example, in response to the arrival of allied forces on the Admiralty Islands during World War II, local people built a kind of airstrip, destroyed their religious and traditional possessions, and awaited the arrival of new riches from afar.[69] Prophets announced that the world was ending or changing.[70] Among the Trans-Fly peoples of New Guinea, entire villages destroyed their ritual cult houses and upset and destabilized conventional gender roles in anticipation of an expanded, brighter, richer and more powerful future, albeit one that they did not understand. These peoples were ineffective in controlling their dealings with the other,[71] and utopias of this kind were the result. They often failed, but were no less significant in prompting change.

What is remarkable about these Cargo Cults is that they were prompted by external connections—hegemonic and conquering states from the outside—which resulted not in the scapegoating of *internal* enemies but in the fearful, ambivalent representation of imaginals that promised a future of wealth and power. Mary Douglas (1970), a British structuralist who was interested in how notions of purity and danger got transposed onto categories of nature and culture in the social imagination of humans, argued long ago for a theory of grid/group control relations that supports the effort to conceptualize how and why moral panics scapegoat and victimize in the United States and complex modern nations. "Group" in contemporary life is difficult to define. Increasingly, moral values and fears have become the boundary conditions for saying who is and who is not a moral, full citizen and human being. If Cargo Cults define futures by way of unknown or unknowable outsiders, sexual panics fuel cultural anger toward those inside society who pose serious risk, and the panics are experienced phenomenologically as threatening the future or the reproduction of one's own society, so that the folk devils must therefore be identified, incarcerated, exiled, or destroyed.

Sexual Scandals, Media, and Modernity

Although sexual panics target enemies within a group, in the modern period, the media, first in print and then in radio and on television and now on the Internet, play an enormous role, sometimes to paradoxical effect, in actually spreading fearful imagery and ideas far into the culture.[72] The literature on moral panics has, since its inception,[73] been confused, ambivalent, and contradictory regarding the relationships between media and panics.[74] Stuart Hall and colleagues (1978) argue that media only reproduce and sustain moral panics originating with public officials (the police, for example). Hall thus assigns a greater historical specificity to social regulatory processes and begins the trend of detailing the role of the media that goes beyond mechanistic and reifying notions of moral panics driven by media and other social institutions that were never sustainable.[75] Watney was particularly skeptical about a mechanistic reliance on media, suggesting that larger social and imaginative processes must operate to explain "the overall ideological policing of sexuality, especially in matters of representation."[76] Hier has also been critical of the conflation of "media discourse and social perception," but even more so, he has critiqued the failure to theorize how social perception is connected to collective action.[77]

When great sexual fears drive media to broadcast and exaggerate fears beyond their local source, these panics have the effect of massaging the feared moral decay through social and political tactics or media into everyday speech and habits. Take note, however, of the paradoxical effect of some media panics. Seemingly it is as if a moral campaign meant to slander a public figure or depose him or the effort to remove a hated political group from opposition has the reverse effect of purposely spreading the dangerous knowledge, forbidden meanings, and corrupt practices into the general population, entirely counter to the presumed aim of containing or stamping them out. The moral panic of sodomites in Holland seems to have had this unintended historical effect, as did the great masturbation fear.

Consider the classic illustration of how print media fermented sexual panics during the London trial of Oscar Wilde in the early 1890s. As is well known, the accusations of sodomy brought by Lord Douglas, the younger lover of the famed playwright (Wilde being a married man with children), opened perhaps the first media scandal of the modern period, massaged by newspapers around the world.[78] It was not just the sexual transgression (perhaps more common than was known) that was at stake. Indeed, masculinity, social-class stability, and the emergence of a modern sense of internalized homophobia (that is, the sense of self-hatred created through same sex desire that tormented and then provoked the accusation of sexual victimization) were surely a paradigmatic cultural message.[79] The Wilde trial criminalized "sodomy" ("unnatural sex") and homosexual identity and also formed the basis of a large-scale production of knowledge and meanings associated with naming "the vice that dared not speak its name." Victorians of the time paradoxically may have had their sexual attitudes altered, their vocabulary expanded, and their private lives exposed to same-sex desires and behaviors that should have scandalized the moral guardians of the times.[80] The effect was to speed up social change in the cultural meanings surrounding sexuality and homosexuality. This example seems counter to the effort to regulate sexual scapegoats, but that is the Foucaultian paradox—panics inflame policing and control while concomitantly spreading new sexual meanings and cultural practices via late 19th-century print media.

A century later in the United States, a similar process seems to have occurred surrounding the extramarital sexual scandal of President Bill Clinton. Similar to the trial of Wilde, the world was saturated day after day with the shocking details of the scandals, including, for example, discussions of telephone calls Clinton had while being fellated, thus introducing concepts (particularly "oral sex") that were previously taboo for the mass media and presumably unknown to small-town America where the Cold War had surrendered its grasp on sexuality very slowly. Will we come to see the paradigmatic effect of the Clinton scandal like that of Oscar Wilde's—actually opening up a broader, more sustained dialogue about sexuality in the United States? Whatever the answer, critics have seen in the spectacle an example of how difficult it is to create a "winning script" for media spin, even when the public sees a moral panic as politically inspired.[81] Janice Irvine has suggested that the attempted impeachment of President Bill Clinton over his sexual adultery provoked "sexual shame," while the panic "prompted widespread sexual dialogue" about oral sex and adultery.[82] This panic in the late 20th century was fanned on television, radio, and the Internet, not just in the newspapers as was the case in the Wilde trial. One effect of this was that the public was much more skeptical of sexual surveys and polls.[83] Thus, the political risk of a political campaign using moral panics is the indirect change in producing counterhegemonic discourse.

My own sense is that the 1980s ushered in new discursive possibilities because of the AIDS pandemic and media coverage that constantly massaged public opinion, introducing terms such as "anal intercourse" for the first time. Presidents Reagan and George H. W. Bush could never bring themselves to utter the term "gay" or "homosexual" in public. Notably, it was President Clinton who did so in the context of the policy on gays in the military that came to be known as "Don't ask, don't tell."[84] Surely, Foucault (1980) would see in these paradoxical effects of what Reagan would not say and Clinton would, the demonstration of his view that sexual discourse shatters silence, increases social control by the state, incites self-regulation and preoccupation with the sexuality of the normative self, and hence heightens both the power of "sex" and its threat to society. At any rate, it is clear that sexual conservatives and Republican strategists seized on the Monica Lewinsky scandal as a way of undermining Clinton's moral authority and destroying political opposition to their own political agenda.[85] One thing is clear: as Clinton's approval ratings stayed in the 60 to 70 percent level throughout the trial, public opinion recognized a distinction between the political office and the private citizen. Ironically, some believe that the American people proved once and for all that there is but a tenuous connection between what they expect of the president as a political leader and what they want to know about his private life.

Panics can turn into cultural spectacles such as the Wilde and Clinton trials. Spectacles are cultural events that take on social importance, inciting new kinds of talk and action so as to constitute a cultural happening–a unique marker and historical cohort event[86] in the lifetimes of individuals and societies. Everything is defined with respect to the trial of Clinton, before and after, in media lingo. Surely in contemporary society, and particularly today's television and Internet media, sex panics have an entertainment value (of course the Wilde and Clinton sexual scandals are exmaples) and voyeur or curiosity capital that "sells" or markets products, whether newspapers or books, television products, souvenirs, and kitsch memorabilia. Media mogul Rupert Murdoch exploited this in the AIDS epidemic.[87] Nearly twenty years later, as Frank Rich (2004) argues, far from being merely a cog in the machines of capitalism, Rupert Murdoch's FOX news is the "true cultural elite" through the sensationalizing of media events ranging from Britney Spears's escapades, the so-called Janet Jackson "wardrobe malfunction" on primetime, and so on (see Herdt, chapter 5).

Historically, sexual spectacles incite fearful feelings and a sense of danger to society and concomitantly compel novel forms of public declarations such as sightings of strange and ominous events, confessions, and accusations of guilt of sexual congress with devils or practice of witchcraft. These declarations broke the silence surrounding topics such as witchcraft during the Renaissance period or, later, drugs and sodomy. These are all processes of radical social change long known to social study.[88]

The power of the media to influence sexuality and sex research in a new and significant way came when Alfred Kinsey published his infamous sex studies (*Sexual Behavior in the Human Male* in 1948 and *Sexual Behavior in the Human Female* in 1953). A zoologist and researcher profoundly interested in nature and natural variation, Kinsey also wrapped himself in the cloak of scientific objectivity (he often wore a white clinician's smock when interviewing) and appealed to the authority of the medical doctor in achieving his success in stalking the dragon of sex in mid-century American society. The near panic that ensued from the publication of his first book in 1948, resulting in accusations that he was promoting communism and moral depravity, cost him his funding from the

Rockefeller Foundation and no small amount of personal stress and pathos, precipitating ill health and premature death. In fact, Kinsey as a personality became the object of a moral panic in his own time—not unlike a messianic figure or prophet who cries out for reform and liberation—and then targeted as a folk devil. James Jones's (1997) biography of Kinsey attests to this, as well as the superb 2004 film *Kinsey*, which has done more than any other Hollywood movie to awaken Americans to the repetitive idée fix (Freud would call it a "repetition compulsion") of moral panic in their sexual lives. Kinsey was like Freud, Malinowski, Margaret Mead, and other academic sexual progressives of the modern period, not only in being a "sexual enthusiast,"[89] but also in seeing himself as a reformer of attitudes, mores, and institutions, as all Kinsey's biographies agree.[90] Fifty years later, significant right-wing Web sites slander Kinsey as "evil" and the "cause" of sexual immorality in our time, causing no end of continuing difficulties to the well-respected Kinsey Institute at Indiana University.[91]

The Kinsey studies illustrate, as Gagnon (2004) has repeatedly suggested, the difficult social politics, changing historical mores, and ethical and scientific problems associated with sexual morality in small-town America. Kinsey exposed the subterranean underside of American life that both shamed and titillated Americans[92] and hence revolutionized the study of sexuality.[93] But Kinsey did not truly understand the political opposition he would engender (he was, after all, a zoologist) and could never formulate an adequate political response to the panic. A generation would pass until the next and more statistically significant survey of sexual behavior would take place in the United States. Not surprisingly, its team would have a much better strategic response.[94] However, that did not stop the wrath of then-Senator Jesse Helms, who blocked its funding, accusing the scientific investigators of "perversions" and having "promoted marijuana," among other such scurrilous accusations. Notwithstanding this last example, the fact is, American academics have handled sexual panics surrounding media and science poorly due to the absence of an articulated vision or conception of precisely who the enemy is—the purveyors, not victims, of panics.

Simon Watney has famously complained of media exploitation of panics. He wrote: "the theory or moral panics is unable to conceptualize the mass media as an industry which is intrinsically involved with excess."[95] He chafes at the notion that media cannot distinguish between "real" panics and their "representations" or that media moguls such as Rupert Murdoch could care less about whether local sensitivities are violated by their exploitation of scandals and panics. However, Watney continues, "Moral panics seem to appear and disappear, as if representation were not the site of permanent ideological struggle over the meaning of signs."[96] I shall return to this view later, but I want to point out that sexual panics go beyond representation, a notion that preoccupied social and cultural theory in the 70s and 80. Moral panics in their awful sweep do material damage, undermine careers, incite riots, and kill people. As a panic picks up momentum, in stories of mass sexual abuse of children by adults,[97] for example, media frenzy takes over, and the cultural spectacle becomes a form of capital for media consumption. The point is not the difference between real and unreal representation—all of these messages and scripts are "real" parts of the process of empowering some individuals and groups and dehumanizing others. Panics are instrumental to a broader production of cultural anger out of which churns the neopolitical order today.

Moral panics overwhelm individual rights and require a new attention to the role that sexual panics play in perpetuating structural violence and reproducing forms of inferior citizenship. As these subjectivities emerge into consciousness and social expression, they unleash powerful energy, titillate and entertain, creating the sense of cultural spectacle, provoking a new power (Foucault might have called it the "biopower") previously contained in a repressed or tabooed discourse such as "virginity" or "sodomy" or the oral sex of presidents. All of these forces of moral regulation ultimately disempowered the self; that is, mechanisms come into place that emotionally and ideologically connect state and nonstate agents, institutions, and the victimized cultural imaginals. Not only do panics expose the limitations of individualism and rights precisely at the moment that market capitalism is becoming the most sophisticated, synthetic, and hegemonic entity capable of promoting packaged sex, but panics also reveal "an emphasis on the moral deviant/degenerative to engage a morally responsible 'ethos,' which is co-opted to refashioning of the self."[98]

Sexual Panics and Structural Violence

Human societies across time and space often have experienced times of dread, anxiety, fear, panic, disgust, depression, and denial to such an extreme degree that social collapse seemed possible. Some of these events may simply be random, as when natural disasters result in ecological collapse, depopulation, and social decline,[99] as Hurricane Katrina revealed.

Linked to such histories are the politics of adaptation, survival, and colonization amid the usual fault lines of structural inequalities (such as racism, for example). While examining a variety of forms of social deviance, including sexuality, Stanley Cohen and others in this line of theory were not primarily concerned with structural violence as a determinant of panics, as we think of these today. Cohen's (2002) retrospective reveals cases of sexualized panics, particularly sexual abuse, and these are not without interest. Hall and his colleagues (1978) did look at the effect of media panics' impact on racism. Clearly, in the modern period, systematic forms of discrimination within and across societies have been pivotal in the production of panics.

Moral panics expose the ideologies, hierarchies, and social fissures of societies, typically registered, as with many human phenomena, along the lines of systemic forms of structural violence. Nowhere is this more pernicious than in the reproduction of sex and gender differences.[100] Medical anthropologist Paul Farmer has defined poverty, racism, and inadequate health care as among the greatest threats to common human dignity.[101] A recent review adds homophobia, heterosexism, ableism, classism, and xenophobia to the list of forms of discrimination and dehumanization that result in violence against the self and sexuality.[102] AIDS has been particularly shaped by the social disparities of society.[103] Farmer has also raised the fundamental question of how or through what mechanisms "social forces ranging from poverty to racism become embodied in individual experience?"[104] As will now be apparent, I view sexual panics today as among the most pivotal mechanisms—political, economic, and religious—that reproduce structural violence of all kinds: they serve to embody fear, disgust, and social exclusion in speech, meanings, and practices.[105] Teunis and Herdt (2006) have examined several critical cases linking sexual inequality to systematic structural violence, including gay-straight alliances in schools, people with disabilities, young women of color in classrooms teaching sexual education, gay men involved in circuit parties—all of which reveal moral panics, pivoting on the violation of norms and normative citizenship.

Connecting the literature on moral panics in the United Kingdom and the emergence of a cultural model dealing with sexual panics in the United States is the work of Gayle Rubin (1984). Her classic paper anticipated the structural violence analyses to be followed in the 90s through Lisa Duggan.[106] Cohen's work preceded the problematic of heteronormativity, sexual citizenship, and the politics of using moral panics to "coerce people into normality," that distinguished the deep, organic analysis of Rubin. Her influential critique of feminist resistance to sexuality analysis laid the groundwork for the new thinking of the 90s by feminists and those who followed.[107]

In the modern period, Rubin understood that sexual panics were a means of inflicting structural regulation on categories of people. By examining what she called "sexual hierarchies" or ideologies, including those of medicine, on contemporary thought, her anthropological perspective raised critical questions about the role that normativity and cultural anger play in the management of sexual citizenships in societies:

> All these hierarchies of sexual value–religious, psychiatric, and popular—function in much the same way, as do ideological systems of racism, ethnocentrism, and religious chauvinism. They rationalized well being of the sexually privileged and the adversity of the sexual rabble. It is difficult to develop a pluralistic sexual ethics without a concept of benign sexual variation. Variation is the property of all life. . . . Yet sexuality is supposed to conform to a single standard. One of most tenacious ideas about sex is that there is one best way to do it, and that everyone should do it that way.[108]

In what must surely be one of the more trenchant and prescient reviews in social science, Rubin specifically examines how a new wave of sexual panic has threatened to unleash powerful forces of structural violence in the United States after 1977: "Right-wing opposition to sex education, homosexuality, pornography, abortion and premarital sex moved from the extreme fringes to the political center stage" as these crusaders "discovered that these issues had mass appeal." [109] She goes on to say that sexual reaction played a role in the election of 1980, through organizations such as the Moral Majority. Rubin, writing in the context of a growing AIDS pandemic, later identified a coming moral panic launched by the right wing on AIDS as among the real threats of our times.[110] She concludes that "AIDS will have far reaching consequences" for sexuality in general and homosexuality in particular.[111] How much this was true has been born out in Herdt (1997), Levine (1998), Watney (1987), and Rubin (1997) herself, writing on the impact of the epidemic that was to devastate the gay ("leather") community in San Francisco.

In the 1980s, the influential work of Simon Watney (1987) explored deep links between sex panics and sexual structural violence through examination of the panic of the AIDS epidemic. As noted, Watney was skeptical about the concept of moral panics, suggesting that they could not account for either the imaginative processes of conscious and unconscious meanings that formed the "deeper resonances" of panics. He believed that the panics themselves always linked to a preexisting process of victimization. Watney recalls that no less a figure than William F. Buckley, Jr., then the editor of the *National Review*, a darling of the neoconservative movement, and friend to Ronald Reagan, called for the incarceration of gay men.[112] It is useful in this context to recall that Herek's (2004) definitive study of sexual prejudice sees homophobia as a form of structural violence that seeks scapegoats by relationship to the object regarded as the greatest risk—homosexuals to heterosexual men.

Panics and the Disruption of Rights

Structural violence and sexual prejudice constitute powerful historical forces that have worked in tandem to provoke moral and sexual panics in late modern societies. The work in this field came before the emergence of a notion of sexual rights, although reproductive health and rights had been growing for years.[113] The introduction of sexual rights into debates about moral and sexual panics surely suggests a fundamental change about the identity and representation of the advocate for the sexually oppressed, the sexual scapegoat. Sexual rights have now come to mean the right of access to the highest standard of sexual health care.[114] One who willingly speaks out on behalf of rights, who no longer passively accepts incarceration, policing, or exile, is a new kind of social agent in the context of a sexual panic. To recall the words of famed gay African American writer James Baldwin, "The victim who is able to articulate the situation of the victim has ceased to be a victim; he, or she, has become a threat."[115]

What was added to critical studies of sexual panic was a new concept of rights, conceptualized as "human rights" as famously ushered in by declarations of the United Nations after World War II, a new and historically distinctive development that began to increase in importance in the last part of the 20th century.[116] An emphasis on social justice and liberationist pedagogy, often referenced to the work of Paulo Freire (1970), anticipated the U.N. declarations. However, Freire never explicitly examined sexuality as "a common striving toward awareness of reality . . . for the education process or for cultural action of a liberating character."[117]

Seen in historical and cultural perspective, there is good reason why sexualized moral panics could not have been distinctive analytical or theoretical concerns prior to the 1990s. The human rights paradigm did not arise by accident; it was the product of intense changes in societies, including in the United States, which have increasingly challenged traditional notions of sexuality. This is augmented by the cultural growth of "recreational" sex since the 1960s,[118] giving rise to what Giddens (1992) has called "plastic sex"—that is, malleable forms of intimacy. Watney (1987) has long insinuated that it was the change in perception of sexual desires and the migration of people in and between sexual cultures that provoked panics. Such a paradigm is in stark contrast to the sexual reform movements of the 1960s and 70s—a period in which Gagnon (2004) suggests that there was a significant increase in sexual behavior. While the middle class accepted this trend, goaded by the feminist movement and the changes associated with egalitarian sexual relations,[119] such changes were never accepted by neoconservatives and fundamentalists.[120] Panics have repeatedly surrounded new forms of intimate relationships, such as the threat to feminists by sadomasochistic sex, predicted by Rubin (1984), the controversies surrounding HIV in the African American community,[121] and, most recently, the threat of transgender individuals.[122] All are indicators of social change; they signify the emergence of new "sexual markets" that socially organize these diverse forms of sexuality[123] to challenge traditional definitions of citizenship.

The "sexual revolution" of the 1960s, the second in the 20th century, was famously associated with the invention of the birth control pill around 1964, which ushered in recreational sex. However, a large-scale stream of new social movements, led by second-wave feminism and the rise of the gay liberation movement, sowed the seeds of a cultural reaction a generation later,[124] the so-called Reagan revolution of "economics and cultural values"[125] that intensified the cultural anger of neoconservatives. These issues are reviewed in chapter 2 by Diane DiMauro and Carole Joffe. As the AIDS/HIV moral panic transformed into a social movement in the late 1980s, a reaction to the medical hegemony of doctors and government and public health scientists and claims for a new self-help formation based on the women's health movement of the 1970s, activists, followed by academics[126] began to study sexuality and reproductive health, identities, and behaviors with new funding. New support for grassroots community-based organizations helped to advance sexual rights.[127]

As mapped out in Teunis and Herdt (2006), it was during this period that significant changes began to occur in the construction of public health, political, and policy debates surrounding sexuality: namely, the transition from identity-based sexual movements, such as the gay and lesbian movement in the post–World War II phase in the mid to late 1960s, to the sexual health movement of the 1980s and 90s. In fact, science in general, and social science in particular, were silent or reluctant to address this gap or to respond to the challenges of explicit or implicit government-sponsored sexual inequality, at least until the World Conference on Human Rights in Vienna in 1993.[128] Note, for example, the very slow response of academics to the AIDS crisis in the United States, with the psychologists responding earlier than anthropologists.[129]

The now-famous Cairo and Beijing conferences of the mid-1990s changed the face of human rights in a positive way and influenced cultural forces such as moral panics. The International Conference on Population and Development (ICPD), held in Cairo in 1994 was an historic turning point in bringing a broad spectrum of reproductive rights into the global arena. ICPD created a Programme of Action to promote gender equality and girls' education, influencing sexual and reproductive behavior in very significant ways.[130] The ability to have free choice in reproductive decisions and "the right to attain the highest standard of sexual and reproductive health"[131] was a critical achievement of these events. The following year in Beijing, the Fourth World Conference on Women placed sexuality front and center in the discussion of sexual rights. Included in the declaration were the words "Full respect for the integrity of the person, . . . consent and shared responsibility for sexual behavior and its consequences."[132]

The rise of American hegemony, unilateralism, and militarism since the end of the Cold War have all played a role in the conflict between sexuality, rights, and U.S. power. Since the 1980s, U.S. internal policy opposition to abortion and women's reproductive rights solidified.[133] Elements of the U.S. opposition to the Beijing conference statements on women's rights included collusion with the Vatican and fundamentalist Islamic regimes, introduction of welfare reform legislation in 1996 (which mandated an "Abstinence-Only" sex education policy) designed to further destabilize reproductive rights and health, especially of poor and minority women and families. Meanwhile, sexual conservatives became increasingly aggressive in the use of the media and the media-based moral panics related to such issues as gays in the military, and the rise of phony science,[134] by local and national political coalitions of sexual and moral conservatives.

Under the current government of President George W. Bush we have witnessed the rise of a new level of cultural anger marshaled to promote moral panics internally and in global politics. Girard (2004) has studied these manifestations of cultural anger or backlash; they include the re-imposition of the "Global Gag Rule" as Bush's first act in office,[135] asser-tion of his opposition to gay marriage—later to take the form of a pro-posed constitutional amendment—and promotion of Abstinence-Only as the triumph of sexual education policy in the 21st century. Each of these three actions reveals major contradictions in U.S. policy externally and/ or internally; each of them has become a wedge issue filled with fear and a moral panic market campaign to influence attitudes, regulate sexually, deny rights, and enforce new policies.

Notably, the mainstreaming of this rights-based approach, as Petchesky (2000) has well argued, began with a negative perspective by focusing on what rights were missing, removed, or under threat. While this "deficit" approach lends itself to the analysis of citizenship, the negative rights approach is a reaction to the continuous cycle of moral panics that has plagued the arena of reproductive and sexual rights. The Vienna Confer-ence of 1993 on social and economic development marked a change in re-garding "sexual violence" as a violation of human rights; it secured for the first time insertion of "sexuality" into the language of human rights.[136] U.S. policy should focus on attaining positive rights and on what is needed to assure full human potential in development, health, and social justice.[137] In Brazil, for example, access to full sexual and reproductive health care is regarded as a new right of the citizen.

In 2000, a new International Covenant on Economic, Social and Cul-ture Rights (ICESCR) included sexual orientation protection for the first time. Although not ironclad, Alice Miller[138] points out, this new advance helped pave the way for recommendations that assure a rights-based ap-proach to sexual health[139] by the U.N. Special Rapporteur on the Right to Health, providing larger recognition of sexual rights as human rights. Increasing resistance from the Vatican, fundamentalist Islamic countries, and the United States also produced new strategic tools and alliances across diverse movements to promote rights as a global trend.[140]

Much more discussion has been directed toward the United States in this current of change. In the United States, the 2001 surgeon general's report on sexuality may be seen as a watershed of American sexual health policy and a reaction to the events of the 1990s. The report, titled "Call to Action to Promote Sexual Health and Responsible Sexual Behavior," advocated new levels of support for research, public awareness, and intervention. This report was not officially approved either by the Clinton or Bush administrations. It must be remembered that the surgeon general's report was necessary in part because of the federal government's official policy on Abstinence-Only education, a policy largely bereft of scientific credibility.[141]

Regarding the role of sex research and moral panics, it is useful to remember that there have been only two preoccupations over the past half-century: first, teen pregnancy and population control from the late 1950s to the 70s, followed by AIDS/STD sexual-risk behavior research in the 1980s and 90s, which led to the Abstinence-Only policy as reviewed in chapter 2 by DiMauro and Joffe.[142] Public- and private-sector funding of sexuality research/sexual-policy formation in these arenas has significantly supported both the emergence of rights and interest group coalitions to support them as well as the concomitant backlash of moral panic.

Teen pregnancy, especially among young women of color, very clearly became a broad theme that fueled cultural anger and a variety of loosely related moral panics.[143] Racist notions of who was and was not a fit parent, who was and was not a "welfare queen," and the like were powerful mechanisms of moral and sexual regulation bearing on young African American women as unwed mothers or as "welfare" mothers. These debates helped to shape gender rights in the United States.[144] By the mid-1990s this focus was increasingly transformed into a debate about the moral imperative to replace comprehensive sexual education with Abstinence-Only policy, as per the 1996 Welfare Reform legislation, which chartered Abstinence-Only sex education to such a degree that critics referred to it as "ignorance-only." These debates disrupted an open discourse about sexuality in the schools, placed young people at risk of sexually transmitted diseases (STDs), and increased the risk of unintended pregnancy.[145] Ultimately these policies have been exported into the global order via the 2001 "Gag Rule," and Abstinence-Only policies or ABC (Abstinence, Be Faithful, Wear Condoms) policies in such major cultural regions as Africa, where sexual citizenship is now being contested in a variety of societies.[146]

The assault on sexual rights in the 1980s was driven by the perception of risk associated with HIV, triggering new scapegoating of individuals and groups that constituted the pandemic.[147] Safe sex campaigns were meant to counter stigma and marginalization of gays, bisexuals, Haitians, commercial sex workers, and hemophiliacs, and with some exceptions these efforts were successful in spite of enormous social pressures exerted from extremist organizations and in the absence of U.S. government support until Surgeon General C. Everett Koop began to speak.[148] Central to these debates was not only the tabooed arena of homosexuality, but also the illicit and immoral areas of hidden desires and practices.[149] Attacks on these public health campaigns were common, and attacks on the funding of "prohomosexual" campaigns continue to the present, as witnessed by attacks on government-funded research studies at such institutions as the University of California, San Francisco. To many observers, it was the assault on desire itself,[150] on sexual minority men,[151] and on the reconstitution of sexual citizenship.[152] Dowsett has reviewed these important events and contrasted them in a significant Australian case study.[153]

Indeed, in my view, so important is the invention of sexual rights as a framework connecting academic theory with advocacy innovatively[154] that we ought to think of the period of the end of Cold War and the beginning of the postmodern and more global order as conditioned by the rise of a new paradigm of sexual and reproductive rights. These include the agenda of having rational goals or pedagogy and human rights advocacy,[155] and the creation of rights as "irreconcilable subjectivities"[156] with social laws and conventions in some places. Feminist scholars and activists, following the historic Beijing and Cairo conferences of the mid-1990s, which were set up in part as a response to the efforts of gay, lesbian, and, later, sexual orientation activists including those looking for transgender rights following the AIDS pandemic in the 1980s, have been instrumental in rights advocacy. Critics of the "rights model" have impugned its "individualist" bias, argued that it is not universal, and criticized its polarization of public and private discourses. However, leading activist scholars remind us that rights, in the sense of "liberty" or "choices," are dependent on broader structural or "enabling" conditions such as social welfare, economic security, and political freedom.[157]

Looking back, it seems obvious that this emergent model of sexual rights was seldom applied to analysis of the continuing waves of sexual panics that have occurred over the past decade or so. The difficulty of conceptualizing the purveyors of moral and sexual panics occurs throughout the early literature on the subject, as noted by Rubin (1984), Watney (1987), and Goode and Ben-Yehuda (1994), and there are significant theoretical and historical reasons for this gap. In part, the problem hinges on the distance between the academy and activists (which Rubin and Watney, respectively, among others tried to bridge),[158] as related to the long, slow response to AIDS by academics, and the lag created by research that includes social hierarchies of sexuality and social justice today.[159] We have not specifically tied the cultural politics of producing moral panics to the mobilization and formation of new interests in politics.

Some analysts see fundamentalists and sexual conservatives losing ground on issues of sexual diversity, identity inclusion, recreational sex, and the cultural values that promote this social justice in society.[160] Their means of reaction has increasingly been to stir up emotional fear, hate, anger, and disgust in ways that push their agendas into broader social, economic, and policy arenas.[161] It was too early to see this trend in the 1980s in spite of the work that first examined moral and sexual panics, though Rubin (1984) had many forward-thinking ideas about what might ensue from thinking about the consequences of the AIDS epidemic for sexuality in general. Today, however, it is possible to go further in understanding the role that a newly fashioned uses of cultural anger plays in late modern politics.

Cultural Anger and Sexual Scripts

Throughout this chapter I have suggested that moral and sexual panics are related to the cultural anger associated with perceptions of social safety risk and security in American society and throughout the world. Panics, as they emerge in a complex society such as that of the United States, are means of generating insipient ideologies of cohesion that can override other forms of difference, whether of class, race, nationality, or religious orientation. Media in local, national, and global settings have a vested interest not only in mainstreaming sex and its marketing, but also in massaging the opinions and fears of the public. Political and religious groups must learn how to massage or "spin" their stories in order to gain support in the effort to win or lose sexual citizenship. Panics in this model fuel anger as a general process of forming collective narratives and cultural scripts. These scripts are vital to the political and media strategies. But how are they different? Moral conservatives and fundamentalists seek to shape government and exert control over the governance of the self.

The work of journalist Thomas Frank (2004) on cultural anger provides a suggestive clue as to the direction that social and cultural analysis might take. Frank's book, *What's the Matter with Kansas?* Is a political study of how the state of Kansas historically changed from being extremely progressive to a bastion "red state" (neoconservative), destroying

the opportunities for decent wages and education and housing. In particular, Frank has written of what he calls "cultural anger" in the Republican
and neoconservative movement; the use of "yeoman righteousness" and
anti-elitist, anti-intellectual and antisexual rhetorical structures as "the
blunt instrument of propaganda" in the effort to win hearts and votes in
the heartland.[162] The targets of this political usurpation are working-class
and aspiring lower-middle-class wage earners, whose rights and well being are dependent on health care and educational programs that typically
require government support or direction. The effect draws on the illusion
of moral panics to gain popular control of the electoral process through
the subversive use of misleading rhetoric—reminding us strikingly of
George Lakoff's (2004) argument that Republicans strategists used these
emotional rhetorical devices successfully in recent years. Frank's ideas,
especially surrounding the pivotal role of "authenticity" sought in "small
town" ideologies that oppose the "endless acts of hubris" that character-
ize wealthy urban "blue state" liberals, is a promising means of analysis
in studying the role of the systematic use of moral panics today to gain
working-class support for free market capitalism solutions, such as tax
cuts for the rich.[163] The paradox of this political position and its negative
effects on wage earners suggests an historical view.

American sexuality history is relatively brief by the standards of Western Europe, and yet the genealogy of American moral panics reveals a rich
and complex history and set of contradictory themes, such as virginity,
abstinence, and antihomosexuality rhetoric and fears that re-cycle sexual
preoccupations and social conflicts, periodically erupting into the now-
familiar tsunamis of sexualized movements and sex panics. These panics
reveal a flaw in the personal sexual morality (premarital intercourse, masturbation, unintended pregnancy, abortion, homosexuality, and prostitution) of individuals. This is typified by the middle-class American historical concern that sex is individual, "natural," or "innate" (more or less, as
a product of gender, race, and class) but also subject to moral "choice"
and "free will," though this concern is pivoted not on the middle class
but rather people of color and the colonized.[164] Christian fundamentalism
has played and continues to play a large role—although its rhetoric and
scripts are changing.[165]

A brief glance at how progressive movements, ideologies, and emotional rhetoric in the United States have changed since the 1870s helps
us to understand the fundamental point that political liberalism has
never been the same as sexual liberalism in this country.[166] Traditionally,

19th-century progressive movements were viewed as an effort to control big business.[167] Progressive movements during this time involved broad changes from the grassroots that linked moral and economic reforms with the rise of workers' rights and the labor movement. States such as Kansas, which were once regarded as the seat of progressivism, had reversed course completely by a century later, while the issues had changed as much as their economies had declined. Progressive efforts were directed as much at individuals as at institutions and grew from the optimistic belief that things were mutable and could be changed.[168] Environmentalism as a simple theory of human development was one source of these optimistic beliefs. Moral reforms arise from the same efforts; for example, the adoption by the State of Kansas of prohibition was largely as a result of the efforts of temperance advocates such as Carrie A. Nation.[169] Alcoholism, like other social ills of the time, was real, not illusory, but the fears extended into moral campaigns, such as treating prostitution as a "social evil."[170] Margaret Sanger began her proreproductive rights magazine, *Woman Rebel*, in 1914 in the face of opposition by postal authorities.[171] Progressive support for this and other forms of control of pleasure and leisure surely compromised the reform movement. Later, Progressive support of the labor movement and Wobblies drew strong social reaction in progressives' effort to organize wage earners in cities such as Spokane.[172] Overall, middle-class reformers had little success in shaping workers and the elite alike.[173] Ironically, progressives opposed the election of Franklin Delano Roosevelt (Jane Addams voted against him[174]) because of his support for the expansion of big government and lack of a progressive vision. Throughout this long period, progressive reform was not very supportive of women's rights, sexual and reproductive support, and protection of rights. There was a distinctively antidemocractic element in this progressive transformation.

Today, the link between panics and cultural anger has taken on a very different political form not known before. "Authenticity," that is, what counts as natural, normal, innate, is pivotal to how the public reacts to politics generally, as one can see in the presidential campaigns of 2008, and, more specifically, in sexuality and sexual panics. The appeal to emotionality and cultural scripts that stereotype segments of the society are critical to this change. Frank's (2004) account of neoconservative reactions suggests that sexual innatism in folk ideologies of sexuality and gender is pivotal to the production of cultural anger. Authentic social living and, indeed, authentic sexuality, is something that is "natural" as well as "God given" and also inexplicably "just happens." Sex drives for men and mothering for women are normal and natural; these are not learned or planned or scripted. They are just there; they are real, and they are not performed. We can look at the Monica Lewinsky scandal during the Clinton Administration to ask if this same rhetorical structure was what bedeviled the Republican strategists who wanted to "get Clinton?" We can wonder if this is a key reason even the red-state voters never turned against Clinton during the sexual scandal: it was a "normal and natural thing" for a man to do, and it was a "normal and natural thing" for Hillary to "stick by her man." No qualified social constructionist theorist since Freud, and certainly not following Kinsey, could possibly accept such an simplistic view—and none would—and yet this is what ordinary people are taught to believe and, in fact, believe if we are to accept Frank's account at face value. Surely we can understand in such a symbolic and rhetorical frame the obviousness that follows from the current president of the United States saying "Marriage between a man and a woman is the pillar of civilization" (Herdt, chapter 5).

From this perspective, not much has changed in the worldview of sexual conservatives, and it appears that none of the last fifty years of social constructionism have done the least bit of good. This does not mean that the media simply mirrors this view. Educated and professional people obviously have more complex and sophisticated views, as suggested by their support for a variety of initiatives such as reproductive choice. And the blue states presumably support a more Catholic, if not a more constructionist view, that sexuality is, whatever else we might grant it to be or be made up of, a performance in context with social actors that respond to the cues and scripts of their respective communities.

This is all true except that a lot has changed: the use of orchestrated cultural anger to fire up moral and sexual panics seems to be growing; it seems that it is becoming a regular stratagem and political tactic in the so-called culture wars (once called the "sex wars"[175]). Culture wars are, however, the wrong concept for this process and, according to Lakoff (2004), the old idea accepts a rhetorical structure that is misleading and undermining of the root causes of sexual change in the post–Cold War period. As Duggan argues repeatedly, the economic neoconservative agenda has increasingly parted company from the cultural complaints of the neoliberal view over the past twenty years.[176] The larger view Duggan advocates as part of the "more visible conflict among elites" in cultural politics is, on one side, that the residual strategy of cultural traditionalism deployed during the late 20th-century culture wars—energetic attacks against "multiculturalism" and "permissiveness" was intended to shrink the funding bases as well as the popular support for sites of nonmarket politics—the arts, education, and social services.[177]

What I want to suggest is that cultural anger has propelled panics in a significant new way—more pernicious, more grassroots in character than the culture wars of the past sketched by Duggan. The neoliberal response, according to Duggan, is to support diversity and tolerance narrowly defined and within a global framework. In other words, the culture wars have undermined the social egalitarian process in the United States, but these have not touched the occurrence of the structural violence which moral panics continue to impact and perpetrate.

But from where did this pervasive cultural anger come? There have long been cycles of sexual purity movements and great scares, as previously stated, in American history,[178] while sexual panics also have been seen in Western Europe since the early 18th century.[179] Politically, sexuality was becoming the increasing focus of what Thomas Frank (2004) has so aptly called "cultural anger" directed toward such debates concerning homosexuality, abstinence, prostitution, bisexuality, and so on. While Frank did not explain the sources of this cultural anger, he did posit a generalized use of "baiting" tactics and economic fear and greed in the late 1990s and into the early 21st century. He implicitly recognized how sexual panics were increasing in number and frequency in elections, legislatures, and courtrooms. However, Lisa Duggan suggests a compelling source: a "precarious consensus" regarding the balance between regulation of sexual behavior and representations, as in art and the artistic and personal expression of sexual feelings, especially in private. This balance remained "substantially intact right up to the 1980s, when conflict broke out all over the place."[180] She suggests that antipornography crusades and the antigay hysteria fanned by AIDS "fueled a revitalized activism among gay people and advocates of humane health care."[181]

In the case study on the moral panic of gay and lesbian marriage in chapter 5, I examine how cultural politics and policy debates on marriage equality rights (gay and lesbian marriage) in the United States and around the world inserted not only moral panics into the presidential election of 2004, but also more generally unleashed cultural anger and backlash concerning what are "real" marriage, family, adoption, and the moral values of society. Underlying this discourse, I believe, is a deeper and more fundamental cultural script that stems from thinking of sexuality as sin or disease or both, from the 19th century onward.[182] To put it in value terms, are homosexuals *fit* to be married? Are they *fit* to be parents? *Fit* to adopt children? Or even *fit* to be citizens?[183] Such are the moral questions and sentiments that underlie small-town life in the United States, as clearly revealed in the significant ethnography of rural Oregon by Arlene Stein.[184] Thus, through a sequence of parochial and nationalist concerns, including quite traditional Christian value coalitions in the United States, we begin to understand how the definition of citizenship in its full political, economic, and social sense is itself at stake in fueling cultural anger.

But while cultural anger has merit, it can only take us so far in the analysis of the complex, disparate, and often multidimensional features of these sexual panics and their ability to destabilize scientific knowledge, the pedagogy of sexuality education, and progress in providing for democracy and social justice to all segments of society. Scripts, that is, sexual script theory, in the social and psychoanalytic writings of Gagnon and Simon, Robert Stoller, and in the long run especially John Gagnon provide the missing link for this work.[185] Like the sociological idea of a master narrative or landmark narrative (more focused than the anthropological concept of "worldview" and its successor, "sexual life ways,"[186]), scripts have the ability to organize a variety of divergent areas of meaning and action. Additionally, script theory is useful in articulating three distinct levels of meaning and action: individual, interpersonal, and cultural.

The power of scripts to articulate and coordinate social life and subjectivity cannot be underestimated. Here I want to suggest that cultural anger provides a powerful mechanism for the coordination of rhetorical action across individuals, situations, and communities. The role of powerful scripted emotions, such as rage, anger, fear, and shame are evident in this long history; Rubin (1984) repeatedly refers to it in her seminal analysis of sexual hierarchies and moral values. Lisa Duggan's 1995 work explored the emotional reactions to what she calls "sexual dissent" in the context of the "porn wars."[187] Janice Irvine's 2002 work has greatly illuminated the systematic use of emotional scripts to provoke political reactions (including fear and shame) and thus exert control over institutions and events surrounding sex education. In a new analysis in chapter 7 she deepens her contribution in this arena.

What I have suggested is that as proponents of sexual rights gained increasing political power in the United States, fundamentalists, sexual conservatives, and bigots increasingly reacted with organized forms of cultural anger—in the extreme form, sexual panics. Sometimes these panics have served as what I have previously defined as a "moral shock," goading coalition of opponents to rights into antiwoman, antigay, or antisexual campaigns. Irvine has noted this: American extremist organizations have effectively "scripted the public conversation on sexual education through rhetorical frames which organize ambivalence, confusion, and anxieties."[188] In the book *Talk about Sex*, Irvine goes further in thinking about the contribution of sexual shame to the rise of cultural anger and moral panics in the United States.

To conclude, panics are characteristic of states that experience times of divided public opinion, changing social, economic and political circumstances, and a clash between state mechanisms of control and the free expression and individual elaboration of sexuality. The clash often initiates a regime of increased scrutiny and threat to rights and even the removal of sexual and reproductive rights. In the United States, this change over the past century must be seen in relation to the rise of being a superpower state, the uneasy balance between state security and militarization, masculinity, sexual freedom, and the Cold War. This uneasy balance can also be seen in the post–Cold War period in response to new challenges to reproductive rights and sexuality that have gained force through the use of a well-scripted cultural anger that attempts to undue rights and thus uphold the contradictions of class privilege and dismantle underclass benefits. The trend under the George W. Bush Administration is to extend these cultural scripts of anger toward sexual change abroad, which has a global impact. Abstinence-Only sex education and antiabortion rights campaigns are the most salient examples of this effort, but antihomosexual campaigns have risen in their power and impact. Time will tell how effective these neoconservative moral panics were in global politics. However, this book raises the question of a need for new study of these questions in sexual politics. The need for a new social progressive movement is obvious, and the effort to counter such trends has already begun.

NOTES

1. I wish to thank the Ford Foundation (New York) for its long-term support of the National Sexuality Resource Center that has indirectly provided resources for this project, and the Rockefeller Foundation for the Bellagio residency in summer 2006 that allowed me the time and space needed to complete the writing.

2. Gayle Rubin, "Thinking Sex: Notes for a Radical Theory of the Politics of Sexuality." In *Pleasure and Danger: Exploring Female Sexuality*. C. S. Vance, ed. (New York: Routledge and Kegan Paul, 1984), 143.

3. The term comes from Lisa and Richard Kim, 2005, "Beyond Gay Marriage," *The Nation*, July 25(1): 24–27.

4. Sean P. Hier, "Conceptualizing Moral Panic Through a Moral Economy of Harm," *Critical Sociology* 28:3 (2002): 311–34.

5. Janice Irvine, 2005, "Anti-Gay Politics Online: A Study of Sexuality and Stigma on National Websites," *Sexuality Research and Social Policy* 2: 3–22.

6. Dr. Nancy Kendall, personal communication.

7. Simon Watney, *Policing Desire: Pornography, AIDS and the Media* (Minneapolis: University of Minnesota Press, 1987), 25.

8. Kenneth Thompson, *Moral Panics* (London: Routledge, 1998).

9. Hier, "Conceptualizing Moral Panic," 322.

10. Thomas Frank, *What's the Matter with Kansas?* (New York: Metropolitan Books, 2004).

11. Hier, "Conceptualizing Moral Panic," 321.

12. Watney, *Policing Desire*.

13. Lisa Duggan, *The Twilight of Equality* (Boston: Beacon, 2003).

14. Charles Critcher, *Moral Panics and the Media* (Buckingham, UK: Open University Press, 2003).

15. Paul Farmer, *Pathologies of Power* (Berkeley: University of California Press, 2003).

16. Stanley Cohen, *Folk Devils and Moral Panics*, 3rd ed. (New York: St. Martin's, 2002 [1972]), vii.

17. Critcher, *Moral Panics*, 11ff.

18. Watney, *Policing Desire*, 38–57.

19. Cohen, *Folk Devils*, vii.

20. After James Jasper; cited in Janice Irvine, *Talk about Sex*, (Berkeley: University of California Press, 2002) 176–77.

21. Gilbert Herdt and Robert Kertzner, "I Do, But I Can't: The Impact of Marriage Denial on the Mental Health and Sexual Citizenship of Lesbians and Gay Men in the United States," *Sexuality Research and Social Policy: Journal of the NSRC* 3:1 (2006): 33–49.

22. Thomas Laqueur, *Solitary Sex: A Cultural History of Masturbation* (New York: Zone Books, 2003).

23. Alan Hunt, "Great Masturbation Panic and the Discourses of Moral Regulation in Nineteenth- and Early Twentieth-Century Britain," *Journal of the History of Sexuality* 8:4 (1998): 579–81.

24. Frank, *What's the Matter with Kansas?*

25. Cohen, *Folk Devils*, xxvii.

26. Gilbert Herdt, *Same Sex, Different Cultures* (Colorado Springs: Westview, 1997).

27. Watney, *Policing Desire*, 41.

28. Critcher, *Moral Panics.* Erich Goode and Nachman Ben-Yehuda, *Moral Panics: The Social Construction of Deviance* (Oxford, UK: Wiley-Blackwell, 1994). Stuart Hall et al., *Policing the Crisis: Mugging, the State and Law and Order* (London: Palgrave Macmillan, 1978). Watney, *Policing Desire.*

29. Edwin H. Sutherland, "The Diffusion of Sexual Psychopath Laws," *American Journal of Sociology,* 56:2 (1950): 142–48.

30. See Critcher, *Moral Panics,* 11f, who critiques these dimensions; Goode and Ben-Yehuda, Moral *Panics,* 33–40; Thompson, *Moral Panics*; and Hall, *Policing the Crisis.*

31. Goode and Ben-Yehuda, *Moral Panics.*

32. Cohen, *Folk Devils,* xxx.

33. Angela McRobbie and Sarah Thornton, "Rethinking 'Moral Panic' for Multi-Mediated Social Worlds," *British Journal of Sociology* 46:4 (1995): 562.

34. Rubin, "Thinking Sex," 163. This article received the notion of "moral panic" not through Cohen's work but through Jeffrey Weeks, *Sexuality and Its Discontents* (London: Routlege and Kegan Paul, 1985), 14–15, who defined this as "the political moment of sex, in which diffuse attitudes are channeled into political action and from there into social change." Presumably, Weeks borrowed the notion from Cohen's prior work.

35. George Chauncey, "The Postwar Sex Crime Panic," in *True Stories From the American Past*, William Graeber, ed. (New York: McGraw-Hill, 1993). See also Rubin's own masterful essay, "Elegy for the Valley of the Kings: AIDS and the Leather Community in San Francisco, 1981–1996," in *In Changing Times*, Martin P. Levin et al., eds. (Chicago: University of Chicago Press, 1997).

36. John Gagnon, "T. Laqueur, Solitary Sex: A Cultural History of Masturbation," *Archives of Sexual Behavior* 34:4 (2005).

37. McRobbie and Thornton, "Rethinking 'Moral Panic," 562.

38. We have to wonder what role sexuality and the famed pedagogical homosexuality in Greece may have played in slandering the reputation of Socrates as well; see Kenneth Dover, *Greek Homosexuality* (Cambridge: Harvard University Press, 1987).

39. I. F. Stone, *The Trial of Socrates* (New York: Anchor Books, 1988) 211.

40. Hunt, "Great Masturbation Panic," 609.

41. Weeks, *Sexuality and Its Discontents.*

42. Hunt, "Great Masturbation Panic," 598.

43. Michel Foucault, *The History of Sexuality* (New York: Pantheon, 1980); Theo Van der Meer, "Dutch Gay Bashers," *Culture, Health and Sexuality* 5 (1994 [2003]).

44. For the domino theory of sexual peril, see Rubin, "Thinking Sex."

45. Stanley Kurtz, "The Libertarian Question," *National Review Online*, April 30, 2003.

46. Cohen, *Folk Devils*.

47. Goode and Ben-Yehuda, *Moral Panics*, 57–62.

48. *New York Times Magazine* (December 12, 1955).

49. A teacher who apparently had been having homosexual relations was so shaken up by reading the news of the spreading scandal that he rose from his unfinished breakfast and drove straight to San Francisco, never reporting to school that day and never returning to Boise. Cited in Rubin, "Thinking Sex," 145.

50. Didi Herman, *The Antigay Agenda: Orthodox Vision and the Christian Right* (Chicago: University of Chicago Press, 1997).

51. Eve Sedgwick, "How To Bring Your Kids Up Gay," *Social Text* 29 (1991).

52. Watney, *Policing Desire*, 56.

53. Watney, *Policing Desire*, 51.

54. Janice Irvine, *Talk about Sex*.

55. Goode and Ben-Yehuda, *Moral Panics*, 8.

56. Chauncey, "The Postwar Sex Crime Panic."

57. Cynthia Enloe, *The Morning After: Sexual Politics at the End of the Cold War* (Berkeley: University of California Press, 1993), 5.

58. Judith Levine, *Harmful to Minors* (Minneapolis: University of Minnesota Press, 2002), 44.

59. Cohen, *Folk Devils*, xiv–xv.

60. Levine, *Harmful to Minors*.

61. Marty Klein, *America's War on Sex: The Attack on Law, Lust and Liberty* (New York: Praeger, 2006).

62. John D. D'Emilio and Estelle B. Freedman, *Intimate Matters: A History of Sexuality in America* (New York: Harper and Row, 1988).

63. Paul Farmer, *AIDS and Accusation* (Berkeley: University of California Press, 1992). Rubin, "Thinking Sex." See also Gilbert Herdt and Shirley Lindenbaum, *The Time of AIDS* (Thousand Oaks, CA: Sage, 1990); Rubin, "Elegy for the Valley of the Kings."

64. Steven Epstein, "The New Attack on Sexuality Research: Moral Panic and the Politics of Knowledge Production," *Sexuality Research and Social Policy* 3:1 (2006). François Girard, "Global Implications of U.S. Domestic and International Policies on Sexuality," Working Paper, No. 1, International Working Group on Sexuality and Social Policy, Sociomedical Sciences Department, Mailman School of Public Health. (Columbia University, New York, 2004). Irvine, *Talk about Sex*

65. Carole Joffe, The *Regulation of Sexuality: Experiences of Family Planning Workers* (Philadelphia: Temple University Press, 1986), 12.

66. Carole Joffe, *Doctors of Conscience: The Struggle to Provide Abortion before and after* Roe v. Wade (Boston: Beacon Press, 1995).

67. William Saletan, *Bearing Right: How Conservatives Won the Abortion War* (Berkeley: University of California Press, 2003).

68. Goode and Ben-Yehuda, *Moral Panic*, 228.

69. Peter Lawrence, *Road Belong Cargo* (New York: Humanities Press, 1964).

70. Vittorio Lantanari, *Religions of the Oppressed*, L. Sergis, trans. (New York: Knopf, 1959).

71. Gilbert Herdt, *Secrecy and Cultural Reality* (Ann Arbor: University of Michigan Press, 2003).

72. Janice Irvine, "Anti-Gay Politics Online: A Study of Sexuality and Stigma on National Websites," *Sexuality Research and Social Policy* 2 (2005).

73. Cohen, *Folk Devils*.

74. Critcher, *Moral Panics and the Media*.

75. McRobbie and Thornton, "Rethinking 'Moral Panic.'"

76. Watney, *Policing Desire*, 41.

77. Hier, *Conceptualizing Moral Panic*, 313.

78. D'Emilio and Freedman, *Intimate Matters*.

79. Watney, *Policing Desire*, 24.

80. David Halperin, *One Hundred Years of Homosexuality*.

81. Benjamin Shepard, "In Search of a Winning Script: Moral Panic vs. Institutional Denial," *Sexualities* 6:1 (2003):54–59.

82. Irvine, *Talk about Sex*, 196. The passage merits quoting:
The dynamics surrounding President Clinton's impeachment offer some insight into how public reaction might undermine the intensions of conservative speakers. Rather than singularly reinforcing sexual shame and reticence, Clinton's affair prompted such widespread sexual dialogue that one headline proclaimed, "in a matter of days, a change in culture" in which "Americans have actually debated the definition of duality, made 'oral sex' part of the public conversation, and speculated about the most private elements of the President's life in ways. . . . Inconceivable as. . . . [In] Harry Truman's day or even Ronald Reagan's."

83. John Gagnon and William Simon, *Sexual Conduct: The Social Sources of Human Sexuality* (London: Hutchinson, 2005 [1973]), 279.

84. Shepard; reviewed in Herdt, chapter 5.

85. Frank Rich. *The Greatest Story Ever Sold* (New York: Penguin, 2006).

86. Glen H. Elder, "Adolescence in the Life Cycle," in *Adolescence in the Life Cycle: Psychological Change and Social Context,* S. E. Dragastin and G. H. Elder Jr., eds. (Washington, D.C.: Hemisphere/Halsted Press, 1975).

87. Watney, *Policing Desire*, 15. Ron Bayer and David L. Kirp, 1992. "The Second Decade of AIDS: The End of Exceptionalism?" in *AIDS in the Industrialized Democracies: Passions, Politics and Policies*, edited by Ron Bayer and David L. Kirp (New Brunswick, NJ: Rutgers University Press, 1992), 361–84.

88. For example, on witchcraft, see Robert A. Levine, *Culture, Personality and*

Behavior (Chicago: Aldine, 1973); specifically as a moral panic, see Goode and Ben-Yehuda, *Moral Panics*, 144–84; on drugs, see Goode and Ben-Yehuda, *Moral Panics*, 205–22; on sodomy, see D'Emilio and Freedman, *Intimate Matters* and Weeks, *Sexuality and Its Discontents*.

89. Paul Robinson, *The Modernization of Sex* (New York: Harper and Row, 1976).

90. James Jones, *Alfred Kinsey: A Public/Private Life* (New York: Norton, 1997).

91. Judith Reisman is a ring leader, having written a bogus book about Kinsey; she was once awarded $734,000 to study pornography by the Justice Department during the Reagan Administration, has gone on to be the cheerleader of the anti-Kinsey movement, employing articles, books, and websites to propagate unfounded accusations that Kinsey was a pedophile, while also advancing works such as *The Pink Swastika*, which argues that the Holocaust was the creation of the German homosexual movement and believes that gay youth programs in the United States ought to be compared to Hitler youth. Daniel Radosh, "The Culture Wars," *The New Yorker*, December 6, 2004, p. 48.

92. Gilbert Herdt, "Kinsey," *International Encyclopedia of the Social Sciences*, *2nd ed., W. A. Darity*, ed. (Detroit: Macmillan Reference, 2008), 269–70.

93. Gagnon and Simon, *Sexual Conduct*.

94. Edward O. Laumann et al., *Social Organization of Sexuality: Sexual Practices in the United States* (Chicago: University of Chicago Press, 1994).

95. Watney, *Policing Desire*, 41.

96. Watney, *Policing Desire*, 41.

97. Levine, *Harmful to Minors*.

98. Hier, *Conceptualizing Moral Panic*, 328.

99. Anthony F. C. Wallace, *Culture and Personality*, 2nd ed. (New York: Random House, 1969); see, especially, the reformulation of prophecy and cognitive dissonance.

100. Gilbert Herdt, "Sexual Development, Social Oppression, and Local Culture," *Sexuality Research and Social Policy* 1 (2004):1–24,

101. Farmer, *AIDS and Accusation*, 8.

102. Niels Teunis and Gilbert Herdt, eds. *Sexual Inequalities and Social Justice* (Berkeley: University of California Press, 2006).

103. Rafael M. Díaz, "In Our Own Backyard: HIV Stigmatization in the Latino Gay Community," in Teunis and Herdt, eds.

104. Farmer, *AIDS and Accusation*, 30.

105. Teunis and Herdt, *Sexual Inequalities*.

106. Duggan, *The Twilight of Equality*. Lisa Duggan and Nan Hunter, *Sex Wars: Sexual Dissent and Political Culture* (New York: Routledge, 1995).

107. Sonia Correa and Richard Parker, "Sexuality, Human Rights, and Demographic Thinking," *Sexuality Research and Social Policy* 1 (2004). Miriam Maluwa et al., "HIV and AIDS-Related Stigma, Discrimination, and Human Rights,"

Health and Human Rights 6 (2002). Rosalind P. Petchesky, *Global Prescriptions: Gendering Health and Human Rights* (New York: Margrave, 2003).

108. Rubin, "Thinking Sex," 152–54.

109. Rubin, "Thinking Sex," 147.

110. Rubin, "Thinking Sex," 163.

111. Rubin, "Thinking Sex," 164. The most detailed review of this era remains the journalistic account by Randy Shilts, *And the Band Played On* (New York: St Martin's 1987).

112. Watney, *Policing Desire*, 92.

113. Joffe, *The Regulation of Sexuality*.

114. Ignacio Saiz, "Bracketing Sexuality: Human Rights and Sexual Orientation—A Decade of Development and Denial at the U.N.," *Health and Human Rights* 7:2 (2004).

115. Watney, *Policing Desire*, 37.

116. Saiz, "Bracketing Sexuality." Richard Parker et al., *Framing the Sexual Subject: The Politics of Gender, Sexuality and Power* (Berkeley: University of California Press, 2002).

117. Paolo Freire, *Pedagogy of the Oppressed* (New York: Continuum, 1970), 106–107.

118. Laumann et al., *Social Organization of Sexuality*.

119. Pepper Schwartz and Philip Blumstein, *Couples* (New York: Marrow, 1983).

120. Girard, *Global Implications*.

121. See Cohen, chapter 3.

122. Paisley Currah, *Transgender Rights* (Minneapolis: University of Minnesota Press, 2006).

123. Ed Laumann et al., *The Sexual Organization of the City* (Chicago: University of Chicago Press, 2004).

124. Steven Epstein, "Gay and Lesbian Movements in the United States: Dilemmas of Identity, Diversity and Political Strategy," in *The Global Emergence of Gay and Lesbian Politics*. B. D. Adam et al., eds. (Philadelphia: Temple University Press, 1999).

125. Duggan, *The Twilight of Equality*.

126. Epstein, "Gay and Lesbian Movements."

127. Dowsett, chapter 4.

128. Rosalind Petchesky, "Sexual Rights: Inventing a Concept, Mapping an International Practice," in *Framing the Sexual Subject*, R. Parker et al., eds. (Berkeley: University of California Press, 2000).

129. Herdt and Lindenbaum, *The Time of AIDS*.

130. Geetanjali Misra and Radhika Chandiramani, *Sexuality, Gender and Rights: Exploring Theory and Practice in South and Southeast Asia*. (New Delhi, India: Sage Publications, 2005), 18.

131. United Nations, Economic and Social Council, Committee on Economics,

Social, and Cultural Rights, General comment 14, UN Doc. No. E/C/ 12, 1994, paragraph 7.3.

132. UN 1994, Paragraph 96.

133. Girard, *Global Implications.*

134. Issues long promoted by the Family Research Council; see Epstein, "The New Attack." Klein, *America's War on Sex.*

135. Clinton suspended the "Global Gag Rule" after years of prior Republican use of this mechanism of sexual and reproductive rights limitation.

136. Petchesky, "Sexual Rights," 83.

137. Sonia Correa and Rosalind Petchesky, "Reproductive and Sexual Rights: A Feminist Perspective," in *Populations Policies Reconsidered: Health, Empowerment and Rights,* Gita Sen et al., eds. (Cambridge: Harvard University Press, 1994). Correa and Parker, "Sexuality, Human Rights and Demographic Thinking,"; Herdt, "Sexual Development"; Teunis and Herdt, *Sexual Inequalities.*

138. Alice Miller 1998.

129. Misra and Chandiramani, *Sexuality, Gender and Rights,* 20.

140. Saiz, "Bracketing Sexuality."

141. Douglas Kirby, *Emerging Answers: Research Findings on Programs to Reduce Teen Pregnancy* (SIECUS Reports, 2001). These developments are surveyed in chapter 2 by DiMauro and Joffe.

142. DiMauro and Joffe, chapter 2; see also Teunis and Herdt, *Sexual Inequalities.*

143. Anna M. Smith, "The Politicization of Marriage in Contemporary American Public Policy: The Defense of Marriage Act and the Personal Responsibility Act," *Citizenship Studies* 5 (2001).

144. Reviewed in Jessica Fields, *Risky Lessons: Sex Education and Social Inequality* (New Brunswick, NJ: Rutgers University Press, 2008). Joffe, *Doctors of Conscience.*

145. Irvine, *Talk about Sex.*

146. See Girard, *Global Implications.* Wieringa, chapter 6.

147. See Dowsett, chapter 4; Watney, *Policing Desire.*

148. Levine, *Harmful to Minors.*

149. Herdt and Lindenbaum, *The Time of AIDS*; Parker et al. *Framing the Sexual Subject.*

150. Watney, *Policing Desire.*

151. Díaz, "In Our Own Backyard."

152. Gary Dowsett, *Practicing Desire: Homosexual Sex in the Era of AIDS* (Stanford: Stanford University Press, 1996). Richard Parker and Peter Aggleton, "HIV and AIDS-Related Stigma and Discrimination: A Conceptual Framework and Implications for Action," *Social Science and Medicine* 57 (2003). Richard Parker, *Beneath the Equator: Cultures of Desire, Male Homosexuality, and Emerging Gay Communities in Brazil* (New York: Routledge, 1999).

153. Dowsett, chapter 4.

154. Petchesky, *Global Prescriptions*. Saiz, "Bracketing Sexuality."

155. Alice Miller, "Easy Promises: Sexuality, Health, and Human Rights," *American Journal of Public Health* 91:6 (1998).

156. Cindy Patton, "Foreword," in *RePlacing Citizenship: AIDS Activism and Radical Democracy*, Brown, M. P., ed. (New York: Guilford Press, 1997), xvii.

157. Correa and Petchesky, "Reproductive and Sexual Rights," 107.

158. The late Martin Levine, a sociologist who pioneered the study of HIV risk among gay men, was one of these scholars; the groundbreaking conference he chaired tells the story (Levine et al., *In Changing Times*).

159. Teunis and Herdt, *Sexual Inequalities*.

160. Gagnon, *An Interpretation of Desire*; Gagnon, "T. Laqueur, Solitary Sex."

161. Girard, *Global Implications*.

162. Frank, *What's the Matter with Kansas*, 16–18.

163. Frank, *What's the Matter with Kansas*, 27.

164. Hunt, "Great Masturbation Panic."

165. See D'Emilio and Freedman, *Intimate Matters*; Herman, *The Antigay Agenda*; Glenda Russell, *Voted Out: The Psychological Consequences of Anti-Gay Politics* (New York: New York University Press, 2000).

166. Michael McGerr, *Fierce Discontent: The Rise and Fall of the Progressive Movement in America, 1870–1920* (New York: Free Press, 2003). Gagnon, personal communication.

167. McGerr, *Fierce Discontent*, 79.

168. McGerr, *Fierce Discontent*, 80.

169. McGerr, *Fierce Discontent*, 83.

170. McGerr, *Fierce Discontent*, 85.

171. McGerr, *Fierce Discontent*, 271.

172. McGerr, *Fierce Discontent*, 145.

173. McGerr, *Fierce Discontent*, 146.

174. McGerr, *Fierce Discontent*, 315.

175. Duggan and Hunter, *Sex Wars*. A. Stein, Shameless, pp. 111ff, refers to the emotional cultural war.

176. Duggan, *The Twilight of Equality*, 11.

177. Duggan, *The Twilight of Equality*, 21.

178. D'Emilio and Freedman. *Intimate Matters*.

179. Laqueur, *Solitary Sex*. Van der Meer, "Dutch Gay Bashers."

180. Duggan and Hunter, *Sex Wars*, 76.

181. Duggan and Hunter, *Sex Wars*, 77.

182. Herdt, "Sexual Development."

183. Evan Wolfson, *Why Marriage Matters* (New York: Simon & Schuster, 2004).

184. Arlene Stein, *The Stranger Next Door* (Boston: Beacon, 2001).

185. Gagnon and Simon, *Sexual Conduct*; Stoller, *Sexual Excitement*.

186. Gilbert Herdt, *Third Sex, and Third Gender: Beyond Sexual Dimorphism in Culture and History* (New York: Zone Books, 1996).
187. Duggan and Hunter, *Sex Wars*, 5.
188. Irvine, *Talk About Sex*, 8.

REFERENCES

Bayer, Ron and David L. Kirp. 1992. "The Second Decade of AIDS: The End of Exceptionalism?" In *AIDS in the Industrialized Democracies: Passions, Politics and Policies*. Edited by Ron Bayer and David L. Kirp. New Brunswick, NJ: Rutgers University Press.

Chauncey, George. 1993. "The Postwar Sex Crime Panic." In *True Stories from the American Past*. Edited by William Graeber. New York: McGraw-Hill.

Cohen, Cathy J. 1999. *The Boundaries of Blackness: AIDS and the Breakdown of Black Politics*. Chicago: University of Chicago Press.

Cohen, Stanley. 2002 [1972]. "Introduction." In *Folk Devils and Moral Panics*. 3rd ed. New York: St. Martin's.

———. 1972. *Folk Devils and Moral Panics*. New York: St. Martin's.

Condon, Bill, dir. 2004. *Kinsey*. 20th Century Fox.

Correa, Sonia and Richard Parker. 2004. "Sexuality, Human Rights, and Demographic Thinking." *Sexuality Research and Social Policy* 1: 15–38.

Correa, Sonia and Rosalind Petchesky. 1994. "Reproductive and Sexual Rights: A Feminist Perspective." In *Populations Policies Reconsidered: Health, Empowerment and Rights*. Edited by Gita Sen, Adrienne Germaine, and Lincoln Chen. Cambridge: Harvard University Press.

Critcher, Charles. 2003. *Moral Panics and the Media*. Buckingham, U.K.: Open University Press.

Currah, Paisley. 2006. *Transgender Rights*. Minneapolis: University of Minnesota Press.

D'Emilio, John D. and Estelle B. Freedman. 1988. *Intimate Matters: A History of Sexuality in America*. New York: Harper and Row.

Díaz, Rafael M. 2006. "In Our Own Backyard: HIV Stigmatization in the Latino Gay Community." In *Sexual Inequalities*. Edited by Niels Teunis. Berkeley: University of California Press.

Douglas, Mary. 1970. *Natural Symbols*. London: Cresset.

Dover, Kenneth. 1987. *Greek Homosexuality*. Cambridge: Harvard University Press.

Dowsett, Gary. 1996. *Practicing Desire: Homosexual Sex in the Era of AIDS*. Stanford: Stanford University Press.

Duggan, Lisa. 2003. *The Twilight of Equality*. Boston: Beacon.

Duggan, Lisa and Nan Hunter. 1995. *Sex Wars: Sexual Dissent and Political Culture*. New York: Routledge.

Duggan, Lisa and Richard Kim. 2005. "Beyond Gay Marriage." *The Nation*, July 25(1): 24–27.

Elder, Glen H., Jr. 1975. "Adolescence in the Life Cycle." In *Adolescence in the Life Cycle: Psychological Change and Social Context.* Edited by Sigmund E. Dragastin and Glen H. Elder Jr. Washington, D.C.: Hemisphere/Halsted.

Enloe, Cynthia. 1993. *The Morning After: Sexual Politics at the End of the Cold War.* Berkeley: University of California Press.

Epstein, Steven. 2006. "The New Attack on Sexuality Research: Moral Panic and the Politics of Knowledge Production." *Sexuality Research and Social Policy* 3(1): 1–12.

———. 1999. "Gay and Lesbian Movements in the United States: Dilemmas of Identity, Diversity and Political Strategy." In *The Global Emergence of Gay and Lesbian Politics.* Edited by Barry D. Adam, Jan W. Duybendak, and Andre Krouwel. Philadelphia: Temple University Press.

Farmer, Paul. 2003. *Pathologies of Power.* Berkeley: University of California Press.

———. 1992. *AIDS and Accusation.* Berkeley: University of California Press.

Fejes, Fred. 2000. "Murder, Perversion, and Moral Panic: The 1954 Media Campaign Against Miami's Homosexuals and the Discourse of Civic Betterment." *Journal of the History of Sexuality* 9(3): 305–347.

Fields, Jessica. 2008. *Risky Lessons: Sex Education and Social Inequality.* New Brunswick, NJ: Rutgers University Press.

———. 2006. "Knowing Girls: Gender and Learning in School-Based Sexuality Education." In *Sexual Inequalities and Social Justice.* Edited by Niels Teunis and Gilbert Herdt. Berkeley: University of California Press.

Foucault, Michel. 1984. "Truth and Power." In *The Foucault Reader.* Edited by Paul Ravionow. New York: Pantheon.

———. 1980. *The History of Sexuality.* New York: Pantheon.

Frank, Thomas. 2004. *What's the Matter with Kansas?* New York: Metropolitan Books.

Freire, Paolo. 1970. *Pedagogy of the Oppressed.* New York: Continuum.

Gagnon, John H. 2005. Personal communication. October 12.

———. 2005. "T. Laqueur, Solitary Sex: A Cultural History of Masturbation." *Archives of Sexual Behavior* 34(4): 471–73.

———. 2004. *An Interpretation of Desire.* Chicago: University of Chicago Press.

Gagnon, John H. and William Simon. 1973. *Sexual Conduct: The Social Sources of Human Sexuality.* London: Hutchinson.

Giddens, Anthony. 1992. *The Transformation of Intimacy: Sexuality, Love and Eroticism in Modern Societies.* Stanford: Stanford University Press.

Girard, François. 2004. "Global Implications of U.S. Domestic and International Policies on Sexuality." Working Paper, No. 1, International Working Group on Sexuality and Social Policy, Sociomedical Sciences Department, Mailman School of Public Health. Columbia University, New York.

Goode, Erich and Nachman Ben-Yehuda. 1994. *Moral Panics: The Social Construction of Deviance*. Oxford, U.K.: Wiley-Blackwell.

Gusfield, Joseph. 1986. *Symbolic Crusade*. Chicago: University of Illinois Press.

Hall Stuart, Charles Critcher, Tony Jefferson, John Clarke, and Brian Robert. 1978. *Policing the Crisis: Mugging, the State and Law and Order*. London: Palgrave Macmillan.

Halperin, David. 1990. *One Hundred Years of Homosexuality and Other Essays on Greek Love*. New York: Routledge.

Herdt, Gilbert. 2008. "Kinsey." *International Encyclopedia of the Social Sciences,* 2nd ed. Edited by William A. Darity. Detroit: Macmillan Reference.

———. 2004. "Sexual Development, Social Oppression, and Local Culture."*Sexuality Research and Social Policy* 1: 1–24.

———. 2003. *Secrecy and Cultural Reality*. Ann Arbor: University of Michigan Press.

———. 1997. *Same Sex, Different Cultures*. Colorado Springs: Westview.

———. 1996. *Third Sex, Third Gender: Beyond Sexual Dimorphism in Culture and History*. New York: Zone.

Herdt, Gilbert and Robert Kertzner. 2006. "I Do, But I Can't: The Impact of Marriage Denial on the Mental Health and Sexual Citizenship of Lesbians and Gay Men in the United States." *Sexuality Research and Social Policy: Journal of the NSRC*. 3(1): 33–49.

Herdt, Gilbert and Shirley Lindenbaum. 1990. *The Time of AIDS*. Thousand Oaks, CA: Sage.

Herek, Gregory M. 2004. "Beyond 'Homophobia:' Thinking about Sexual Stigma and Prejudice in the Twenty-First Century." *Sexuality Research and Social Policy* 1(2): 6–24.

Herman, Didi. 1997. *The Antigay Agenda: Orthodox Vision and the Christian Right*. Chicago: University of Chicago Press.

Hier, Sean P. 2002. "Conceptualizing Moral Panic Through a Moral Economy of Harm." *Critical Sociology* 28(3): 311–34.

Hunt, Alan. 1998. "Great Masturbation Panic and the Discourses of Moral Regulation in Nineteenth- and Early Twentieth-Century Britain." *Journal of the History of Sexuality* 8(4): 575–616.

Irvine, Janice. 2005. "Anti-Gay Politics Online: A Study of Sexuality and Stigma on National Websites." *Sexuality Research and Social Policy* 2: 3–22.

———. 2002. *Talk about Sex*. Berkeley: University of California Press.

Joffe, Carole. 1995. *Doctors of Conscience: The Struggle to Provide Abortion before and after Roe v. Wade*. Boston: Beacon.

———. 1986. *The Regulation of Sexuality: Experiences of Family Planning Workers*. Philadelphia: Temple University Press.

Jones, James H. 1997. *Alfred C. Kinsey: A Public/Private Life*. New York: Norton.

Kempadoo, Kamala. 2000. "Introduction: Globalizing Sex Workers' Rights." In *Global Sex Workers: Rights, Resistance, and Redefinition.* Edited by Kamala Kempadoo and J. Doezama. New York: Routledge.

Kendall, Nancy. 2006. Personal communication. April 23.

Kim, Lisa and Richard Kim. 2005. "Beyond Gay Marriage." *The Nation.* July 25(1): 24–27.

Kinsey, Alfred, Wardell B. Pomeroy, Clyde E. Martin, and Paul Gerhard. 1953. *Sexual Behavior in the Human Female.* Philadelphia: W. B. Saunders.

Kinsey, Alfred, Wardell B. Pomeroy, and Clyde E. Martin. 1948. *Sexual Behavior and the Human Male.* Philadelphia: W. B. Saunders.

Kirby, Douglas. 2001. *Emerging Answers: Research Findings on Programs to Reduce Teen Pregnancy.* SIECUS Reports.

Klein, Marty. 2006. *America's War on Sex: The Attack on Law, Lust and Liberty.* New York: Praeger.

Kurtz, Stanley. 2003. "The Libertarian Question." *National Review Online,* April 30, 2003.

Lakoff, George. 2004. *Don't Think of an Elephant: Know Your Values and Frame the Debate: The Essential Guide for Progressives.* White River Junction, VT: Chelsea Green.

Lantanari, Vittorio. 1959. *Religions of the Oppressed.* Translated by L. Sergis. New York: Knopf.

Laqueur, Thomas. 2003. *Solitary Sex: A Cultural History of Masturbation.* New York: Zone.

Laumann, Edward O., Stephen Ellingson, Jenna Mahay, Anthony Paik, and Yoosik Youm. 2004. *The Sexual Organization of the City.* Chicago: University of Chicago Press.

Laumann, Edward O., John H. Gagnon, Robert T. Michael, and Stuart Michaels. 1994. *Social Organization of Sexuality: Sexual Practices in the United States.* Chicago: University of Chicago Press.

Lawrence, Peter. 1964. *Road Belong Cargo.* New York: Humanities Press.

Levine, Judith. 2002. *Harmful to Minors.* Minneapolis: University of Minnesota Press.

Levine, Martin. 1998. *The Life and Death of the Homosexual Clone.* New York: NYU Press.

Levine, Martin, Peter M. Nardi, and John H. Gagnon, eds. 1997. *In Changing Times: Gay Men and Lesbians Encounter HIV/AIDS.* Chicago: University of Chicago Press.

Levine, Robert A. 1973. *Culture, Personality, and Behavior.* Chicago: Aldine.

Maluwa, Miriam, Peter Aggleton, Richard Parker. 2002. "HIV and AIDS-Related Stigma, Discrimination, and Human Rights." *Health and Human Rights* 6: 1–18.

McGerr, Michael. 2003. *Fierce Discontent: The Rise and Fall of the Progressive Movement in America, 1870–1920*. New York: Free Press.

McRobbie, Angela and Sarah Thornton. 1995. "Rethinking 'Moral Panic' for Multi-Mediated Social Worlds." *British Journal of Sociology* 46(4): 559–74.

Miller, Alice. 1998. "Easy Promises: Sexuality, Health, and Human Rights." *American Journal of Public Health* 91(6): 861–64.

Misra, Geetanjali and Radhika Chandiramani. 2005. *Sexuality, Gender and Rights: Exploring Theory and Practice in South and Southeast Asia*. New Delhi: Sage.

Parker, Richard. 1999. *Beneath the Equator: Cultures of Desire, Male Homosexuality, and Emerging Gay Communities in Brazil*. New York: Routledge.

Parker, Richard and Peter Aggleton. 2003. "HIV and AIDS-Related Stigma and Discrimination: A Conceptual Framework and Implications for Action." *Social Science and Medicine* 57: 13–24.

Parker, Richard, Regina Barbosa, and Peter Aggleton, eds. 2002. *Framing the Sexual Subject: The Politics of Gender, Sexuality and Power*. Berkeley: University of California Press.

Patton, Cindy. 1997. "Foreword." In *RePlacing Citizenship: AIDS Activism and Radical Democracy*. Edited by Michael P. Brown. New York: Guilford.

Petchesky, Rosalind P. 2003. *Global Prescriptions: Gendering Health and Human Rights*. New York: Palgrave.

———. 2000. "Sexual Rights: Inventing a Concept, Mapping an International Practice." In *Framing the Sexual Subject*. Edited by Richard Parker, Regina Maria Barbosa, and Peter Appleton. Berkeley: University of California Press.

Radosh, Daniel. 2004. "The Culture Wars." *New Yorker*. December 6. p. 48.

Rich, Frank. 2006. *The Greatest Story Ever Sold*. New York: Penguin.

———. 2004. "On 'Moral Values,' It's Blue in a Landslide." *New York Times*. November 14: Arts & Leisure, 1, 8.

Rights of the Body and Perversions of War: Sexual Rights and Wrongs Ten Years Past Beijing. 2005. Conference paper: Universidad Peruana Cayteano Heredia. Lima, Peru.

Robinson, Paul. 1976. *The Modernization of Sex*. New York: Harper and Row.

Rubin, Gayle. 1997. "Elegy for the Valley of the Kings: AIDS and the Leather Community in San Francisco, 1981–1996." In *In Changing Times: Gay Men and Lesbians Encounter HIV/AIDS*. Edited by Michael P. Levine, Peter M. Nardi, and John H. Gagnon. Chicago: University of Chicago Press.

———. 1984. "Thinking Sex: Notes for a Radical Theory of the Politics of Sexuality." In *Pleasure and Danger: Exploring Female Sexuality*. Edited by Carole S. Vance. New York: Routledge and Kegan Paul.

Russell, Glenda M. 2000. *Voted Out: The Psychological Consequences of Anti-Gay Politics*. New York: New York University Press.

Saiz, Ignacio. 2004. "Bracketing Sexuality: Human Rights and Sexual Orientation—A Decade of Development and Denial at the U.N." *Health and Human
Rights* 7(2): 49–80.

Saletan, William. 2003. *Bearing Right: How Conservatives Won the Abortion War.*
Berkeley: University of California Press.

Schwartz, Pepper and Philip Blumstein. 1983. *Couples.* New York: Marrow.

Sedgwick, Eve. 1991. "How to Bring Your Kids Up Gay." *Social Text* 29:18–27.

Shepard, Benjamin. 2003. "In Search of a Winning Script: Moral Panic vs. Institutional Denial." *Sexualities* 6(1): 54–59.

Shilts, Randy. 1987. *And the Band Played On.* New York: St Martin's.

Smith, Anna M. 2001. "The Politicization of Marriage in Contemporary American Public Policy: The Defense of Marriage Act and the Personal Responsibility Act." *Citizenship Studies* 5(3): 303–20.

Stein, Arlene. 2006. Shameless: Sexual Dissidence in American Culture. New
York: NYU Press.

———. 2001. *The Stranger Next Door.* Boston: Beacon.

Stoller, Robert J. 1979. Sexual Excitement. New York: Random House.

Stone, I. F. 1988. *The Trial of Socrates.* New York: Anchor.

Sutherland, Edwin H. 1950. "The Diffusion of Sexual Psychopath Laws." *American Journal of Sociology* 52: 142–48.

Teunis, Niels and Gilbert Herdt, eds. 2006. *Sexual Inequalities and Social Justice.*
Berkeley: University of California Press.

Thompson, Kenneth. 1998. *Moral Panics.* London: Routledge.

United Nations. "The Beijing Declaration and the Platform for Action." New
York: United Nations.

United Nations. 1994. *Economic and Social Council. Committee on Economic, Social, and Cultural Rights*, General comment 14. The right to the highest atone-
able standards of health. U.N. Doc No. E/C 12.

———. 1994. "Report of the International Conference on Population and Development." Cairo, Egypt. U.N. Doc No. A CONF. 171/13/18 October.

Vaid, Urvashi. 1995. *Virtual Equality.* New York: Anchor.

Van der Meer, Theo. 1994 [2003]. "Dutch Gay Bashers." *Culture, Health and Sexuality* 5: 153–66.

Wallace, Anthony F. C. 1969. *Culture and Personality.* 2nd ed. New York:
Random.

Watney, Simon. 1987. *Policing Desire: Pornography, AIDS and the Media.* Minneapolis: University of Minnesota Press.

Weeks, Jeffrey. 1985. *Sexuality and Its Discontents.* London: Routlege and Kegan
Paul.

———. 1981. *The Making of the Modern Homosexual.* London: Hutchinson.

Wolfson, Evan. 2004. *Why Marriage Matters.* New York: Simon and Schuster.

2

The Religious Right and the Reshaping of Sexual Policy
Reproductive Rights and Sexuality Education during the Bush Years

Diane di Mauro and Carole Joffe

This chapter chronicles the impact on sexuality policy in the United States of the rise of the Religious Right as a significant force in American politics. Using a case study analysis of abortion-reproductive rights and sexuality education, it narrates the story of how U.S. policy debates and practices have changed since the 1970s as sexual conservatism rose in prominence and sexual progressives declined in power. We argue that these developments were especially evident during the presidency of George W. Bush. The Religious Right's appeal to traditional moral values and its ability to create moral panics about sexuality are addressed, specifically with regard to abortion and sexuality education. Ultimately, political meddling and moral proscriptions, disregard for scientific evidence, and the absence of a coherent approach regarding sexual and reproductive health rights have undermined sexuality policy in the United States. The chapter ends on a cautious note of optimism, suggesting that the Religious Right may have overreached in its attempt to control sexuality policy.

The United States has a long history of sexual conservatism dating back to its Puritan founders, who put in place a regulatory framing of moral and sexual behaviors and values. This framing dictated an appropriate socialization of children within the family, as well as appropriate roles and behaviors for heterosexual couples, strictly within the confines of marital relationships. Since then, the United States has seen a number of historical periods of fluctuating progressive and regressive moments pertaining to sexuality[1]—for example, the first sexual revolution in the early twentieth century during the Progressive Era (1890–1913) was followed by the repressive dictates of legally sanctioned moral authorities during the post-Prohibition period of the late 1940s.[2]

Since the 1970s—and especially since 2000, when George W. Bush first became president—the United States has experienced another wave of political dominance by sexual conservatives. This article demonstrates the unprecedented abilities of actors associated with the Religious Right to reshape policies in the areas of sexuality education and reproductive rights. The origins of this development—and, indeed, of the movement now referred to as the Religious Right—were set in motion some thirty years ago, primarily as a reaction to the women's liberation and gay rights movements of that era and the significant changes they ignited in sexual values, behaviors, relationships, and social policies.

The women's liberation and gay rights movements challenged virtually every aspect of normative sexuality of the time, primarily by asserting the legitimacy of sex outside marriage, sex separated from procreation, and homosexuality. "The Myth of the Vaginal Orgasm,"[3] an essay that critiqued conventional heterosexual understandings, was one of the best-known feminist statements of the period. These two new movements also called into question prevailing notions of family life. Demands for a more equitable division of labor within households were expressed in another key document of the times, "The Politics of Housework,"[4] as well as in demands for increased male involvement in child rearing and calls for state-funded child care centers, all of which struck a nerve with those committed to traditional conceptions of family life.

Not surprisingly, given the emotionally charged nature of the issues involved, a countermovement initially referred to as the New Right (and later, the Religious Right) arose in response to these developments.[5] The New Right's mobilization around issues of domestic policy as a response to the provocations of feminists, gays, and other progressives differentiated it from the Old Right, which had historically focused largely on foreign policy.[6]

The first such campaign of this new movement, in fact, was not specifically about sexuality but focused on a child care bill passed by Congress that authorized $2 billion for states to use for childcare—one of the first legislative victories of feminism. This bill was ultimately vetoed by then-president Richard Nixon in 1971, partly in response to a massive outpouring of letters from alarmed housewives, organized mainly through their churches, who had been stirred to action by New Right operatives with dire warnings that the government was going to take over care of their children.[7] As a New Right spokeswoman later reflected on this successful effort to derail the childcare bill, "The opening shot in the battle over the family was fired in 1971."[8]

This new force in American politics greatly expanded in 1973, becoming both more structured and more visible in response to the Supreme Court decision *Roe v. Wade,* which recognized a legal right to abortion.[9] Opposition to *Roe* galvanized hundreds of thousands of previously apolitical people, many of them congregation members who organized the effort through their churches. The explosive issue of abortion served as what Rosalind Petchesky termed a "battering ram" for a wide range of other issues that would also receive attention from social conservatives in the years ahead: sexuality education, teenage pregnancy, welfare policies, and out-of-wedlock births.[10]

Early leaders of the New Right—such as Richard Viguerie, one of the originators of direct-mail campaigns, and Paul Weyrich, a conservative Republican Party operative—realizing the electoral potential of religious voters, moved effectively to bring these newly politicized individuals into the Republican Party. In 1979, a meeting between Weyrich and the Reverend Jerry Falwell led to the formation of the Moral Majority.[11] The instrumental role that religious conservatives affiliated with the New Right played in the election of Ronald Reagan in 1980—"the Christian Right's coming out party" as one writer put it—marked the recognition of this movement as a key constituency of the Republican Party.[12] Subsequently, a number of Religious Right–affiliated groups formed—such as Focus on the Family, the Christian Coalition, the Family Research Council, the Concerned Women of America, and the Traditional Values Coalition— and became increasingly influential in circles in Washington, D.C. Indeed, by 2006, noted political commentator Kevin Phillips stated that the two elections of George W. Bush, in 2000 and 2004, "mark the transformation of the GOP into the first religious party in U.S. history."[13]

With the advent of the HIV/AIDS pandemic during the 1980s, the Religious Right became even more noteworthy for its reassertion of religious faith and values, as well as the accompanying cultural anger[14] that targeted feminists and homosexuals as the primary sources of the supposed sexual degeneracy evident in the United States. Campaigns against gay parenting and, above all, opposition to marriage equality for lesbians and gay men have become signature issues for such key organizational entities of the Religious Right as Focus on the Family and the Family Research Council.

The Religious Right's mobilization in response to changes in Americans' sexual behavior along with the corresponding legal and policy developments (e.g., the legalization of abortion) is viewed by many as a classic instance of a moral panic. The originator of the term, British sociologist Stanley Cohen, defined a moral panic as "a condition [that] . . . emerges to become defined as a threat to societal values and interests. . . . [A]t times . . . it has . . . serious and long-lasting repercussions and might produce such changes as those in legal or social policy or even in the way society conceives itself."[15]

This article discusses this moral panic over changing sexual behavior by offering case studies of two key issues: abortion-reproductive rights and sexuality education. These areas have been targets of the Religious Right from its inception and, consistent with Cohen's formulation, continue to be among the most crucial sites for contestation and political retrenchment. At the time of this writing, near the end of the George W. Bush presidency, the Religious Right has been highly successful in cutting back earlier gains not only in terms of abortion rights but also with regard to contraception—an issue long regarded as common ground between opponents and supporters of abortion. With respect to sexuality education, the Right has been similarly successful in reshaping the content and intent of such programs and, in the process, steering millions of dollars to religiously affiliated organizations that promote abstinence-only-until-marriage education at the expense of contraceptive information.

Before proceeding to detailed examinations of the cases, the authors note some common themes that run through the attacks of the Religious Right on sexuality-related issues. Although these lines of attack have been evident since the early mobilization of the Religious Right in the 1970s, they have reached new heights following the election of George W. Bush.

Personnel Actions That Reward the Political Base

First and most crucial has been the administration's rush to reward the Religious Right with key appointments and massive funding for its desired programs. It would be naive to ignore the fact that all presidential administrations to one degree or another favor their supporters with jobs and desired programs—but the extent to which this favoritism occurred immediately after Bush first came into office, as well as the manner in which such appointments were made, appear truly without precedents.

Historian Garry Wills gives an account of the personnel policies in the first administration of George W. Bush:

> For social services, evangelical organizations were given the same right [as K Street lobbyists were for economic legislation] to draft bills and install the officials who implement them. Karl Rove had cultivated the extensive networks of religious right organizations, and they were consulted at every step of the way as the administration set up its policies on gays, AIDS, condoms, abstinence programs, creationism, and other matters that concerned the evangelicals. All the evangelicals' resentments under previous presidents, including Republicans like Reagan and the first Bush, were now being addressed.
>
> She [Kay James, head of the White House Office of Personnel] knew whom to put where, or knew the religious right people who knew. . . . The evangelicals knew which positions could affect their agenda, whom to replace, and whom they wanted appointed. This was true for the Centers for Disease Control, the Food and Drug Administration, and Health and Human Services—agencies that would rule on or administer matters dear to the evangelical causes.[16]

Furthermore, as a number of observers have pointed out, the appointment procedures used to fill important government posts and advisory committees violated all previous norms of professionalism.[17] Those named to positions relating to reproductive and sexual health policies were often chosen on the basis of their adherence to prolife positions rather than on their professional credentials. Furthermore, such vetting took place even in areas removed from sexuality and reproduction. Scientists being considered for various appointments—such as, for example, the advisory panel for the National Institute for Drug Abuse—were asked whether they had voted for President Bush and where they stood on various social issues, such as abortion.[18]

An example of the extremes to which this kind of ideological purity was applied by Bush operatives is offered by journalist Rajiv Chandrasekaran in his account of the personnel decision making for the Iraq Coalition Provisional Authority.[19] Similar to Bush Administration appointees in the domestic sphere, positions for the Coalition Provisional Authority were recruited from Religious Right circles and queried about their positions on abortion. Chandrasekaran noted that the first director of health services was Frederick Burkle, a distinguished physician who was a specialist in disaster relief with extensive experience in Kurdish Iraq. Burkle was shortly replaced by James Haverman, a nonphysician whose main professional experience before taking the Iraq post was running a Christian adoption agency that sought to discourage women from having abortions. Chandrasekaran described how Iraq's ruined hospitals went unattended while Haverman initiated a no-smoking campaign and prioritized the privatization of the Iraq healthcare system.

Another aspect of these personnel policies was the Bush Administration's willingness to attack the perceived enemies of the Religious Right and remove them from office or, in the case of researchers, to withdraw government support for their work. In a well-publicized case, Elizabeth Blackburn, a distinguished cell biologist at the University of California, San Francisco, was removed from the President's Council on Bioethics because of her support for stem cell research. She was replaced by a relatively obscure political scientist who had compared the harvesting of stem cells to slavery.[20]

But nowhere was this willingness to go after ideological enemies made clearer than in the notorious case of the so-called hit list that was assembled in 2003 to target sexuality researchers at odds with the Right's agenda.[21] In this case, staff members at the Traditional Values Coalition, one of the leading organizations affiliated with the Religious Right, made available to sympathetic members of Congress a list of 157 researchers and their projects that had been funded through the National Institutes of Health (NIH). The projects in question focused on topics that the Traditional Values Coalition found particularly objectionable, such as, for example, studies of prostitution or of HIV in particularly hard-hit communities. Even before the existence of the hit list was revealed, sympathetic staffers at NIH had warned its potential grantees to cleanse their proposals of such provocative phrases as "sex worker" and "men who have sex with men" in the title pages and abstracts of their grants (which were accessible to the public).[22]

Attacks on Scientific Integrity

Ideologically driven personnel decisions, in turn, led to the second theme evident in the Bush Administration's treatment of sexuality-related issues: the willingness to allow politics to trump scientific findings. Whether it was the discredited claim that abortion causes breast cancer posted on a government website by antiabortion operatives within the federal

bureaucracy or the patently false statement in a federally funded abstinence-only program that HIV can be transmitted by sweat and tears,[23]
the Bush Administration repeatedly legitimated the use of misleading and
false evidence to support the outcomes it desired. In one of the most notorious comments on the approach to science in the Bush Administration,
journalist Ron Suskind told of an encounter with a Bush senior adviser
who contrasted the reality-based community of conventional scientists
with the current White House: "We're an empire now, and when we act,
we create our own reality."[24]

Indeed, the disdain for scientific integrity displayed during the Bush
presidency across a wide variety of fields—going well beyond sexuality
and reproductive health—prompted an unprecedented move by the Union
of Concerned Scientists to issue a statement in February 2004 denouncing the Bush Administration's policies on science. Ultimately, more than
10,000 members of the U.S. scientific community signed this statement,
including forty-eight Nobel Laureates.[25]

Breaching the Church-State Barrier

The near disappearance of the line separating church and state is a third
common thread in the Religious Right's involvement in sexuality-related
issues and policies. Even before the full-throttle promotion of faith-based
services that has hallmarked the Bush Administration, high-profile instances of church-state violations had been perpetrated by the Religious
Right. For example, the Reagan years saw one of the earliest manifestations of abstinence-only programming: the creation of so-called chastity
centers under the Adolescent Family Life Act.[26] Under this act, religious
groups received public funding to urge teens to be sexually abstinent
and they did so by promoting religious doctrine. This breach of church-
state separation resulted in litigation that ultimately went to the Supreme
Court. In *Bowen v. Kendrick,* the court ruled that public money cannot be
used to pay for religious activities in a publicly funded sexuality education program.[27] But under the Bush Administration, funding of religious
groups has grown exponentially. Besides funding noncontroversial faith-
based social services, the church-state boundary was violated by the huge
influx of monies given to religious groups for both abstinence-only programs and crisis pregnancy centers, which counsel against abortion. These
programs, too, have been the subject of litigation because of violation of
church-state separation.[28]

Traditional Views on Sexuality

Fourth, in its approach to sexuality-related issues, the Religious Right has promoted a highly traditional—some would say neopuritanical—view of sexuality, one that does not reflect the behaviors or values of most Americans in the twenty-first century. As the very phrase "abstinence only until marriage" implies, the Religious Right condemns sexual activity before marriage, as well as opposes gay marriage while demonizing homosexual behavior. Although the abstinence-only campaign is typically thought to be targeted at teenagers, sexual conservatives within the U.S. Department of Health and Human Services revised the abstinence campaign in fall 2006 to include unmarried adults ages twenty to twenty-nine—even though well over 90 percent of people in this age group have been found to be sexually active.[29] Additionally, as the recently stepped-up attack on contraception in Religious Right circles suggests, the prevailing view for these groups is that all sexual activity within marriage must be open to the possibility of procreation.[30]

In practical terms, such views of sexuality have resulted in an often single-minded warning on the dangers of the health risks of sexual behavior (especially for youth) with no acknowledgment of the pursuit of sexual pleasure as an inalienable right, along with an inflexible condemnation of nonmonogamous relationships. In fact, fears of promiscuity led a number of prominent members of the Religious Right to speak out against the promising new vaccine for the human papillomavirus, which can cause cervical cancer, because this vaccine is most effective when given to girls around the age of thirteen.[31]

Internationalism

Fifth, sexuality-related policies have served as vehicles to internationalize the efforts of the Religious Right. This tactic is, in fact, long-standing; in 1984, at a United Nations (U.N.) conference on population in Mexico City, the Reagan Administration announced its controversial policy stipulating that no U.S. foreign aid would fund family-planning services in countries or agencies that used their own monies for abortion services or even counseled about abortion. After the Clinton Administration overturned the Mexico City policy, George W. Bush reinstated the policy (often referred to as the Global Gag Rule) immediately on taking office. The Bush Administration also implemented policies on AIDS education and prevention in Africa that are heavily weighted with abstinence-only provisions—provisions that many critics decry as not only unrealistic but also certain to lead to illness and death that otherwise could have been prevented. Furthermore, the Bush Administration's appointments of Religious Right partisans to various delegations to the United Nations and other international bodies have also permitted a renewed attack on contraceptive services in other countries.[32]

The Scope of This Chapter

Though our research presents, from a sexually progressive viewpoint, an admittedly demoralizing account of the damage done to sexuality-related policies by the Religious Right in the United States, especially during the presidency of the second Bush, we will also offer some cause for (cautious) optimism. In the classic manner of the hubris that typically accompanies successful social movements, it appears that the Religious Right may have overreached in its attempt to remake sexuality policy in the United States. We return to this point at the end of this article.

This essay is not offered as a full analytic account of the moral panics precipitated by sexual and reproductive issues since the 1970s—such an account would necessarily include additional, separate sections on gay and lesbian issues (especially marriage equality) and on the HIV/AIDS pandemic. Instead, this chapter is primarily historically descriptive in demonstrating that political struggles over sexuality rights in the United States have again become intensified arenas of contestation, illustrated by the Religious Right's attacks on reproductive rights and sexuality education.

Reproductive Rights in the United States

How Struggles around Reproductive Rights Have Unfolded since *Roe v. Wade* (1973)

A teenage boy in Texas was sentenced to life imprisonment with no possibility of parole for forty years for causing the stillbirth of twins. The young man had stomped and beaten on his girlfriend's stomach, at her request, because the two feared the consequences of an unwanted pregnancy. In a similar case in Michigan, a young man caused his girlfriend to miscarry after hitting her in the abdomen with a baseball bat. Both of these incidents occurred in states with parental notification laws for abortion.[33]

A group calling itself the NAAPC (the National Association for the Advancement of Preborn Children) filed suit in California to stop research on stem cells.[34] The acronym NAAPC is an obvious attempt to claim identification with one of the oldest and most illustrious civil rights groups in the United States, the NAACP (the National Association for the Advancement of Colored People).

Websites at two U.S.-government-supported agencies, the Centers for Disease Control (CDC) and Prevention and the National Cancer Institute (NCI), posted misleading information about the effectiveness of condoms (CDC) and the alleged link between abortion and breast cancer (NCI).[35]

At the height of the holiday shopping season, prolife groups mounted a boycott against American Girl, a manufacturer of very popular dolls, because the company makes charitable contributions to Girls Inc., a nonprofit organization for girls and young adolescents that supports comprehensive sex education, legal abortion, and gay rights.[36]

The above incidents illustrate the remarkable extent to which reproductive issues have become a key flashpoint of contemporary American politics and culture. Since 2000 and the first presidential term of George W. Bush, battles over abortion and related issues have been particularly intense; American society has experienced an unprecedented intrusion of the ascendant Religious Right far beyond the issue of abortion into multiple areas of everyday life. But abortion remains the overriding issue of concern for the movement. The attack of the Religious Right on abortion from 1973 to the present has been multifaceted and extremely effective.

Cliché though it may be, the abortion situation in the United States can be described accurately as a war—a war, moreover, with many fronts. This article will analyze a number of those fronts, including the courts, the U.S. Congress, the state legislatures, U.S. popular culture, and the front lines of abortion provision. This analysis of reproductive rights in the United States concludes with a discussion of the spread of abortion to other issues.

A War with Many Fronts

The courts. The judiciary is one of the prime sites where the Religious Right has been rewarded by Republican presidents for its support. Starting with the presidency of Ronald Reagan, litmus tests have been imposed on judicial nominations for Supreme Court justices, as well as those for lower courts.[37] The Religious Right's ability to act as broker in the selection of Supreme Court nominees was in full display in summer 2005, when the movement convened a number of what it called judicial Sundays, when pastors and congregants across the country took part in a teleconference with White House officials and high-ranking Republican legislators to discuss possible nominees.[38] Religious Right leaders, such as James Dobson of Focus on the Family, were among the first to demand the withdrawal of the nomination of Harriet Miers, a Bush ally whom Dobson and his colleagues did not trust as being sufficiently conservative.

Among the key Supreme Court rulings on abortion have been the *Harris v. McCrae* decision in 1980, which ruled that poor women had no right to a federally funded abortion,[39] and the *Webster v. Reproductive Health Services* decision in 1989, which ruled that restrictions on abortion services—such as parental notification or consent for minors seeking abortion and state-ordered scripts that physicians must read to patients—do not impose an undue burden on women seeking abortions.[40]

The *Planned Parenthood of Southeastern Pennsylvania v. Casey* decision in 1992 reaffirmed the essential constitutional right to an abortion, much to the relief of the abortion rights community. The decision did, however, abolish the trimester framework of the original 1973 *Roe* decision and upheld several restrictions on abortion.[41] Although the Supreme Court ruled narrowly against a ban on so-called "partial birth abortion"[42]— a rarely used technique known in medical terms as "intact dilation and extraction"—in the *Stenberg v. Carhart* case in 2000, a newly reconfigured Court with two Bush appointees reheard an almost identical case, *Gonzales v. Carhart*, in fall 2006. To the dismay of the abortion rights community, the Court upheld the ban, in spite of various medical groups' testimony that in some instances, the disputed technique was the safest option. The reproductive freedom movement was also shocked that with this decision the Court overturned precedent and found that an exception to protect women's health was no longer constitutionally necessary in abortion law.[43]

Congress. The House and Senate have actively sought to intervene in abortion care in a way that is not applied to any other medical procedure. For example, besides passing the ban on partial birth abortion, an action that led to the Supreme Court hearings mentioned above, legislators have introduced measures on fetal pain requiring—against the medical community's best scientific judgment[44]—anesthesia for the fetus after a certain point in gestation. But the most unprecedented instance of congressional interference into medical practice came in 1996, when the Residency Review Committee for Obstetrics and Gynecology of the Accreditation College of Graduate Medical Education (ACGME) stipulated that residency programs in this field should offer routine training in abortion procedures with an opt-out clause for those who had moral or religious objections. For the first time ever, Congress held hearings on an ACGME standard and essentially nullified this new requirement by stating that no ob-gyn residency was at risk of losing funds if this stipulation was not followed.[45]

State legislatures. Since *Roe v. Wade,* state legislatures have annually considered hundreds of bills whose intent it is to restrict, if not eliminate, abortion provision—and many of these bills have become law. Empowered by the *Webster* decision, a majority of states now have either parental-notification or parental-consent laws for minors who wish to have an abortion. Additionally, a number of states have passed onerous TRAP (Targeted Regulation of Abortion Providers) laws: These bills, which do not apply to any other areas of health care, require physicians who provide abortion services to comply with complicated and cumbersome requirements mandating, for example, the number of parking spaces, the rate of airflow, or the width of doorways for the buildings in which they work.[46] A number of these laws have passed judicial scrutiny—often thanks to highly conservative judges vetted by the Religious Right. Even when some of these bills ultimately are overturned in the courts, dealing with them is very costly and time consuming for the abortion-providing community, so these laws can serve as a disincentive that keeps some potential abortion providers from offering this service at all.

U.S. popular culture. To a remarkable degree, the antiabortion movement has been successful in its campaign to stigmatize abortion within U.S. popular culture. Positive or even neutral portrayals of abortion in television and film have been nearly absent, typically because of networks' fear of organized protests to advertisers from the Religious Right.[47] Meanwhile, starting in 1985 with a widely distributed video, *The Silent Scream,*[48] a brilliant piece of antiabortion propaganda that misleadingly claimed to portray a late-term abortion, the fetus emerged as a cultural figure in its own right.[49] Such disparate events as the rise of routine ultrasonography in pregnancies (and the increasing availability of ultrasounds in nonmedical settings such as shopping malls); the rise of fetal medicine;[50] and a strategic campaign by the Religious Right to insert the fetus as an independent actor into various legislation[51] have combined to promote the notion of an adversarial relationship between the fetus and its potential enemy—the woman who would abort.

The Religious Right has skillfully capitalized on the power of ultrasounds. In response to urging from Religious Right organizations, more than $30 million of public funding has been given to pregnancy resource centers, also known as crisis pregnancy centers, during the Bush Administration.[52] These monies, in many cases, have been used to purchase ultrasound machines as a means of convincing pregnant women not to abort. A recently announced strategy of the antiabortion movement is working for legislation that would compel abortion-providing facilities to offer each patient the opportunity to see an ultrasound of the fetus she is carrying.[53]

Yet another indication of the stigmatized position of abortion in American culture is its linguistic suppression. The word "abortion" is increasingly shrouded in silence—even among its advocates. "I support a woman's right to choose" or "I support choice" are commonly used formulations by politicians, who, in spite of their belief in abortion rights, feel the need to employ such euphemisms. At the same time, use of the word "choice" itself is criticized by many within the reproductive rights movement because the term suggests that abortion is a consumer item that can be freely chosen by all women, whereas the reality is that abortion is decreasingly available to many American women—especially those made vulnerable by race, poverty, or age.[54]

On the front lines of abortion provision. The most consequential impact of the war against abortion—but also the least visible to many Americans—occurs on a daily basis at the facilities that offer abortion services. There, beleaguered healthcare professionals and their staff have to manage the consequences of the various restrictions and laws that govern abortion provision in their states. Beyond that, they face enormous security concerns that occur in no other area of American medicine. Since 1993, seven members of the abortion-providing community have been murdered, six at their workplaces and one in his home. Thousands more have been terrorized, the clinics where they work have been vandalized and firebombed, and in 2000 more than half of all abortion providers experienced some form of antiabortion harassment.[55]

Moreover, the daily challenges abortion providers face go well beyond security and compliance with complicated regulations. The stigma and marginalization that have come to surround abortion care in many communities[56] mean that providers often confront such difficulties as hospitals who refuse privileges to abortion doctors, landlords who refuse to renew leases, and vendors who refuse to provide essential services such as laundry. These refusals are often engineered by groups and individuals affiliated with the Religious Right.

The Spread of the Abortion War to Other Issues

Emboldened by its electoral successes, especially since the 2000 election of George W. Bush, the Religious Right in the United States has extended its assault on reproductive issues beyond abortion to a variety of other areas. These new terrains provide a number of ways for this movement to expand its influence and further its various objectives. One of the most notable developments has been the emergence of embryo politics—an effort, on many fronts, to define the meaning of life in ways that are at odds with conventional understandings. So, for example, by its reference to human embryos as preborn or microscopic Americans,[57] the Religious Right has attacked not only stem cell research but also assisted reproduction techniques that use embryos, such as in vitro fertilization. Through various legislative measures—such as the Unborn Victims of Violence Act of 2004 (Laci and Conner's Law), which states that the murderer of a pregnant woman can be charged with two crimes, or an amendment to a children's health bill that mandated healthcare to a fetus but not to the woman carrying the fetus[58]—the Right is attempting to lay the groundwork for an eventual legal (and cultural) recognition of the personhood of the unborn, an action that would render abortion illegal.[59]

Such efforts on the part of the Religious Right to control the meanings of life extend to end-of-life issues as well. Euthanasia, physician-assisted suicide, and other right-to-die issues have long been targets of this movement. These issues came to a head in spring 2005 with the notorious case of Terri Schiavo. President Bush and Republican legislators, seeking to please their extreme right-wing base, made unprecedented intrusions into the decision of a Florida man to withdraw a feeding tube from his brain-dead wife. In what was to prove a massive political miscalculation, Tom DeLay, then second in command in Congress, exclaimed to a gathering of the Family Research Council, "One thing that God has brought to us is

Terri Schiavo, to help elevate the visibility of what is going on in America."[60] Bill Frist, a physician who was then majority leader in the Senate and a 2008 presidential aspirant, disgraced himself (and helped derail his presidential chances) by claiming, on the basis of watching television footage of Schiavo in her hospital bed, that he disagreed with the diagnosis of brain death given to the patient—a diagnosis that was later confirmed by autopsy.[61]

The case ultimately involved the highly unusual and irregular spectacle of Congress passing a bill—which George W. Bush signed after taking a jet to the White House in the middle of the night—specifically tailored to one event. The Schiavo case was notable for the visible presence at the dying woman's hospice of some of the key players in the most violent wing of the antiabortion movement; indeed, in an eerie echo of the most extremist antiabortion politics, these leaders issued calls for the deaths of judges who did not prevent the removal of the feeding tubes.[62]

The Religious Right's aggressive campaign against emergency contraception (EC) is both an outgrowth of embryo politics as well as a suitable vehicle for the movement's escalation to a war against contraception itself. Emergency contraception is a higher-than-normal concentration of oral contraception that, if taken within seventy-two hours of unprotected intercourse, is effective in preventing pregnancy. Although health professionals point to the fact that EC prevented an estimated 51,000 abortions in 2000 alone,[63] the Religious Right has reframed EC itself as an abortifacient. This reframing is based on the unconventional definition of pregnancy that the movement has been increasingly using. Whereas the consensus in the medical community is that pregnancy commences with the implantation of a fertilized egg in the uterus, the Right now argues that pregnancy begins with the fertilization of an egg. Even though most experts agree that EC works by inhibiting ovulation, abortion opponents claim that this drug causes an abortion because it cannot be proven that EC does not ever inhibit implantation of a fertilized egg.[64]

The Religious Right fought assiduously to prevent this drug from being approved for over-the-counter (OTC) status by the U.S. Food and Drug Administration (FDA), a move that would make EC more readily available to American women. The arguments mounted by Religious Right spokespersons went beyond insisting that the drug was an abortifacient; with no evidence whatsoever, the group claimed that easier access to this drug would increase promiscuity among adolescent women—a claim that has been disproved by researchers.[65] In spite of overwhelming consensus by the FDA's own advisory panel of experts that this drug is safe for OTC status, the agency, bowing to pressure from the Right, repeatedly denied this application. Several high-ranking FDA officials, including Susan Wood, director of the Office of Women's Health, resigned in protest over this capitulation.[66] Ultimately, in the face of widespread negative publicity and with two women senators stalling the nomination of a new head of the FDA, the agency finally reached a compromise position in summer 2006, allowing the drug to have OTC status for women ages eighteen and over.

Though elements of the antiabortion movement have long opposed regular contraception as well as EC, this opposition was mainly covert for fear of alienating the vast majority of Americans who use birth control. However, more recently, such opposition has become more open. The opposition to contraception is based on moral grounds as well as the alleged health consequences of contraceptive use. For example, after hosting a conference in fall 2006 titled "Contraception Is Not the Answer," a Pro-Life Action League spokesperson commented on the organization's website that "the entire edifice of sexual license, perversion and abortion is erected upon the foundation of contraception."[67] The organization Focus on the Family posted on its website, "Modern contraceptive inventions have given many an exaggerated sense of safety and prompted more people than ever before to move sexual expression outside the marriage boundary."[68] As with EC, some within the Religious Right are increasingly reframing various forms of "regular" birth control, in particular oral contraception ("the Pill") as a form of "abortion."[69]

This growing movement against contraception is revealed most dramatically in pharmacies: an increasing number of pharmacists affiliated with the Religious Right have been refusing to fill prescriptions for EC and, in some cases, regular oral contraception. (The chain of Wal-Mart pharmacies, often the only pharmacy available to rural women, only recently reversed its long-standing policy of refusing to stock EC; one can speculate that this shift occurred because of an intensifying period of public criticism, both domestically and globally, of numerous Wal-Mart policies.) These well-publicized cases, which have included pharmacists refusing birth control to married women as well as single ones, occasionally accompanied by strident lectures, have led to a flurry of contradictory legislation in the states—with some states passing legislation compelling pharmacies to fill such prescriptions and more conservative states affirming the right of pharmacists to refuse to fill them.[70]

This pharmacy refusal movement, in turn, has led to a broader health-care worker refusal movement associated with the Religious Right. These instances include cases of ambulance workers who have refused to transport women in need of an emergency abortion to a hospital, nurses who have refused to dispense EC at public health clinics, and doctors who will not perform sterilizations. In some cases, health workers have refused to perform services for some patients that they are willing to do for others. For example, in one well-publicized case, a lesbian was refused insemination services at a clinic that performed this service for couples and straight women. In another case, a single straight woman who wished to adopt a child was denied the necessary physical exam by a doctor who did not believe single women should have the right to adopt.[71] In such cases, where health workers selectively dispense desired services, the issue is not necessarily embryo politics but rather the regulation of sexual activity to which Religious Right devotees object. The current widespread phenomenon of hospital mergers between Catholic and non-Catholic facilities has only exacerbated this problem of reproductive health services being selectively offered or not offered at all.[72]

U.S. Foreign Policy

Reproductive politics have become a central part of U.S. foreign policy as well as domestic policy. The Global Gag Rule mentioned earlier in this article has meant the loss of millions of dollars in aid for reproductive healthcare to countries in the developing world. Similarly, President Bush, in each year of his presidency, has refused to release funds appropriated by Congress for the UN Population Fund (UNFPA), a move strongly supported by his Religious Right base. The stated reason for this freezing of funds is that UNFPA monies are used to support coercive abortion and sterilization in China—a claim that has been repeatedly disproved, including by a team sent by the U.S. Department of State. The International Women's Health Coalition (IWHC), one of the premier watchdog groups in the area of reproductive health, has pointed out that $161 million from the United States has been withheld at a time when over half a million women die as a result of pregnancy or childbirth each year, and over 350 million couples lack access to contraception: "the Administration . . . den(ies) safe motherhood services, contraceptives, fistula repair, and HIV/AIDS prevention services to women in 140 developing countries worldwide."[73]

Numerous other examples exist of the centrality of antiabortion themes in the involvement of the United States in international health issues. For example, the World Health Organization, in response to the nearly 70,000 women per year who die from illegal abortions and the nearly 19 million women each year who seek illegal abortions, sought to place mifepristone—a pill used for early abortions—on its essential medicines list. This list officially recommends drugs to which doctors worldwide should have access. The United States lobbied hard against the bill, stalled the process, and ultimately was defeated.[74]

The United States under George W. Bush has also acted unilaterally or with a small bloc of other countries at various UN meetings, pushing hard for an antiabortion and anticontraception agenda. In 2002, in one of the more bizarre such coalition efforts, the U.S. delegation, in alliance with Iran, Iraq (less than a year before the country was invaded by the United States), Libya, Sudan, and the Vatican, tried to block consensus at a special session on children. Whereas the vast majority of delegates—recognizing the realities of sexual abuse, sex work, early marriage, and consensual sex among teenagers—supported contraceptive education and services, including HIV/AIDS prevention, the abovementioned coalition unsuccessfully pushed for an abstinence-only approach.[75] Although the Bush Administration's support for international AIDS work—known formally as the President's Plan for AIDS Relief—has drawn praise for the $15 billion that has been committed to this work, the plan has also been widely criticized for its ideologically driven limitations. For example, a considerable amount of the allocated funds are for abstinence and be-faithful programs, an approach that most international experts think is not realistic for most of those at risk for HIV and AIDS. Moreover, the Bush Administration has insisted that condoms be promoted only for high-risk sexual encounters and has discouraged the provision of needle exchanges, an approach that many in the field have found effective.[76]

The Impact of the Religious Right on Sexual and Reproductive Issues

What has been the cumulative impact of these unrelenting attacks by the Right on reproductive issues since 1973, especially during the George W. Bush years? The strategies and attitudes mentioned earlier in this article—payback appointments and deployment of resources, disdain for science, blurring of church-state separation, outdated understandings of gender roles—have worked together to significantly weaken reproductive rights and services in the United States. In the international realm, official U.S. policies have similarly eroded the promise of both much-needed medical services and sexual rights.

With specific regard to abortion, *Roe v. Wade* still stands, but its future status is precarious, and even if abortion remains legal, this victory may be hollow. Currently, 87 percent of all U.S. counties are without an abortion provider, which, given U.S. population distribution, means that one out of three women live in counties without abortion services.[77]

Medical institutions, particularly residencies in obstetrics and gynecology, have done an imperfect job of training in abortion procedures—often, as already discussed, because of external political pressures. As a result, many abortion care facilities have difficulties in finding an adequate number of qualified providers. In many communities, local obstetrician-gynecologists who are personally supportive of abortion rights may feel constrained from providing abortions, fearing both sanctions from colleagues and possible violence from pro-lifers. Therefore, clinics that provide abortions often must rely on doctors who fly in from other locations.[78] Although the actual number of individual abortion providers in the United States is unknown, what is known is that the number of identified abortion-providing facilities has steadily declined. Between 1996 and 2000, for example, the number of such facilities declined by 11 percent.[79]

Predictably, the most vulnerable women in U.S. society—women of color, those with low income, the young, and those residing in rural areas—have been affected most by the difficulties in gaining access to abortion services. The Hyde Amendment, originally passed in 1976, forbids the use of public funding to pay for abortions, and only nineteen states allow the use of Medicaid funds for this purpose.[80] Although abortion rates in general saw a considerable decline during the 1980s and 1990s, disparities between the poor and the nonpoor were noteworthy. The Guttmacher Institute, the leading research organization that tracks reproductive health events, recently gave this stark assessment: "The abortion rate among women living below the federal poverty level . . . is more than four times that of women living above 300 percent of the poverty level."[81] Although there may appear to be a contradiction between the statements that poor and disproportionately minority women, on the one hand, have more trouble gaining access to abortions and, on the other, have higher rates of abortions than nonpoor women, this seeming contradiction can be explained by the growing gap between the two groups' access to contraception. The institute also documented that poor women of color are those most likely to experience a delay in obtaining an abortion, thus complicating the search for someone who will perform the procedure (many abortion-providing clinics do not offer services for women who are past the first trimester of pregnancy) and making it more costly.[82]

For teenagers, such delays are often a function of parental-notification or parental-consent requirements. Although no firm data exist on how widespread the phenomenon is, a number of accounts document behavior similar to that occurring in the pre-*Roe* (1973) era, with desperate individuals attempting to perform their own abortions. The combination of the stigma currently associated with abortion in many communities, along with the restrictive regulations now in place, has meant that teenagers especially are vulnerable to engaging in this behavior, often with tragic consequences.[83]

Although much of the attention of the culture wars has been focused on abortion, in fact, the Religious Right's attacks on contraception have been equally consequential. The opponents of birth control have not been effective in culturally stigmatizing birth control, but they have been very effective in cutting off state and federal public funding for family planning services, with such actions often occurring without much public notice. The Religious Right has steadfastly opposed Title X of the Public Health Service Act,[84] the main government program that provides contraception to low-income women, since the creation of the program in 1970—and there is a long history, starting with Ronald Reagan, of appointing anti-abortion ideologues to run the Office of Family Planning, which administers the program.[85] In such a hostile environment, Title X funding has remained flat and currently is woefully inadequate to meet the needs of its low-income constituency. In some cases, states have allowed the use of Medicaid funds to pay for such services. Yet since 1994, more than half of all states have cut funding for family planning, in some cases having instead redirected funds to crisis pregnancy centers.

As with abortion, therefore, a wide disparity exists between contraceptive use for poor versus nonpoor women. A recent report from the Guttmacher Institute showed fewer low-income women using any contraceptive method in 2002 than in 1995; over the same period of time, "[T]he unintended pregnancy rate among poor women increased by 29 percent, even as it fell by 20 percent among women with higher incomes."[86] In short, given these growing disparities in both abortion rates and birth control usage, one can meaningfully speak of two Americas when it comes to women's ability to control their fertility. The common ground that most Americans believe in no matter where they stand on abortion—the desirability of the prevention of unwanted pregnancies—has been sabotaged by the systematic defunding of contraceptive services that has been demanded by the Religious Right.

Furthermore, reproductive health and reproductive rights have been ground zero in the war against science waged by the Bush Administration and its allies. As Chris Mooney, one of the leading observers of this phenomenon, put it, "Where religious conservatives may once have advanced their pro-life and socially traditionalist views through moral arguments, they now increasingly adopt the veneer of scientific and technical expertise."[87] Accordingly, what many have decried as "junk science" has been deployed by Religious Right–affiliated spokespeople to argue for a postabortion syndrome, which posits significant, long-term mental health effects of abortion—a claim long disputed by the American Psychological Association; for discredited links between breast cancer and abortion; and for the alleged ineffectiveness of condoms as protection against HIV and other sexually transmitted infections.[88] As the next section of this article will discuss, abstinence-only sexuality education curricula have been exposed by government investigators as being rife with inaccuracies. Crisis pregnancy centers, which receive millions of dollars of public funding, have similarly been shown by investigators to give inaccurate information to teenage callers on such matters as the effect of abortion on future fertility as well as breast cancer.[89]

This war on science has also included an attack on individual scientists who are out of step with the administration's collusion with the Religious Right on crucial issues. In addition to the development of the hit list discussed earlier in this article, other actions have included a clampdown on the number of scientists within the federal bureaucracy who are allowed to work with the World Health Organization or to attend international health conferences. For example, in 2004, more than 150 government researchers were prevented from traveling to the International AIDS Conference in Bangkok;[90] this decision was made, one journalist reported, "after the organizer of the conference refused a request by the United States to invite the evangelist Franklin Graham to give a speech promoting faith-based solutions to the AIDS epidemic."[91] Stem cell research has been held back at the federal level because of George W. Bush's actions since taking office and is progressing only in a few individual states. All these actions, not surprisingly, have led to a demoralization among government scientists, with many leaving their positions.[92]

Internationally, the developing world remains highly dependent on funding from the United States for reproductive healthcare services but deeply frustrated by the ideologically driven constraints imposed as individuals affiliated with the Religious Right have taken charge of many aid programs. At the same time, the Religious Right's ability to place its allies into key roles as advisers and delegates to U.N.-related functions concerning reproductive health has enabled a further long-standing goal of that movement, to engage in "disruptive diplomacy," as a recent report put it— that is, to weaken the United States' collaborative efforts with that international body.[93]

The Movement for Reproductive Rights

How has the reproductive rights movement in the United States responded to these assaults by the Religious Right? Initially, the fight for abortion rights in the United States was part of a larger struggle for sexual and reproductive freedom that was a crucial component of the feminist and gay rights movements of the 1960s and 1970s. Those who fought for legal abortion, for example, also worked against sterilization abuse of women of color, for the ability of poor women to have children and raise them in dignity, for the legitimacy of lesbian and gay relationships, for deeper understandings of women's sexuality, and so on. The continual attack on legal abortion since the 1973 *Roe v. Wade* decision, however, has put the reproductive rights movement on a very defensive basis, with a perhaps inevitable narrowing of focus onto the maintenance of legal abortion. What once was a vibrant grassroots movement gradually became entrenched in large bureaucratic organizations such as Planned Parenthood, National Organization for Women, and NARAL Pro-Choice America.[94]

However, a number of events are currently rejuvenating the abortion rights movement and returning it to its roots as a broader-based entity. The first such event is the globalization of the reproductive freedom movement. The historic UN conferences at Cairo and Beijing in the mid-1990s and the follow-up events, most recently in 2004 and 2005 at the United Nations, have brought U.S. activists into contact with thousands of their counterparts elsewhere, including those in the developing world, and expanded U.S. activists' understanding of reproductive rights into a larger framework of human rights.[95]

Second, in spite of continual complaints by veteran activists that the abortion rights movement has not captured the imagination of a new generation, the March for Women's Lives, held in spring 2004 in Washington, D.C., clearly challenged this belief. The march not only was thought to be the largest political gathering ever in the United States (with an estimated participation of more than a million) but also included a sizable presence of young women, many of whom were women of color. Using the frame of reproductive justice, many of this newer generation of activists have aligned themselves with other struggles for social justice by expanding the scope of their groups beyond abortion itself while remaining committed to keeping abortion legal and accessible in the United States.[96] Among the most prominent of such new groups is the SisterSong Women of Color Reproductive Health Collective, which primarily represents women from five ethnic populations: Asian American and Pacific Islander, Black and African American, Latina, Middle Eastern and Arab American, and Native American and indigenous. Besides legal abortion, the individual organizations in this collective work on such issues as HIV/AIDS services, midwifery, services for incarcerated women, teen pregnancy, and screening for sexually transmitted diseases.[97]

Third, as the authors will discuss further in the conclusion of this article, the escalating actions of the Religious Right may arguably provide the most potential for reviving a vibrant reproductive rights movement. Just as the feminist and gay rights movements of the 1970s and the *Roe v. Wade* decision stimulated the emergence of a strengthened Religious Right, so, too, might the broad-based attack of the latter on a wide range of issues, especially contraception, spur a similar mobilization response from the reproductive rights movement.

Sexuality Education: A Politically Charged Arena

A History of Debate and Controversy, 1905–2006

The historical tracing of sexuality education in the United States is a path of controversy and debate, as was aptly shown by Irvine[98] and Moran.[99] These reviews illustrated that this history can be viewed as a progressive narrowing of formalized opportunities for teaching about sexuality in the public schools, a curriculum currently guided by ideological intentions to impose on students a traditional moral view of sexuality.

Evident from the very first attempt to introduce a sexuality education curriculum into the U.S. public school system—initiated in 1905 by the American Society for Sanitary and Moral Prophylaxis (in response to a much-exaggerated venereal disease epidemic)—debate on the issue has taken place on a "shifting social, cultural, and political terrain . . . a controversial backdrop against which educators have instructed American youth about sexuality."[100] The predominance of controversy surrounding sexuality education has historically overshadowed an essential and, to this date, unattainable requirement for its success—namely that such education be guided by a rational, coherent national discussion taking place not only within the school system but also in the larger public arena regarding its objectives and the training of its instructors, as well as the design, implementation, and evaluation of its curriculum. Most striking is the fact that no such public discussion has ever taken place as part of this process to answer the question, "What values and knowledge about sexuality should be taught to the next generation?" What little discussion has taken place in the age of abstinence-only education focuses on the limitation of students' access to information about sexuality, lest adolescents would be encouraged to run (sexually) amok.

By the 1940s and 1950s, family experts joined the social hygienists in celebrating early marriage and domesticity by providing gender education: that is, teaching students traditional, gender-appropriate behavior for what supposedly constituted masculinity, femininity, fatherhood, and motherhood within a framework of middle-class values and conformity.[101] By the 1960s and 1970s, sexuality education curricula incorporated the concept of freedom of personal choice regarding orientation and access to contraception, primarily due to increased sexual freedom regarding premarital intercourse and cohabitation—as well as the back-to-back legislative decisions of March 1972 (*Eisenstadt v. Baird*, which extended the right to purchase and use contraceptives to unmarried people) and January 1973 (*Roe v. Wade*). Equally important in triggering these changes was the emerging youth countercultural and women's liberation movements, themselves "product[s] of a confluence of social trends including growth in women's college attendance and labor force participation, delayed marriages, and a spirit of opposition nourished in part by the civil rights movement, and later opposition to the Vietnam War."[102] During this period, sexuality education experienced the beginning of its most progressive era, one that began with the 1964 founding of the first national organization to support sexuality education—SIECUS, the Sexuality Information and Education

Council of the United States. With the support and promotional efforts of SIECUS and like-minded, newly trained sexuality educators graduating from health education programs, a national campaign to support sexuality education was launched, one that pressed for a comprehensive, value-neutral framework without moralistic condemnation and that was based on factual information regarding contraception, a critique of gender role socialization, and the promotion of sexuality as a natural force of human life.[103]

Yet, once again, opposition was swift, as the John Birch Society, MOMS (Mothers Organized for Moral Stability) and POSSE (Parents Opposed to Sex and Sensitivity Education) condemned SIECUS's efforts, claiming, "Sexuality education was part of a deeper conspiracy to weaken America's moral fiber in preparation for a communist takeover."[104] By 1968, the use by these groups of the threat of sexuality education mobilized concerned citizens to forge a new right movement committed to social and sexual issues, a movement that would in turn lead the crusade against sexuality education in the coming decade.

This New Right movement, which emerged in the 1970s, gained considerable strength with the advent of the 1980s and the HIV/AIDS pandemic. Although the term "Religious Right" would come into use only in later decades, the movement always had a strong religious and, specifically, Christian evangelical base. Initially, however, the incorporation of HIV/AIDS curricula nationwide—truly intended to decrease HIV risk—was indicative of a more comprehensive sexuality education approach taking hold across the country, one that incorporated educational (and, at that time, innovative) objectives designed to confront and repel sexism, homophobia, stigma, and discrimination. The progressive moment proved short lived as traditional and religious political viewpoints began to exploit the life-and-death urgency of HIV and AIDS to invigorate another conservative backlash. This AIDS-related backlash focused on controlling sexuality by demonizing targeted risk groups, particularly gay men and prostitutes, and warning of the dangers of unrestrained sexual impulse, especially among adolescents. Conservative organizations and their spokespeople effectively and strategically exaggerated the risk of transmission and contagion among gay people, promoting the view of HIV/AIDS as just retribution and a sign of God's wrath for the sexual depravity produced by the sexual revolution in the 1960s and 1970s.[105]

It was at this juncture that conservative organizations followed a new tactic in their approach to opposing sexuality education—namely, the championing of a new, so-called morally superior version of sexuality education—rather than working to eliminate it in the nation's schools. Initially, this abstinence-only education approach emphasized the benefits of delaying the onset of first sexual intercourse until marriage and provided little, if any contraceptive information. Ironically, prior to the late 1980s and early 1990s, sexuality education programs were not very widespread in the nation's schools—the programs became more prevalent only in response to the HIV pandemic taking hold in the United States, the resulting increase in HIV/AIDS education for grades K–12, and, in response, the conservative backlash that initiated the abstinence-focused educational approach. For conservatives, HIV/AIDS became the sexual panic of sexuality education, providing the necessary moral boost to promote abstinence-only education as a viable means for protecting youth and supporting traditional family values.[106] From the 1980s and continuing to the present, a vast network of conservative organizations mobilized, spurred by the ascendancy of conservatism and a reassertion of religious faith and values newly reemerging in the United States.

During this period, the conservative movement instituted its most successful strategy for opposing sexuality education: the use of language and emotion to seize the rhetorical higher ground by framing the issue as one between good and evil.[107] Right-wing opponents of comprehensive sexuality education claimed that it promoted promiscuity, abortion, and homosexual recruitment and that those who opposed such education represented a responsible, morally appropriate position.[108]

From the mid-1980s through the mid-1990s, this large, powerful conservative network continued to grow, working primarily at the legislative level. By 1996, the Religious Right had been successful in getting its sexuality education platform enshrined in federal legislation in the form of Clinton's welfare reform legislation, the 1996 Temporary Assistance for Needy Families Act. This legislation initially provided $50 million for an even more rigid educational approach than the 1981 Adolescent Family Life Act, now called abstinence-only-until-marriage education programs. From the passing of the bill up until 2005, every state except California adopted an abstinence-only education approach—one developed without community discussion or public debate. This trend was accompanied by the codification of federal abstinence-only guidelines that have differentially affected state, district, and school policies as dictated by disparate state mandates, recommendations, funding needs, accountability requirements, and community pressures.[109]

By the end of the 1990s, the oppositional camps engaged in the battle over sexuality education were solidified as those promoting abstinence-only-until-marriage education versus those supporting comprehensive sexuality education.[110] The disparity between the two could not have been greater. Comprehensive education seeks to promote a positive view of sexuality, to provide students with information and skills about taking care of their sexual health, and to help them acquire skills to make responsible decisions.[111] Such curricula are designed to provide age-appropriate information as well as opportunities for students to explore attitudes and develop skills with regard to physical anatomy and bodily functions; social, individual, and family relationships; society and culture; decision making; skill building to resist social and peer pressure; and contraception. Additionally, comprehensive curricula typically contain an emphasis on abstinence with the intent to delay the onset of first sexual intercourse. It is important to note that the term "comprehensive" is often applied to a range of sexuality education curricula; for some professionals, these curricula can be considered as long as they provide information about the use of contraceptives without focusing on the risks they pose. Also, the extent to which comprehensive curricula do in fact reflect progressive values about sexuality and gender differs significantly across the spectrum.[112]

Abstinence-only curricula, conversely, posit that a mutually faithful monogamous relationship in the context of marriage is the expected standard of human sexual activity and that "sexual activity outside of the context of marriage is likely to have harmful psychological and physical effects."[113] These curricula dictate abstinence until (heterosexual) marriage, provide little factual contraceptive information, and may even emphasize condom failure, the threat of death or serious illness (such as breast cancer or mental breakdown) from abortion and homosexuality, and the potential reversibility of homosexuality through faith and religious commitment.

Since 2005 however, abstinence-only education, as well as the Bush Administration's support of it, has systematically come under attack by a wide ranging informal coalition of professionals, legislators, researchers, and organizations. From 2005 to the present, in addition to California, another sixteen states[114] have opted out of the $50 million, in direct response to both the effective advocacy efforts on the part of such coalition and to the findings of evaluative research that has seriously questioned the effectiveness of this "educational" approach.[115] Another indication of its increasing unpopularity, is the recent (and very first) Congressional

ITHACA COLLEGE LIBRARY

hearing conducted on April 28, 2008, by Congressman Waxman, Chair of the House Committee on Oversight and Government Reform, on the effectiveness of abstinence-only education. A multitude of witnesses testified to the ineffectiveness of such approach–including the American Academy of Pediatrics, the Institute of Medicine, and the American Public Health Association–and emphasized that continued federal support for such approach not only did not comport with the evidence but also that it was potentially dangerous to children. While these developments are certainly encouraging, progress has been slow moving on the proposed Responsible Education About Life Act (REAL)[116]—formerly the Family Life Education Act—which would provide federal funding for comprehensive sexuality education programs that include information on both abstinence and contraception and condoms, in spite of support by more than 125 national and state organizations, including medical, civil rights, faith-based, family planning, educational, public health, reproductive rights, and HIV and AIDS service organizations. First introduced in March 2007 by Rep. Barbara Lee, REAL has been referred to the Subcommittee on Health and no vote on it has been yet scheduled.

Where Are the Youth in All of This?

Curiously, in the U.S. education system seldom is it affirmed that the primary goal of sexuality education is the right of youth to know about human sexuality—nor it is understood as an inherent "right to know." This inadequacy has historical roots in the long-standing attitude among adults that in setting educational objectives for youth concerning sexuality their primary responsibility, whether in their capacity as parent, teacher, or administrator, is to protect youth from potential harm as opposed to providing youth with appropriate services and sufficient information with which to make decisions and protect themselves. Logically, this view assumes that those in the position to know what youth need are also those who determine the parameters of knowledge itself, as well as the parameters of access to that knowledge.

An interesting illustration of the significant implications of this primary difference is to look at the issue of public support for abstinence-only versus comprehensive education. This support (or the lack of it) is indicative of the view that adolescents must be protected. For example, if one were to ask, "Why is there no public opposition to abstinence-only education or visible support for comprehensive sexuality education?"—myriad responses might be offered. Whereas recent surveys have demonstrated significant public support for comprehensive education over abstinence-only education[117] this support has not translated into either tangible public opposition to abstinence-only education or into visible support for comprehensive education. Acknowledging the very active advocacy network supporting comprehensive programs, one response would highlight the lack of funding and organizational support necessary to position an effective counterpoint to the cohesive, conservative opposition; another response would point to political apathy.

Closely related to the issue of adult attitudes toward youth is the profound discomfort and ambivalence toward speaking about sexuality that in general prevails between parents and children and, by extension, between teachers (other than health educators specifically trained to conduct sexuality education) and students. In fact, in spite of the sexual saturation evident in the media and popular culture in the United States, public discussions of the relative merits of comprehensive education versus abstinence-only education are curiously absent. Supporting this view of the significance of adult attitudes toward youth is the theory that posits two dominant and distinct positions regarding the sexual maturity of adolescents: a process of dramatization on the one hand and a process of normalization on the other.[118]

The former view sees adolescent sexuality as a psychological, medical, and familial drama in which teen sexual urges are overpowering and difficult to control, given that teens lack self-regulatory capacities—and, consequently, their access to information about sexuality needs to be carefully circumscribed. This view also prioritizes the rights of parents as gatekeepers to their children's knowledge, an attitude not unlike the withholding of information from girls and women in the abortion arena. The second view presents a very different perspective, one that "treats adolescents as the owners of their own bodies and the agents of their own sexual behavior, [and is accompanied by a commitment] to provide them with access to the information and resources they need to exercise this rightful ownership . . . and agency over their sexual behaviors,"[119] including knowledge about their anatomy, contraceptive methods, and decision-making processes.

Despite the aforementioned caveats, adults with adequate knowledge and access to resources—especially parents—could and should be the sources of information regarding sexuality as well as permission giving for children. However, as long as parents, teachers, religious leaders, politicians, and others view adolescent sexuality primarily as a source of danger (of unwanted pregnancy, disease, moral corruption, and the road to hell), public voices in support of comprehensive sexuality education programs will remain, at best, ambivalent and considerably less audible than those supporting abstinence-only education. Needless to say, parents often lament that adolescents in the United States are already maturing too rapidly and hence abstinence-only programs might be viewed as an appropriate slowing-down mechanism, especially in light of the sexual saturation of U.S. popular culture. A more rational, informed approach would be to address the degrading and exploitative aspects of that culture—seeking to undermine its impact when possible—while acknowledging that adolescents both are capable of and have rights to mutually respectful and pleasurable sexual relations, assisted by easy access to a wide range of information and resources.

Current Trends: More of the Same or Turning Tide?

The dire view for sexuality education in the United States: Impact at state and local levels. The increasing mobilization and consolidation of conservative groups seeking to undermine comprehensive sexuality education has resulted in effective oppositional tactics at the local, state, and national levels. The ramifications of such political entrenchment nationwide are dramatic and powerful. During 2005, the federal government spent $170 million on abstinence-only education;[120] an increasing amount of this support was provided to religious organizations. Throughout the United States, in a period of vastly shrinking federal resources for state and local social service agencies, abstinence-only education programs have been replacing more comprehensive ones prompted by the incentive of available federal support. Currently, 86 percent of public school districts that have a policy to teach sexuality education require that abstinence be promoted; 35 percent require abstinence to be taught as the only option for unmarried people and either prohibit the discussion of contraception altogether or limit discussion to its ineffectiveness.[121] Strikingly, only 21 percent of junior high and 55 percent of high school instructors teach the correct use of condoms,[122] whereas the proportion of sexuality education teachers who teach abstinence as the only way to prevent pregnancy and sexually transmitted diseases increased from one in fifty in 1988 to one in four in 1999.[123] Instead of framing sexuality education as a means of promoting healthy adolescent sexuality, U.S. policy engenders an ever-increasing sexual illiteracy, especially among youth, who end up resorting to the Internet as their primary source of sexuality information.[124]

Impact in the classroom. Abstinence-only curricula typically rely on misleading, inaccurate, and incomplete information by which to warn youth of the dangers of any and all sexual activity. Even more significant—and indicative of the interest to promote social change in tune with a conservative agenda—is the inclusion in such curricula of information regarding traditional gender roles and male-female relationships. Examples are plentiful in this regard: the inclusion of gender-stereotypic information about male-female differences (e.g., males desire casual sexual activity from any and all women whereas women agree to sexual activity to get love); an emphasis on traditional gender roles as the norm within marriage (e.g., will the wife work after marriage or will the husband be the sole breadwinner?); and the normalizing of heterosexuality.[125]

At present, the continuing and compelling mobilization of conservative and religious forces opposing comprehensive sexuality education continues to dominate the political arena, especially at the local level. In their most extreme actions, these forces rely on perpetuating a far-reaching climate of fear, ignorance, and intimidation in the classroom and in the community, whereas at a more moderate end, they employ increasingly subtle strategies to undermine other types of educational efforts. In either case, the result includes an uneven development and implementation of programs, self-censorship in the classroom, a blanding of the curriculum, and a cursory teaching of only those topics regarded as safe and uncontroversial. Self-censorship in the schools occurs through the outsourcing of instruction; for example, schools increasingly are hiring consultants from outside organizations to teach sexuality education so that should controversy erupt, any ensuing public attention can be diverted away from the school itself. An increase is also evident in legislated teaching via state law in opposition to homosexuality and abortion, especially in schools in southern states.[126] In the end, given such tactics and increasingly hostile environments, many school districts find it much easier to implement an abstinence-only education curriculum, thereby circumventing controversy and opposition and, in the process, gaining access to government funding.

Exporting abstinence-only abroad. According to Human Rights Watch reporting on abstinence-only HIV/AIDS programs in Uganda, "The United

States is using its unparalleled influence to export abstinence-only programs that have proven to be an abject failure in its own country."[127]

The abstinence-only policies of the U.S. government—based on the framework established in its domestic legislation for sexuality education—have become part and parcel of all U.S. global HIV-prevention efforts, regardless of the position or views of its international partners. For instance, the United States Leadership Against HIV/AIDS, Tuberculosis and Malaria Act of 2003 focused on fourteen countries in sub-Saharan Africa and the Caribbean that have been severely affected by AIDS, requiring "the expenditure of 33 percent of HIV prevention funds on abstinence-only programs that exclude consideration of other approaches to HIV prevention."[128]

Nowhere has such policy exportation been more keenly promoted than in Uganda, whose government has been heralded for its success in dramatically decreasing the prevalence of HIV in Ugandans[129] in the 1990s via a comprehensive public-education approach known as ABC: Abstain, Be Faithful, and use Condoms. Yet recent analyses indicate that Uganda's success cannot be solely attributed to ABC. For one, the Ugandan government did not implement abstinence-only education on a large scale until 2001, when the United States began intently promoting these programs internationally. More significantly, the decline in HIV has been credited to the government's comprehensive approach to HIV prevention, which has been in place for more than a decade and has emphasized a range of strategies, including positive behavior change, high-level political leadership, condom use, and widespread HIV testing—all of which no doubt contributed to diminishing HIV prevalence in the country. Human Rights Watch notes, "Nothing in the demographic or historical records suggests that abstinence education as conceived by the United States is what contributed to Uganda's HIV prevention success."[130] Moreover, at the 2005 Annual Retrovirus Conference in Boston, Massachusetts, a presentation on research from the Rakai district in Uganda indicated that condom use, coupled with premature death among those infected more than a decade ago with the AIDS virus—not the ABC approach—was responsible for the decline in HIV infection.[131]

For all practical purposes, ABC has been effectively changed to AB (Abstain and Be Faithful) in the years since 2001, according to the new policy of the Uganda AIDS Commission (UAC). This shift coincides with the active participation of conservative Bush Administration appointees as technical advisers placed at the Uganda Ministry of Education by the

U.S. Agency for International Development to oversee the Presidential Initiative on AIDS Strategy for Communication to Youth.[132] What is now evident in the Uganda approach is the large-scale distribution of school-based education materials that contain "numerous falsehoods about condoms, a caution that premarital sex is against religion and norms of all cultures in Uganda and considered a form of deviance or misconduct."[133] More recent developments are even less encouraging, such as the issuance of a nationwide recall of all free government condoms in October 2004 by the Ugandan Ministry of Health, allegedly in response to failed quality control tests. New requirements for postshipment quality-control testing have continued to create a national shortage of condoms in keeping with the ministry's intent to be "less involved in condom importation but more involved in awareness campaigns [focusing on] abstinence and behavior change."[134]

These more recent developments—including reports of newly increasing infection rates in the country—portend a difficult future ahead for HIV prevention efforts in Uganda. As the UAC director general, Dr. Kihumuro Apuuli, has publicly stated, despite the increasing financial support from the donor community, the rate of people acquiring HIV/AIDS is still increasing; 130,000 Ugandans became infected in 2005, compared with 70,000 in 2003.[135]

On a More Positive Note: Trends and Developments

Evaluative research. A number of organizations—including the American Academy of Pediatrics;[136] the American Medical Association;[137] the Centers for Disease Control and Prevention;[138] the Institute of Medicine;[139] the Society for Adolescent Medicine[140]—have each published research analyses supporting the effectiveness of comprehensive education.[141] These organizations have cited evidence that comprehensive sexuality education programs providing information about both abstinence and contraception can help delay the onset of sexual activity in teenagers, reduce their number of sexual partners, and increase contraceptive use when they become sexually active.[142]

Many of these programs are using excellent resource curricula and material reviewed and highlighted by such organizations as SIECUS and Advocates for Youth. For example, currently in use in a number of states across the United States are developmental guidelines for implementing sexuality education from kindergarten through twelfth grade[143] as well as a number of sexuality education curricula whose primary objective is preventing pregnancy and sexually transmitted infections: Reducing the Risk,[144] Teen Talk,[145] Teen Outreach Program,[146] Be Proud Be Responsible,[147] Becoming a Responsible Teen,[148] and Safer Choices.[149]

More recently, independent evaluative research has seriously questioned the effectiveness of abstinence-only programs[150] and has demonstrated how and why abstinence-only education is scientifically unsound[151]—that it has little impact on behavior change,[152] that its withholding of essential health information is morally problematic because it fails to equip youth to make informed decisions, and that it promotes questionable and inaccurate opinions.[153] More specifically, according to Human Rights Watch,

> government-funded evaluations in at least twelve U.S. states as well as a federally mandated independent evaluation authorized in 1997 indicate that abstinence-only programs show no long-term success in delaying sexual initiation or reducing sexual risk-taking behaviors among program participants and that program participants are less likely to use contraceptives once they become sexually active.[154]

In December 2004, the Committee on Government Reform of the U.S. House of Representatives issued the Waxman Report (known more formally as the Content of Federally Funded Abstinence-Only Education Programs), one of the most widely disseminated reviews of abstinence-only programs. Named after Congressman Henry Waxman from California, who has taken a strong and consistent stand against the Bush Administration's misuses of science, the report concluded that abstinence-only programs contain "false information about the effectiveness of contraceptives and the risk of abortion, blur religion and science, treat stereotypes about boys and girls as scientific fact, and contain scientific errors."[155] It is important to note, however, that most existing comprehensive sexuality education programs could not pass any efficacy test either, primarily because evaluation researchers have set the minimum standard for what could be considered an effective program as requiring ten to fourteen hours of class time, a luxury simply not available in public schools.

Organizational support for comprehensive programs. Professional organizations have played and continue to play a significant role in both alerting the public to the deficient abstinence-only education policy promoted by the U.S. government and augmenting the public's knowledge of the issues at hand—and, in the process, helping to expand support for comprehensive education. A significant recent example of such support is the position paper issued by the Society for Adolescent Medicine urging the U.S. government to abandon this policy as "current U.S. federal law and guidelines regarding abstinence-only funding are ethically flawed and interfere with fundamental human rights."[156] In its indictment of the Bush Administration, the report emphasized the human right to sexual health information and the obligation of governments to provide accurate information to their citizens; the report also called for a science-based government policy regarding sexual and reproductive health education.

Another important example of organizational support for comprehensive education is the National Coalition to Support Sexuality Education, convened by SIECUS in 1990, which now consists of more than 140 national organizations committed to medically accurate, age-appropriate comprehensive education; their members represent a broad constituency of education advocates, healthcare professionals, religious leaders, child and health advocates, and policy organizations, including the American Public Health Association, Girls Inc., the National Medical Association, the National Urban League, and the YWCA, among others. The National Coalition is a strong supporter of recent legislative efforts to reimplement comprehensive sexuality education in schools, such as the Responsible Education About Life Act,[157] which was introduced in both the House of Representatives and the U.S. Senate and, if enacted, would provide $206 million a year to states for medically accurate, age-appropriate, comprehensive education that would include information about both abstinence and contraception from both a values and a public health perspective.

On an individual level, the camps of support and opposition to comprehensive sexuality education are not always clearly delineated, nor do they line up neatly. In fact, recent media attention has been directed to support for sexuality education coming from an unlikely source—a young Christian activist from the small, conservative town of Lubbock, Texas. Shelby Knox, a member of the Lubbock Youth Commission attending the local high school, unsuccessfully advocated for the Lubbock school system to replace its abstinence-only program with a more comprehensive approach;[158] her video-documented activist journey has made a considerable impact in public circles, however.[159]

The Battle Ahead

At present, the field of sexuality education has been seriously and effectively hobbled in continuing its mission, having little political clout to develop relevant sexuality education policy or expand the public's understanding of sexuality and its relationship to human fulfillment and public health. With the increasing demonstration of the ineffectiveness of the abstinence-only approach and an increasing number of states declining federal support for such programs, perhaps the "chickens are coming home to roost" and the tide is beginning to turn, providing an important opportunity to capitalize and expand on existing support for comprehensive sexuality education and, in the process, promote much-needed sexual literacy among the general population. For such expansion to occur, the following developments would be paramount: (1) a national information-media campaign targeting not only the general public but also diverse communities and constituencies across the United States to identify potential venues of support for sexuality education and expand the cohort among parents, health practitioners, and religious and community leaders who are willing to actively and publicly work for it and (2) an increase in the capacity of national advocacy organizations working at both national and state levels, as well as local organizations working across communities, to develop appropriate communication strategies to refine public advocacy in support of comprehensive sexuality education.

Part and parcel of this dual-pronged approach is the framing of comprehensive sexuality education and its health agenda in terms of a human rights perspective focused on the negative rights of freedom from discrimination, stigma, and abuse, as well as the positive rights of self-actualization and the enrichment for society of recognizing diversity in sexuality and family structures. Such an approach not only would help build support for sexuality education but also would contribute to building the foundation for a human rights culture in the United States.

In terms of youth, this sexual rights approach to sexuality education would, by necessity, bring adolescents themselves to the foreground as the primary beneficiaries of such programs. In this view, sexuality education would ensure access to an educational opportunity for youth that went beyond teaching about risk behaviors and preventive measures to assisting young people in the process of self-actualization and in becoming capable of maintaining mutually respectful and sexually satisfying relationships and experiences with others.

Regardless of what transpires over the next five to ten years regarding this issue, one can be sure the battle for sexuality education will remain contentious, with much at risk. After all, not only the future of American youth and their ability to function as sexually healthy and empowered individuals is at jeopardy, but also the future prospects of sexual rights being valued as human rights in American political culture.

Conclusion

The intent of this article has been to document the political struggles over sexuality rights in the United States that became intensified arenas of contestation since the rise of the Religious Right in the 1970s, and particularly so during the presidency of George W. Bush from 2000 to 2008. Drawing on the examples of reproductive rights and sexuality education, this article suggests that the outcome of these struggles can be characterized largely by the waning of sexual rights and serious inequities in sexual and reproductive health.

Sobering as this account has been, however, we see a ray of hope in the evident overreaching of the Religious Right that occurred in the last years of the Bush presidency. We have noted the difficulties the movement has experienced in its attempt to extend abortion politics to a range of other issues. This was particularly true in the public's repudiation of government intervention in the Schiavo case, which raised "right to die" issues. Some 82 percent of the American public, including many self-identified evangelicals, told pollsters they felt such intervention was inappropriate.[160] The Religious Right's campaign against contraception is similarly out of touch with the values of the vast majority of Americans: birth control is used at some point by 98 percent of all heterosexually active women in the United States.[161] As the Religious Right's attempt to restrict birth control, particularly through pharmacists' refusals, has become more widely known, these campaigns have backfired in the court of public opinion. Indeed, a poll conducted in the summer of 2007 concluded that "voters overwhelmingly describe themselves as dissatisfied with the country's approach to reproductive health issues; by 58 percent to 24 percent they say the country is headed off on the wrong track rather than the right direction on issues such as sexuality education, contraception, unintended pregnancy and abortion." The poll also noted Americans' "strong desire" for a greater emphasis on prevention, with particular support for comprehensive sex education.[162]

Similarly, with respect to stem cell research, the Religious Right is significantly out of step with the majority of Americans. The veto by President Bush in July 2006–the first in his presidency after five years in office–of a stem cell bill passed by Congress was notable for the ensuing panic among politicians who would be facing voters in fall 2006. Indeed, on this bill, some of the most stalwart opponents of abortion in the Senate broke not only with President Bush but also with their Religious Right base to support this measure.[163] In the one state (Missouri) in which the issue of stem cell research was on the ballot, voters approved such research.

Such unpopular moves by the Religious Right offer progressives a crucial opportunity to make evident to the American public the oft-disguised theocratic agenda of the movement. A society in which women cannot control their fertility, in which promising research on diseases is held back, in which young people are lied to about life and death matters, and in which homosexuality is demonized is simply not acceptable to the majority of Americans in the 21st century. Indeed, given the dynamic nature of moral panics that scholars have pointed to,[164] perhaps it is not too far fetched to expect a new moral panic to arise among Americans in reaction to the unacceptable intrusions of the Religious Right into the most private spheres of people's lives.

Abortion is the primary reproductive issue about which Americans appear to remain genuinely conflicted–while a majority of Americans support legal abortion, they also support considerable restrictions on the procedure, which can make access difficult, especially for the young and the poor. The best defense for its supporters–morally as well as strategically–is to frame abortion as one essential component of a larger platform of valued rights and services shared by a significant portion of the U.S. population. Such a platform includes universal health insurance that covers contraception, abortion and prenatal and obstetric care; affordable child care; and support for sexual diversity and self-determination. With regard to sexuality education, this platform would be dictated not by Religious Right proponents who deny health information to youth in the name of morality, but by those parents, teachers, school administrators, and community and religious leaders who support age-appropriate comprehensive sexuality education and are willing to work for its implementation in schools nationwide. Such a platform would make clear the meanings of reproductive and sexual justice and the threat the Religious Right poses to the kind of society in which most Americans wish to live.

In conclusion, in spite of the concrete and negative ramifications that the actions of the Religious Right have had on sexuality-related policy, the current epoch should be considered as yet another time in flux, with both regressive and progressive aspects, rather than one of hegemonic conservatism. The continual resistance to the sexual conservatives' position on the part of sexuality advocates and scholars working in the fields of reproductive rights and sexuality education, as well as those supporting marriage equality, are visible testimonies to the shifting terrain of sexual politics in the United States. Furthermore, we are encouraged by the number of critiques that have begun to appear of the Religious Right from well-known evangelical leaders who decry the movement's tunnel-vision focus on abortion and homosexuality to the exclusion of issues such as poverty and the environment.[165] However, we have no illusions that the Religious Right as a force in American politics is "over," as some giddily proclaimed after the 2006 election in which Democrats made considerable gains.[166] Even if weakened at the national level, this movement will remain strong in various locales, especially in certain "red" states. Nonetheless, writing in the waning months of the George W. Bush presidency, we voice cautious optimism that this epoch will be seen by historians as the zenith of the Religious Right's influence on sexuality-related policies, both domestic and foreign–and more significantly, that these scholars will report that this shameful era was followed by a restoration of integrity in these crucial areas of government action.

NOTES

The authors wish to acknowledge the helpful contributions of Gilbert Herdt and Rosalind Petchesky to this article, as well as the insightful comments the National Sexuality Resource Center reviewers provided in evaluating its previous version. We also are grateful for the excellent technical assistance of Alexandra Slessarev and Kate Cosby. Previously published in a different form in *Sexuality Research and Social Policy* (4)1:67–92 (2007). Used by permission of the publisher.

1. The use of the word "fluctuating" is intentional here. The rise of sexual conservatism, although existing since the inception of the republic, does not have a specific movement or origin—nor did it or does it take place in a linear sequence of regressive actions imposed by a dominant political power. Rather, sexual conservatism has fluctuated between ascendancy and decline within U.S. culture in a pattern contingent on historical conditions and circumstances.

2. G. Chauncey, *Gay New York: Gender, Urban Culture, and the Making of the Gay Male World 1840–1940* (New York: Basic Books, 1994).

3. A. Koedt, "The Myth of the Vaginal Orgasm," in *Radical Feminism*, A. Koedt, E. Levine, and A. Rapone, eds. (New York: Quadrangle, 1973), 198–207.

4. P. Mainardi, "The Politics of Housework," in *Sisterhood Is Powerful*, R. Morgan, ed. (New York: Vintage, 1970), 447–55.

5. C. Lo, "Countermovements and Conservative Movements in the Contemporary U.S." *Annual Review of Sociology* 8 (1982), 107–34.

6. J. Hardisty, *Mobilizing Resentment: Conservative Resurgence from the John Birch Society to the Promise Keepers* (Boston: Beacon, 1999).

7. C. Joffe, *Friendly Intruders: Childcare Professionals and Family* Life (Berkeley: University of California Press, 1979).

8. O. McGraw, *The Family, Feminism, and the Therapeutic State* (Washington, D.C.: Heritage Foundation, 1980).

9. *Roe v. Wade*, 1973.

10. R. Petchesky, *Abortions and Women's Choice: The State, Sexuality, and Reproductive Freedom* (Boston: Northeastern University Press, 1990).

11. J. Micklethwait and A. Wooldridge, *The Right Nation: Conservative Power in America* (New York, Penguin, 2004).

12. E. Kaplan, *With God on Their Side: How Christian Fundamentalists Trampled Science, Policy, and Democracy in George Bush's White House* (New York: New Press, 2004).

13. K. Phillips, *American Theocracy: The Peril and Politics of Radical Religion, Oil, and Borrowed Money in the Twenty-First Century* (New York: Viking, 2006).

14. T. Frank, *What's the Matter with Kansas? How Conservatives Won the Heart of America* (New York: Henry Holt, 2004).

15. S. Cohen, *Folk Devils and Moral Panics: Creation of Mods and Rockers* (London: MacGibbon & Kee, 1972), 9.

16. G. Wills, "A Country Ruled by Faith," *New York Review of Books* 53, November 16 (2006), 8.

17. C. Mooney, *The Republican War on Science* (New York: Basic Books, 2005); M. Specter, "Political Science: The White House vs. the Laboratory" *New Yorker*, March 13 (2006), 58–69.

18. Mooney, *The Republican War.*

19. R. Chandrasekaran, *Imperial Life in the Emerald City: Inside Iraq's Green Zone* (New York: Knopf, 2006).

20. Specter, "Political Science."

21. S. Epstein, "The New Attack on Sexuality Research: Morality and the Politics of Knowledge Production" *Sexuality Research and Social Policy: Journal of NSRC* (3)1 (2006), 112.

22. S. Epstein, "The New Attack on Sexuality Research," 112.

23. H. Waxman, *The Waxman Report: The Content of Federally Funded Abstinence-Only Education Programs*, Washington, D.C.: Committee on Government Reform, Special Investigations Division, U.S. House of Representatives, December 2004.

24. Mooney, *The Republican War*, 243.

25. Mooney, *The Republican War*, 243.

26. K. Luker, *When Sex Goes to School: Warring Views on Sex—and Sex Education—Since the Sixties* (New York: Norton, 2006).

27. *Bowen v. Kendrick*, 1988.

28. D. Henriques and A. Lehren, "Religion for Captive Audiences, with Taxpayers Paying the Bill." *New York Times*, December 10 (2006), A1, A18.

29. S. Jayson, "Abstinence Message Goes beyond Teens," *USA Today*, October 31 (2006), A1.

30. R. Shorto, "Contra Contraception," *New York Times*, May 7, 2006, http://www.nytimes.com/.

31. R. Stein, "For Some, There Is No Choice," *Washington Post*, July 16 (2006), A6.

32. P. Chamberlain, *Undoing Reproductive Freedom: Christian Right NGOs Target the United Nations* (Cambridge: Political Research Associates, 2006).

33. E. Cardenas, "Teen Must Serve Pro-Life Center," *Detroit News*, September 30, 2005, http://www.detnews.com/.

34. L. Uttley, "The Politics of the Embryo," *American Progress*, http://www.americanprogress.org/.

35. Committee on Government Reform—Minority Staff, Special Investigations Division, United States House of Representatives, "Politics and Science in the Bush Administration." November 2003, http://democrats.reform.house.gov/.

36. N. Sanchez, "American Girl Boycott: Groups Pick a Fight with a Doll over Messages to Girls," *Kansas City Star*, November 21 (2005), B5.

37. M. McKeegan, *Abortion Politics: Mutiny in the Ranks of the Right* (New York: Free Press, 1992).

38. D. Kirkpatrick, "DeLay To Be on Christian Telecast on Courts," *New York Times*, August 3, 2005, http://www.nytimes.com/.

39. Petchesky, *Abortion and Women's Choice*.

40. D. Garrow, *Liberty and Sexuality: The Right to Privacy and the Making of Roe v. Wade* (New York: MacMillan, 1994).

41. D. Garrow, *Liberty and Sexuality*.

42. Center for Reproductive Rights, n.d, "Stenberg v. Carhart: Background Information," http://www.crlp.org/crt_pba_carhart.html.

43. *Gonzales v. Carhart*, 2007.

44. S. Lee et al., "Fetal Pain: A Systematic Multidisciplinary Review of the Evidence," *Journal of the American Medical Association* 294 (2005), 947–54.

45. A. Foster, J. van Dis, and J. Steinauer, "Educational and Legislative Initiatives Affecting Residency Training in Abortion," *Journal of the American Medical Association* 290 (2003), 1777–78.

46. Center for Reproductive Rights, "Targeted Regulation of Abortion Providers (TRAP): Avoiding the Trap," April 2004, http://www.crlp.org/pub_fac_trap.html.

47. T. Weitz and A. Hunter, "*Six Feet Under* Brings Abortion to the Surface," in *21st-Century Sexualities: Contemporary Issues in Health, Education and Rights*, G. Herdt and C. Howe, eds. (London: Routledge, 2007), 69–73.

48. *The Silent Scream*, DVD, directed by B. Nathanson (1984; Brunswick, OH: American Portrait Films).

49. R. Petchesky, "Fetal Images: The Power of Visual Culture in the Politics of Reproduction," in *Reproductive Technologies: Gender, Motherhood, and Medicine*, M. Stanworth, ed. (Minneapolis: University of Minnesota Press, 1987), 57–80.

50. M. Casper, *The Making of the Unborn Patient: A Social Anatomy of Fetal Surgery* (New Brunswick, NJ: Rutgers University Press, 1998).

51. Uttley, "The Politics of the Embryo."

52. M. Kaufman, "Pregnancy Centers Found To Give False Information on Abortion," *Washington Post*, July 18 (2006), A8.

53. S. Simon, "Abortion Foes Energized by Their Losses," *Los Angeles Times*, November 9 (2006), http://www.latimes.com/.

54. C. Joffe, "It's Not Just Abortion, Stupid: Progressives and Abortion," *Dissent* 51 (2005), 91–96.

55. S. Henshaw and L. Finer, "The Accessibility of Abortion Services in the United States," *Perspectives on Sexual and Reproductive Health* 35:1 (2003), 16–24.

56. C. Joffe, *Doctors of Conscience: The Struggle to Provide Abortion before and after* Roe v. Wade (Boston: Beacon, 1995).

57. D. Murdock, "The Adoption Option," *National Review*, August 27, 2001, http://www.nationalreview.com/.

58. Uttley, "The Politics of the Embryo."

59. American Civil Liberties Union, "Religious, Women's Health, Rights Organizations Declare Opposition to SCHIP Extension to Fetuses," May 7, 2002, http://www.aclu.org/.

60. D. Kirkpatrick and S. Stolberg, "How Family's Cause Reached the Halls of the Library of Congress," *New York Times*, March 22 (2005), A1.

61. J. Eisenberg, *Using Terri: The Religious Right's Conspiracy to Take Away Our Rights* (San Francisco: HarperCollins, 2005).

62. M. Goldberg, *Kingdom Coming: The Rise of Christian Nationalism* (New York: Norton, 2006).

63. Henshaw and Finer, "The Accessibility of Abortion."

64. C. Page, *How the Pro-Choice Movement Saved America: Freedom, Politics, and The War on Sex* (New York: Basic Books, 2006).

65. J. Couzin, "Plan B: a Collision of Science and Politics," *Science* 310 (2005), 38–39; C. Harper et al., "The Effect of Increased Access to Emergency Contraception among Young Adolescents," *Obstetrics and Gynecology* 106 (2005), 483–91.

66. A. Wood, J. Drazen, and M. Greene, "A Sad Day for Science at the FDA," *New England Journal of Medicine* 353 (2005), 1197–99.

67. Pro-Life Action League, "Contraception Is Not the Answer," *Pro-Life Action League Homepage Archive*, October 4, 2006, http://www.prolifeaction.org/.

68. Shorto, "Contra-Contraception," ¶8.

69. Page, *How the Pro-Choice Movement*, 14–15.

70. R. Stein, "Health Workers' Choice Debated," *Washington Post*, January 30 (2006), A1.

71. Stein, "For Some, There Is No Choice;" R. Stein, "Seeking Care and Refused," *Washington Post*, July 16 (2006), A6.

72. MergerWatch, "Hospitals and Religious Restrictions," 2006, http://www.mergerwatch.org/hospital_mergers.html.

73. International Women's Health Coalition [IWHC], "Bush's Other War," 2006, http://www.iwhc.org/resources/bushsotherwar/index.cfm, 1.

74. IWHC, "Bush's Other War," 1.

75. IWHC, "Bush's Other War," 1.

76. D. Jamison and N. Padian, "Where AIDS Funding Should Go," *San Francisco Chronicle*, May 23 (2006), A23.

77. Henshaw and Finer, "The Accessibility of Abortion."

78. Joffe, *Doctors of Conscience.*

79. Henshaw and Finer, "The Accessibility of Abortion."

80. ACLU, "Public Funding for Abortion," July 21, 2004, http://www.aclu.org/reproductiverights/lowincome/16393res20040721.html.

81. H. Boonstra et al., *Abortion in Women's Lives* (New York: Guttmacher Institute, 2006), 20.

82. H. Boonstra et al., *Abortion in Women's Lives*, 20.

83. C. Joffe, "Reproductive Regression," January 23, 2006, http://www.tompaine.com/articles/2006/01/23/reproductive_regression.php.

84. Title X, Public Health Service Act, 42 U.S.C. § 300 (1970).

85. After the November 2006 election, George W. Bush continued this tradition. See the Election Epilogue section at the end of this article for details.

86. J. Frost, A. Sonfield, and R. Gold, "Estimating the Impact of Serving New Clients by Expanding Funding for Title X," *Occasional Report No. 33* (New York: Guttmacher Institute, 2006), 7.

87. Mooney, *The Republican War*, 208.

88. Mooney, *The Republican War*, 208; Specter, "Political Science."

89. Kaufman, "Pregnancy Centers."

90. Mooney, *The Republican War*, 62.

91. Specter, "Political Science."

92. Specter, "Political Science."

93. Chamberlain, *Undoing Reproductive Freedom,* 4.

94. C. Joffe, T. Weitz, and C. Stacey, "Uneasy Allies: Pro-Choice Physicians, Feminist Health Activists and the Struggle for Abortion Rights," *Sociology of Health and Illness* 26 (2004), 775–96.

95. Petchesky, "Fetal Images."

96. Joffe, "It's Not Just Abortion."

97. Y. Silliman et al., *Undivided Rights: Women of Color Organize for Reproductive Justice* (Boston: South End, 2004).

98. J. Irvine, *Talk about Sex: The Battles over Sex Education in the United States* (Berkeley: University of California Press, 2002).

99. J. Moran, *Teaching Sex: The Shaping of Adolescence in the 20th Century* (Boston: Harvard University Press, 2000).

100. L. Rotskoff, "Sex in the Schools: Adolescence, Sex Education and Social Reform," *Reviews in American History* 29 (2001), 311.

101. Moran, *Teaching Sex.*

102. R. Petchesky, personal communication, August 10, 2006.

103. Irvine, *Talk about Sex.*

104. Moran, *Teaching Sex,* 285.

105. Innumerable examples of such exaggeration can be found on the hate-crime.org website at http://www.hatecrime.org/subpages/hatespeech/hate.html.

106. The first legislative success in promoting abstinence-only education took the form of the Adolescent Family Life Act of 1981. Although the new legislation benefited from the explicit support of the Reagan Administration, it was side-tracked by a lawsuit instituted by the ACLU on the basis that it failed to incorporate secular language.

107. I. Dickman, *Winning the Battle for Sex Education* (New York: Sexuality Information and Education Council of the United States, 1982); D. di Mauro and D. Haffner, *Winning the Battle: Developing Support for Sexuality and HIV/AIDS Education* (New York: Sexuality Information and Education Council of the United States, 1990).

108. Hatecrime.org, 2007, http://www.hatecrime.org/subpages/hatespeech/hate.html.

109. N. Kendall, presentation, Fellow's Conference, Sexuality Research Fellowship Program, Arlie Conference Center, Warrenton, VA, 2006.

110. Abstinence-only-until-marriage and comprehensive sexuality education will henceforth also be identified as abstinence-only and comprehensive education.

111. Sexuality Information and Education Council of the United States [SIECUS], *Developing Guidelines for Comprehensive Sexuality Education* (New York: SIECUS, 2000).

112. Kendall, presentation.

113. Welfare Reform Act, 1996.

114. At present the additional sixteen states who have rejected federal funds for abstinence-education are: Arizona, Colorado, Connecticut, Iowa, Maine, Montana, New Jersey, New Mexico, New York, Ohio, Rhode Island, Virginia, Washington, West Virginia, Wisconsin, and Wyoming.

115. Mathematica Policy Research Inc., Impacts of Title V, Section 510 Abstinence Education Programs (Princeton, 2007); Mathematica Policy Research Inc., The Evaluation of Abstinence Education Programs Funded under Title V Section 510 (Princeton, 2002); Santelli et al., "Abstinence and Abstinence-Only Education: A Review of U.S. Policies and Programs" *Journal of Adolescent Health* 38 (2006), 72–81. There are probably additional states that have already or plan to opt out but do not make this information public for a variety of reasons, including not wanting to draw attention to the fact that no organization in their state applied for such funding, that receiving such money might compromise an upcoming gubernatorial election, etc.

116. S. 972 and H.R.1653

117. Henry J. Kaiser Foundation, Sex Education in America: A Series of National Surveys of Students, Parents, Teachers, and Principals (Menlo Park, CA: Henry J. Kaiser Foundation, 2000); Kaiser Family Foundation and the Kennedy School of Government, "Sex Education in America," NPR.org., November 29, 2004, http://www.npr.org/. According to the second report (Kaiser Family Foundation and the Kennedy School of Government, 2004), 93 percent of parents of junior high students and 91 percent of high school students believe it is important to have sexuality education as part of the school curriculum; 95 percent of parents of junior high students and 93 percent of high school students believe that birth control and other methods of preventing pregnancy are appropriate topics for sexuality education programs in schools; only 30 percent of American adults agree with the statement "The federal government should fund sex education programs that have 'abstaining from sexual activity' as their only purpose." As indicated in the 2000 Henry J. Kaiser Foundation Report, the majority of Americans favor more comprehensive education over abstinence-only; at least three quarters of parents say that in addition to abstinence, sexuality education should cover how to use condoms and other forms of birth control, abortion, sexual orientation, pressures to have sex, and the emotional consequences of having sex.

118. Schalet, "Must We Fear Adolescent Sexuality?" *Medscape General Medicine* 6:4 (2004), 1–22, http://www.medscape.com/.

119. Schalet, "Must We Fear Adolescent Sexuality?" 12.

120. Although currently a number of streams of federal dollars are available for abstinence-only education, much of the support to states is provided via Title V (2005), which must be matched by state funds (for every four dollars in federal money, the state must provide three dollars or an equivalent in services). See

http://www.nonewmoney.org/main.htm for a brief history of legislative support for abstinence-only education in the United States.

121. D. J. Landry, L. Kaeser, and C. L. Richards, "Fetal Pain: A Systematic Multidisciplinary Review of the Evidence," *Journal of the American Medical Association* 294 (1999), 947–54.

122. Santelli et al., "Abstinence and Abstinence-Only."

123. J. F. Darroch, J. F. Frost, and S. Singh, "Differences in Teenage Pregnancy Rates among Five Developed Countries: The Roles of Sexual Activity and Contraceptive Use," *Family Planning Perspectives* 33 (2001), 244–50; Darroch, Frost, and Singh, *Teenage Sexual and Reproductive Behavior in Developed Countries: Can More Progress Be Made?* (New York: Allen Guttmacher Institute, 2001), http://www.guttmacher.org/pubs/eurosynth_rpt.pdf.

124. Kaiser Family Foundation, *Generation RX.com: How Young People Use the Internet for Health Information: A Kaiser Family Foundation Survey* (Menlo Park: Kaiser Family Foundation, 2001).

125. Sexuality Information and Education Council of the United States [SIECUS], "Special Edition: Sexuality Education, A Decade of Controversy," *SIECUS Report* 38:6 (2003, Fall).

126. SIECUS, "Special Edition."

127. Human Rights Watch, "The Less They Know, the Better: Abstinence-Only HIV/AIDS Programs in Uganda 17:4A (2005), http://hrw.org/reports/2005/Uganda0305.Uganda0305.pdf., 5.

128. Human Rights Watch 2005, 8–9.

129. According to UNAIDS (2005), HIV prevalence among antenatal clinic (ANC) female attendees (data available from Uganda on an annual basis since 1985) "in Kampala, the major urban area increased from 11 percent in 1985 to 31 percent in 1990. Beginning in 1993, HIV prevalence among ANC women began to decline in Kampala reaching 8.3 percent in 2002. In 1991, 28 percent of ANC women tested who were less than 20 years of age were HIV positive. This rate declined to 6 percent in 2001. Sentinel surveillance of ANC attendees outside of Kampala began in 1989. Median HIV prevalence declined from 13 percent of ANC women tested in 1992 to 4.7 percent in 2002" (UNAIDS, "Country Assessments").

130. Human Rights Watch 2005, 7; S. A. Cohen, "Beyond Slogans: Lessons from Uganda's Experience with ABC and HIV/AIDS," *The Guttmacher Report on Public Policy* 6:5 (2003), http://www.guttmacher.org/pubs/tgr/06/5/gr060501.pdf.

131. S. Russell, "Uganda's HIV Rate Drops, but Not from Abstinence: Study Concludes Basis of Bush Policy Apparently Irrelevant," *Sfgate.com*, February 24, 2005, http://www.sfgate.com/.

132. See F. Girard, "Global Implications of U.S. Domestic and International Policies on Sexuality," working paper, International Working Group on Sexuality

and Social Policy, Sociomedical Sciences Department, Mailman School of Public Health, Columbia University, New York, 2004.

133. Human Rights Watch 2005, 3.

134. Human Rights Watch 2005, 4.

135. Thought Theater, "Abstinence: Uganda HIV Rate Suggest Failure," 2007, http://www.thoughttheater.com/2006/05/ abstinence_uganda_hiv_rates_su.php.

136. "Adolescents and Human Immunodeficiency Virus infection: The Role of the Pediatrician in Prevention and Intervention," *Pediatrics* 107 (2001), 188–90.

137. Report of the Council on Scientific Affairs, Action of the AMA House of Delegates 1999 Interim Meeting, CSA Report 7-1-99 (Chicago: AMA, 1999).

138. "State-Specific Birth Rates for Teenagers—United States, 1990–1996." *Morbidity & Mortality Weekly Report* 46 (1997), 838–42.

139. *No Time To Lose: Getting More from HIV Prevention* (Washington, D.C.: National Academies Press, 2000).

140. "Abstinence-Only Education Policies and Programs: A Position Paper of the Society for Adolescent Medicine," *Journal of Adolescent Health* 38 (2006), 283–87.

141. M. Howell and A. Feijoo, *Science or Politics? George W. Bush and the Future of Sexuality Education in the United States* (Washington, D.C.: Advocates for Youth, 2001), http://www.advocatesforyouth.org/publications/factsheet/fsbush.pdf.

142. C. Dallard, "Abstinence Promotion and Teen Family Planning: The Misguided Drive for Equal Funding," *The Guttmacher Report on Public Policy* 5 (2002), 103; D. Kirby, "Understanding What Works and What Doesn't in Reducing Adolescent Sexual Risk-Taking," *Family Planning Perspectives* 33 (2001), 276–81; J. Manlove, A. Papillio, and E. Ikramullah, *Not Yet: Programs to Delay First Sex among Teens* (Washington, D.C.: National Campaign to Prevent Teenage Pregnancy, 2004).

143. National Guidelines Task Force, *Guidelines for Comprehensive Sexuality Education: Kindergarten–12th Grade* (New York: Sexuality Information and Education Council of the United States, 1991).

144. Advocates for Youth, "Reducing the Risk," http://www.advocatesforyouth.org/programsthatwork/1reducingrisk.htm.

145. Teen Pregnancy Coalition, "Teen Talk," http://www.teenpregnancycoalition.org/programs/teentalk/index.htm.

146. Advocates for Youth, "Teen Outreach Program," http://www.advocatesforyouth.org/programsthatwork/19top.htm.

147. Advocates for Youth, "Be Proud Be Responsible," http://www.advocatesforyouth.org/programsthatwork/14bpbr.htm.

148. Advocates for Youth, "Becoming a Responsible Teen," http://www.advocatesforyouth.org/programsthatwork/12bart.htm.

149. "Safer Choices," *Advocates for Youth*, http://www.advocatesforyouth.org/programsthatwork/4saferchoices.htm. Advocates for Youth, "Science and Success: Sex Education and Other Programs That Work To Prevent Teenage Pregnancy, HIV and Other Sexually Transmitted Diseases," 2007, http://www.advocatesforyouth.org/publications/ScienceSuccessES.pdf.

150. Mathematica Policy Research Institute, "Impacts of Four"; Santelli et al. "Abstinence and Abstinence-Only."

151. D. Kirby, *Emerging Answers: Research Findings on Programs to Reduce Teen Pregnancy* (Washington, D.C.: National Campaign to Prevent Teen Pregnancy, 2001); Kirby, "Understanding What Works"; D. Kirby "Effective Approaches to Reducing Adolescent Unprotected Sex, Pregnancy and Childbearing," *Journal of Sex Research* 39 (2002), 51–57.

152. Hauser, *Five Years of Abstinence-Only-until-Marriage Education: Assessing the Impact* (Washington, D.C.: Advocates for Youth, 2004).

153. Santelli et al., "Abstinence and Abstinence-Only."

154. Human Rights Watch 2005, 72. The studies cited in the report are Goodson et al. (2004), Hauser (2004), and Mathematica Policy Research Institute Inc. (2002). Additionally, see Cochrane Collaborative Review Group on HIV Infection and AIDS (2004).

155. Waxman, *The Waxman Report*, 3–4.

156. Society for Adolescent Medicine, "Abstinence-Only Education," 86.

157. Responsible Education About Life Act, HR 768, 109th Cong. (2005) and S 368, 109th Cong. (2005).

158. J. Fields and D. L. Tolman, "Risky Business: Sexuality Education and Research in U.S. Schools," *Sexuality Research and Social Policy: Journal of NSRC* 3:4 (2006), 63–76.

159. A narrative of this attempt has been presented in the widely acclaimed 2005 documentary, *The Education of Shelby Knox*, produced by independent filmmakers Marion Lipschutz and Rose Rosenblatt. The film follows Shelby, a devoutly, self-proclaimed abstinent girl living in Lubbock, Texas, as she reconciles her religious beliefs with her commitment to comprehensive education and human rights; as the film demonstrates, by the end of the school year, both the mayor and the policy chairman of the city's Youth Council resigned, citing pressures from adults as their reason for leaving. In the film, the last words on the issue were spoken by the mayor of Lubbock: "Sexuality education is a very controversial issue; it will be dealt with at some time in the very near future. To what degree, I don't know."

160. CBS News, "Political Fallout over Schiavo," March 23 (2005), http://www.cbsnews.com/.

161. W. D. Mosher et al., "Use of Contraceptives, Use of Family Planning Services in the United States: 1982–2002," *Advance Data from Vital and Health*

Statistics 350, Atlanta: Centers for Disease Control and Prevention, December 10, 2004, http://www.cdc.gov/nchs/data/ad/ad350.pdf.

162. National Women's Law Center, "Memo to Interested Parties," Peter D. Hart Research Associates, 2007, http://www.nwlc.org.

163. S. Stolberg, "First Bush Veto Maintains Limits on Stem Cell Use," *New York Times*, July 20 (2006), A1, A16.

164. Ben-Yehuda, *The Politics and Morality of Deviance: Moral Panics, Drug Abuse, Deviant Science and Reversed Stigmatization* (Albany: SUNY Press, 1990).

165. R. Balmer, *Thy Kingdom Come: How the Religious Right Distorts the Faith and Threatens America: An Evangelist's Lament* (New York: Basic Books, 2006); D. Kuo, *Tempting Faith: An Inside Story of Political Seduction* (New York: Free Press, 2006); J. Wallis, *God's Politics: Why the Right Gets It Wrong and the Left Doesn't Get It.* (San Francisco: HarperSanFrancisco, 2005).

166. N. Kristof, "A Modest Proposal for a Truce on Religion," *New York Times*, December 3 (2006), Section 14, 13.

REFERENCES

Adolescent Family Life Act. 1981. Title XX of the Public Health Service Act, U.S. Department of Health and Human Services, http://opa.osophs.dhhs.gov/titlexx/oapp.html (accessed Feb. 6, 2007).

Advocates for Youth. 2007. "Science and Success: Sex Education and Other Programs That Work to Prevent Teenage Pregnancy, HIV and Other Sexually Transmitted Diseases," http://www.advocatesforyouth.org/publications/ScienceSuccessES.pdf (accessed Feb. 6, 2007).

American Academy of Pediatrics. 2001. "Adolescents and Human Immunodeficiency Virus Infection: The Role of the Pediatrician in Prevention and Intervention." *Pediatrics* 107: 188–90.

American Civil Liberties Union. 2002. *Religious, Women's Health, Rights Organizations Declare Opposition to SCHIP Extension to Fetuses.* ACLU website, May 7, http://www.aclu.org/reproductiverights/fetalrights/16418prs20020507.html (accessed Sept. 26, 2006).

———. 2004. *Public Funding for Abortion.* ACLU website, July 21, http://www.aclu.org/reproductiverights/lowincome/16393res20040721.html (accessed February 3, 2007).

American Medical Association—Council on Scientific Affairs. 1999. *"Report of the Council on Scientific Affairs"* (Action of the AMA House of Delegates 1999 Interim Meeting, CSA Report 7-1-99). Chicago: AMA.

Balmer, R. 2006. *Thy Kingdom Come: How the Religious Right Distorts the Faith and Threatens America: An Evangelist's Lament.* New York: Basic Books.

Ben-Yehuda, N. 1990. *The Politics and Morality of Deviance: Moral Panics, Drug Abuse, Deviant Science and Reversed Stigmatization.* Albany: SUNY Press.

Boonstra, H., R. Gold, C. Richards, and L. Finer. 2006. *Abortion in Women's Lives.* New York: Guttmacher Institute.

Bowen v. Kendrick, 487 U.S. 589 (1988).

Bruckner, H., and P. Bearman. 2005. "After the Promise: The STD Consequences of Adolescent Virginity Pledges." *Journal of Adolescent Health* 36: 271–78.

Cardenas, E. 2005. "Teen Must Serve Pro-Life Center," *Detroit News* Sept. 30, http://www.detnews.com (accessed Sept. 26, 2006).

Casper, M. 1998. *The Making of the Unborn Patient: A Social Anatomy of Fetal Surgery.* New Brunswick, NJ: Rutgers University Press.

CBS News. (2005). "Political Fallout over Schiavo." *CBSnews.com,* March 23, http://www.cbsnews.com (accessed Dec. 6, 2006).

Center for Reproductive Rights. 2004. "Targeted Regulation of Abortion Providers (TRAP): Avoiding the TRAP." *Crlp.org,* April, http://www.crlp.org/pub_fac_trap.html (accessed Jan. 2, 2006).

———. n.d. "*Stenberg v. Carhart:* Background information," http://www.crlp.org/crt_pba_carhart.html (accessed July 25, 2006).

Centers for Disease Control and Prevention. 1997. "State-Specific Birth Rates for Teenagers—United States, 1990–1996." *Morbidity & Mortality Weekly Report* 46: 838–42.

Chamberlain, P. 2006. *Undoing Reproductive Freedom: Christian Right NGOs Target the United Nations.* Cambridge, MA: Political Research Associates.

Chandrasekaran, R. 2006. *Imperial Life in the Emerald City: Inside Iraq's Green Zone.* New York: Knopf.

Chauncey, G. 1994. *Gay New York: Gender, Urban Culture, and the Making of the Gay Male World 1840–1940.* New York: Basic Books.

Cochrane Collaborative Review Group on HIV Infection and AIDS. 2004. "Evidence Assessment: Strategies for HIV/AIDS Prevention, Treatment and Care." San Francisco: University of California, San Francisco Institute for Global Health, July, http://www.igh.org/Cochrane/pdfs/EvidenceAssessment.pdf (accessed Sept. 26, 2006)

Cohen, S. 1972. *Folk Devils and Moral Panics: Creation of Mods and Rockers.* London: MacGibbon & Kee.

Cohen, S. A. 2003. "Beyond Slogans: Lessons from Uganda's Experience with ABC and HIV/AIDS." *The Guttmacher Report on Public Policy* 6(5), http://www.guttmacher.org/pubs/tgr/06/5/gr060501.pdf (accessed July 26, 2006).

Committee on Government Reform—Minority Staff, Special Investigations Division, U.S. House of Representatives. 2003. "Politics and Science in the Bush Administration," http://democrats.reform.house.gov/features/ politics_and_science/pdfs/pdf_politics_and_science_rep.pdf (accessed Sept. 26, 2006).

Cooperman, A. 2006. "Church Urged to Disinvite Obama." *Washington Post*, November 30: A04.

Couzin, J. 2005. "Plan B: A Collision of Science and Politics." *Science* 310: 38–39.

Dallard, C. 2002. "Abstinence Promotion and Teen Family Planning: The Misguided Drive for Equal Funding." *The Guttmacher Report on Public Policy* 5: 103.

Darroch, J. F., J. F. Frost, and S. Singh. 2001a. "Differences in Teenage Pregnancy Rates among Five Developed Countries: The Roles of Sexual Activity and Contraceptive Use." *Family Planning Perspectives* 33: 244–50.

———. 2001b. *Teenage Sexual and Reproductive Behavior in Developed Countries: Can More Progress Be Made?* New York: Guttmacher Institute, November, http://www.guttmacher.org/pubs/eurosynth_rpt.pdf (accessed Sept. 26, 2006).

D'Emilio, J., and E. Freedman. 1997. *Intimate Matters: A History of Sexuality in America.* New York: Harper & Row.

Dickman, I. 1982. *Winning the Battle for Sex Education.* New York: Sexuality Information and Education Council of the United States.

di Mauro, D., and D. Haffner. 1990. *Winning the Battle: Developing Support for Sexuality and HIV/AIDS Education.* New York: Sexuality Information and Education Council of the United States.

Eisenberg, J. 2005. *Using Terri: The Religious Right's Conspiracy to Take Away Our Rights.* San Francisco: HarperCollins.

Eisenstadt v. Baird, 405 U.S. 438 (1972).

Epstein, S. 2006. "The New Attack on Sexuality Research: Morality and the Politics of Knowledge Production." *Sexuality Research and Social Policy: Journal of NSRC* 3(1): 1–12.

Fields, J., and D. L. Tolman. 2006. "Risky Business: Sexuality Education and Research in U.S. Schools." *Sexuality Research and Social Policy: Journal of NSRC* 3(4): 63–76.

Foster, A., J. van Dis, and J. Steinauer. 2003. "Educational and Legislative Initiatives Affecting Residency Training in Abortion." *Journal of the American Medical Association* 290: 1777–78.

Frank, T. 2004. *What's the Matter with Kansas? How Conservatives Won the Heart of America.* New York: Henry Holt.

Frost, J., A. Sonfield, and R. Gold. 2006. "Estimating the Impact of Serving New Clients by Expanding Funding for Title X." *Occasional Report No. 33.* New York: Guttmacher Institute.

Garrow, D. 1994. *Liberty and Sexuality: The Right to Privacy and the Making of Roe v. Wade.* New York: MacMillan.

Girard, F. 2004. "Global Implications of U.S. Domestic and International Policies on Sexuality" (working paper no. 1). New York: International Working Group on Sexuality and Social Policy, Sociomedical Sciences Department, Mailman School of Public Health, Columbia University.

Goldberg, M. 2006. *Kingdom Coming: The Rise of Christian Nationalism.* New York: Norton.

Gonzales v. Carhart, 127 S.Ct.1610 (2007).

Goodson, P., B. Pruitt, E. Buhi, K. Wilson, C. Rasberry, and E. Gunnels. 2004. *Abstinence Education Evaluation: Phase 5 Technical Report.* College Station: Department of Health and Kinesiology, Texas A&M University.

Hardisty, J. 1999. *Mobilizing Resentment: Conservative Resurgence from the John Birch Society to the Promise Keepers.* Boston: Beacon.

Harper, C., M. Cheong, C. Rocca, P. Darney, and T. Raine. 2005. "The Effect of Increased Access to Emergency Contraception among Young Adolescents." *Obstetrics and Gynecology* 106: 483–91.

Harris v. McCrae, 448 U.S. 297 (1980).

Hatecrime.org, 2007, http://www.hatecrime.org/subpages/hatespeech/hate.html (accessed Feb. 6, 2007).

Hauser, D. 2004. *Five Years of Abstinence-Only-until-Marriage Education: Assessing the Impact.* Washington, D.C.: Advocates for Youth.

Henriques, D., and A. Lehren. 2006. "Religion for Captive Audiences, with Taxpayers Paying the Bill." *New York Times,* December 10: A1, A18.

Henry J. Kaiser Foundation. 2000. *Sex Education in America: A Series of National Surveys of Students, Parents, Teachers and Principals.* Menlo Park, CA: Henry J. Kaiser Foundation.

Henshaw, S., and L. Finer. 2003. "The Accessibility of Abortion Services in the United States, 2001." *Perspectives on Sexual and Reproductive Health* 35(1): 16–24.

Howell, M., and A. Feijoo. 2001. *Science or Politics? George W. Bush and the Future of Sexuality Education in the United States.* Washington, D.C.: Advocates for Youth, January, http://www.advocatesforyouth.org/publications/factsheet/fsbush.pdf (accessed Sept. 26, 2006).

Human Rights Watch. 2005. "The Less They Know, the Better: Abstinence-Only HIV/AIDS Programs in Uganda." *Human Rights Watch,* 17(4A): 1–79, http://hrw.org/reports/2005/uganda0305/uganda0305.pdf (accessed Sept. 26, 2006).

Institute of Medicine—Committee on HIV Prevention Strategies in the United States. 2000. *No Time To Lose: Getting More from HIV Prevention.* Washington, D.C.: National Academies Press.

International Women's Health Coalition. 2006. "Bush's Other War," http://www.iwhc.org/resources/bushsotherwar/index.cfm (accessed Dec. 8, 2006).

Irvine, J. 2002. *Talk about Sex: The Battles over Sex Education in the United States.* Berkeley: University of California Press.

Jamison, D., and N. Padian. 2006. "Where AIDS Funding Should Go." *San Francisco Chronicle,* May 23: A23.

Jayson, S. 2006. "Abstinence Message Goes beyond Teens." *USA Today,* October 31: A1.

Joffe, C. 1979. *Friendly Intruders: Childcare Professionals and Family Life.* Berkeley: University of California Press.

———. 1995. *Doctors of Conscience: The Struggle to Provide Abortion before and after* Roe v. Wade. Boston: Beacon.

———. 2005. "It's Not Just Abortion, Stupid: Progressives and Abortion." *Dissent* 51: 91–96.

———. 2006. "Reproductive Regression," *Tompaine.com*, January 23, http://www.tompaine.com/articles/2006/01/23/reproductive_regression.php (accessed Jan. 11, 2007).

Joffe, C., T. Weitz, and C. Stacey. 2004. "Uneasy Allies: Pro-Choice Physicians, Feminist Health Activists and the Struggle for Abortion Rights." *Sociology of Health and Illness* 26: 775–96.

Kaiser Family Foundation. 2001. *Generation RX.com: How Young People Use the Internet for Health Information: A Kaiser Family Foundation Survey.* Menlo Park, CA: Kaiser Family Foundation.

Kaiser Family Foundation and the Kennedy School of Government. 2004. "Sex Education in America," *NPR* November 29, http://www.npr.org (accessed Jan. 11, 2006).

Kaplan, E. 2004. *With God on Their Side: How Christian Fundamentalists Trampled Science, Policy, and Democracy in George W. Bush's White House.* New York: New Press.

Kaufman, M. 2006. "Pregnancy Centers Found to Give False Information on Abortion." *Washington Post*, July 18: A8.

Kehrl, B. 2005. *States Abstain from Federal Sex Ed Money. Stateline.* November 29, http://www.stateline.org (accessed Jan. 11, 2006).

Kendall, N. 2006. Presentation at Fellows' Conference, Sexuality Research Fellowship Program, Arlie Conference Center, Warrenton, VA, October.

Kirby, D. 2001a. *Emerging Answers: Research Findings on Programs to Reduce Teen Pregnancy.* Washington, D.C.: National Campaign to Prevent Teen Pregnancy.

———. 2001b. "Understanding What Works and What Doesn't in Reducing Adolescent Sexual Risk-Taking." *Family Planning Perspective* 33: 276–81.

———. 2002. "Effective Approaches to Reducing Adolescent Unprotected Sex, Pregnancy and Childbearing." *Journal of Sex Research* 39: 51–57.

Kirkpatrick, D. 2005. "DeLay To Be on Christian Telecast on Courts." *New York Times*, August 3, http://www.nytimes.com (accessed Dec. 8, 2006).

Kirkpatrick, D., and S. Stolberg. 2005. "How Family's Cause Reached the Halls of Congress." *New York Times*, March 22: A1.

Koedt, A. 1973. "The Myth of the Vaginal Orgasm." In *Radical Feminism* edited by A. Koedt, E. Levine, and A. Rapone. New York: Quadrangle.

Kristof, N. 2006. "A Modest Proposal for a Truce on Religion." *New York Times*, December 3: Section 4, p. 13.

Kuo, D. 2006. *Tempting Faith: An Inside Story of Political Seduction.* New York: Free Press.

Landry, D. J., L. Kaeser, and C. L. Richards. 1999. "Abstinence Promotion and the Provision of Information about Contraception in Public School District Sexuality Education Policies." *Family Planning Perspectives* 31: 280–86.

Lee, S., H. Ralston, E. Drey, J. Patridge, and M. Rosen. 2005. "Fetal Pain: A Systematic Multidisciplinary Review of the Evidence." *Journal of the American Medical Association* 294: 947–54.

Lipschutz, M., and R. Rosenblatt. (Producer/Directors). 2005. *The Education of Shelby Knox* [Motion picture]. Cine Qua Non/Incite Pictures.

Lo, C. 1982. "Countermovements and Conservative Movements in the Contemporary U.S." *Annual Review of Sociology* 8: 107–34.

Luker, K. 2006. *When Sex Goes To School: Warring Views on Sex—And Sex Education Since the Sixties.* New York: Norton.

Mainardi, P. 1970. "The Politics of Housework." In *Sisterhood Is Powerful.* Edited by R. Morgan. New York: Vintage.

Manlove, J., A. Papillio, and E. Ikramullah. 2004. *Not Yet: Programs To Delay First Sex among Teens.* Washington, D.C.: National Campaign to Prevent Teenage Pregnancy.

Mathematica Policy Research Institute Inc. 2002. *The Evaluation of Abstinence Education Programs Funded under Title V Section 510.* Princeton, NJ.

———. 2007. "Impacts of Four Title V," *Section 510 Abstinence Education Programs,* Princeton, NJ.

McGraw, O. 1980. *The Family, Feminism, and the Therapeutic State.* Washington, D.C.: Heritage Foundation.

McKeegan, M. 1992. *Abortion Politics: Mutiny in the Ranks of the Right.* New York: Free Press.

MergerWatch. 2006. "Hospitals and Religious Restrictions," http://www.merger-watch.org/hospital_mergers.html (accessed Dec. 8, 2006).

Micklethwait, J., and A. Wooldridge. 2004. *The Right Nation: Conservative Power in America.* New York: Penguin.

Mooney, C. 2005. *The Republican War on Science.* New York: Basic Books.

Moran, J. 2000. *Teaching Sex: The Shaping of Adolescence in the 20th Century.* Boston: Harvard University Press.

———. 2003. "Sex Education and the Rise of the New Right." *Reviews in American History* 31: 283–89.

Mosher, W. D., G. M. Martinez, A. Chandra, J. C. Abma, and S. J. Willson. 2004. "Use of Contraceptives, Use of Family Planning Services in the United States: 1982–2002." *Advance Data from Vital and Health Statistics,* No. 350. Atlanta: Centers for Disease Control and Prevention, December 10, http://www.cdc.gov/nchs/data/ad/ad350.pdf (accessed Jan. 2, 2006).

Murdock, D. 2001. "The Adoption Option." *National Review*, August 27, http:// www.nationalreview.com (accessed July 25, 2006).

National Guidelines Task Force. 1991. *Guidelines for Comprehensive Sexuality Education: Kindergarten–12th Grade*. New York: Sexuality Information and Education Council of the United States.

National Women's Law Center. 2008. "Memo to Interested Parties," Peter D. Hart Research Associates. April 13, http://www.nwlc.org (accessed April 13, 2008).

Page, C. 2006. *How the Pro-Choice Movement Saved America: Freedom, Politics and the War on Sex*. New York: Basic Books.

Petchesky, R. 1987. "Fetal Images: The Power of Visual Culture in the Politics of Reproduction. In *Reproductive Technologies: Gender, Motherhood and Medicine*. Edited by M. Stanworth. Minneapolis: University of Minnesota Press.

———. 1990. *Abortion and Women's Choice: The State, Sexuality and Reproductive Freedom*. Boston: Northeastern University Press.

———. 2003. *Global Prescriptions: Gendering Health and Human Rights*. London: Zed Books.

Phillips, K. 2006. *American Theocracy: The Peril and Politics of Radical Religion, Oil, and Borrowed Money in the Twenty-First Century*. New York: Viking.

Planned Parenthood of Southeastern Pennsylvania v. Casey, 505 U.S. 833 (1992).

Pro-Life Action League. 2006. "'Contraception Is Not the Answer,' Says League." Homepage Archive, *Pro-Life Action League*, October 4, http://www.prolifeaction.org/home/2006/cinta3.htm (accessed Feb. 2, 2007).

Responsible Education About Life Act, H.R. 768, 109th Cong. (2005) and S. 368, 109th Cong. (2005).

Roe v. Wade, 410 U.S. 113 (1973).

Rotskoff, L. 2001. "Sex in the Schools: Adolescence, Sex Education and Social Reform." *Reviews in American History* 29: 310–18.

Russell, S. 2005. "Uganda's HIV Rate Drops, but Not from Abstinence: Study Concludes Basis of Bush Policy Apparently Irrelevant." *SF Gate*, February 24, http://www.sfgate.com (accessed Sept. 26, 2006).

Sanchez, N. 2005. "American Girl Boycott: Groups Pick a Fight with a Doll over Messages to Girls." *Kansas City Star*, November 21: B5.

Santelli, J., M. Ott, M. Lyon, J. Rogers, D. Summers, and R. Schleifer. 2006. "Abstinence and Abstinence-Only Education: A Review of U.S. Policies and Programs." *Journal of Adolescent Health* 38: 72–81.

Schalet, A. (2004). "Must We Fear Adolescent Sexuality?" *Medscape General Medicine*, 6(4), 1–22, December 30, http://www.medscape.com/viewarticle/494933 (accessed Sept. 26, 2006).

Sexuality Information and Education Council of the United States. 2000. *Developing Guidelines for Comprehensive Sexuality Education*. New York: Sexuality Information and Education Council of the United States.

Sexuality Information and Education Council of the United States. 2003. "Special Edition: Sexuality Education, a Decade of Controversy." *SIECUS Report*, 38:6, Fall.

Shorto, R. (2006). "Contra-Contraception." *New York Times*, May 7, http://www. nytimes.com (accessed Dec. 8, 2006).

Silliman, Y., M. Fried, L. Ross, and E. Gutierrez. 2004. *Undivided Rights: Women of Color Organize for Reproductive Justice*. Boston: South End.

Simon, S. 2006. "Abortion Foes Energized by their Losses." *LA Times*, November 9, http://www.latimes.com (accessed Dec. 1, 2006).

Smith, D. S. (Producer), and B. Nathanson, B. (Director). 1984. *The Silent Scream* [DVD]. Brunswick, OH: American Portrait Films.

Society for Adolescent Medicine. 2006. "Abstinence-Only Education Policies and Programs: A Position Paper of the Society for Adolescent Medicine." *Journal of Adolescent Health* 38: 283–87.

Specter, M. 2006. "Political Science: The White House vs. the Laboratory." *New Yorker*, March 13: 58–69.

Stein, R. 2006a. "Health Workers' Choice Debated." *Washington Post*, January 30: A1.

———. 2006b. "For Some, There Is No Choice." *Washington Post*, July 16: A6.

———. 2006c. "Seeking Care and Refused." *Washington Post*, July 16: A6.

Stenberg v. Carhart, 530 U.S. 914 (2000).

Stolberg, S. 2006. "First Bush Veto Maintains Limits on Stem Cell Use." *New York Times*, July 20: A1, A16.

Thought Theater. 2007. "Abstinence: Uganda HIV Rates Suggest Failure," http:// www.thoughttheater.com/2006/05/abstinence_uganda_hiv_rates_su.php (accessed Feb. 6, 2007).

Title V, Elementary and Secondary Education Act, 20 U.S.C. 7201 *et seq.* (2005).

Title X, Public Health Service Act, 42 U.S.C. § 300 (1970).

UNAIDS, Joint United Nations Programme on HIV/AIDS. 2005. Uniting the world against AIDS: Uganda, http://www.unaids.org/en/Regions_Countries/ Countries/Uganda.asp (accessed Feb. 6, 2007).

Unborn Victims of Violence Act of 2004, 18 U.S.C. § 90A-1841 (2004).

United States Leadership Against HIV/AIDS, Tuberculosis and Malaria Act of 2003. Sections 402(b)(3) and 403(a), http://rpc.senate.gov/_files/ L23HEALTHfr051503.pdf (accessed Feb. 6, 2007).

Uttley, L. 2005. "The Politics of the Embryo." *American Progress*, July 19, http:// www.americanprogress.org (accessed Jan. 2, 2006).

Wallis, J. 2005. *God's Politics: Why the Right Gets It Wrong and the Left Doesn't Get It*. San Francisco: Harper.

Waxman, H. 2004. *The Waxman Report: The Content of Federally Funded Abstinence-Only Education Programs*. Washington, D.C.: Committee on Government Reform, Special Investigations Division, U.S. House of Representatives, December.

Webster v. Reproductive Health Services, 488 U.S. 1003 (1989).

Weitz, T., and A. Hunter. 2007. "*Six Feet Under* Brings Abortion to the Surface." In *21st Century Sexualities: Contemporary Issues in Health, Education and Rights*. Edited by G. Herdt and C. Howe. London: Routledge.

Welfare Reform Act, § 510(b)(2) (1996). U.S. Social Security Administration, http://www.ssa.gov/OP_Home/ssact/title05/0510.htm (accessed Feb. 6, 2007).

Wills, G. 2006. "A Country Ruled by Faith." *New York Review of Books* 53, November 16: 8–12.

Wood, A., J. Drazen, and M. Greene. 2005. "A Sad Day for Science at the FDA." *New England Journal of Medicine* 353: 1197–99.

3

Black Sexuality, Indigenous Moral Panics, and Respectability

From Bill Cosby to the Down Low

Cathy J. Cohen

I promised myself that I would no longer discuss the ranting and raving of Bill Cosby that occurred over four years ago. For those who do not remember, it was May 17, 2004 when Bill Cosby, speaking at Constitution Hall in Washington D.C. at a commemoration of the 50th anniversary of *Brown v. Board of Education*, began his attack on poor black people and black youth. Actually, Cosby's comments were largely focused on the issue of faulty parenting among the black poor; however, at the center of his disgust were poor black children and black young people whom he characterized as deviants, resulting from the pathological choices of their parents. While his running commentary on black people and the black poor, which has lasted now for five years and culminated in the publication of the book *Come on, People: On the Path from Victims to Victors* with Alvin Poussaint, is too long to recount in this chapter, I do want to include a few notable comments from his initial speech.[1] Below I highlight quotes from Mr. Cosby's initial speech in 2004 because I believe that speech fueled the flames for the current media-facilitated moral panic about the black poor, black youth culture, black parenting, and, specifically, the absence of a heteronormative two-parent nuclear black family being voiced by numerous leaders in black communities.[2]

COSBY ON THE BLACK POOR: "Lower economic people are not holding up their end in this deal. These people are not parenting. They are buying things for kids–$500 sneakers for what? And won't spend $200 for 'Hooked on Phonics.'"

"We as black folks have to do a better job. Someone working at Wal-Mart with seven kids, you are hurting us. We have to start holding each other to a higher standard. We cannot blame white people."

COSBY ON BLACK YOUTH CULTURE: "People putting their clothes on backwards: Isn't that a sign of something gone wrong? . . . People with their hats on backwards, pants down around the crack, isn't that a sign of something, or are you waiting for Jesus to pull his pants up? Isn't it a sign of something when she has her dress all the way up to the crack and got all type of needles [piercings] going through her body? What part of Africa did this come from? Those people are not Africans; they don't know a damn thing about Africa."

COSBY ON CIVIL RIGHTS: "Brown versus the Board of Education is no longer the white person's problem. We have got to take the neighborhood back. We have to go in there–forget about telling your child to go into the Peace Corps–it is right around the corner. They are standing on the corner and they can't speak English."

COSBY ON LITERACY: "Basketball players–multimillionaires–can't write a paragraph. Football players–multimillionaires–can't read. Yes, multimillionaires. Well, *Brown v. Board of Education*: Where are we today? They paved the way, but what did we do with it? That white man, he's laughing. He's got to be laughing: 50 percent drop out, the rest of them are in prison."

COSBY ON POOR BLACK WOMEN: "Five, six children–same woman–eight, ten different husbands or whatever. Pretty soon you are going to have DNA cards to tell who you are making love to. You don't know who this is. It might be your grandmother. I am telling you, they're young enough! Hey, you have a baby when you are twelve; your baby turns thirteen and has a baby. How old are you? Huh? Grandmother! By the time you are twelve you can have sex with your grandmother, you keep those numbers coming. I'm just predicting."

COSBY ON THE SONS AND DAUGHTERS OF POOR, BLACK, UNMARRIED MOTHERS: "[W]ith names like Shaniqua, Taliqua and Mohammed [!] and all of that crap, and all of them are in jail.

COSBY ON BLACKS SHOT BY POLICE: "These are not political criminals. These are people going around stealing Coca-Cola. People getting shot in the back of the head over a piece of pound cake and then we run out and we are outraged, [saying] 'The cops shouldn't have shot him.' What the hell was he doing with the pound cake in his hand?

Initially, my reluctance to engage Mr. Cosby and his continuous outbursts about the failings of poor black parents and their children stemmed from the fact that others had already plowed that path and, truthfully, he seemed far too easy a target.[3] I mean how difficult is it to discredit someone "preaching" about faulty parenting who admitted to having an affair and then found himself embroiled in a legal paternity battle over whether he was the father of a child from the acknowledged affair?[4] He seemed in many ways too easy to dismiss.

More recently, however, my reluctance to engage the Cosby rant has less to do with Cosby's own internal failings and more to do with the conflicted feelings his commentary evokes for me. Let me be clear, Cosby's attacks on the poor are, at worst, fundamentally wrong. He provides no structural context when demeaning the choices and behaviors of poor black parents, and instead he belittles this group of people about which he claims to be concerned. At best, Cosby has stumbled onto some partial truths, conjuring up images of poor young black people and their parents that are incomplete in their details of the economic and political challenges that poor black people face but that are hauntingly familiar as I look out the window of my house, visit my relatives, or drive through many poor black neighborhoods. Moreover, the Cosby rant has been given a kinder, more rational presentation by other individuals, most notably Barack Obama.

It was Senator Obama, who in his 2008 Father's Day speech told the black congregation at Apostolic Church of God in Chicago and the world, through media coverage, that black fathers bore a significant role in perpetuating the troubles facing black communities and black children:

Of all the rocks upon which we build our lives, we are reminded today that family is the most important. And we are called to recognize and honor how critical every father is to that foundation. They are teachers and coaches. They are mentors and role models. They are examples of success and the men who constantly push us toward it. But if we are honest with ourselves, we'll admit that what too many fathers also are is missing–missing from too many lives and too many homes. They have abandoned their responsibilities, acting like boys instead of men. And the foundations of our families are weaker because of it. You and I know how true this is in the African-American community. We know that more than half of all black children live in single-parent households, a number that has doubled–doubled–since we were children.[5]

Noting the similarity to Cosby's criticisms of black men and black families, Julie Bosman of the *New York Times* writes, "His [Obama's] themes have also been sounded by the comedian Bill Cosby, who has stirred debate among black Americans by bluntly speaking about an epidemic of fatherless African-American families while suggesting that some blacks use racism as a crutch to explain lack of economic progress."[6]

So, whether I like it or not, it is Cosby's partial truths and their replication and refinement that continue to make him a difficult but necessary subject for me. I find it necessary to deal with Cosby's partial truths because the images of failing black people he presents resonate, not surprisingly, with many white people, but also, and more importantly for me, with many black people (I dare say myself included). Thus, those interested in providing a more complex and layered image and understanding of the lives of poor and young people must endure and engage the Cosbys of the world. This chapter is far too short to allow me to delineate fully a more accurate picture of the lives of poor black people than Cosby has offered. Instead, I will try to address one part of the Cosby phenomenon, namely why so much rage and fear seems to exist among either middle-class black people or older black people toward those younger and poorer in black communities.

The concept of moral panics, which is the focus of this book, will be the lens through which I explore this trend. Using both Bill Cosby's rage and the hysteria surrounding the down low as a starting point, I want to rethink the nature of moral panics, in particular those that emerge around sex in marginal communities. In this particular case I am interested in the development of moral panics in black communities, driven by what some have deemed the deviant behavior of other group members. I am especially interested in trying to think through how moral panics possibly work differently within marginalized or oppressed communities.

Many accounts of moral panics represent them as irrational, overreactions to lesser events exaggerated by the media. The history of marginalized communities, however, puts into question the irrationality of community panic given the past actions of a disapproving state and public against members of marginalized groups. Moreover, while much of the moral panic literature, starting with Stanley Cohen and moving forward, either explicitly states or implicitly assumes that much of the targeting, blaming, and shaming of a group comes from people external to the targeted group, today we see the continued tradition of black leaders attempting to police group members engaged in what is thought to be deviant, destructive, and dangerous behavior and norms, often tied to sex.[7] This policing corresponds with what I have deemed the secondary marginalization of those most vulnerable in oppressed communities.

While the question of indigenous moral panics around sexual norms and behavior is the centerpiece of this chapter, I am also interested in the absence of panic in those same communities when objective circumstances and "facts" suggest that mass mobilization and alarm is called for. For example, why does there still seem to be little pervasive panic in black communities about the spread of HIV and AIDS among black people or at least focused on those groups hardest hit by the epidemic—black gay men and heterosexual black men who have sex with men. Undoubtedly, the response of community stakeholders has as much to do with perceptions of who is at risk in this epidemic and their status and membership within black communities as it does with the dearth of resources available to adequately respond to this crisis. An exploration of this phenomenon should provide greater insight into indigenous moral panics.

Last, in this chapter I will focus less on historical and academic treatments of black deviance and more on the continued moral panic around black sexuality that is evident today in the public, manifest in what I believe to be a troubling trend, namely, the increasing public demonization of certain segments of black communities rooted in an attack on their sexual behaviors, patterns of intimacy, and family structures. Not surprising, as with all moral panics, I believe such attacks are not only about concerns relating to sexual behavior but also embody the anxiety of the black middle-class threatened with incurring even greater losses under the conservative political environment that exists today under the Bush Administration. Before I delve into a discussion of the fragile position of the black middle class and our evolving understanding of moral panics, let me start by extending my comments on Bill Cosby and then turn my attention to the media coverage of the phenomenon known as the down low.

Bill Cosby

While there are many things one might ponder after reading any one of Bill Cosby's diatribes against the poor, one important thing to notice about Cosby's construction of black deviance is the way sexuality is mixed with ideas of criminality and cultural deviance. Thus, for Cosby and others concerned with deviance in black communities, sexual deviance is an important dimension but only one dimension of a totalizing deviant lifestyle. His rendition of the failures of the black poor and black young people in particular sound amazingly like earlier cultural theories of the "underclass" in black communities.[8]

These theories argue that it is not the structural limitations that the poor face that dictate their behavior, but it is instead their non-normative cultural values and behaviors that facilitate the intergenerational cycles of poverty and their alienation from mainstream society. According to these theories and Cosby, these are disreputable people that cannot be helped simply by providing them with jobs, government support, or quality education. They need a cultural revolution that starts from within.

The implications of such an analysis of poverty and/or deviance for those concerned with helping to secure the sexual and human rights of marginalized individuals is that our work must begin and end with an emphasis on recognizing the multiple and intersecting identities under which people exist and through which they are marginalized, necessitating a political analysis that highlights one's full humanity across multiple dimensions and not just in the sexual realm. What is needed is an intersectional approach to sexual rights much in line with the work on sexual citizenship.[9] The foundation to this approach is the recognition that one's sexual decisions and behaviors impact not only our private relationships but also, and possibly more importantly, our public/political status and rights both nationally and within communities. Furthermore, our public and legal status before the state also shapes our sexual decision-making. For example, being in the military might shape who someone is willing to have sex with independent of desire. Similarly, receiving assistance from the state might influence an individual's reproductive choices.

Beyond Cosby's individual comments and his totalizing analysis of deviant behavior in black communities, what is just as interesting is the response his words garnered throughout black communities. Far from being uniformly reprimanded for his public belittling of black people, and specifically the black poor, Cosby was largely supported and hailed as a truth teller among black elites. Black leaders from Jesse Jackson to Cornel West to Kwame Mfume to Skip Gates all went on record saying that while it was hard to hear, Cosby had spoken the truth about young black people and far too many poor black parents—a truth that it was claimed most people in black communities quietly shared.[10] Harvard scholar Skip Gates in his August 1, 2004 *New York Times* op-ed piece on Cosby wrote, "Any black person who frequents a barbershop or beauty parlor in the inner city knows that Mr. Cosby was only echoing sentiments widely shared in black communities."[11]

It is the joining of forces against the black poor by those with access to the media and indigenous resources and power within black communities that is particularly alarming and fascinating to me. By now I have grown accustomed to, though no less disturbed by, the constant maligning of the black poor by those from outside of black communities. Whether it is Ronald Reagan's infamous phrase "welfare queen" or the overwhelming rejection by the white public of welfare programs perceived as helping poor black people, on a daily basis one is reminded of the contempt held for poor black people across large swaths of American society.[12] However, in this chapter I want to explore indigenous black responses to the black poor through the framework of moral panics, paying close attention to the heightened condemnation of black poor people or young black people by those Michael Eric Dyson calls the "Afristocracy."[13]

We need to take one more detour before turning our attention to moral panics—a quick discussion of the down low.

The Down Low

From my vantage point, a process of indigenous moral panic is involved in the hysteria around the constructed phenomenon of black men on the down low and their purported threat to black women: summed up by the recent subtitle in *Essence* magazine on this subject—"They're Bi and they Lie." In the down-low panic, black men are being "called out" by black women or other black men who in their pasts were also on the down low. These down-low black men are represented as engaging in deviant and dangerous sexual behaviors, threatening the lives of black women. Here I am referring to the idea or belief that has been circulating for some time that black women are at greater risk for HIV than other women, in large part because some unknown number of black men, and seemingly only black men by the reports, are having unprotected sex with men and then returning home to have unprotected sex with women—presumably black women. These men labeled as being on the down low do not identify as gay or bisexual but heterosexual, further complicating intervention strategies and the sexual safety of black women.

Many people identify the starting point for this panic with the publication of J. L. King's book, *On the Down Low: A Journey Into the Lives of Straight Black Men Who Sleep with Men*.[14] That book may be one marker of the beginning of this panic, but the panic has grown far beyond the writings of J. L. King. There is no denying that the idea of black men on the down low has taken off and been embraced by the media leading to coverage of the topic in the *New York Times Magazine* and on popular television shows such as *ER*, *Law and Order* and even the *Oprah Winfrey Show*. There was a period of time when you could not pick up a magazine aimed at black women—like *Essence* magazine—that did not include some mention of or story about black men on the down low.

I had one such encounter with the hysteria surrounding this moral panic at a tapping of the *Oprah Winfrey Show* about AIDS. I was in the audience, there to support a good friend who was going to serve as the expert doctor for the show. The focus of the show was AIDS in America with an emphasis on the increasing rates of infection among women, especially black women. The celebrity draws for the episode were Magic Johnson and his wife, Cookie, who were there to discuss their experience of living with Johnson's HIV and AIDS diagnosis as well as his new initiative to end AIDS in black communities. Also on the program was Reverend Eugene Rivers from Boston.

Reverend Rivers is known for his willingness to take controversial stands and offer a different and often contested perspective about politics in black communities. For example, Rivers is one of the most prominent black ministers to publicly and vocally support and work with George W. Bush's Administration. At this taping, Rivers was not short on words when describing the sexual pathology of far too many young people in black communities as well as black men who sleep with men as well as women. He argued that in the black community, "there is a culture of promiscuity that says we must celebrate big pimping, booty popping, and bootylicousness." He continued stating that "this culture is promoted and accepted, and it demeans black women in ways that are absolutely absurd. . . . The black community and America in general has to confront this crisis because we are now reducing a generation of young women to a biological underclass."[15] He concluded by suggesting that black men who have sex with men and then with black women, possibly infecting these women with HIV, are committing murder and should be put in jail.

Unfortunately, Rivers did not seem concerned about the lack of evidence currently available proving that black men supposedly on the down low are the cause of the rising rates of HIV and AIDS among black women. In fact, the Centers for Disease Control and Prevention (CDC) note on their website that there is no evidence to support the theory that down low behavior is the reason for the increasing rates of HIV among black women. Specifically, CDC states,

> The phenomenon of men on the down low has gained much attention in recent years; however, *there are no data* to confirm or refute publicized accounts of HIV risk behavior associated with these men. What is clear is that women, men, and children of minority races and ethnicities are disproportionately affected by HIV and AIDS and that all persons need to protect themselves and others from getting or transmitting HIV.[16]

The reality, of course, is that there are a number of factors that contribute to the higher rates of HIV and AIDS among black women, including higher infection rates among male heterosexual partners because of male-to-male sexual activity and the exchange of contaminated blood through the use of "dirty" needles.

Again, there is much that can be said about Rivers's comments and the lack of complexity in his statements; my interest is really in the response his uninformed accusations received. To my surprise, many in the audience applauded Rivers for his comments with many black women in the audience nodding in agreement and some saying "that is right!" Oprah said something to the effect that Rivers had her head spinning and then began to offer her own stories about the wayward values and behaviors of black youth today. She offered anecdotal stories of female students at an unnamed historically black female college telling her that young black women accept being called a "bitch and ho." She decried how older black people have failed this younger generation by not teaching them their history, and then she contrasted young black people with Jewish youth whom she said understand and take to heart their history. Finally, she raised the issue of black men on the down low and voiced her frustration that these men who say they are not gay will not accept their sexual preference and stop infecting black women.

Largely missing from this "discussion" of sexuality and young people in black communities was any clear, evidence-based oppositional voice. A few of the show's participants attempted to point out that the crisis of the down low is yet another media- and profit-motivated crisis that has linked two phenomenon—the rising rates of HIV among black women and the acknowledgement that some black men have sex with men and also identify as heterosexual and continue to engage in heterosexual relationships—without any evidence to prove that there is a causal link between the two. That perspective was drowned out with the "common knowledge" (at least according to Rivers and Oprah), that sex in black communities (at least among the marginal) is out of control and now threatening the lives of more respectable people, specifically heterosexual women.

There was little support among audience members for the black woman living with AIDS who stood up and tried to explain that the down low panic that is taking place across black communities—on television, on the radio and at dinner tables—is one that is filled with a rhetoric of blame, a rhetoric of blame that does nothing to help "protect" black women because all this discourse does is shut down any honest communication about the complexity of sex in any community, including black communities. Instead, the focus of this discussion was on personal responsibility and blame, blaming black men who have sex with men and women and gently blaming black women for not demanding that the men they have sex with use a condom.

So instead of a productive and open discussion about what we need to do to stem the devastation of HIV and AIDS in black communities and especially among black women and girls, we find ourselves contributing to a discussion that presumes the deviant sexuality of black men, reinforcing and reconstructing the old narrative that sexuality in black communities is always deviant, always dangerous, and always irresponsible. The idea of deviant sexuality in black communities is a familiar trope; this time it is being disseminated throughout black communities, most notably by members of the black elite with access to national audiences and constituencies that extend far beyond black Americans.

The Black Middle Class, Respectability, and Moral Panics

As a number of scholars have written, one of the most significant strategies for mobility in black communities has been one focused on promoting the respectability of black people.[17] Historian Evelyn Brooks Higginbotham explains this strategy, noting that "African Americans' claims to respectability invariably held subversive implications[:] . . . the concept of respectability signified self-esteem, racial pride, and something more. It also signified the search for common ground on which to live as Americans with Americans of other racial and ethnic backgrounds."[18] She continues, "the politics of respectability constituted a deliberate, highly self-concession to hegemonic values. While deferring to segregation in practice, adherents of respectability never deferred to it in principle."[19]

The ideal of acceptance through adherence has influenced the politics and scholarship of black communities for centuries. For example, scholars from W. E. B. Du Bois to William Julius Wilson have engaged in rigorous research, attempting, in part, to explain why some individuals in black communities have not been able to secure economic and social advancement as might be expected based on the experiences of other African Americans and some ethnic groups.[20] These researchers have also devoted a significant amount of their writing to detailing differences in class, culture, and status within African American communities. Usually, the language is not as blunt as calling some undeserving and others respectable and worthy of advancement and acceptance, but if one reads between the lines, that is a central part of their message.

Ironically, a reliance on respectability and relative positioning can be thought of as even more critical for African Americans who have secured some mobility but find it threatened in politically hostile times. For example, where once the expansion of the black middle class was routinely touted by the Clinton Administration, under the Bush Administration, the continued expansion of the black middle class seems questionable in the face of a massive downturn in the economy and rising layoffs from state and city government agencies that previously had been an important route to economic advancement on the part of black Americans. Similarly, the most recent attack on affirmative action, aided significantly by the Bush Administration, threatens access to higher education for African Americans and the job opportunities that result from such capital. Furthermore, the Bush Administration has gone to great lengths to reconfigure the politics of black representation at least as is manifested through administration appointments such as Condoleezza Rice. These black appointees are much more likely to emphasize personal responsibility over structure when discussing the lived condition and politics of black communities.

All these factors and many more suggest that the relative access and mobility experienced by the black middle class in our post-segregated society is susceptible, if not to serious roll-backs, at least to significant constraints in the future. Many believe, therefore, that a politics of respectability may be the one effective strategy for continued expansion of the black middle class in a political environment dominated by the Christian Right and the Bush Administration. It is not surprising, therefore, that in our current political environment, African Americans with some access to power, mobility, and status and those aspiring to secure such resources are feeling especially anxious about what they perceive to be the bad or deviant behavior of other group members. I am referring to behaviors that are thought to threaten the status and mobility of other black people, putting into question the politics of respectability as an effective political strategy for advancement by, in particular, the black middle class.

This concern provides the context for understanding data from a survey of African Americans age thirty and over that found that 50 percent of black adults believe that "the behavior of too many young black Americans threatens the progress of respectable black people who are trying to do the right things."[21] Furthermore, the "deviant" behavior of black youth is especially puzzling to more mature black Americans when they consider the opportunities they believe this group enjoys. Specifically, 80 percent of survey respondents indicated that they believe young black Americans today have more opportunities available to them than when they were growing up. Over 50 percent of African Americans thirty and over believe this generation has *many more* opportunities than they had. Older black Americans are essentially frustrated by two conflicting perceptions: 1) that young black people's behavior is deviant (indeed, they have been told this repeatedly by black leaders they trust), and 2) that the same youths have better opportunities than they ever had. The contradiction leads them to engage in a language of moral panic over young black people.

One consequence of such fragility in terms of social mobility tied to the heightened narrative of the internal undermining of black mobility by other black people is the intensified secondary marginalization of those in black communities thought to compromise the status of those with greater access. As argued in my book *The Boundaries of Blackness*, in the postindustrial era we face a period of advanced marginalization wherein members of marginal communities have taken on the daily, face-to-face responsibility of policing individuals in their group that have less resources and power. The proliferation of black welfare case workers meant to regulate and police the actions of those on welfare, who are disproportionately women of color, is one example of this form of indigenous policing.

Of course, there are more informal means of community policing. Mary Pattillo discusses the policing of black youth by the black middle class who move into poor and working-class black neighborhoods through a process of gentrification.[22] It is not surprising in such instances to have the new middle-class black homeowners routinely call the police as a means of controlling the behavior of their working-class and poor black neighbors.[23] In these examples, indigenous moral entrepreneurs take on the responsibility of policing the public behaviors of group members, especially those behaviors thought to diminish the respectability of the community. Cathy Cohen notes, "targeted members of oppressed communities are thus confronted with a *secondary process of marginalization*, this time imposed by members of their own group."[24]

I contend that the comments of black opinion-makers such as Bill Cosby, Oprah Winfrey, Reverend Eugene Rivers, and even Barack Obama are examples, to varying degrees, of black elites attempting to police the boundaries of acceptable blackness especially as it relates to sexual behavior. Moreover, it is the partial and familiar truths and images found in all of their comments that generate support for their analysis on the part of many in the larger black community. Most members of black communities were raised to understand what it takes to exist and survive in a fundamentally racist societal structure. These individuals then look around, often at the behavior of young people, and see community members engaging in what they believe to be nonnormative sexual norms and behavior. Thus confronted with behaviors that seem not only detrimental to advancement if one is to play by the established rules, but also fundamentally dangerous and harmful to any type personal happiness and success, many black Americans instinctively gravitate to the uncomplicated and available narrative that these young people in all of their totality are out of control.

The repetition of a narrative by those inside and outside black communities that there exists another out-of-control/ pathological subgroup in black communities generates what might be called an indigenous moral panic in black communities. This panic then serves as a catalyst for actions meant either to eliminate the behaviors or designate them as something foreign and unacceptable to respectable black people. Rarely is there an investigation as to whether the narrative is true or a defense of those who stand accused of nonnormative actions, instead the focus is on eliminating the behavior or at least making such actions invisible or less visible to those in the dominant group.

Let me underscore three points that I believe to be critical in understanding the response of many black people to what they consider deviant behavior, especially as manifested by young people. First, much of the frustration voiced by the black middle class and its periphery is motivated by their interest in protecting the class mobility they have secured through hardwork and "good moral fiber" or, more specifically, acceptance and adherence to a normative value structure developed to sustain the power of some dominant group members. However, that is not the only explanation for the disgust articulated by many black people with contemporary behaviors and values. Some of their angst is generated by a true and deep concern for the future of many poor black people and young black people. Again, a survey of black Americans over thirty indicates that 70 percent of respondents believe that "both young black and young white people suffer from the wrong morals concerning important things like sex and work."[25] Thus, some of the anxiety of black Americans is rooted in the belief that this entire generation of young people has lost its moral compass. Black Americans may believe that all young people are in trouble; they also know that the consequences for such misguided behavior will be much more severe for black youth.

Most in black communities know firsthand the difficult conditions that face the more vulnerable members of society. They are clear about the discrimination and inconsistencies inherent in the criminal justice system. They understand that such problems result in the exponential expansion of incarcerated young black people. Members of black communities experience directly and hear the statistics regarding the disproportionate impact of HIV and AIDS in black communities. Black Americans also have firsthand knowledge of the unemployment rates in black communities that are double those among comparable white Americans. Furthermore, they did not need Bill Cosby to tell them about the 50 percent high school drop-out rate among black males in public high schools. In fact, recent data indicate that 53 percent of black Americans thirty and over believe that "although black youth are making some bad decisions, they also face substantial discrimination which limits their opportunities."[26] In some manner, it is the concern for black youth that fuels the panic of older black Americans.

The second point that is critical in understanding the response of many black people to what they consider deviant behavior is that although most black Americans understand the structural constraints many black youth face, we cannot minimize the difficulty of producing an accessible structural analysis that has the same power as the "I pulled myself up by my boot-straps and so can you" story when trying to explain the popularity of personal responsibility narratives in black communities. It is not that black people do not understand and recognize the structural conditions that inhibit the choices and possibilities of poor people, especially poor black people. The problem is that a structural analysis has little traction today, especially, as it is pitted against the counterfactual of black people who have seemingly "made it." In the absence of a logical, accessible, and easily communicated structural analysis, it seems reasonable that black Americans would opt for the personal responsibility explanations of Cosby and others when trying to make sense of their fragile success and the deemed failure of those young black people and poor people seen cursing in public, hanging out on the street, seeming never to work or go to school, having children out of wedlock, and being portrayed on TV primarily as criminals or rappers.

In the post–civil rights era, significant segments of black communities, especially those that grew up under and struggled against Jim Crow segregation, have decided that things are not as bad for this generation as in the past and thus they do not want to hear or promote the stories of a racist structure or discriminatory system. They seem especially reluctant to make that defense when images of black people making bad *individual* decisions about school, work, relationships, sex, and childbearing seem to be everywhere. The nuanced nature of systemic discrimination in a neo-Liberal order in which dejure segregation has been eliminated is hard to notice and point out when the narrative disseminated again and again by the dominant communication machinery is one of progress and a color-blind society.

Third, there is also the historical understanding of the consequences of deviance that black people carry with them. Contrary to Oprah's claim that black youth do not know their history, black Americans, possibly more than any other group, have experienced and remember how a white supremacist state will construct a group as deviant to justify their continued oppression and secondary status. In the history of black people, governments, organizations, vigilante groups, and average citizens have referenced what was believed to be the abnormal and deviant sexual behavior of black Americans as a reason to deny them full citizenship status and rights. Whether it is denying enslaved Africans the right to marry or forcing the sterilization of black women or limiting the financial support women could receive from the state, sex and the constructed image of an untamed black sexuality has continuously been a lynchpin for policies of deprivation and dehumanization targeting African Americans.

Given the black communities' understanding of this history, it comes as no surprise that deep concern or feelings of panic emerge among many in black communities when the general public starts to construct the sexual behaviors of some black people as outside the norm. And instead of mounting a rigorous reply to such accusations, increasing numbers of black community members and opinion-makers have engaged in a strategy of indigenous policing or truth-telling, agreeing with those located outside of black communities that something is fundamentally wrong with the patterns and practices of some marginal but significant portion of black Americans. It is this indigenous or internal process of community policing motivated in part by what I think can be labeled "historically rational group panic" that can augment our understanding of moral panics.

Moral Panics

Many traditional theories of moral panics, such as Stanley Cohen's canonical work *Folk Devils and Moral Panics*, focus on understanding the construction of a moral panic.[27] In these works, moral panics are conceptualized as rule-breaking by a vulnerable or relatively powerless group whose actions and impact are exaggerated through media reports and rumor. It is important to note that not only are the facts of the story distorted or exaggerated, but also, more importantly, the implications of the story are inflated, suggesting that a moral code has been broken that threatens societal progress and agreed-on norms. In his work on moral panics surrounding child predators, Philip Jenkins reminds us that the objective facts of a situation do not need to change for a moral panic to emerge. Instead, the framing and public understanding of a situation or phenomenon can change without the reality of an event or change in trend.[28]

The ability for a moral panic to develop also lies in the preexisting feelings and attitudes of others toward the group being targeted as "folk devils." In Cohen's rendition, it is the media who are the originators and main culprits in the construction of moral panics. He suggests that there are many factors for exaggerated reporting, such as the need to create news as well as the bias and sensationalism that exists in news organizations. Thus, the fuel for such panics is contagious reporting when multiple news organizations repeat not only the specific story line but also the supposed implications of such actions for the larger society. Jenkins also notes the significance of competing interest groups and stakeholders in shaping the framing of events, implications, and response. Finally, in much of the research on moral panics, the response to the construction of folk devils is explored through the reaction of the larger public as well as social control units, often those associated with the state, such as the police and the courts.

My contention is that exploring the development of moral panics in marginal communities provides a different understanding of how they are created as well as who is responsible for controlling such deviant actions. First, moral panics that develop in marginal communities, especially those concerned with the presumed deviant behavior of group members, confound the idea that moral panics originate or gain their strength from outsiders or enemies. In the case of the moral panics around the sexual decisions and behaviors of young black people or men on the down low, most of the "experts" and stakeholders fueling the exaggerated fear in black communities are other black people. Undoubtedly, the media plays a central role in spreading rumors or emphasizing certain frames, but their stories are legitimized by public figures thought to be rooted in black communities.

Second, moral panics in marginal communities challenge the often-presumed irrationality of moral panics. For example, the fear and deep concern of African American for what is believed to be the nonnormative sexual behaviors of community members is not only a reaction to the internalization of patriarchal heteronormative values about what constitutes proper sexual conduct, but it is also a reaction to the knowledge that the idea of black deviant sexuality has been used continuously as a justification for the secondary status of African Americans. Thus, far from being irrational, a community-based panic might be appropriate if we acknowledge the fact that the status and progress of black Americans continues to be tenuous.

Third, moral panics in marginal communities also point to a different set of responders. Unlike Cathy Cohen, whose research focuses on formal units of social control such as the police and courts to rectify the situation, moral panics in marginal communities take on an individual bent with community members demanding different or improved behaviors from other community members. Any assistance from formal structures outside of those communities is understood as auxiliary to the strategy of individual responsibility and respectability. One reason for the secondary role given to outside initiatives and efforts might also be knowledge-based. Specifically, African Americans also have knowledge of the ineffective work of government institutions, not to mention the restrictive requirements that often accompany such policies and programs, to aid truly those most marginal in black communities. Thus, when that knowledge is coupled with the power of the individual responsibility narrative, it is not surprising that the respectability strategy is the dominant discourse from many black opinion leaders today.

The Absence of Panic: Respectability and AIDS in Black Communities

In June 2006, the Chicago AIDS Foundation held a standing-room-only panel and forum to discuss the devastating rates of HIV and AIDS in black communities. I had the honor of not only being in the room for the discussion, but also being one of the participants on the panel. After participating in the discussion, I can write with confidence that what continues to panic many individuals pursuing research, advocacy, and political work around HIV and AIDS in black communities is the seeming absence of panic around this epidemic in black communities. The lack of forceful mobilization continues to be baffling when one looks at the numbers. For example, African Americans make up approximately 13 percent of the U.S. population, yet in 2005 African Americans accounted for 49 percent of newly diagnosed HIV cases and 50 percent of all diagnosed AIDS cases in the country.[29] The rate of AIDS diagnoses for blacks is about ten times the rate for whites and three times that for Latinos.[30] Black women account for 67 percent of all AIDS cases among women in the United States. Their rate of new AIDS cases is twenty-three times that of white women in the United States. Black men are eight times more likely to be infected with HIV/AIDS compared to white men.[31]

According to the Centers for Disease Control and Prevention, African American youth are the largest group of young people who are HIV positive. For example, while they make up only 17 percent of those aged thirteen to nineteen years old in the United States, they account for 70 percent of all HIV/AIDS diagnoses among the same age group in 2006.[32] Similarly, black youth ages twenty to twenty-four comprise 16 percent of that age group in the United States and 57 percent of that age group diagnosed with HIV/AIDS in 2006.[33] A recent CDC study of men who have sex with men found that an "increase in diagnoses was especially high among males between the ages of 13 and 24, with an annual increase of 12.4 percent[,] [c]ompared to 1.5 percent for men overall. The annual increase was still higher among young African-American men who have sex with men, nearly 15 percent."[34]

Not surprisingly, some of the new numbers have created quite a scare among those fighting HIV/AIDS in black communities. With numbers in some segments of black communities—like those among black gay men— that rival the rates of infection witnessed in sub-Saharan Africa, AIDS activists in black communities are still trying to figure out how to mobilize our communities around this epidemic and the threat it poses. Of course, one of the oft-cited barriers to mobilization has been the preoccupation, especially among leaders, with preserving the public perception of respectability among good "god-fearing" black people. Too often worried that highlighting the growing epidemic of AIDS would turn the spotlight on drug use, men having sex with men, and sex work in black communities, too many leaders, advocates, church people, and radicals were quiet about AIDS and only joined the discussion when forced. Those choices and behaviors were and continue to be unforgivable. But how do we explain the willingness of those same black leaders to speak out about the "deviant" lifestyle of the black poor and many black young people? How do we understand their willingness to tell partial truths about some marginal members of black communities and not others?

This is a sad story about the importance and weight given to some members of black communities over others. For many black opinion leaders, there are some black lives that can be redeemed and saved while there are others that are beyond reconciliation. The willingness to speak out about perceived deviant behaviors while demeaning those groups being targeted also suggests that these individuals are seen as salvageable at some level; they are full members of black communities who have lost their way and need only middle-class guidance to get them back on track.

The silence that we have and continue to experience around the risk of AIDS, in particular, for black gay men and black men who have sex with men is a clear marker that these individuals no longer have standing in black communities. As I have previously written, the indigenous construction of their membership in black communities has not only been questioned but also revoked. We should be clear, therefore, that the moral panic surrounding the down low is not about saving the lives of black men, but instead about protecting respectable black women who have followed the rules of proper sexual behavior and thus do not "deserve" to be threatened with HIV.

Conclusion: Respectability and Mobilization— What Can We Do?

Given the reality of the quest for respectability in the black community at a time when there are escalating rates of HIV and AIDS, we have to figure out what we can do. Specifically, what can people who work on sex in the midst of moral panics do to secure the sexual rights of those most marginalized in black communities? First, we have to use an intersectional approach to address issues of sex and intimacy in black and other marginal communities. The securing of sexual rights in vulnerable and marginalized black communities is a complicated task that is not only about sex but also involves a commitment to a broader social justice agenda that will promote the full humanity of black people in this country. While sexual rights have to be at the center of such struggles, we must have an intersectional approach that makes evident the ways sexual rights are connected to other human rights such as economic advancement and racial justice in this country.

For example, the retreat from comprehensive sex education in the public schools may be one of the most significant attacks on challenging HIV and AIDS in black communities as well protecting the sexual rights people of color. Public schools are one of the few places—other than prisons—where we have a chance to intervene in the lives of significant numbers of black and Latino children, challenging and changing how they think about sex; how they think about themselves; and how they think about HIV and AIDS. But, increasingly, across the United States state and city governments have either refrained from requiring comprehensive sex education in public schools or they have required that abstinence become a central part, if not the dominant component, of the sex education curriculum. This, of course, means that young people in public schools are receiving incomplete, inaccurate, and often unrealistic information about sex, when, in fact, they need programs and resources that will empower them to make healthy sexual decisions.

The teaching of comprehensive sex education to young black people must be a critical issue for activists. I would, however, caution against becoming so focused on the provision of comprehensive sex education that we ignore the other failings found in far too many public schools that educate young black and Latino children. These children's sexual rights are secured not only through the provision of comprehensive sex education but also through a quality education that will lessen their economic dependency among other things. When thinking about the sexual rights of marginalized people, our analysis has to be broad and intersectional.

Second, while nearly everyone doing AIDS work in the United States understands, or at least can articulate, that it is misguided to talk about AIDS in disadvantaged communities and communities of color without also talking about prisons, I am not sure our work reflects this insight. The statistics scream out at us, highlighting that the expansion of the prison industrial complex in this country has come largely at the expense of black and Latino communities and black and Latino young people. A recent study by the PEW Center on the States found that there are 2.3 million people in incarcerated in the United States. The study also noted that a

> close examination of the most recent U.S. Department of Justice data (2006) found that while one in 30 men between the ages of 20 and 34 is behind bars, the figure is one in nine for black males in that age group. Men are still roughly 13 times more likely to be incarcerated, but the female population is expanding at a far brisker pace. For black women in their mid- to late-30s, the incarceration rate also has hit the one-in-100 mark.[35]

Increasingly, the data make clear the connection between incarceration and the AIDS epidemic in the United States. It was reported by Brent Staples in the New York Times that "in any given year, 35 percent of the people with tuberculosis, nearly a third of those with hepatitis C and 17 percent of the people with AIDS pass through jails and prisons."[36] Yet in spite of these staggering numbers, most authorities that run correctional facilities ban the use of condoms. Staples adds that more than 95 percent of the nation's prisons do not allow or make available condoms to prisoners.[37] Now if varying reports that estimate that over half of all those in prison are having sex are factored into these figures, then one can begin to see the risk to which government officials are willing to expose men and women (disproportionately people of color) in prison.

It is, therefore, very clear from such figures that those struggling to end AIDS in black communities must broaden their lens of analysis and engage in far reaching social justice politics. If for no other reason than sheer numbers, anyone concerned about AIDS in communities of color in particular, has to be concerned about the expansion of the prison industrial complex. AIDS activists have to advocate not only for the distribution of condoms in prison, but also they need to have an analysis of prisons. What is the work that we need to pursue around prisons, incarceration, and sexual rights? The end goal is to make sure that those incarcerated have access to condoms and sex education and that they can engage in recognized sexual relations and receive adequate healthcare. Or are those demands only one part of a broader social justice movement that sees its goal as abolishing prisons and stopping the mass incarceration of black and Latino youth?

Let me be clear, absent an understandable and cohesive analysis, there are many things those working on sexual rights amid moral panic can do. In particular, those who are researchers can continue to produce the evidence-based research needed by policy makers, educators, activists, and the media. Scholars, however, must also be prepared and willing to repackage that same information into a form that is accessible while rigorous. Fundamentally, we have to find ways to tell evidence-based stories that accurately represent the lives of those under attack while also touching the hearts of those unsure of what to do and where to stand on issues. Researchers must also be willing to surrender our research—at least a bit—to respond to the direct needs of nongovernmental organizations and others on the frontline of struggle. This means connecting to movements that might be able to hold us accountable.

Those working in NGOs have to remember that the pursuit of sexual rights in black communities is not only about winning policy interventions but also about being a part of a larger movement intent on societal transformation. If activists do not pay attention to some of the larger trends and structural contexts in which crisis and panic take hold, then we may win certain battles, even one day finding a cure for AIDS, without truly liberating affected communities, and in particular communities of color, from their secondary status in society. If we leave in place such factors as poverty, racism, mass incarceration, and political disempowerment, those factors will prove to be fertile ground for the next health, social, and moral epidemic.

Finally, I speak from experience in suggesting that we also have to deal with our own moral ambivalence around sex and its intersection with race, gender, class, and nationalities that create different and various sexual subjects. I believe that all of us working on sex and sexual rights in the United States would benefit from greater racial literacy, allowing us to tell a nuanced story of sexual rights and moral panics in communities of color. For example, in previous work, I have attempted to explain the lack of mobilization around AIDS in black communities by focusing almost exclusively on black leaders and their concern with status and mobility, while avoiding the uncomfortable truth that personal decisions must figure into our analysis of the spread of AIDS and HIV in black communities as well as our response to this crisis. Here is where Bill Cosby's partial truths must be addressed if we are to move forward realistically, effectively, and ethically.

When Bill Cosby talks about a black woman with eight children from eight different men and when the *New York Times* conjures up the image of black men on the down low possibly infecting black women or when the Bush Administration spews statistics about black teens having more sexual partners than teens from other racial and ethnic groups and having the highest rates of sexually transmitted diseases, HIV, and AIDS, I find myself struggling with my own panic and respectability impulse not only because I know the lived consequences of such statistics, images, and experiences for black people in this society, but also because of issues of shame—shame of what other groups think of *my* people.

All of these factors suggest to me that those of us working on sex and sexual rights might benefit from being able to differentiate between the irrational moral panic of outsiders and the internal and indigenous panic of insiders conditioned through a history of oppression. However, even after making those distinctions, we must push past our hesitation and find our moral voice, guided by an intersectional approach to sexual rights, one that recognizes that sexual rights in communities of color will never be fully secured without a mass movement that includes an analysis of racism, sexism, class, homophobia, and heterosexism, systems that limit the sexual decisions we can make and, more importantly, the lives we can lead.

NOTES

1. Bill Cosby and Alvin F. Poussaint, *Come on, People: On the Path from Victims to Victors* (Nashville: Thomas Nelson, 2007).

2. http://www.blackcommentator.com/93/93_cover_cosby.html.

3. Michael Eric Dyson, *Is Bill Cosby Right? Or Has the Black Middle Class Lost Its Mind?* (New York: Basic Books, 2005).

4. Autumn Jackson, the woman who accused Cosby of being her father and requesting $40 million for her silence about his paternity, was convicted of extortion with two others in 1997.

5. Barack Obama's Father's Day Speech, http://my.barackobama.com/page/community/post/stateupdates/gG5nFK
June 15, 2008.

6. Julie Bosman, "Obama Sharply Assails Absent Black Fathers," June 16, 2008, http://www.nytimes.com.

7. Stanley Cohen, *Folk Devils and Moral Panics: The Creation of the Mods and Rockers, Third Edition* (New York: Routledge, 2002).

8. Oscar Lewis, "The Culture of Poverty," in *On Understanding Poverty: Perspectives from the Social Sciences.* D. P. Moynihan, ed. (New York: Basic Books, 1968); Charles Murray, *Losing Ground: American Social Policy, 1950–1980* (New York: Basic Books, 1984).

9. David Bell and Jon Binnie, *The Sexual Citizen: Queer Politics and Beyond* (Malden, MA: Polity, 2000).

10. See, for example, Cornel West's comments on NPR at http://www.npr.org; Hamil R. Harris, "Some Blacks Find Nuggets of Truth in Cosby's Speech Others Say D.C. Remarks about Poor Blacks Went Too Far," http://www.washingtonpost.com; and a Fox News interview with the Reverend Jesse Jackson at http://www.foxnews.com/printer_friendly_story/0,3566,124818,00.html.

11. Henry Louis Gates, "Breaking the Silence," *New York Times*, August 1, 2004, Section 4, p. 11.

12. Martin Gilens, *Why Americans Hate Welfare: Race, Media, and the Politics of Antipoverty Policy* (Chicago: University of Chicago Press, 2000).

13. Dyson, *Is Bill Cosby Right?* xiv.

14. J. L. King. *On the Down Low: A Journey into the Lives of 'Straight' Black Men Who Sleep with Men* (New York: Harlem Moon, 2005).

15. http://www2.oprah.com/tows/slide/200610/20061026/slide_20061026_350_109.jhtml.

16. See a brief discussion of the down-low phenomenon and what we do not know about the transmission bridge between women and men who have sex with other men on the Centers for Disease Control and Prevention website at http://www.cdc.gov/hiv/topics/aa/resources/qa/downlow.htm.

17. Evelyn Brooks Higginbotham, *Righteous Discontent: The Women's*

Movement in the Black Baptist Church, 1880–1920 (Cambridge: Harvard University Press, 1993).

18. Higginbotham, *Righteous Discontent*, 188.

19. Higginbotham, *Righteous Discontent*, 193.

20. W. E. B. Du Bois, *The Philadelphia Negro: A Social Study,* 2nd ed. (Philadelphia: University of Pennsylvania Press, 1996); William Julius Wilson, *The Truly Disadvantaged: The Inner City, the Underclass, and Public Policy* (Chicago: University of Chicago Press, 1987).

21. Cathy J. Cohen, *African-American Cosby Study*. National survey of 500 black Americans age thirty and over administered by Knowledge Networks during April 2007. Respondents are part of the Knowledge Networks online research panel. The panel is representative of the entire U.S. population. The completion rate was 61.4 percent. Unlike other Internet research that covers only individuals with Internet access who volunteer for research, Knowledge Networks surveys are based on a sampling frame that includes both listed and unlisted numbers and is not limited to current Web users or computer owners. Panel members are randomly recruited by telephone and households are provided with access to the Internet and hardware if needed. Knowledge Networks selects households using random digit dialing (RDD).

22. Mary Pattillo, *Black on the Block: The Politics of Race and Class in the City* (Chicago: University of Chicago Press, 2007).

23. Cathy J. Cohen, *The Boundaries of Blackness: AIDS and the Breakdown of Black Politics* (Chicago: University of Chicago Press, 1999).

24. Cohen, *The Boundaries of Blackness*, 75.

25. Cohen, *African-American Cosby Survey*.

26. Cohen, *African-American Cosby Survey*. It is important to note that an additional 30 percent of older African Americans believe that "while black youth face some discrimination, most of their problems arise because of *their own bad decisions and behaviors.*" Only 18 percent of older blacks attribute the difficulties black youth face to primarily "things like discrimination and a lack of jobs."

27. Cohen, *Folk Devils and Moral Panics*.

28. Philip Jenkins, *Moral Panic: The Changing Concepts of the Child Molester in Modern America* (New Haven: Yale University Press, 1998).

29. Centers for Disease Control and Prevention [CDC], Fact Sheet: HIV/AIDS among African Americans, June 2007, http://www.cdc.gov/hiv/topics/aa/resources/factsheets/aa.htm.

30. CDC, HIV/AIDS among African Americans.

31. CDC, HIV/AIDS among African Americans.

32. Centers for Disease Control and Prevention, "HIV/AIDS Surveillance in Adolescents and Young Adults (through 2006)," May 21, 2008, http://www.cdc.gov/hiv/topics/surveillance/resources/slides/adolescents/index.htm.

33. CDC, "HIV/AIDS Surveillance."

34. David Tuller, "H.I.V. Diagnosis Rates Continue to Rise among Young Men, African-Americans," June 27, 2008, http://www.nytimes.com.

35. PEW Center on the States. "PEW Report Finds That More Than One in 100 Adults Are behind Bars," February 28, 2008, http://www.pewcenteronthestates.org/news_room_detail.aspx?id=35912.

36. Brent Staples, "Fighting the AIDS Epidemic by Issuing Condoms in the Prisons," September 7, 2004, http://www.nytimes.com.

37. Staples, "Fighting the AIDS Epidemic."

4

The "Gay Plague" Revisited

AIDS and Its Enduring Moral Panic

Gary W. Dowsett

There is and has always been a kind of moral panic surrounding HIV/
AIDS as a social phenomenon, and that moral panic mostly concerns
sexuality generally and homosexuality in particular. HIV/AIDS speaks directly to our confusion about sex, and it especially brings into focus our
decided ambivalence about homosexuality. While male-to-male sexual
transmission of HIV is not the only means of infection, all forms of transmission carry with them some suspicion of deviancy, a deviancy shaped
originally by the first "fallen man" in the epidemic—the homosexual, that
is, the "original" sexual deviant in the modern history of sexuality. The
discovery of what eventually became AIDS among gay men in the United
States placed gay men at the center of the epidemic there, and the world
learned first about what became AIDS through the lens of American culture, bringing the United States' particular take on homosexuality with it
(more later on this topic).

The suspicion of the homosexual even lurks behind the notion of heterosexual HIV transmission—the majority of cases worldwide. For example, as noted by the late anthropologist Carol Jenkins in her analysis
of group rape in Papua New Guinea, HIV transmission occurring to the
women concerned might be heterosexual, but men infected through the
mixing of semen during such events can hardly be regarded as heterosexually infected by other men, nor would homosexual transmission make
sense of such circumstances.[1] Yet, these men are clearly having sex together. In this argument, Jenkins rightly questions the application of that
Western sexuality binary—homosexual/heterosexual—to other cultures.
She is not the only researcher to argue this, as information about sexual

cultures in many countries became increasingly exposed because of HIV/ AIDS and was reported to the many international and regional AIDS conferences held since the pandemic began. If nothing else, this continual flow of research demonstrates remarkable variability in human sexual expression. Yet this application of the heterosexual/homosexual binary conceptualization of human sexuality to HIV transmission has been difficult to undo, despite its patent inadequacies. Why is this? Could it be that the necessity for maintaining the binary is related to protecting heterosexuality from an inherent instability endlessly reflected in an enduring ambivalence toward homosexuality?

Time: 2006; Place: Toronto; Issue: HIV/AIDS;
Situation: S.N.A.F.U.

The global pandemic of HIV infection and the devastating consequences of its usually deadly sequelae, AIDS, have occupied a central place on the world stage for twenty-six years. It is one of the most terrible global catastrophes human beings currently face. Every two years, the world's warriors against HIV/AIDS, including those people living with the infection (hereafter, PLWHA) meet to assess progress, learn the latest in prevention ideas, policy innovation, and treatment progress, and share their experience. The latest death toll is announced (it stands at the time of this writing at around 2 million) and the number of PLWHA is revised (now at around 33 million, with about 2.5 million new infections every year).[2]

In 2006, the biennial conference was held in Toronto, Canada, the third conference held in that country. The United States, where the disease was first diagnosed, with a huge epidemic of its own and one of the powerhouses of scientific research and international funding to fight the pandemic, does not host the conference because of immigration policies prohibiting PLWHA from visiting that country (although, at the time of writing, a moderation of this policy was mooted by President George W. Bush). Some conferences produce good news: in 1996 in Vancouver, a breakthrough in new antiretroviral drugs offered the first indication that eventually AIDS might shift from terminal illness to chronic manageable condition. This has happened in the developed world, but access to these drugs has yet to reach most of the world's PLWHA twelve years later. Other conferences report disappointing news: we still have no certain news about potential vaccines, and deaths and new infections are rising.

Still other conferences leave us with a "steady as she goes" message. Toronto in 2006 was of this last variety, except if one read between lines and listened to quietly emerging news about rapidly increasing HIV infections among men who have sex with men in many developing countries and increases in infection rates in gay communities in the developed world, once regarded as the great success stories in controlling the pandemic.

In a special preconference satellite meeting, epidemiological surveillance data were presented noting these worrying figures, with the conclusion being that the fastest growing sector of the pandemic was, in fact, currently occurring among men who have sex with men. Yet, throughout the conference, expert after expert and activist after activist reported a real failure of effort on the part of government, research, health promotion, and funders in working with this population newly at enhanced risk. Neglect and marginalization were the terms used to describe the overall approach to the needs of that sector. These charges of neglect were not just coming from gay activists; they were noted by Dr. Peter Piot, executive director of the Joint United Nations Programme on AIDS, during the preconference summit and again in his opening plenary address to the conference as a whole. They were also noted by Dr. Chris Beyer of Johns Hopkins University in the first conference plenary session when he presented the usual update on the global epidemiology. Additional sessions organized by the American Foundation for AIDS Research (amfAR), and one titled "Emerging and Re-emerging Epidemics" all attested to fast-growing epidemics among gay men and other men who have sex with men, and all mentioned neglect and failures to act.

Why? The major explanation offered by many senior commentators and trusted experts was "homophobia," in this case meaning structural or societal blockages or obstructions based on prejudice against homosexuality to creating, supporting, and enacting appropriate measures to deal with these fast-growing epidemics. The adequacy of the term "homophobia" will be addressed shortly, but for now let us note that such widespread use of this term gestures toward a shared understanding of some social dynamic that ignores the scientific evidence about how the pandemic is moving and that registers antihomosexual standpoints that preshape any subsequent responses to the exigencies of these epidemics. In essence, there is an underlying moral economy exposed by this assertion of homophobia that confirms for gay men and other homosexually active men from around the world that the global response to HIV/AIDS was, and is still, not a "level playing field" on which all in need equally play.

To comprehend how this global health disaster becomes an artifact of a moral economy and thereby subject to inequitable action, we need to revisit the fundamental nature of things gay in the phenomenon that is HIV/AIDS. For moral economies have purposes, origins, and moments when they manifest, revealing agendas beyond the immediate. One major manifestation of such moral economies is the moral panic.

Invoking Homophobia

The invocation of homophobia as one way to understand the problems in obtaining well-thought-through and planned responses to the HIV pandemic is an interesting one. The term was coined over forty years ago[3] but is now regarded as problematic as Greg Herek has often noted.[4] Once an attribute of individuals with different kinds of fears of homosexuality and self-doubt generated by homosexuality, "homophobia" is now also used to describe (messily) a societal state of mind as well as a description of antigay sentiment, forces, and tactics (henceforth I will call all these "activity" for the sake of brevity) at various levels, individual and collective. It is even sometimes ascribed, incorrectly in my view, to gay people in the term "internalized homophobia" (a catachresis, given that the original term described an "internalized" state in relation to the homophobe). Herek usefully suggests "sexual stigma" and "sexual prejudice" for the more social of the attributes listed above, and the old gay liberation term "internalized oppression" might usefully be resurrected to solve the rest. Whatever else, homophobia is not very useful in understanding the positioning of gay and homosexually active men in terms of HIV/AIDS or in conceptualizing the persecution more broadly of homosexually active men in non-Western countries, because it does not tell us how all this occurs.[5] That said, its ready adoption since the beginning of the pandemic as the common frame for acknowledging prejudice, oppression, neglect, and persecution strengthens claims made by many different actors that antigay activity has been in operation scientifically, politically, and culturally.[6] We can trace not only this dynamic from the beginning of the pandemic, but also see its origins prior to the pandemic as well.

Undoubtedly, antigay activity from the start has profoundly shaped how we understand the pandemic and how we operate within it. At times this has been direct: for example, the earliest mass media tagged the pandemic as the "Gay Plague" even though other populations were infected right from the beginning. At other times it has been less direct: for example, a plea was made at the final plenary session of the XII International AIDS Conference in Geneva in 1998 for gay men to vacate the international HIV/AIDS field because we had done our job. This was suggested even though the pandemic still affected gay and other homosexually active men worldwide at that time and has increasingly done so since, as noted earlier. I would argue that such antigay (more broadly, antihomosexual) activity features as a palimpsest in the HIV/AIDS world—always present but not immediately obvious, always overwritten but never erased, yet endlessly underpinning the pandemic. Certainly, as HIV treatments became more effective in the West and the focus moved to developing country access to treatments, gay men in the West appeared to fall off the agenda internationally as well as in many Western countries. This did not mean that that gay men were rendered nonexistent; rather, the focus on the developing world increasingly brought with it the specter of homosexuality as issues concerning developing country men who have sex with men emerged not just epidemiologically but also stridently in the voices of such men themselves. They increasingly pointed out the absence of their issues from the global HIV/AIDS agenda and invoked homophobia to explain it. This repetition of charges of neglecting of homosexual men, and the doubt such voices caused about the "heterosexuality" of the pandemic, particularly in sub-Saharan Africa and Asia, reminded the HIV/AIDS world that sex between men can never be hidden or normalized into silence. The early lessons of the pandemic remain salient.

One classic example from my own country, Australia, was the first epidemiological categorization of HIV transmission with various tags, one of which was "bisexual transmission." The lunacy of this category should be immediately obvious, as is the poor science behind it. The confusion of sexual orientation with a transmission vector exemplifies the early but ongoing difficulty science has with sexuality. So, too, for heterosexuality, since it is well known to be a less-than-stable state, particularly in its heteronormative form (adult, lifelong, monogamous, and reproductive marriage). Fewer and fewer people seem to live such heteronormativity nowadays. If they do not, then adulterous men are suspect, because, beyond other female partners, they can and do pursue transsexuals as well as female sex workers for sex (the transgender hijra in South Asia and the transsexual sex workers in any major Western city can testify to this).[7] Such men are seen to put their wives at risk and are often regarded, after gay men, as the chief perpetrators in HIV/AIDS.[8] Similarly, bisexually active men were regarded as suspicious from the start of the epidemic as a "bridging" population potentially carrying the virus from gay men to women. This framework underpinned the early fears in Latin America concerning HIV/AIDS about the culture of "machismo" allowing men to penetrate whomever they choose—men, women, or youth. It retains its salience in the frenzy in the United States about African American men on the "down low," a culture of ostensibly heterosexual and usually married men who have sex with men as well.[9] This assumption about bisexually active men is noteworthy not only in its ready adoption, but also because (then and now) we know little about bisexually active men in the West and even less in the rest of world. These formulations assume the virus will travel in one direction; also, no one asks the question, who infected the men in the first place?

In other HIV-affected populations there are suspicions too. While sometime blamed in their own right for "spreading" HIV, injecting drug users are known to employ risky sexual practices when using, and male-to-male sex is not as uncommon among this population as is often thought.[10] Sex work is similarly implicated among this population.[11] Also, we know young people experiment with sex, and sex between young men is not uniformly regarded as unfortunate, particularly when virginity among young women is prized and when institutions prove conducive for same-sex activity (for example, in schools and the military). Men in prison—well, enough said. Finally, from the death of actor Rock Hudson from AIDS and as more and more celebrities "come out" as gay, such as HIV-positive figures like Olympic diving champion Greg Louganis, the specter of the homosexual lurking behind every HIV infection (among men) remains potent. The case of Magic Johnson, an HIV-positive professional basketball player who had to continue to deny that his infection occurred during sex with men, was not an isolated instance. Thereby, HIV/AIDS can never rid itself of the "stain" of the homosexual. These last examples come from the United States, which does seem to have particular problems with HIV/AIDS and homosexuality. Of course, this is not just an issue for the United States, even if the significance of that country's experience of homosexuality and HIV/AIDS and its moral economy concerning sex provides a powerful discursive framing of the pandemic for the rest of us (as the saying in Australia goes, the United States sneezes and we all get a cold!).

Understanding the Moral Panic in HIV/AIDS

Homosexuality is the fundament of all suspicions about sex beyond the normative, and it even casts doubt on the normative itself. As the sexual other, homosexuality is ever-present. The idea that homosexuality might be central to moral panics, not just those concerning HIV/AIDS, is not new. Simon Watney, in his book *Policing Desire*,[12] documented the moral panic that had occurred in Britain during the 1980s, largely constructed through media reports of various events and responses to HIV/AIDS. For example, "'An eighteen year-old Coventry man, who thought he had caught AIDS after drinking from the same bottle as a gay men, punched and killed him'. . . received a three months sentence in what was described as a 'wholly exceptional case.'"[13] Watney offers many more such examples from Britain, and in his third chapter, he frames this discussion within the development of theoretical work in the United Kingdom on defining and understanding moral panics, drawing on Stanley Cohen's work in the 1970s. Also, Stuart Hall's subsequent refinements and Gayle Rubin and Dennis Altman's analyses of moral panics surrounding HIV/AIDS in both the United States and Australia are noted.[14]

Watney links the panic about HIV/AIDS directly and from the outset to the endless Western "scandal" of homosexuality throughout the twentieth century. That scandal is now well researched and understood, most notably through the works of British gay historian Jeffrey Weeks and French gay philosopher Michel Foucault.[15] In HIV/AIDS, it did not take too long to see the scandal rehearsed in the infamous, if transitional, moment of gay-related immune deficiency (GRID), defined in 1981 and abandoned subsequently, focusing on gay "lifestyle" factors, before its re-definition as AIDS and the discovery of HIV as an infectious agent. These are emblematic of a shockingly subjective "science" deploying its moral economy despite the initial incidence of disease in the United States among three other populations: Haitians, heroin users, and those with hemophilia. More directly, the mass media's instant embrace of the "Gay Plague," as mentioned earlier, and the currency that the term enjoyed for so long nails Watney's analysis firmly in place. Weeks also observed early on that HIV/AIDS was notable as a health issue in that its chief victims are blamed for the disease that strikes them.[16] This begs the question: why, when others were so soon infected by HIV (including female sex workers who usually get the blame for spreading sexually transmissible infections), have gay men largely remained at fault/the cause/to blame for HIV/AIDS? Watney's scandal is running at full speed.

This centrality of homosexuality to moral panics about HIV/AIDS was further dissected in the exceptional collection edited by Douglas Crimp in the journal *October* in 1987 (reprinted as the monograph *AIDS: Cultural Analysis/Cultural Activism* in 1988).[17] In that collection, Watney contributed a remarkable chapter, "The Spectacle of AIDS," in which he challenged the moral panics framework, so constituted, as unable to explain fully the British response to the epidemic in the 1980s:

> This is why it is so important to avoid any temptation to think of the ongoing AIDS crisis as a form of "moral panic," which carries the temptation that it is an entirely discrete phenomenon, distinct from other elements and dramas in the perpetual moral management of the home. On the contrary, homosexuality, understood by AIDS commentary as the "cause" of AIDS, is always available as a coercive and menacing category to entrench the institutions of family life and to prop up the profoundly unstable identities those institutions generate.[18]

Here, Watney situates HIV/AIDS within a longer and more substantive social space, much more at the center of the West's "perpetual" struggle with sexuality and social order than in a single moment in history unique to itself. Also, Paula Treichler's enduring characterization of AIDS as "an epidemic of signification" in that same volume remains as true now as it did then, and it speaks of things larger than the media reaction to the pandemic itself or to any temporally discrete social phenomena.[19] Further, Watney argues for a particularity in the moral panic surrounding HIV/AIDS, in that unlike other moral panics, which appear episodic, the moral panic associated with HIV/AIDS has never gone away but is endlessly refreshed, and thus it reveals a debt to the scandal of homosexuality.[20] The current, revitalized discussions on men who have sex with men in the international HIV/AIDS field bear witness to this insight.

An Australian Example

I would like to explore this idea a little further in order to track some continuity between Watney and others' analyses of the late 1980s and more recent events, for it seems to me that what happened in Toronto in

2006 reveals both the continuity of the moral panic about HIV/AIDS and its antihomosexual underpinnings. Over the last twenty-five years, each country has its own awful HIV/AIDS moments that stand out to those of us working in the field who were and are ever watchful and wary of our society's reactions. I want to take one such early moment from Australia to examine the relation between politics and moral panics.[21]

By 1984, the HIV epidemic had been slowly growing, somewhat unnoticed, in Australia since the first AIDS death in 1982. The gay communities in the capital cities had organized in concert an AIDS Action Council in each state and territory by 1983, and these were beginning to undertake HIV-prevention education activities, at first unassisted by government. The national or commonwealth government was slow to find its way (public health was mostly regarded as a state/territory matter rather than federal matter at that time), and there was a feeling we were in a "phony war" during these first few years. Debates occurred about protecting the blood supply by asking gay men not to donate blood, and the gay communities were quick to point out that not all gay men were ill and not all those who were ill were gay men. This early detection by gay activists of the ease with which gay men as a population (that is, homosexuality) could be positioned as the problem underlying HIV/AIDS was prescient and potent in shaping the politics of HIV/AIDS from then on.

The first Australian epidemiological research projects were established around this time, soon followed by the earliest social research projects (with which I was involved), and these were notable for a remarkable cooperation between gay communities, particularly in Sydney and Melbourne, and researchers. Indeed, many of the researchers like myself were also gay, as were the earliest health practitioners, counselors, and social workers looking after PLWHA. At that time, before the development of the HIV-antibody test, syndromic diagnosis was the key to assessing who was infected. Using information about the signs of possible infection (night sweats, skin lesions, etc.), gay men had already begun to conduct community debates, provide information about HIV/AIDS, and change their behavior—from as early as 1981 as we know now.[22] This occurred before the HIV-antibody test was deployed nationwide in 1985, first to protect the blood supply and then to begin the heart-breaking personal and community-wide confirmation of just how big our epidemic was to be in Australia. By then, the die was cast, setting homosexuality at the center of the debate about just what HIV/AIDS is and was to be.

Soon, another event intervened to shape the politics of HIV/AIDS before both the extent and nature of the Australian epidemics and the dynamics of gay men's responsible behavior change would be revealed. Toward the end of 1984, the commonwealth government called an early general election. This progressive (social democratic, or center-Left) Labor Party government had been elected in 1983, and it was pursuing *inter alia* an ambitious and wide-ranging reform of the national health system. The government was being opposed by conservative political forces that also controlled many of the state governments at that time. Then, a timely and classically choreographed moral panic arose about AIDS in the very conservative state of Queensland following the deaths of three babies through blood transfusions from a blood bank donation (then, as now, a fully voluntary donation service in Australia). These were traced to a donation from one infected gay man. The archconservative then-premier (head of government) of Queensland exploited these deaths to launch an all-out attack on the federal government and on gay men. The "yellow" media were rampant in their pursuit of gay men, whose sexual activities were still illegal in most states at that time. Calls for the quarantine of homosexuals arose from various sectors, and other such nonsensical demands were cynically manipulated during the electoral hype by both conservative political forces, including reactionary religious groups, and those running a longer-term antigay agenda in Australia. These moments helped weld HIV/AIDS and gay men together in the public mind, particularly reinforcing the idea of homosexuality as a threat to the health of "innocent" others (babies) and a danger to all (through the blood supply, not just through sex). This event reveals how moral panics are opportune and can become political gifts in the hands of the right manipulator, irrespective of personal values, because they draw on an underlying, extant moral economy.

Interestingly, the commonwealth government's response was to galvanize the national health system in a remarkable policy shift that saw Australia become the first nation to test and protect the national blood supply by using the newly developed HIV-antibody test. Also, funds began to flow to build a national research effort and to initiate widespread prevention by directly funding the gay communities to undertake it themselves. The establishment of these national policy processes and cooperative strategies with the states to implement them were all in place within a short time. This set of maneuvers eventually became the evolving national HIV/AIDS strategies that have guided the Australian response ever since.[23] The response by the then-commonwealth minister for health, Dr. Neal Blewitt, robbed wind from the sails of the conservatives, and the Labor Party federal government was returned to power. This example is offered to indicate that moral panics are not always inevitably and invariably successful in shutting down progressive forces but can reinforce both the political opportunism behind them. This example also confirms Watney's analysis of the foundational part played by always ready, always pensive, antihomosexual discourse in such moments. Indeed, ever since and every so often, Australian governments, state and federal, have been accused of being overly influenced by the "gay lobby" (if so, this would be a world-first for any government); at one point, Dr. Blewitt himself was accused of being gay because of his HIV/AIDS policies.

Like the Gay Plague before it, this event helped to establish the major forces shaping HIV/AIDS as discourse for at least the next ten years and to provide the template for HIV/AIDS activism that continues to this day not just in Australia but also, I would argue, globally. One of the major constituents of that discourse is a sophisticated community-based activism that learned from gay men its main tactics, forms of argument, basic theories (for example, of the state, of sexuality), means of mobilization, its forms of communication and alliance-building activity, and the strategic deployment of its own professionals as both advocates and specialist workers. This activism drew primarily on gay rights agitation from the 1970s on.[24] The pervasiveness and sophistication of gay rights activism involved a canny ability to recognize the anti(homo)sexual underpinnings that still pervade modern medicine despite the removal of homosexuality as a category of illness from the Diagnostic and Statistical Manual of Mental Disorders (DSM) III in 1973, and in public health in terms of inadequate sexual health services (sexually transmitted infection (STI) clinics, etc.), poor staff training in sexuality, and a pervasive heterosexism (they used to ask always if one was "active" or "passive"!).

Gay politics also recognized that the state was not a neutral arbiter of contesting social forces or an unbiased protector of pluralist values, but rather a powerful force regulating sexual and social life; and, unlike second-wave feminism in Australia, gay politics did not get into bed with the state until the HIV epidemic forced a collaboration.[25] Other features now so familiar as to appear HIV/AIDS-generated (rather than gay) were a preparedness to use direct action (for example, civil disobedience) as well as electoral pressure, a claim to solidarity and shared identity, and a collective or community mobilization with a capacity to draw on its own for expertise (gay lawyers, doctors, researchers, politicians, public servants, and so on). These became familiar strategies for all involved in HIV/AIDS, and one cannot imagine the notion of an "HIV identity" (the PLWHA) without its predecessor in "gay man." Similarly, the AIDS Coalition to Unleash Power (ACT-UP) is only conceivable in the context of post-Stonewall gay activism. The conception of HIV/AIDS as more than a health issue is dependent partly on previous theoretical work on sexuality as a social issue, not just a personal proclivity, one that is constituted in conflict and struggle (the work of Jeffrey Weeks and, to a lesser extent, Michel Foucault, was already known to gay activists and scholars in Australia by the early 1980s). Other social movements from the 1960s on had undoubtedly helped form gay men's politics from the 1970s on, namely, the women's, civil rights, and antiwar movements. However, it was gay men who first brought those politics to HIV/AIDS, and this reveals again why HIV/AIDS can never escape the specter of homosexuality.

Various similar events occurred abroad during the 1980s, particularly during the Reagan and George H. W. Bush presidencies in the United States. Even the nomenclature eventually settled on globally by agencies such as the World Health Organization (WHO) and other international players—the now ubiquitous term "MSM" or "Men who have Sex with Men"—was not without its antigay elements. The one and only meeting WHO's Global Programme on AIDS (hereafter WHO/GPA) ever held on gay men and HIV/AIDS in 1989 (for which I was a delegate) was confronted with an attempt to frame the emerging term as "MWM" ("Men who have sex With Men"). This maneuver omitted the obviously uncomfortable "sex" between men from the configuration, regardless of its central role in HIV transmission, and might thereby have applied to "Men who play golf With Men"![26]

It is in this way that the presence of gay men (or homosexuality, more accurately) within HIV/AIDS is sometimes felt in its absence. At many meetings in Geneva at WHO/GPA during the late 1980s and early 1990s (again, I was often a delegate), attempts were made to put male-to-male HIV transmission—and, therefore, prevention—issues on the agenda for developing countries, especially Africa. These were met with a complete denial of homosexuality existing, except as some distasteful postcolonial remnant, and a confident declaration was usually offered that various countries' epidemics were "heterosexual." This is a quite problematic framing of those epidemics, as Cindy Patton noted eighteen years ago in her book *Inventing AIDS*.[27] Any sexuality theorist knows that the very existence of the term "heterosexual" is a Western colonial impost as well, and that term was dependant on the earlier coining of the term "homosexual" and, as such, always reflects its opposite: heterosexuality is definitionally always *not* homosexuality. The term is so very Western in its cultural and scientific origins as to be often inapplicable to other sexual cultures, particularly many in Africa and Asia. Therefore, to call these epidemics heterosexual is patently wrong in terms of epidemiology's description of transmission patterns, and it misunderstands the culturally specific nature of sexual risk-taking and vulnerability to HIV infection in many countries (as Jenkins's example mentioned earlier notes).

Today, of course, we see clear and incontrovertible evidence of MSM epidemics in Africa—denial is no longer possible; in Asia the complex cultural intersections between sex between men and sex between men and women are increasingly recognized, calling for ever-newer conceptions of how the virus will move. Yet, even now, there is significant failure to discern the profound differences between cultures of male-to-male sexual activity from region to region and even within countries.[28] MSM is a sloppy category. It obscures gay men and their specific sexual cultures; it simplistically aggregates quite different manifestations of male same-sex practice; it denudes same-sex activity of meaning by reducing it to behavior; it occasionally even gestures toward a common identity and shared values that are, in practice or discourse, not shared by these same populations of men who enjoy sex with men. Indeed, the very category MSM performs a kind of mopping-up function in the framing of the pandemic within the obsolete Western binary opposition heterosexual/homosexual. It suggests a failure to come to terms with variable human sexual expression rather than its recognition. It leaves in place for the West the false sense of security lying in the virgule between homosexuality and heterosexuality, between gay and straight men in particular—yet every gay man knows that the difference between a gay man and a straight one is a six-pack of beer! In this metonymic usage, MSM itself becomes another refutation of homosexuality.

As the existence of homosexuality elsewhere was being refuted in HIV/AIDS debates during the late 1980s and early 1990s, it became clear in Australia, and in the United Kingdom, that the potential (unrealized now) for more generalized epidemics moving from among gay men to others (read "ordinary" people) was growing, even if this was not strongly supported by "hard" evidence. Yet, the transfer of prevention funding toward general population health education was huge (noted again by Watney in the United Kingdom and in Australia by Richard Feachem).²⁹ This led to an outcry about the "de-gaying" of HIV/AIDS in both countries. Behind this claim lay a clear recognition by gay activists of the ease with which government could and would turn their attention from gay men's prevention needs to others whose claims were politically easier to meet and supported by antigay forces. This was a period during which the "innocent victims" of AIDS were defined by their difference from gay men. Others were "guilty" too, but sex workers could easily be redefined as victims of patriarchy when it suited (although such a tactic has never fully redeemed this population). Even injecting drug users can be redefined as "addicts" (beyond self-control) and therefore warranting help. Gay men, however, had (and have) only themselves to blame for "choosing" their "lifestyle" or engaging in their sinful/unnatural/perverted/sick acts. Compensation by governments to those infected through tainted blood transfusions and blood products thereby further layered guilt on gay men, whose equally accidental crossing of the path of this virus actually first alerted the world to the danger, and whose invention of safe sex as then the only prevention possibility has, indeed, saved many lives no matter what their sexual orientation or vulnerability.³⁰ There has never been a "thank you" for that.

Gay men can read this set of events and many other moments like these until the mid-1990s very well. There are versions in many countries, and it has taken the HIV/AIDS world twenty years to start to use the word they are relatively comfortable with—homophobia—for what gay men have known all along and often complained about to no avail. The source of moral panics about HIV/AIDS right from the start has always been evident in an undercurrent of antigay sentiment. That nomination of those "innocent" victims facilitated a significant antigay agenda in many countries. One wonders whether Zimbabwe's President Mugabe would have been so able to use homosexuality as a political wedge to stay in power had HIV/AIDS not been in play. Yet, Mugabe is not unique, and we neglect others, particularly those in the Asia-Pacific region, whose tardiness and neglect in responding to their MSM epidemics have led to the dramatic increases in HIV prevalence reported at Toronto 2006.

Last, I want to emphasize, along with Watney and others, the key position of the homosexual in any reconceptualization of moral panics everywhere by arguing that the template for moral panics concerning sexuality relies, first, on the concept of sexuality itself, which, following Foucault and Weeks, begins seriously with the segregation and nominalization of the homosexual. Without that identification and segregation, all the other sexual others (the usual targets of sexuality moral panics) cannot be comprehended, nor can sexual normativity be invented and subsequently invested in individually and socially. Unlike the fallen woman who is the victim of sexuality, the homosexual is seen through definition to "escape" power (a nonsense, I know, in Foucault's framework, but bear with me) and engage desire without boundary. Once the homosexual escapes, the door is open for others to do so as well and to do so as a new type of person in pursuance of identity. We see this both in the identification of those other categories of sexual deviancy most focused on in moral panics after homosexuals ("fallen" sex workers [read "women" here, male sex workers are forgotten], errant teenagers, the racially imagined lustful, and, recently, the lurking pedophile) and in the emergence of these categories as pathologized personhood. These can only come after the invention of the homosexual, and the framework relies on the homosexual as originary. There were earlier sexual configurations such as the sodomite and the onanist. There were previous stigmatized identities based in part on presumed sexual attributes (the Bulgars or "Bougre" (French) gave us the word "bugger"). However, the history of sexuality in the West cannot be understood without the homosexual as the cornerstone of its epistemology. The invention of the homosexual, following Foucault, marks the transubstantiation of sexuality into *episteme*. As a consequence, wherever sexuality is concerned, the template for deviation implicitly or explicitly is the homosexual. It is not just that HIV/AIDS struck gay men in the United States first that placed homosexuality at the center of the pandemic, the sexual bases of the pandemic could only draw on prevailing discourses on sexuality, and those predictably were antihomosexual at their core. This is even clearer in the response of the United States to the epidemic.

What of the United States?

If the United States is so influential in framing the discourse on HIV/AIDS, how do its moral panics about the pandemic occur? Many histories of the gay liberation period in the West from 1969 to circa 1981/1982 (the beginning of HIV/AIDS) often assume that there were parallel social movements occurring in the United States, the United Kingdom, Canada, Australia and New Zealand, the Netherlands and Scandinavia, and Germany (then West Germany). Perhaps that single history needs reexamining to see whether such uniformity was the case. Altman captured the pervasive feel of that time in his book, *The Americanization of the Homosexual*.[31] He pinpointed the way it seemed that gay life, as it was being constituted in the Castro in San Francisco and Greenwich Village in New York (to name just two gay social—and sexual—worlds), provided a template for all gay men (at least in the West, for the developing world was not on the map on these grounds at that time). Certainly, it looks like that initially when one visits gay spaces in Sydney, Amsterdam, and New York still.

Yet, differences soon became apparent in the English-speaking world as well as in northwestern Europe. For Australia, a more familiar British style of homosexuality had always been dominant (private school buggery, vicar and choirboy jokes, the camp of the music hall and about royalty, for example, in Queen Mother and Noël Coward jokes). It was also present in the often brutal and always brittle antihomosexual ambience that suffuses sport, the military, and working-class masculinity in Australia, all of which, as I have argued elsewhere,[32] only lightly masks a density of homoerotic practices that pervaded the colonies throughout the nineteenth century[33] and preexisted them in presettlement indigenous life, and which has blossomed throughout the twentieth century into the large, noisy, and very visible gay communities that so successfully negotiated the much-praised Australian response to HIV/AIDS.

There is something queer about Australia. Evidence of sodomy in the Australian colonies in the late nineteenth century was used as proof of social rot requiring criminalization of sex between men in the Labouchére amendment in Britain, which soon after caught out Oscar Wilde.[34] The Wolfenden Report in Britain in 1967 and its subsequent reforms decriminalizing sex between two men in private arguably provided more of a template for subsequent political and legislative change in Australia from the early 1970s on than did the struggle over the DSM III in the United States. So, although gay activism in the 1970s and 80s in Australia also looked to the new gay liberationist examples in the United States, Britain remained a major source of shared ideas and common strategies, for example, significant work done in trade unions by gay activists in both countries eventually brought the social democratic political parties of both countries to a position of supporting gay rights (albeit to varying degrees and with variable success).

Altman's book had an additional, sometimes forgotten subheading: *The Homosexualization of America*. This, perhaps, not only reflects the optimism of the period, but also the extent of the shock the United States seems to have experienced at such a mammoth revelation of same-sex desire on the part of its men (and women). By the early 1970s, the scale of the visible creations of the Castro and the Village rivaled the revelations of homosexual activity in the Kinsey (and other) reports of just over twenty years earlier, and from which scandal, I suspect, "middle America" in particular has never quite recovered.[35] Almost immediately, new persecution of homosexuals occurred during the McCarthy era in the 1950s in the name of preserving the edifice of the "American Dream," always invoked as such by the Right and by the powerful U.S. "establishment," and which is always *not* gay (Walt Whitman notwithstanding!). This anti-homosexual activity, only briefly quieted in the "permissive" 1960s, found new momentum and its old groove in HIV/AIDS, also documented by Altman early in *AIDS in the Mind of America*.[36]

There is no equivalent in Australia of the "American Dream" (and maybe we are poorer for it), but this absence does leave antihomosexual forces in Australia scratching harder for antithetical arguments (usually found in biblical references or in ambiguous claims as to what constitutes the "natural"), as gay people's claims to full citizenship were slowly being achieved throughout the late twentieth century. That is not to say that homosexuals are fully accepted in Australia; tolerance has its costs.[37] Foucault's general notion of the social place of the homosexual is pertinent here:

> Homosexuality is a historic occasion to re-open affective and relational vir-
> tualities, not so much through the intrinsic qualities of the homosexual,
> but because of the "slantwise" position of the latter, as it were, the diagonal
> lines he [sic] can lay out in the social fabric allow these virtualities to come
> to light.[38]

This slantwise position well describes the contemporary place of gay men (maybe not lesbian women) in Australian society. Certainly, not all Australians like homosexuals, but a kind of tolerance not unlike that in northwestern Europe has developed since the 1960s that demands some recognition of the different place gay life occupies in the Antipodes compared with our North American cousins.

On this, Michael Bronski notes that in the United States:[39]

> The specter of homosexuality haunts the mainstream [US] imagination in
> a way that is persistent and unique. This specter is at once phantasmagoric
> and real. It is conjured from the actual lives of gay men and lesbians, from

fears of homosexuality, from real or imagined details of gay sexual activity, from historical prejudice, and from existing but archaic legal codes. More important, it arises from the imaginations of heterosexuals who find homosexuality—and everything it signifies—both frightening lurid and very titillating. . . . Homosexuality carries with it the possibility of escape from the constraints of heterosexuality.

Noting the Kinsey report's documentation of widespread homosexual experience among men (for example, 37 percent of men have some overt homosexual experience to the point of orgasm between adolescence and old age),[40] it may be that actual sexual experience and memories of its pleasures also lie behind the United States' fascination, nay, obsession, with homosexuality beyond just its imagined possibilities. Bronski utilizes the word "escape" also, and that begs the question: to escape from what? Gay liberationists would have answered: heterosexuality. Queer theorists might now more judiciously respond: heteronormativity. However, these formulations rely still on that binary opposition so beloved in sex talk—homosexuality/heterosexuality—and lose sight of all that has gone into rendering this binary problematic, irrelevant, or nonsensical.

It is the increasing lack of distance between homosexual and heterosexual, gay and straight, that registers considerable amounts of "escape" going on. Whether in the ever-increasing list of sexual identity signifiers—gay, lesbian, bisexual, bicurious, transsexual, transgender, intersex, queer, questioning—or, in formulations like Jonathan Dollimore's use of the "proximate" relation of homosexual desire to all forms of desire,[41] homosexuality and its pleasures seem evident on every page of American sexuality, a situation now well documented by queer theorists (e.g., Sedgwick).[42] This would render as a lost cause the "othering" of the homosexual (whether as deviant or as sexual minority) or at least suggest some interesting possibilities about the enormous amount of energy going into sustaining such othering by the United States' Right-wing and fundamentalist religious forces (discussed by other authors in this volume). This suggestion partly recuperates two original characteristics of Weinberg's delineation of homophobia—a secret fear of being homosexual and repressed envy—and strengthens it as an irrational fear psychologically situated deeply within some people.[43] These characteristics register compromises and pleasures forgone and ambiguous erotic possibilities in the very bodies they inhabit, exposing those virtualities then exemplified in those who have already "escaped," most obviously gay men.

Here, we might turn to gender to amplify the argument. In social theory, gender is one the major structural frameworks that orders daily life, its relations, practices, institutions, and discourses. The gender order elaborates and secures tremendous social inequalities in each society, and institutionalized heterosexuality (or heteronormativity), as the primary mechanism organizing relations between the sexes, must be regarded as fundamental to that social order.[44] For this reason, Watney once argued that gender is heterosexist.[45] Second-wave feminism alerted us to the part played in all societies by the gendered division of labor, both inside and outside domestic relations, with its inequitable allocation of social resources, rewards, and burdens. Escaping heteronormativity would seem to be a major preoccupation of second-wave feminism and of contemporary gender theory and politics. Therefore, it is not surprising that women, their rights in relation to work and career, parenting, and abortion (childbearing and rearing are major components of heteronormativity) and, in particular, lesbians (as the most wayward of women) form a central target of Right-wing strategies concerning gender and sexuality. As heteronormativity comes under pressure from within, or is even reckoned to need renovation, the increasing blurring of the boundary between heterosexual and homosexual provides further avenues for escape. The homosexual woman shines light on one major escape route for women. Gay men also demonstrate the possibility for different kinds of relations with women as well as with men.[46] The homosexual man exemplifies a tantalizing possibility of escape for those men who find heteronormativity stultifying (remember: patriarchy does not benefit all men equally and many men are bored by straight sex, too). Foucault captured this dangerous possibility well:[47]

> I think that what most bothers those who are not gay about gayness is the gay life-style, not sex acts themselves. It is the prospect that gays will create as yet unforeseen kinds of relationships that many people cannot tolerate.

The gender order is fragile indeed.

Homosexuality among men often provides a primary target in any moral panic about sexuality, as gay men are "fallen men," failing in their duty to the gender order and also undermining patriarchy by mining the rich vein of anal desire and pleasure quarantined by homosociality and sustained therein through homophobia (following Sedgwick).[48] One does not have to classify homophobia only as a psychological or emotional disorder, tempting though this is[49] or move beyond that to a more social formulation; it is becoming obvious that social relations, particularly heterosexual social relations, are unraveling to reveal the homoerotic substrate beneath them. This substrate is evident in the scene in the much-lauded film *Brokeback Mountain*, when Ennis (Anus?), played by Golden Globe winner and Australian actor, the late Heath Ledger, while making love to his wife Alma, turns her over to penetrate her from behind. Her face registers some disquiet or discomfort, maybe both; and it is not clear whether this penetration is achieved anally or vaginally. This is deliberately left uncertain, and heterosexuality is rendered as such at the same time. Such uncertainty is also evident in the growing interest in anal intercourse in heterosexual pornography. Anuses are, remarkably, non-gender-specific parts of the human anatomy and undoubted erogenous zones. Any man penetrating an anus cannot be unaware of that human singularity and his own potential for (capacity for? experience in?) similar pleasures. Indeed, a colleague in the United States now tells me that the newest growth genre [sic] in pornography is "pegging": the use by women (at least, for the moment, only women) of strap-on dildos to penetrate their male partners.[50] This practice is not new in gay men's pornography, but, again, "proximity" is glaringly obvious. As the *cordon sanitaire* surrounding heterosexual men's anuses loosens in anal pleasures, heteronormativity needs to fight harder for its moral economy as its foundations crumble.

In registering alarm about this, the religious Right in the United States is quite correct about the importance of homosexuality's slant-wise position; they do "read the tea leaves" well and, therefore, move to ensure that slant-wise position and all those seen as part of this social change are marginalized, kept from view, persecuted, and punished whenever possible. What is at stake in the challenge to the gender order and to the deployment of sexuality mounted by feminism and queer theory, by women's movement activism, and gay men's ever-growing sexual cultures is more than domestic order and sexual conformity. A mammoth structure of power, privilege, inequality, exploitation, and abuse is unraveling, for it is rife with crisis tendencies. Critical elements of that challenge must be tackled particularly when a new opportunity arises, and HIV/AIDS provided and continues to provide an unparalleled opportunity for attack on one of the most worrisome and vulnerable populations—gay men. It is not that others affected by HIV/AIDS are not marginalized, stigmatized, or persecuted. They are; but I am arguing they can only be so mistreated because of the ease with which the homosexual can be mistreated first.

It is not surprising that President Reagan never mentioned HIV/AIDS throughout most of his presidency in the 1980s. This was no oversight; it was screamingly deliberate.[51] This omission testifies to the centrality of homosexuality in the U.S. epidemics and the specific terror homosexuality produces in that country. It is not surprising either that former President Clinton's more realistic and compassionate response to HIV/AIDS had to be counterpoised to perpetuating inequality for homosexual people through his "don't ask, don't tell" policy in the U.S. military. Now, HIV infection among racial minorities in the United States is soaring, and many lay this fact directly at the door of homophobia and its link with racism (see Cathy Cohen, chapter 3).[52] Being African American and on the "down low" is the key example here. The African American man becomes yet again a threat to the "American Dream"; this time not by exercising his prodigious sexual talent to entice white women and endanger white ascendancy but by being homosexually active and hence escaping heteronormativity also. It is beginning to look like everyone wants to desert the "Titanic" of heteronormativity, leaving only white, heterosexual, privileged men and "their" women behind, desperately rearranging the deck chairs (by keeping marriage heterosexual, promoting abstinence education, rolling back abortion rights, etc.).

Can the same be said of Australia during the 1980s to 1990s? Those documenting the history of HIV/AIDS in Australia can plot the multiple instances where gay men and antigay activity drove the agenda. Both need to be recognized here. There were times and places—the epidemics worked differently in different parts of the country—when Australian gay men were able to change national and local policies and programs effectively and with considerable sophistication. One marker might give some idea of these achievements: all Australian states and territories had legalized (with some differences) sex between men by 1997, and many had included not just sexuality or sexual orientation but also HIV/AIDS as a category covered by antidiscrimination legislation. The extent of this social change is not unique to Australia (New Zealand, Canada, and the United Kingdom achieved similar changes, although the timing and sequence were different; while, it must be noted, the rest of Europe was often far ahead on some things), and this shows how the politics of sexuality and HIV/AIDS play out differently outside the United States.

Does this achievement of social change mean antigay activity does not exist in Australia? Of course not, as the occurrences of gay bashing,[53] and the opposition of the recent conservative and—unfortunately—the new

Labor federal governments to gay marriage attest. That said, the commonwealth, state and territory governments are not seriously at war with Australian gay people, and HIV/AIDS has been marked by a collaborative partnership approach, even if at times that partnership is a tense and ongoing contest. References to homosexuality on stage and screen, in carnival or celebration, on snowfield or in surf, cause far less kafuffle in Australia on a day-by-day basis than would appear the case in the United States. Funding for HIV/AIDS prevention and research, national health program support for HIV treatment, and social services for PLWHA were not in any more serious danger under the previous neo-Liberal regime than was any other aspect of human services and public sector program delivery, nor have these radically changed under the new government so far. HIV prevalence does not differentially affect any sector of the Australian population on racial or ethnic bases. Indeed, while the health outcomes for indigenous Australians are shockingly worse than for nonindigenous people, including sexually transmissible infections, this is not true for HIV/AIDS, and there is a National Indigenous Sexual Health Strategy operating alongside the national HIV/AIDS strategy. The same cannot be said of any national approach to the shockingly high levels of HIV infection among African and Latino Americans in the United States.

It is, of course, in this very struggle of the "sex wars" (now termed the "culture wars") in the United States that we see not only antigay activity but also the complex and resilient response of gay and lesbian people and of racial and ethnic minorities. I mention that because the history of sexuality can be mapped not only through the construction of the homosexual, but also through the resistance and resilience of homosexuals themselves. These responses are also part of an activist *habitus* that has a long history, one that provided a fundamental basis for HIV/AIDS activism, as noted earlier. In this way, as Watney noted, the history of sexuality provides an explanation that is central to understanding moral panics about HIV/AIDS. Irrespective of other forms of HIV transmission and other populations affected by HIV/AIDS, the specter of the homosexual lurks behind every population at risk through quiet presence or shrill absence, behind every minority disproportionately affected through their deviation from assumptions about normativity, through the so-called heterosexual epidemics looking increasingly queer as time moves on, and through the activist template provided by gay rights advocates right from the start that sustains a unique international HIV/AIDS politics.

Back in Toronto. . .

The frequent invocation of homophobia at the Toronto XVI International AIDS Conference in 2006 as a major tool in understanding the dynamics of the global response (namely, inaction concerning MSM) might also be regarded as further evidence that homosexuality lurks as fundament behind the moral panic of HIV/AIDS. Yet this does not work in the way one might expect. Recuperating homophobia from its psychological origins to describe a social disposition (that is, as a society-wide historical dynamic like racism) is a dubious maneuver. It suggests a shared consciousness operating at cultural level and even across cultures and countries. Given that homophobia means very little unless it manifests in practical consequences, for example, in acts of violence, vilification, or punishment, how are we to understand this operating at the level of the social: how is a collective psychological phobia produced and made manifest? The term explains nothing about its construction as a social dynamic, and then, even if we could explain that, how it might be countered. In other words, homophobia cannot provide any avenue for counteraction; it contains no strategy for its defeat. Therein lies the uselessness of the term despite its seeming salience in HIV/AIDS discourse, for it robs us of any strategy for response. This deployment of homophobia is in this way ironically homophobic, for it keeps everything in its place.

Do we need any further evidence than the speeches of Bill and Melinda Gates (their foundation is now one of, if not the, largest donors of funds globally to fight HIV/AIDS) at the opening ceremony at the Toronto conference, during which Ms. Gates spoke eloquently of the structural blockages to responding well to the pandemic and nominated *inter alia* homophobia; while in the same speech, when listing those populations that face the stigma and neglect such structural blockages produce, she failed to add gay men and other men who have sex with men—a very telling absence! An oversight or deliberate omission? We shall never know. The governor-general of Canada, Her Excellency, the Right Honourable Michaëlle Jean, included both terms in her passionate address, as did every other opening ceremony speaker. So, maybe it is an American thing after all. Melinda Gates, for all the good works of the Gates Foundation, is still locked into the moral economy of the United States, and it speaks though her. One can forgive someone new to the field, but to every gay man and to every MSM activist from the developing world in that vast opening ceremony hall however, it was HIV/AIDS business as usual!

NOTES

I would like to acknowledge the contribution of my colleagues Murray Couch and Michael Hurley from La Trobe University and the research assistance of Andrew Lavin. Gil Herdt offered wise and timely advice, both editorial and theoretical. My thanks go to them all. The original stimulus for this chapter arose from an invitation from Gil to be part of a panel discussion at "Sexual Rights and Moral Panics": the Fifth Biennial Conference of the International Association for the Study of Sexuality, Culture and Society, held in San Francisco in 2005. My thanks go also to Niels Tunis and the conference organizing committee for support to attend that conference.

1. Carol Jenkins, "The Homosexual Context of Heterosexual Practice in Papua New Guinea," in P. Aggleton, ed., *Bisexualities and AIDS* (London: Taylor and Francis, 1996).

2. UNAIDS, *AIDS Epidemic Update, December 2007* (Geneva: UNAIDS, 2007).

3. George Weinberg, *Society and the Healthy Homosexual* (New York: Doubleday Anchor, 1973).

4. Gregory M. Herek, "Beyond 'Homophobia': Thinking about Sexual Prejudice and Stigma in the Twenty-First Century," *Sexuality Research and Social Policy: A Journal of the NSRC* 1 (2004): 6–24.

5. Gary W. Dowsett, "HIV/AIDS and Homophobia: Subtle Hatreds, Severe Consequences and the Question of Origins," *Culture, Health and Sexuality* 5 (2003): 121–36.

6. Dennis Altman, *AIDS in the Mind of America* (New York: Anchor/Doubleday, 1986); Ralph Bolton, ed., *The AIDS Pandemic: A Global Emergency* (New York: Gordon and Breach, 1989); Cindy Patton, *Sex and Germs: The Politics of AIDS* (Boston: South End, 1985); Simon Watney, *Policing Desire: Pornography, AIDS and the Media* (London: Methuen, 1987).

7. Azizul Haque, Gary Dowsett, and Shale Ahmed, "Researching the Dimensions of MSM Activity in Dhaka, Bangladesh, To Assess the Risk of HIV/STD Transmission and Develop Prevention Programs," poster presentation to XVI International AIDS Conference, Barcelona, 7–12 July 2000.

8. Gary W. Dowsett, "Some Considerations on Sexuality and Gender in the Context of HIV/AIDS," *Reproductive Health Matters* 11 (2003): 1–9.

9. Benoit Denizet-Lewis, "Living (and Dying) on the DownLow," *New York Times Magazine*, 3 August 2003, section 6: 28–37.

10. Seth C. Kalichman, Timothy Heckman, and Jeffrey A. Kelly, "Sensation Seeking as an Association between Substance Use and HIV-Related Risky Sexual Behavior," *Archives of Sexual Behavior* 25 (1996): 141–54.

11. Peter A. Newman, Fen Rhodes, and Robert E. Weiss, "Correlates of Sex Trading among Drug-Using Men Who Have Sex with Men," *American Journal of Public Health* 94 (2004): 1998–2003.

12. Simon Watney, *Policing Desire.*

13. Simon Watney, *Policing Desire,* 9.

14. Noted in Simon Watney, *Practices of Freedom: Selected Writings on HIV/AIDS* (Durham: Duke University Press, 1994).

15. Michel Foucault, *The History of Sexuality—Volume I: An Introduction,* R. Hurley, trans. (Harmondsworth: Penguin, 1978); Jeffrey Weeks, *Sexuality and Its Discontents* (London: Routledge and Kegan Paul, 1985).

16. Jeffrey Weeks, *Sexuality* (Chichester: Ellis Horwood, 1986).

17. Douglas Crimp, ed., "AIDS: Cultural Analysis, Cultural Activism," *October* 43 (Winter 1987); reprinted as *AIDS: Cultural Analysis, Cultural Activism* (Cambridge: MIT Press, 1988).

18. Watney, "The Spectacle of AIDS," in Crimp, *AIDS,* 75.

19. Paula Treichler, "AIDS, Homophobia and Biomedical Discourse: An Epidemic of Signification," in Crimp, *AIDS.*

20. Watney, *Practices of Freedom.*

21. For a full account of this period, see John Ballard, "The Politics of AIDS," in H. Gardner, ed., *The Politics of Health: The Australian Experience* (Melbourne: Churchill Livingstone, 1989): 349–75.

22. Australian Gonococcal Surveillance Program, "Changing Patterns of Gonococcal Infections in Australia, 1981–1987," *Medical Journal of Australia* 149 (1988): 609–12.

23. Commonwealth of Australia, *National HIV/AIDS Strategy: A Policy Information Paper* (Canberra, 1989); Commonwealth of Australia, *National HIV/AIDS Strategy, 1993–94 to 1995–96* (Canberra, 1993); Commonwealth of Australia, *National HIV/AIDS Strategy: Partnerships in Practice, 1996–1997 to 1998–1999* (Canberra, 1996); Commonwealth of Australia, *National HIV/AIDS Strategy: Challenges and Changes, 1999–2000 to 2003–2004* (Canberra, 2000); Commonwealth of Australia, *National HIV/AIDS Strategy: Revitalising Australia's Response 2005–2008* (Canberra, 2005).

24. At that time in Australia, as elsewhere, there was a split between lesbian activism and gay men's activism, so I am really referring to gay men's activism at this point—HIV/AIDS was soon to change that.

25. Discussed in Gary W. Dowsett, "Pink Conspiracies: Australia's Gay Communities and National HIV/AIDS Policies, 1983–96," in Anna Yeatman, ed., *Activism and the Policy Process* (Sydney: Allen and Unwin, 1998); and developed further in Gary W. Dowsett, "Governing Queens: Gay Communities and the

State in Contemporary Australia," in M. Dean and B. Hindess, eds., *Governing Australia: Studies in Contemporary Rationalities of Government* (Melbourne: Cambridge University Press, 1998).

26. One never gets the sense that the United Nations is terribly antigay in its HIV/AIDS efforts, but there have been only a few official U.N. meetings specifically on gay men and HIV/AIDS ever since, despite growing epidemics the world over becoming obvious from the late 1980s on.

27. Cindy Patton, *Inventing AIDS* (New York: Routledge, 1990).

28. Gary W. Dowsett, Jeffrey Grierson, and Stephen McNally, *A Review of Knowledge about the Sexual Networks and Behaviours of Men Who Have Sex with Men in Asia* (Melbourne: La Trobe University, Australian Research Centre in Sex, Health and Society, 2003, monograph series #59).

29. Richard G. A. Feachem, *Valuing the Past...Investing in the Future: Evaluation of the National HIV/AIDS Strategy 1993–94 to 1995–96* (Canberra: Commonwealth of Australia, 1995).

30. Michael Callen, *How to Have Sex in an Epidemic* (New York: News from the Front Publications, 1983).

31. Dennis Altman, *The Homosexualization of America, the Americanization of the Homosexual* (New York: St Martin's Press, 1982).

32. Gary W. Dowsett, *Practicing Desire: Homosexual Sex in the Era of AIDS* (Stanford Calif: Stanford University Press, 1996).

33. Robert Hughes, *The Fatal Shore* (London: Collins Harville, 1987).

34. Walter J. Fogarty, "'Certain Habits': The Development of a Concept of the Male Homosexual in New South Wales Law, 1788–1900," in R. Aldrich and G. Wotherspoon, eds., *Gay Perspectives: Essays in Gay Culture* (Sydney: University of Sydney, Department of Economic History, 1992): 59–76.

35. Alfred C. Kinsey, Wardell B. Pomeroy, and Clyde E. Martin, *Sexual Behavior in the Human Male* (Philadelphia: W.B. Saunders, 1948); and Alfred C. Kinsey, Wardell B. Pomeroy, Clyde E. Martin, and Paul H. Gebhard, *Sexual Behavior in the Human Female* (Philadelphia: W.B. Saunders, 1953).

36. Dennis Altman, see note 6.

37. Gary W. Dowsett, "Johnnie comes marching . . . where: Australian Gay Men, Masculinity, HIV/AIDS, and Sex," *Culture, Health and Sexuality* 5 (2003): 237–248.

38. Michel Foucault, *Essential Work of Foucault, Vol. 1*, ed. P. Rabinow, trans. R. Hurley et al. (New York: New Press, 1998): 138, quoted in B. T. Heiner, "The Passions of Michel Foucault," *Differences* 14 (2003): 22–52.

39. Michael Bronski, *The Pleasure Principle: Sex, Backlash, and the Struggle for Gay Freedom* (New York: St Martin's Press, 1998): 16.

40. Alfred Kinsey et al., 1948, see note 40: 560.

41. Jonathan Dollimore, *Sexual Dissidence: Augustine to Wilde, Freud to Foucault* (Oxford: Clarendon Press, 1991).

42. Eve Kosofsky Sedgwick, *Between Men: English Literature and Male Homosocial Desire* (New York: Columbia University Press, 1985).

43. George Weinberg, see note 4.

44. R. W. Connell, *Gender and Power* (Sydney: Allen and Unwin, 1987); also, R. W. Connell, *Gender* (Cambridge: Polity, 2002).

45. Simon Watney, "The Banality of Gender," *Oxford Literary Review* 8 (1986): 13–21.

46. Gary W. Dowsett, "I'll show You Mine, if You'll show Me Yours: Gay Men, Masculinity Research, Men's Studies, and Sex," *Theory and Society* 22 (1993): 697–709.

47. Michel Foucault, quoted in Leo Bersani, "Foucault, Fantasy, and Power," *GLQ* 2 (1995): 11.

48. Eve Kosofsky Sedgwick, see note 47.

49. Martin Kantor, *Homophobia: Description, Development, and Dynamics of Gay Bashing* (Westport, Conn: Praeger, 1998).

50. Elizabeth Bernstein, PhD, Columbia University, personal communication.

51. Randy Shilts, *And the Band Played On: Politics, People, and the AIDS Epidemic* (Harmondsworth: Penguin, 1988).

52. Colin Robinson, "Psst: Homophobia causes AIDS! Pass it on," *The Scarlet Letters* 3 (2006): 7–11 [Newsletter of the Institute for Gay Men's Health, Gay Men's Health Crisis, New York, and the AIDS Project of Los Angeles].

53. Stephen Tomsen, "'A Gross Overreaction': Violence, Honour and the Sanctified Heterosexual Male Body," in S. Tomsen and M. Donaldson, eds., *Male Trouble: Looking at Australian Masculinities* (North Melbourne: Pluto Press, 2003): 91–107.

———————

5

Gay Marriage
The Panic and the Right[1]

Gilbert Herdt

There can be no civilization until homosexual men are
allowed to marry.

—Michel Foucault, 1961

Marriage between a man and a woman is the pillar of
western civilization.

—George W. Bush, 2004

The great fear of "gay marriage" in the United States is associated in many
people's minds with the radiant faces of the thousands of lesbian and gay
couples standing on the steps of city hall in San Francisco, waiting to be
married by Mayor Gavin Newsom. It was early 2004 and the mayor himself instructed the press that he was spurred on to this revolutionary act
by reaction to President George W. Bush's January 20, 2004, State of the
Union address. In the president's speech he had referred to the 1996 Defense of Marriage Act (DOMA), that restricts marriage to a man and a
woman, as "the most fundamental, enduring institution of our civilization." Bush was also quoted as stating that marriage between a man and
a woman was a "pillar of civilization," a phrase that could be found in
sexual and religious conservatives' tirades against marriage rights in the
months leading up to this point. The stage was set for a classic moral
panic provoked by sexual politics and assisted by the media, except that
in this case, it was clear that the rights of individuals (gay men and lesbians) were at stake and were the object of a well-coordinated effort to
scapegoat them. The history and culture of this panic, its contribution to
the election in 2004, and its aftermath, frame this chapter.

Media attention at the city hall that February focused on the masses lining up to marry from all over the country. Advocates were thrilled with the mayor's bold move, and their actions led to a large turnout and media attention. There were endless photographs in the newspapers, on television, and online that showed crowds of men and women, not only from within the Bay Area, but also others who had come from around the country to be married. Governor Arnold Schwarzenegger was opposed, but even those who supported marriage rights for lesbians and gays voiced concerns. Diane Feinstein, California's senior senator and a former mayor of San Francisco, for example, remarked dryly that the Massachusetts court decision from late 2003 that led to the legalization of same-sex marriage in that state and the San Francisco marriages were "too much, too fast, too soon." Her comment lost her support among gay men and lesbians, but many mainstream politicians agreed with the sentiment. Critics and many Christian fundamentalists, Catholics included, found evidence in the mayor's action to support the pope's fear that a new sexual decadence was going to break down the family. Other sexual conservatives felt that these "freak" marriages were sort of a lark to gays, an adolescent impulsive thing, which were compared to the "media circus" of Britney Spears's less-than-twenty-four-hour marriage and annulment in Las Vegas. The San Francisco warning shot was heard elsewhere. Marriages were also performed for a time in Sacramento, California, Portland, Oregon, New Paltz, New York, and Washington State as well, before the courts and opposition politicians shut them down.

Thus, gay marriage as a moral and sexual panic flashed into the American landscape and ultimately rolled out the presidential election year of 2004 that reelected George W. Bush. Many political commentators on the Left, such as famed *New York Times* editorialist Frank Rich,[2] clearly suggest that the moral panic of marriage rights helped send Bush back to office. Through the political strategy of Karl Rove, President Bush's chief White House advisor, frightening the Christian Right and fundamentalist voters in the "red states," with sermons denouncing this "devil practice" on the Sunday immediately proceeding the election, a larger-than-ever voter turnout tipped the balance against more progressive candidates in a variety of states in which gay marriage was a hot-button issue. Following the San Francisco gay marriage ceremonies, the election year was embroiled in a variety of tactics to support and oppose these rights. The controversy continued to unfold on television and radio talk shows, on caravan bus trips across the country to advance gay marriage, through endless polls, and through countless legislative and judicial measures. However, the roots of this panic were laid long before and galvanized in popular reaction to the 2003 U.S. Supreme Court decision *Lawrence v. Texas* that struck down states' sodomy laws in the United States. Gay marriage became a panic in large measure because of its political efficacy as a wedge issue in the elections of 2004 and, to a lesser extent, the congressional elections that followed in 2006. By May 2008, the California Supreme Court had legalized same-sex marriage in a landmark decision that opponents vowed to fight.

Who could have imagined that marriage, surely among the stodgiest and least controversial of topics—seemingly essential and a necessary part of the heteronormativity of the human condition—could have become the object of such a swift and divisive moral panic at the end of the modern period and late market capitalism? As Foucault's 1961 quotation above makes clear, so fundamental is the institution of marriage to Western civilization that no true sexual progress could be made in society until its forms were expanded to provide for gays and lesbians. Nevertheless, few observers, straight or gay, anticipated the way in which marriage would come to signify the stigma of exclusion through promotion of an institution (marriage) to normalize and prompt conformity to being straight. By defining marriage as the privilege of citizenship to which only heterosexuals were entitled, as the Bush Administration did, and then following this with a 2004 marriage promotion law alleged to help couples develop interpersonal skills that sustain "healthy marriages," a new stage of the battle for marriage rights was determined. Thomas Frank,[3] an anti-Bush political journalist, anticipated this upheaval and the exploitation of the class basis of voting against gay and lesbian rights. The Bush Administration has subsequently put Americans' tax money where its mouth was: the federal government provided $1.5 billion to promote marriage "especially" among low-income communities without much opposition.[4] In the view of other critics, such as Frank Rich,[5] marriage was the normal state of things in the blue states as much as the red states, but the values expressed belonged to those of the mainstream, not Christian fundamentalists, who opposed marriage rights for lesbian, gay, bisexual, or transvestite (LGBT) people. James Carville (once President Clinton's chief political strategist) captured the difference best when he joked on television, "I was opposed to gay marriage until I found out I didn't have to have one!"

Foucault seems to have anticipated some of these late modern sexual politics, and from his historical researches (especially *The History of*

Sexuality) he was, of course, no stranger to moral panics in the earlier modern period. Foucault's writing imagined the ways in which homophobia was at the base of many forms of sexual prejudice and even of mainstream sexuality. In the immortal words of David Halperin,[6] there could be no orgasm without ideology! Social conventions squeeze people and their sexual scripts, making exciting what is forbidden and forbidding what is exciting. Foucault's prescient remark that there "can be no civilization until homosexuals have the right to marry" is surely a surprise to many students of Foucault, since the great French scholar, like most of his French peers, such as feminist Simone de Beauvoir and her lover, the French existentialist philosopher Jean-Paul Sartre,[7] disdained marriage as a bourgeois prison that led to the entrapment of individuals via middle-class mediocrity. Bush's self-proclaimed pillar must come down or yield to homosexual marriage, because, in Foucault's view, we cannot claim to have an authentic civilization. Civil unions and domestic partnership benefits certainly suggested a middle ground between these views, but this moderation was ignored in the moral panic of gay marriage that shaped up in 2004: one was either for or against lesbians and gays having the right to marry. And anyway, private focus groups around the United States suggested to marriage advocates at the time that the public believed the distinction between a "civil union" and "real marriage" was a "trick;" that is, in ordinary peoples' minds there is only one *real* form of marriage, that which is based on church weddings—further evidence of a conspiracy of "Liberals" ("humanist" doctors, lawyers, academics, and policy-makers, who collude with gays for the "special rights" about which fundamentalists spread fear in their media campaigns.)[8] As I shall note later, these attitudes not only were evidence that homophobia, as Herek[9] has stated, dies hard, but also that the U.S. trajectory of marriage still differs greatly with that of Canada and Western Europe, wherein the Netherlands, Belgium, Spain, and Norway have made same-sex marriage entirely legal.

Progressive reporters, such as Thomas Frank, had been saying all along that a great backlash against gay marriage was being managed by neo-conservatives, prepackaged in "media talking points" to script what moral conservatives ought to say on talk shows such as *The O'Reilly Factor*: "In one end you feed an item about, say, the menace of gay marriage, and at the other end you generate, almost mechanically, an uptake of middle-American indignation, angry letters to the editor, an electoral harvest of the most gratifying sort."[10] This media panic underscored that deeply imbedded homophobia, as Glenda Russell observes time and again, is a political reality.[11] Yet, to many lesbians and gay men, denial of marriage signified second-class citizenship—or none at all. It was especially worrying to some LGBT critics[12] that conservatives, including fundamentalists at Focus on the Family, were promoting marriage for regulatory purposes that suited their own essentialized political ends. Indeed, a *Christian Science Monitor* reporter quotes them, ironically, as defining marriage as "a natural thing" that must be seen as "the natural law present in marriage."[13]

The ensuing political rhetoric and passions stirred up an intense difference of opinions among neoliberal allies, especially second-wave feminists, not to mention within the LGBT community itself. Early on, Michael Warner, for example, echoed a powerful sentiment in some quarters when he lamented, "There were cogent reasons that the gay movement for decades refused to take the path on which it is now hell-bent."[14] More conservative gay advocates, such as Andrew Sullivan, supported the imperative for gays to have marriage rights in order to achieve social acceptance.[15] Clearly the right to marry was highly problematic for gay and reproductive rights advocates, who saw in this political and generational divide or, perhaps even more, cultural divide, the opening for opportunist political tactics employed by extreme Christian conservatives and sexual neoconservatives to divide and conquer the public.

In my view, the ensuing political reaction in the 2004 election constituted one of the most important and dramatic chapters in the use of cultural anger and moral panics to reduce and restrain the rights of individuals in recent American history. A social and historical transformation had occurred between the period of the nascent and emerging sexual identity movements in the 1960s and 70s, right up to the time of the presidential election of 2004. It was unthinkable a generation ago that the issue of gay marriage would be taken seriously. True, opinion polls had continued to rise, and significantly so, in favor of homosexuality following the early 90s fiasco of "Don't Ask, Don't Tell" policy (see below), though the majority of those polled continued to be in the negative. However, attitudes toward gay marriage were even more persistently negative until late, when mid-2008 California field polls showed for the first time a majority in favor of same-sex marriage in that state. The brunt of the historic change is that the train of gay and lesbian rights had left the station and had become sufficiently important and achievable, due to their movement being powerful enough, that U.S. politics would drift into a moral panic. While this chapter does not pretend to explain the sources of this panic in recent years in the United States or the sources' vicissitudes in the 2004 election, I do hope to elucidate some of the events and reactions that went into shaping the cultural logic and narratives of this change.

Anti-Gay Campaigns since the Cold War

A series of important political and historical changes since the Cold War are central to the moral panic of gay marriage and to the assault on gay rights surrounding sexual rights. These mid-century and later changes involved intense compression of gender roles and antihomosexual campaigns of the Cold War that had been in place since the late 1940s, followed by post-Cold War reactions that began to unwind these political forces after the demise of the Soviet Union.[16]

As lawyer and policy analyst François Girard[17] has argued persuasively, American policy for the past quarter century has been insensitive to sexual and reproductive rights and to "rights" as a framework more broadly. The reasons for this opposition are complex, but they certainly have to do with the rise of neoconservativism over the past generation. The contestations surrounding rights for women's reproductive choices, homosexuality, and comprehensive sex education have long involved perceived threats to morals, and thus a concomitant backlash against expansion of sexual rights, typically through antiwoman and antihomosexual campaigns that emerged after post World War II that challenged and changed gender roles and masculinity, intimate relationships, and sexual identity movements.[18] As these changes took hold in sexuality, marriage, and the family, a gathering storm of reaction at first unsettled and then galvanized neoconservative and sexual conservatives, roughly beginning with the Reagan presidency and beyond. It is notable that conservative Barry Goldwater, iconic in the Republican Party at the time of Reagan's ascendancy, profoundly disagreed with the growing influence of Christian conservatives in the party and eventually parted company, actually supporting integration of gays into the military.[19] In hindsight, these transformations were broadly built from the earlier, Cold War structure of sexual and gender prejudices intertwined with new fears and reactions to sexual movements and the advent of the HIV epidemic.[20] Thus, by the early 1990s, the United States was in the position of being the last remaining superpower, with a legacy of gender and sexual compression that had fueled the moral panics identified earlier in the introduction to this book.

Reaction to the famed Kinsey Reports in 1948 and 1952, for example, not only marked the beginning of a terrible escalation in moral panics surrounding sex and homosexuality in particular, but also the deployment of mass media to fan the flames of public sexual illiteracy. Time after time the conservative critics complained of how Kinsey's work would weaken the "moral fiber" or "moral fabric" or some such moral cliché, because of Kinsey's assertion that homosexuality, premarital sex, and masturbation were far more common than previously believed. Anticommunists then jumped on the bandwagon of an anti-Kinsey media campaign.[21] Congressman Joe McCarthy famously accused the politically conservative Kinsey himself of being a communist. The recent film *Kinsey* fairly accurately portrays the social atmosphere of the times, complete with the McCarthy witch-hunt that Kinsey was unprepared to handle. A tidal wave of moral panic reactions was unleashed in those days of Cold War fear.

Consider the following story: "A virulent moral sickness is attacking American society. Its obvious symptoms may be seen at any newsstand in large cities or small. American society is becoming mentally and emotionally ill with an unrestrained sex mania." The date of this quote is 1958; its source—the influential *Christian Times*, was cited by legal scholar Didi Herman to illustrate the prevalent conservative fear about how "young people were being taught to glorify all forms of sexuality and perversion."[22] What is remarkable is that the 1958 op-ed was widely accepted; and it is even more remarkable that one can read similar comments (noted below) right through the 2004 election year campaign rhetoric of opponents to gay marriage.

After World War II, masculinity expanded, and so did canonical gender roles, at the expense of intimacy. That is, during this period, a powerful gender binary, in Marge Garber's sense, was amplified into the cultural forms of American society and then reified through the first impact of mass television shows, thus achieving an apex of dualistic tendencies via institutions and their gender roles in the family, church and school, policies, identities, and, of course, popular culture during the Eisenhower years.[23] The modernization of sexuality, as Paul Robinson has distilled its primary notions of "sexual drive," "sexual morality," and "reproduction" (especially as these emphasized male/female difference), added to the binaries "homosexual" versus "heterosexual," was at its zenith.[24]

During the heyday of rising antihomosexual rhetoric, communism was frequently mentioned in the same narratives with sexual perversion. In Herman's analysis, in the 1920s and 30s, the first wave of attack against

Catholics led to the second wave of attack against Jews. Right-wing attacks on communities of faith then fanned out to include what they called
the "cult of homosexuality" by the 1950s and early 1960s. The greatest
threat to the American nation was the Communist menace of the Soviet
Block, the emasculator of strong warriors. To be accused of communism
in the 40s and 50s was symbolic castration, if not, in fact, generative of
psychological impotence. The accusation of homosexuality was a de facto
accusation of communism pure and simple; the difference was elided in
the moral campaign against Alfred Kinsey and his followers. This same
rhetorical structure, all other things being equal, was at first anti-Semitic
and sometimes anti-Catholic and later targeted Jews as Marxist sympa-
thizers and effeminate, "intellectual effete," a phrase Spiro Agnew (a red
basher and McCarthy-era figure) was fond of promoting. By the 21st century, the phrase would come to mean liberal "urban decadents" in the so-
called blue states.[25] However, in these moral panics, unlike the Communists and homosexuals, at least the Jews and Catholics had faith, even if
their god was not Christ. Worst of all was a Jew who was homosexual and
Communist, a monster in conspiracy to ruin masculinity! It is remarkable that earlier capitalist and fascist rhetoric shared the common enemy
of Communist/homosexual/Jew. Today, these other dangerous marginals
have largely dropped out of extreme Christian fundamentalist hate literature and are no longer acceptable as the objects of moral panics, leaving
homosexuals as the last enemy: other.

The historical legacy of antihomosexuality contained in the Cold War
and the period leading up to this time was productive of moral panics.
A key to their analysis is the patriarchal masculinity the rhetoric and binaries and moral panics produced. A new warrior was created—strong,
silent, emotionally unexpressive; sometimes angry; an over-socialized,
sometimes alienated heterosocial man. He had to marry, have children,
objectify women, and hate homosexuals. Tennessee Williams captured the
images in his classic play, *Cat on a Hot Tin Roof*, in which the protagonist is suspected of being homosexual and lives in a childless marriage.
American men during the period were drafted to fight in the Korean War
and later the Vietnam War; they were drafted to fight on Madison Avenue as the" Man in the Gray Flannel Suit," selfless but coddled smokers
and two-fisted drinkers; the flotsam of capitalism. This masculinity was
of course not confined to the United States. The extraordinary fact of the
then two superpowers is how uncannily their gender roles mirrored aspects of the reproductive purity and antihomosexual bias of the Nazis.

Soviet masculinity under Stalin and American masculinity under General Eisenhower were alike in more ways than they differed.[26] Homosexuality was illegal and was punished, though homosexuals were more closeted in the military then now. Abortion was illegal. Sex educators were suspect. And traditional gender roles underlay these stereotypes and Cold War expectations of conformity. These are the hallmarks of a wave of panics that compressed equality and privacy.[27]

Ironically, the collapse of the Soviet Union as arch enemy and the emergence of American unilateral policy a la George H. W. Bush, appears to have shifted neoconservative attitudes about sexuality in the United States[28] toward more "traditional values" platforms in areas such as abstinence, antihomosexuality, antiabortion, and heteronormativity marriage in the mid-1990s. Moreover, media campaigns increasingly employed "cultural anger"[29] in the images of average people's voices and faces to mobilize American public opinion against these marginals and in removal of their rights.

Following the ascendancy to power of President Ronald Reagan in the early 1980s and to the present government of George W. Bush, a new agenda was built on this history of moral panics and "traditional values" that was opposed to sexuality. The new regime of sexual conservatism[30] extolled an extreme Christian coalition agenda on sexuality, fundamentally challenging the role of sexual/reproductive health, education, and rights in the United States, while also promoting a neoconservative economic agenda of free markets and global world trade.[31] Such a paradigm stands in marked contrast to the sexual reform and effort to de-essentialize sexuality in the 1960s and 1970s, a period in which John Gagnon has argued that there was a "significant increase in normative and non-normative sexual behavior."[32] The 1960s witnessed, after all, the rise of the second sexual revolution of the 20th century, the period that consolidated the emergence of "recreational sex"[33] as the reigning paradigm of the middle class. This transformation disquieted many but profoundly offended the moral brigade of extreme right-wing Christians.[34] The collapse of the liberal consensus, the assault on the "New Deal," and the growth of economic neoliberalism all fed into this transformation of American political ideology.[35] Concomitant assaults on public health and social services and attacks on science continued to escalate during this era.[36]

Consider, for example, the link between antiwomen prolife campaigns and antigay campaigns since the 1970s. The clamor surrounding *Roe v. Wade* (1973) and the intense conflicts over abortion rights and access to clinics and good reproductive healthcare since the landmark decision of the Supreme Court is well known and has been brilliantly analyzed by DiMauro and Joffe.[37] The critical connections to antigay campaigns in this period was demonstrated in the classic essay of Rubin,[38] but has been amplified via the regulation of nonprocreative sexualities since the 1990s.[39] What led to the escalation of the violence in this arena—the bombing of birth control clinics, the assassinations of medical doctors, the death threats to care takers and mothers themselves—in retrospect may be seen as the infusion of cultural anger by a variety of major right-wing organizations.[40] These were all the classic signs of a moral panic that becomes rabid with potential to destroy the social fabric.

Antipornography campaigns during the 1980s provided another antisexual panic in the transition to the HIV pandemic that became the leading headline for years to follow. The AIDS epidemic provided new contradictions and support for attempts to regulate sexuality in the media and popular culture.[41] Moral panics in this period targeted homosexuality, often by conflating the dangers of both pornography and homosexuality as synonymous moral degeneracy. In some sense that trend has continued up to the present.

In the 1980s and early 90s, federal government policy shifts increasingly politicized sexual health research and public health measures, particularly in the arena of HIV/AIDS and reproductive health and abortion rights.[42] HIV was itself to become a great fear, lending itself to a panic and witch-hunt of Haitians, sex workers, and homosexuals.[43] The U.S. government and public health service were doing little or nothing to respond, and the president himself was silent until a conservative Mormon doctor, who happened to become the U.S. surgeon general, eventually decided that HIV was a disease not a moral sickness.[44] Paradoxically, it was the rising AIDS movement[45] that enabled the reaction to medical authority and science, the creation of self-help medical knowledge networks, the use of AIDS monies to fund grassroots LGBT community-based organizations, and the stimulation of new and more sweeping research on homosexuality. All emanated from the panic of AIDS.[46]

In tandem, a new wave of reaction began to ferment at the grassroots level by sexual conservatives: the growing panic stirred up against sexual education. Sex education, once a matter of "plain vanilla" public discussion in schools, became increasingly political, controversial, and objectionable to sexual conservatives.[47]

Sexual conservatives were growing in numbers,[48] both in the United States (during Ronald Reagan's presidency) and in the United Kingdom.[49] Two new extraordinary elements were added: first, a reassertion of religious faith and values in reaction to liberalism and Great Society programs of the 1960s that implicitly supported the sexual revolution through advanced welfare capitalism, much of which has subsequently been rolled back or suspended altogether.[50] The tolerant attitude of this era associated with this affluent governmental expansion and related events of expressive social movements in the 1960s and 70s came under attack during the Reagan government. Second, the moral panic of the early 1980s was explicitly antihomosexual in association with people and these individuals were treated as a disease or diseased. The AIDS panic fueled the engine of a new essentialism, and a new kind of sexual scapegoating, that would target, in succession, Haitians, sex workers, homosexuals, and bisexuals. And, as indicated in the Introduction, this targeting is not over.[51] The accusation and stigma of AIDS in the United States and abroad was contagious and left academics and advocates alike breathless and unable to keep up with the catastrophe.[52]

Thus, a powerful cultural anger directed toward homosexuals in particular, but also toward abortion clinics, reproductive health doctors, and eventually sex educators and sex education programs in the public schools, must be seen not as the same story but rather as part of the same historical and cultural sequence of events that formed the temper of the times.[53] The political use of the antigay and antiwoman rhetoric, moral campaigns, and organizational mechanisms that infused sexual conservatives in the 1980s[54] was to install neoconservative power and agendas at the grassroots level and build this force into an effective electoral strategy.[55] Mobilization of grassroots fundamentalist religious and political networks of working and middle-class people in the 1990s became the explicit agenda of the Republican Party and the framers of Newt Gingrich's "Contract with America"—moving through the election of President Clinton and a new Republican majority in Congress in 1994.[56]

Over the decades of these conservative sexual and gender transformations, antisodomy laws that criminalized homosexuality remained powerful and widespread in the United States. Enter here the problem of sexual rights in public/private space in Supreme Court decisions, bringing into focus powerful contradictions between sexual normality and homosexuality as identified within state laws that exoticized "sodomy" as unnatural and diseased—and a threat to the public. The counter-reaction against the McCarthy witch-hunt, in the 1960s emergence of a gay and lesbian movement, followed in the 1980s by a new queer movement and "Act Up," critical to grassroots reactions to the prior era.[57] Gay activists were particularly angered by the seminal decision in the State of Georgia case brought to the Supreme Court, *Bowers v. Hardwick* (1986), which sustained this antigay rhetoric. The Supreme Court's historic decision ruled that local custom and community values determine what is a threat to the public, even when the activity is between consenting adults in private.

However, some corrections occurred in progressive areas. In 1961 Illinois became the first state to repeal sodomy laws and was soon followed by other state repeals as well as city ordinances, such as San Francisco's landmark 1975 law to protect gay rights.[58] *Bowers v. Hardwick* kept the lid on homosexual freedom, activities of a political nature, and also fueled the moral panics that ensued, including the "Gays in the Military" battle that is discussed below. In sexual transactions in the United States, the rule of silence remained: do it, but don't talk about it. For people in most places, the idea of marriage for people of the same sex was a bitter, far-fetched dream, if not in fact a joke. An entire generation came of age hoping for the advance of sexual rights following the gay liberation movement of the 1960s and 70s, only to feel thwarted by subsequent laws and moral panics that checked further progress up to the 1990s. The emergence of a sexual subjectivity of the "closet," as Sedgwick has suggested, depended on a concomitant social order that resonated of moral and sexual panics— signaling to the self to remain hidden.[59]

During the 1990s, roughly concurrent with the Clinton presidency following the Reagan and Bush Sr. administrations, enormous transformations in the cultural, historical, and political conditions of marriage discussions began. The transition through the George H. W. Bush presidency was associated with continued neoconservative activism and a smaller flurry of antihomosexual campaigns.[60] Indeed, recall that Pat Buchanan, in the 1992 presidential race, announced his decision to launch "a religious war, a culture war, a war for the soul of America" that promoted traditional family values and evangelical Christianity against homosexuality in an appeal that had all the markings of a classic moral panic.[61] The presidential election year of 1992 notably saw Bush Sr. employ antigay tactics prominently in his unsuccessful bid for reelection.

The Clinton Era: Gays in the Military

The "Don't Ask, Don't Tell" policy under the Clinton government in the early 1990s provoked a rash of new antigay campaigns and occasional panics. Building on the momentum of antigay rhetoric in the 1992 campaign, President Bill Clinton's push to legalize military service for gay men and lesbians provoked an immediate firestorm of reaction. Clinton had gained victory in the election having made several promises to support gay issues, since lesbians and gay men were actively involved in the Democratic Party's 1992 convention and they pushed for change on several fronts. Conservatives never forgave Clinton. Their unsuccessful attempts to invoke impeachment a few years later, following disclosure of the Monica Lewinski sexual scandal, surely revealed the depth of political feeling leading up to the precarious installment of George W. Bush in the White House eight years later.[62]

President Clinton's call for a change in policy to allow gays to serve openly in the military was an historic step away from this past, and while critics believe that it led to the undermining of public confidence in Clinton, the ensuing debate was truly revolutionary. To give a sense of the magnitude of this problem, between 1982 and 1992, seventeen thousand gays were dismissed from the military because of homosexuality. Polls gave high support to antidiscrimination attitudes toward gays. Clinton was not the first prominent American politician to raise the issue. In the early 1980s, conservative icon Barry Goldwater had previously criticized the Pentagon for its antihomosexual policies. However, Goldwater's views were regarded as renegade. Clinton's managers supported the change in military policy—believing that lifting the ban would enjoy wide appeal.[63] They clearly saw a parallel in Truman's landmark 1948 Executive Order to end discrimination against African Americans in the armed services. In a Veteran's Day speech in Little Rock, Arkansas, Clinton appealed for the change and then sought to reassure military brass. But his proposal created instantaneous sexual panic, as front-page *New York Times* stories quoted enlisted soldiers in the barracks as fearing that they would be looked at sexually in the shower room, preyed on, or even raped; even a Marine general told of his anxiety about gays being in the shower with him.[64] The Joint Chiefs of Staff, headed by Colin Powell, believed that gays had to remain hidden in order for the U.S. military to remain fit and the most powerful fighting force. As Enloe has concluded, this panic was about more than homosexuality; it was "about the kind of gender order that guarantees this society's national security."[65]

The Don't Ask, Don't Tell policy has been widely examined[66] and its flaws were obvious from the start. The ban covered not only homosexual behavior but also a "propensity" to engage in homosexual conduct, and many enlisted men and officers balked at the policy. The initial media stories are reminiscent of classic smear campaigns and moral panics, with spill-over effects that spread into two other highly gendered, homophobic domains of gender segregated male supremacy: the priesthood, and the Boy Scouts of America (BSA). Notably, the priesthood has recently been the subject of the Vatican's significant new teaching regarding a radical change in its policy prohibiting the recruitment of men who have "tendencies" toward homosexuality.[67] Meanwhile, the military policy was widely viewed as a failure, and its rollback was imminent. The moral is that patriarchy, in such examples, abhors homosexuality, and moral panics are one result.

But it is the moral panic whipped up in the Boy Scouts that is more instructive in providing a lesson about the subsequent attack on gay marriage. The moral and sexual fears fanned by the media and instigated, in part, by the fundamentalist Christian movement (especially the Church of Jesus Christ of Latter Day Saints, which strongly supports the BSA) in the late 1990s, caused the Boy Scouts of America to deny a gay man's right to be a scout master. This ban was extended to a denial that there were gay members of the BSA and a Supreme Court case that justified their actions. In *BSA v. Dale* (2000), the Scouts won the right, as they have put it, to exclude homosexuals as "role models" due to the conflict in values homosexuality represents.[68] The Scouts argued that they had "been so effective for ninety years" by supporting "character development," with values inconsistent with homosexuality. The court statement noted, "Tolerance does not require admission of all forms of behavior as being 'appropriate.'" Scouting was introduced by Lord Robert Baden-Powell (a man preoccupied with male eroticism) in 1910 to promote patriotism, courage, self-reliance, and masculinity—all instantiated in the Scout Oath.[69] A defender of the BSA has written that the Scouts' policy cannot be compared to racism or anti-Semitic feelings because it fundamentally hinges on the fact that homosexual character is "sodomy," "which the Scouts and the great majority of Americans find objectionable."[70] To cap off this rhetoric of panic and the slippery slope logic employed by this author, he concludes, "Homosexuality is akin to adultery and incest and bestiality. It is clearly not akin to being black or Jewish."[71] Is it not fascinating to observe not only that Baden-Powell embodied a mix of purity and militarism with "a strong anti-masturbation element," but also he suggested that with the sexual practice would come weakness, idiocy, and lunacy?[72]

Civil unions and marriage rights were the second major area of Clinton promises and failed policy. A backlash following the messy handling of the Don't Ask, Don't Tell debate, which inspired the White House recognition too late that Clinton and the Democrats, had miscalculated. Polls showed that the public felt negative—the slippery-slope argument that the military would be spoiled by open homosexuality seemed to work. Poll support for Clinton dropped. Neoconservatives then seized on the panic surrounding the issue to begin a new drive to restrict marriage to men and women, and a series of court battles went their way.[73] Today the United States is the lone Western country to practice discrimination against gay men and lesbians—all the other Western powers have integrated gays into their military forces, apparently without a hitch.[74]

Two powerful forces, dominant and resistant discourses and mobilizing political movements, then came into place: a new coalition of sexually conservative/Christian coalition forces that rallied to enact the Defense of Marriage Act (DOMA) in 1996—the "battering ram"[75] to exert draconian laws and reinstate traditional gender norms into American culture. Advocates who have reviewed this period of change differ somewhat on the history and details of political strategy,[76] but by 2005, forty states had enacted legislation or amendments to their state constitutions banning same-sex marriage. Resistant counterhegemonic forces that opposed these trends employed an arsenal of gay lawyers who attempted to create a new language of legal and social reasoning to carry court cases.[77] The critical passage of DOMA in the context of welfare reform—an event that former Surgeon General Jocelyn Elders[78] describes as the low point of the Clinton Administration—was a bitter pill to gay advocates, final proof that the Clinton Administration had abandoned them. Yet DOMA also signified to the nation as a whole the new hegemony of Christian fundamentalist and sexual conservative influence in the United States.[79] These forces were going to promote gay marriage as a moral panic. Ironically, Clinton's support of gay issues probably fueled the anger that conservatives marshaled in their impeachment effort following the disclosure of the Monica Lewinsky affair.

These events of the mid- to late-1990s form the broader social and political context in which we may now understand the highly successful use of "cultural anger" that led to the ascendance of George W. Bush and, in particular, the Republican victory in the 2004 presidential election. The decade that led up to the 2004 election was filled with years in which sexually conservative neoconservatives brilliantly deployed cultural anger through traditional values platforms and campaigns to gain greater restrictions on abortion, reinstate the traditional homophobic conditions of the U.S. military via Don't Ask, Don't Tell policies, pass abstinence-only legislation under the Welfare Reform Act (1996), and adopt DOMA. The cultural anger directed against homosexuals built on prior moral panics but it remained dynamic—in part, the legacy of 1980s reactions to AIDS activism and the rising visibility of gays and sexual minorities in the United States. A new series of sexual panics began to place a wedge of fear into U.S. policy debates, domestic and global.

Anna Smith has reviewed in detail the changes in public policy that have promoted marriage as a form of "patriarchal heterosexuality" that has marginalized gays and lesbians.[80] The review preceded *Lawrence v. Texas* and is notable for the legislation that President Clinton signed into law, particularly DOMA, which imposed federal guidelines on issues once left to the states, and imposed the definition of marriage restricted to a man and a woman. Brief digression into the historical and cultural changes that laid the ground work for that law will enable us to gain deeper understanding of the 2004 panic.

Heteronormative Marriage at the End of the Century

Marriage has a long history of political, legal, economic, and religious reform efforts in the United States, some of which have genuinely resulted in policy change and others that have lingered for decades without success. Since the founding of the republic, marriage has been considered at times a "natural right" and/or a "God-given" right.[81] Nineteenth-century feminist reformers variously viewed marriage as a form of slavery, with divorce the only means to freedom,[82] while later social movements regarded companionate marriage as a higher form of egalitarian relations between the genders. Marriage was denied to slaves in the United States and, subsequently, antimiscegenation laws remained on the books until late in the 20th century. California was the first state to nullify miscegenation laws (1948), and it followed that precedent in legalizing same-sex marriage in the state. Throughout this long American history, however, marriage between people of the same gender has been impossible and remained a utopian dream until very late—the 2004 San Francisco marriages being part of that utopia.

Over the past two centuries, marriage has remained the norm in the United States despite gains in social equality, women's rights, and the opposition to marriage by a variety of radical reformers, including the socialist, free-love, and homophile movements.[83] In their bald form, feminist critiques of marriage since the time of Emma Goldman[84] still regard marriage as a force of patriarchy and male domination. All of the efforts over the past two centuries show that historical analyses of marriage have not dispelled the "connections among marriage, gender hierarchy, citizenship, and sexuality."[85] Single and divorced persons, those who are widowed for one reason or another, and those who have opposed marriage on ideological grounds have generally been disparaged in American society, with a few upper class exceptions.[86]

Queer advocates likewise have long critiqued marriage in support of feminist allies, but their own reasons have to due with heteronormativity in the constitution of marriage as a social contract.[87] Assimilation via marriage or other hierarchical institutions in this view[88] will not end the oppression of gays or change the antigay rhetoric that drives moral conservatives.[89] As Carmen Vasquez warns, "We must stop pretending that our assimilation into this culture will tame the hate-filled hearts."[90]

Clearly, marriage is a key to understanding sexual and gender citizenship—and restriction—in most societies. But what about its other claimed benefits, such as enhanced well-being?[91] Health wise, marriage matters a great deal, although the precise benefits on an individual basis are more difficult to chart than compared to the general population. Current research has repeatedly shown that whatever people's attitudes and views on marriage, it bestows a variety of long-term benefits, including economic, social, legal, and health protections.[92] Numerous studies based on the general population over a period of decades indicate that, on average, married individuals report better mental health, less psychological distress, and lower rates of psychiatric disorder than the unmarried.[93] Marriage is thus uniquely associated with a host of tangible and intangible benefits that, in composite, are linked to and support psychological health, but only so long as the marriage is mutually satisfying.[94]

It must be stated, however, that within the population of the United States there is a large division between those who do not wish to marry, others who live together but without marriage, and those who regard marriage as sacred and the "pillar of civilization." Within heterosexual populations, too, living together without marriage is now very common,[95] a secular trend that has been extended further through late welfare capitalism in Western Europe.[96] Within the LGBT community itself, the divide remains fairly large over the value of marriage and the fear—whether right or wrong—that marriage will normalize and heterosocialize gay men and lesbians,[97] removing what is unique, creative, and human about each of them as individuals and about the gay/lesbian community as a whole.[98]

Antigay campaigns opposing marriage rights have drawn on the historical imagery of homosexuality as pathology. Homosexuals were historically regarded as deviant, in violation of moral, religious, gender, and sexual norms. In the 19th and early 20th centuries, homosexuals were classified as "degenerate" or diseased in a variety of ways.[99] In short, homosexuals are viewed as unfit for marriage and unfit to be parents, according to this historical pathological view. After the 1960s, the LGBT movement gained power and voiced increasing opposition that led, most famously, to the depathologization of homosexuality in the medical profession. In 1972 and 1973 the American Psychiatric Association voted to "declassify" homosexuality as a disease in favor of seeing gay men and lesbians as a normal variant of human sexual expression.[100] The late eminent psychiatrist Judd Marmor, who helped to advance these changes, was often quoted as saying, "If we made our judgments about the mental health of heterosexuals only from the patients we saw in our office, we'd have to assume that all heterosexuals were mentally disturbed."[101] In the subsequent decades it is clear that homosexuality has greatly improved its standing in public opinion polls, with the majority of Americans currently in support of gay and lesbian rights.[102]

However, it is equally clear that two fundamental sources of pathology remain foremost in the minds of Americans: a large number (the latest Pew poll finds that 55 percent) of Americans continue to believe that "gay sex is a sin," and a smaller but still significant number of Americans (perhaps between 20 and 25 percent) believe that homosexuality is an illness or a disease. Polls show rather consistently that there is a strong generational split over this pathology—younger people ages eighteen to twenty-nine endorse positive attitudes about homosexuality at a rate of 72 percent while elders were at 39 percent. The younger group also supported gay marriage upwards of 59 percent more than their elders.[103] The higher support among younger than older people for gay marriage in Pew polls has been consistent.

These pathologizing attitudes about homosexuality in the older generation are not merely the legacy of history; they are, in part, the result of enormous political lobbying and media massaging successfully waged by extreme Right Christian coalition forces, the so-called sexual conservatives.[104] However, the official position on homosexuality of organizations such as the Christian Medical and Dental Society of the United States (which claims 17,000 members) shows that: (1) they believe homosexuality is unnatural, (2) sinful, (3) may result in bodily harm to organs and orifices, and (4) that homosexuality can be effectively changed by "conversion therapy" because it is a choice. These political claims are disputed by scientific research in one way or another.[105] Yet decades of change and reform have failed to make a significant dent in the belief systems of such people.

At the turn of the century, a new and dramatic source of challenge to these received pathologizing attitudes came in the form of European legislation to legalize same-sex marriage. In the Netherlands in 2001 (shortly before 9/11), same-sex marriage was made legal, with complete and full rights following soon thereafter. Subsequently, the Dutch law was followed by other Western European nations: Belgium (full rights), Denmark and Germany (partial rights), and, notably, Spain (full legal rights for marriage and parenting in 2005, and Norway in 2008. The United Kingdom also made civil marriage legal between gays. These new international changes accelerated some of the global LGBT movement efforts to further expedite change in North America, with the highly significant result that Canada, in 2005, changed its federal law to allow full rights. These countries' new laws began to exert a change in the rhetoric. How could gays be pathological if these other countries, our allies, made marriage among them normal? Marriage proponents, including academic experts, argued that marriage was such a good and necessary thing that its benefits were undeniable. Gender, economic, political and legal pressures thus reached a crescendo in the 2004 presidential election—upping the stakes for opposing forces on gay marriage in the United States.

Meanwhile, the panic surrounding gay marriage further polarized American religion, which has long been divided around gays and the question of homosexual rights broadly. Today it is clear that gays and lesbians divide churches and religion more broadly than another other issue in the country. Christian fundamentalists since the Reagan era have always opposed gays and have campaigned in vehement terms around what the late William Dannemeyer called "the right to sodomize"–which is what he says American gays most wanted to achieve.[106] However, in 2003 the Pope clearly escalated the general panic by his teaching, which demanded that all Catholics oppose gay marriage and gay civil unions; this resulted in the U.S. Conference of Catholic Bishops voting to endorse the proposal for a constitutional amendment to prohibit same sex marriage.[107] In some communities the division is huge. As political scientist Cathy Cohen states, "According to religious doctrine, black lesbian and gay members of the community are to be embraced and taken care of in a time of need. However, their gay identity places them outside the indigenously constructed boundaries of both Christianity and blackness as defined by the church."[108] Girard has suggested that leveraging support for abstinence-only legislation by scapegoating gays and gay marriage has further divided the African American community and reproduced the racism and politics of social injustice that marriage rights seeks to end.[109]

One reason that cultural anger has been such a powerful tool to neoconservatives has to do with the immediate success of the Bush Administration's exploiting fear in the aftermath of the 9/11 attacks on New York City's World Trade Center.[110] Cultural anger has taken one form of fear-based violence/military action against perceived enemies of the United States—broadly and vaguely suggestive of conspiracies and plots to destroy the United States literally or through subversion of its values. The post-9/11 world had a new level of fear, creating a wedge between traditionally allied groups and the export of American "cultural values" to "promote democracy" abroad. The throngs of gays marrying in San Francisco in early 2004 was employed subtly to seize on this imagery and a perceived threat within the country to national moral security.

Lessons from the Heartland: "Normality" and Panic 2004

Not long after the San Francisco marriages, an article appearing in USA Today caught my attention while traveling. The story compared the lives of a straight and a gay couple from Kansas (my birth state) on the front page of the "Life" section. The narrative reveals some of the critical elements of the moral panic of gay marriage that has made its way into mainstream and tabloid media. Not only does the story illustrate some of the core cultural scripts that were at play in the discursive battle over marriage rights, but it also demonstrated the quandary of the LGBT movement with regard to the deep cultural wish to marry among people who see themselves as "normal" but lacking in rights.

In February 2004, at the time of the *USA Today* story, polls showed the country strongly against gay marriage rights.[111] The context was heavily laden with the events in San Francisco in which gay and lesbian couples were furiously registering people to marry and the Massachusetts legislature was trying to overturn the recent ruling of the state supreme court that allowed for legal marriage for gays and lesbians, at least temporarily. It will be remembered that during the Super Bowl, only days before the San Francisco spectacle, a mini moral panic broke out across the United States in reaction to the Janet Jackson "wardrobe malfunction" that allowed her breast to be bared during a half-time performance. Somehow the ludicrousness of the national reaction to a bare breast–the sheer moral outrage expressed by millions of viewers, the loss of television sponsors, and number of irate politicians and clergy who said that they would never watch the Super Bowl again, not to mention calls for an official investigation by the government into this bizarre incident, revealed not only the panic-laden character of anything sexual for the American public but also the way in which the trivialization of the national dialogue obscured such weighty issues as the war in Iraq. The point is that there was a depth of cultural anger that was out there and it was easily redirected to the issue of gay marriage.

USA Today's story was titled "Quiet Division in the Heartland: Kansans Are on Both Sides of the Aisle on Gay Marriage."[112] Two large color photos framed the cover page, providing an immediate eye-catching comparison: a straight family of man, woman, and children, and a gay male couple with dogs. Both thirty-something couples were "normal" on first impression—and, after all, they live in the same affluent suburb of Kansas City (Johnson County) that reporter Frank[113] has examined as a case study of "one of the most Republican areas in the nation."[114] The couples are dressed conservatively, and everyone has smiling, clean-cut looks. Each presents as a "family": Brad and Julie Williams with their two children, Mason (aged 6), and Olivia (aged 7) and Kirk Isenhour and Doug Anningare with their pair of pair Irish Setters, Berkley and Beau. The symmetry of the photos is complemented by the fact that both of the families are described as religious, hard working, and seemingly heteronormative, because—as the cultural script unfolds—they both say that they want to be "normal" and "married." The Williamses are "faithful Southern Baptists at church every Sunday. . . . Steering [their] children by the Bible's authority."

Kirk and Doug are "faithful Episcopalians at church every Sunday" who come home to their house in the suburbs complete with a basketball hoop in the driveway. But while the gay couple is expected to be tolerant of their straight church-going neighbors, the feeling is reciprocated only a bit. When the straight couple was asked if they would allow their children to interact with Kirk and Doug, the Williamses could voice only partial acceptance. When asked if they would allow their children to attend a birthday party of a child with "two mommies," they turned fretful and retorted that they "would have to pray on it."

The folks in this conservative town regard homosexuality as an "inborn trait," something to be tolerated, if not pitied, though not necessarily accepted. For example, a neighbor of the gay couple, fifty-three-year-old Laura Casper, said that she "prays for their healing" in her Christ Church. Her praying, though, did not prevent her from saying that the Bible condemns homosexuality: "To pretend this is not sin, not sickness, tells anyone in pain and suffering that there's something God can't handle." Even more progressive local citizens, like sixty-nine-year-old Hayward Spears, a grandfather of seven who lives nearby, draws the line at gay marriage, he said, "Because it's not the right environment for children." Another male neighbor stated he wouldn't mind if a gay teacher taught his seven-year-old son, as long as "they don't flaunt their sexuality." The same man seemed to correct himself when he then remarked that he would not pay higher taxes to cover the health insurance of the domestic partner of such a teacher. And Julie Williams, the mother of the picture-postcard straight family, summed up this attitude by saying that if homosexuals are accepted in schools, Scouts, and even pulpits, "Children could be desensitized to acting this way,"—suggesting that they could learn to tolerate homosexuality or even become gays and lesbians themselves. Her husband also pondered the vague sense that his son, if allowed to accept gays being married, might somehow turn out differently. Thus goes the slippery-slope discourse of gay marriage in the cultural script of these suburban Kansans.

A few months later in 2004, Kansas went on to pass a state constitutional amendment to ban gay marriage, and the two sitting U.S. senators from Kansas and two of its three congressmen all went on record as supporting an amendment to the U.S. Constitution banning marriage rights for gays and lesbians. It is not without interest that this group of congressional representatives has a voting record that includes long and continued opposition to abortion and choice, strong opposition to gays in the military, strong endorsement of DOMA, strong support of abstinence-only sex education, and, more recently, strong support of the Iraqi war—a bundle of seemingly unrelated but actually culturally interwoven stakes in the neoconservative movement that has opposed reproductive and sexual rights in the United States.

The cultural scripts that emerged from this vignette may be tallied as follows: (1) Homosexuality may be a choice or it may be innate and cannot be helped, but it is a choice to express it; (2) God does not approve of homosexuality either way; the Bible says it is a sin; (3) everyone should be married in this wealthy suburb, including the gays, suggesting the script: you can assimilate but not perform your affection, such as kissing in public; (4) tolerance extends to being around gays as long as they don't "flaunt" their sexuality (i.e., expressing affection with each other in public, such as holding hands); (5) straight parents apparently fear the open performance and acceptance of homosexuality because they believe that their children could "catch" the condition or imitate the behavior, turning gay and thus going to social events with gays must be limited; and (6) parents believe that gays and lesbians must not be allowed in positions of moral authority, whether in the schools, church, or Boy Scouts to avoid this outcome in their children. Tolerance is also limited with teachers—they must keep their own sexuality somehow in check, and the community will not pay for the health care of the gay couple, since that would constitute endorsement of this "lifestyle." In practice, these scripts are variants of ideas that have been around for decades—though they are more enlightened than before.

Twenty years ago anthropologist Naomi Quinn suggested that there is a resilient core of cultural meanings that surround the word "marriage" in American culture.[115] She discovered that there are three key cultural meanings involved: promise, dedication and attachment, which connote "effortful and ongoing" goals that are "very difficult over the long run" to sustain.[116] Because marriage is central to American definitions of kinship as well, the meanings of marriage must be understood as extending their group in a broader network of familial and kin relationships.[117] The core virtues of Quinn's analysis can be seen to support family, long-term intimacy, and emotional/sexual attachments that are socially expected and essentially contractual. The brunt of these meanings has the "overriding sense" of being emotional, she suggested, whereby two people are engaging in joint goals. She continued, "Commitment tells a complex story about American marriage," since enduringness and exclusivity organize marital goals through the word "commitment."[118] Marriage is a durable product in American folk psychology. We even refer to this process through phrases such as "we made that the cornerstone," and "our marriage was strengthened," and "marriage is a do-it-yourself project" as part of how Americans talk about the cultural script of being married and staying together.[119] This view of marriage supports the classic analysis of sociologists Robert Bellah and colleagues during the same period.[120] Yet the changes that were beginning to occur in American society, including the increasing trend of heterosexuals living together without being married, were revealing a new split between the generations in how they viewed the meaning of commitment and durability of marriage, which will be examined further below.

The USA Today story also exposes the significant role that the media was to play in this growing moral panic—a vital part of the moral panic of gay marriage in the presidential election. The story of the two sides in the heartland anticipates how the media were to be used and misused in the 2004 election, in part by a highly effective machine created in the White House and in another part by the "sleepwalking journalists"[121] covering such stories at the time.

Pivotal Role of "Activist Judges"

Civil rights and the advancement of rights more broadly in the United States, including marriage rights, have historically been dependent on judicial court decisions in higher and lower courts.[122] The highly litigious history of landmark gay marriage cases in such states as Georgia, Hawaii, Texas, and then Massachusetts, especially, during the presidential primary season of 2004 are instructive because they formed the context of the reactions and media campaigns that contributed to the moral panic of gay marriage that led up to the 2004 presidential campaign.

Immediately following the majority opinion of the Supreme Court in Lawrence v. Texas, in the summer of 2003, the phrase "activist judges" began to reappear in the rhetoric of sexual conservatives. The long roll back of draconian antigay laws—some of them as "sodomy laws" that dated from the 19th century—was inevitable following the 1973 declassification of homosexuality as a disease by the American Psychiatric Association, the rise of the gay and lesbian movement and social rights that emerged during the 1970s, and the terrible years of the AIDS epidemic in the 1980s, and the dramatic increase in popular support for homosexuality during the Clinton presidency in spite of the failure of Don't Ask, Don't Tell policies. The 2003 Supreme Court decision known as *Lawrence v. Texas* struck down all remaining sodomy statutes in the United States. *Lawrence v. Texas* (overturning *Bowers v. Hardwick*—Georgia) was a pivotal moment in this change.[123] The Supreme Court decision voided all sodomy laws on the basis of the right to privacy among consenting adults—a limited ruling in itself—but sufficient to incite a panic. However, interesting enough, polls showed an immediate and dramatic drop in popular support both for homosexuality and for gay marriage following the *Lawrence v. Texas* decision. Moreover, there were efforts to curtail the change in the most conservative states. Meanwhile, a new rhetoric quickly emerged: the charge that "activist judges" were destroying the moral fabric of the United States—a fear that was to become a battering ram ready and able to mobilize sexual and religious conservatives in general. It is notable that President Bush himself took up this rhetorical charge early in the 2004 presidential race.

Prominent Republicans such as Senator Cornyn of Texas went on record as stating, "We must do whatever it takes to stop same sex unions." As Doug Ireland suggests, the Republicans quickly seized upon "gay marriage as a wedge issue against the Democrats."[124] The Republicans had long used gay-baiting tactics to win elections, but the 2004 election raised this rhetorical tactic to a new level. Indeed, to some extent, not just the threat of "gay marriage" but also the threat of "activist judges" would emerge quickly and serve significantly as a wedge issue between sexually conservative blacks and black ministers and whites and middle class ministers who espoused reform. The real change that resulted from this decision, however, had far more to do with the perception that the Court had gone too far and that the politicians had to take back the power to protect "the sacred institution" of marriage. It is notable that the "thirteen states in which 'sodomy' laws were struck down by the Supreme Court were all states that Bush carried in his first election."[125] Their embrace of a new homophobia was decisive in stirring up an angry gay backlash; that is, a cultural anger marshaled to win elections for reasons that promoted a broader economic and political agenda far beyond "pushing the antigay hot button."

The problems posed by marriage rights in the United States clearly expose major contradictions in public attitudes. Sex remains a matter of morality and religious belief, not public health, to many; marriage is perceived to be a "natural" or God-given right that justified current gender, power, social class, and sexual regulations and ideas, perhaps not as much as in the first half of the twentieth century but enough that a moral panic inciting fear of the collapse of marriage was effective in the last campaign. Regarding homosexuality, neoconservatives and sexual and religious conservatives criticize gays and lesbians for "being promiscuous" and "morally unfit" for marriage, while denying them the right and benefits to the institution of marriage, which they strongly extol for the general population.[126]

We cannot underestimate the role played by traditional gender attitudes in the gay marriage panic, including the notion that men are active, masculine, and should be out in the workplace, while women are passive, feminine, and should stay at home rearing children. Sexual conservatives have extolled the traditional values of family, marriage, love and procreative sexuality, guided in a significant sense by conservative patriarchal ideologies of the nation and the genders. Yet the cumulative effect of the erosion of traditional gender roles in economic, social, political, and legal terms is striking, and there can be no doubt that change disrupts the expectations and norms of middle-class people to some extent and may compel a backlash. "Homosexual marriage," when emotionally manipulated in the ways examined by Janice Irvine[127] rings as a hollow and strange idea, an incitement to reaction. Surely many observers will agree that underlying this fear and the larger moral panic of 2004 surrounding gay marriage was heterosexism and homophobia, as suggested by Kitzinger and Wilkinson.[128] Additionally, however, from the anthropological view, one cannot help but wonder if there is the meaning of violation in this heterosexism/homophobia of gender roles should gay men and lesbians be able to marry. This is what the narrative of the Kansas suburban heterosexuals in the USA Today story implied. Other media stories that react to this image provide no rational or reasonable basis in the narratives of sexual conservative advocates and even ordinary people—other than the sense that "it is just plain wrong." Common sense formulations of this kind, as Geertz suggested long ago,[129] are signs of the cultural scripts powerfully at work that have nothing to do with common sense but rather arise from morally embargoed contestations in society.

Looking back to the events of that election, there is good reason to see why this sort of common-sense folk psychology regarding gender and marriage would be on people's minds. Duggan has written a powerful invective against what she calls "conservative marriage politics" that aims to ban gay marriage and promote traditional marriage.[130] She has advocated for the importance of not getting trapped in the "right to marriage" per se. She focuses on how state regulation of households and partnerships affects "safety, prosperity, equality and welfare of all Americans." In her historical analysis, ordinary wage earners' quality of life has been so eroded as to make education and well-being difficult to achieve. Social security benefits, medical decisions, and child custody are among the many issues she sees as having been undermined by twenty-five years of neoconservative government. Duggan argues that sexual progressives need to take back the rhetorical high ground from moral conservatives who have framed the meaning of the "marriage crisis." She suggests that the apocalyptic images that they have fostered may be their undoing—the slippery slope argument. "The moral conservatives' nightmare vision of a flexible menu of options" to marry or live together "might become a route to progressive equality!" Ultimately she argues that the moral conservative strategy is to preserve "gendered marriage."

These same concerns framed the reaction to the even more historic decision of the Massachusetts Supreme Court on November 18, 2003, which held by a 4-3 vote that the ban on gay marriage was unconstitutional. The court instructed the state to make preparations for gay marriage. In a second ruling on February 6, 2004, the court also decreed that only gay marriage would suffice to meet the requirements of the law. Gay and lesbian couples within the State of Massachusetts soon rushed into marriages, attracting people from other states as well. By March 29, the state legislature passed a law banning gay marriage and establishing civil unions in the future; meanwhile, it proposed a vote on a constitutional amendment to this effect.

The marriages continued, however, and this huge change was drawing the highest-level reactions from around the United States, starting with the president. On November 18, 2003, President George W. Bush issued the following statement from the White House: "Marriage is a sacred institution between a man and a woman. Today's decision of the Massachusetts Supreme Judicial Court violates this important principle. I will work with congressional leaders and others to do what is legally necessary to defend the sanctity of marriage." In later speeches, the president was to decry the nefarious decisions of what he called "activist judges" in this arena–a strong initial volley into the 2004 election campaign. The courts and the executive had laid the basis for a strong media frenzy and a moral panic in 2004.

Gay Marriage in the 2004 Election

The combination of these powerful political and cultural dynamics immediately burst on the stage of the presidential election theatre in February and March 2004, resulting in what I have come to regard as the most significant deployment of a moral panic to win an election. The San Francisco marriage ceremonies, combined with the historical Massachusetts Supreme Court decision mandating legal gay marriage there, drew huge and continuous media attention. For days in those two months, television and radio, newspapers and magazines, and the Internet in a variety of forms, including blogs, quickly situated gay marriage as the defining issue of the election. Of course the Iraq War eventually took precedence, both in the news and the campaigns, and the presidential debates centered much more on the war than gay marriage. Still, what matters is how the 2004 election year was framed, was then played out, and how the theme of America being "taken over" by gay marriage, as commentators on the *O'Reilly Factor* expressed it, were fundamental to the public discourse.

The president himself provoked the moral panic of gay marriage and a sense of a runaway train that would ruin Americans' lives by his constant references to "activist judges." It was as if these shadowy judicial figures were antidemocracy, and un-American. As we have seen, this rhetoric referred to pivotal cases involving the legality of gay and lesbian rights to marry in Massachusetts, home state of Bush's challenger, Senator John Kerry, that would destroy the "sacred" institution of marriage. The significance of the associations rendered by Massachusetts—John Kerry and "activist judges" who want to "impose gay marriage"—was not lost on the many opinion articles of the period.[131] There seemed to be pent up reactions to the earlier Supreme Court decision of *Lawrence v. Texas* that struck down sodomy legislation in the United States; the pent-up cultural anger was now being incited into a new call to action of Christian conservatives and neoconservatives that was quite successful in marshalling votes. Mormon Republican Governor Mitt Romney went on to oppose the Massachusetts Supreme Court decision, a pivotal factor in his courting of the extreme Christian Right for a 2008 presidential run.

Again, President Bush himself must be seen as the key instigator in this political theatre of moral panic.[132] In February 2004 speech, the president publicly threw his backing behind a constitutional amendment to ban gay marriage:

After more than two centuries of American jurisprudence and millennia of human experience, a few judges and local authorities are presuming to change the most fundamental institution of civilization. Their actions have created confusion on an issue that requires clarity. On a matter of such importance, the voice of the people must be heard. Activist courts have left the people with but one recourse. If we're to prevent the meaning of marriage from being changed forever, our nation must enact a constitutional amendment to protect marriage in America. *Activist judges . . . have begun redefining marriage by court order, without regard for the will of the people and their elected representatives. On an issue of such great consequence, the people's voice must be heard. If judges insist on forcing their arbitrary will upon the people, the only alternative left to the people would be the constitutional process. Our nation must defend the sanctity of marriage.*

The strident language and historical appeal clearly established a new concern at the highest levels of the government, at the state level creating in a new kind of alignment or political coalition, with sexual conservatives opposed to the extension of marriage rights. Additionally, on other occasions the president criticized the actions of the Massachusetts Supreme Court and questioned the right of gays to marry. It was another moment in the growing moral panic.

The reaction in the media was intense, and a new wave of antigay advertisements, opinion pieces, and political placements in diverse media began to warn of the threat of gay marriage and "special interest groups" (a term used by sexual conservatives to talk about LGBT rights). By the spring of 2004, a growing antigay marriage movement supported by conservative organizations such as Focus on the Family was in place and commanding debate.

Now, perhaps more transparently, we can see in this rhetorical incitement the direct effect of "cultural anger" that Thomas Frank has said underlies the "grab for power" of neoconservatives vis-à-vis working class people, who, as he has shown in his remarkable case study of Kansas, voted against their own interest on matters of the economy, education for their children, and healthcare for themselves.[133] How else to explain the success of neoconservatives time and again in winning office and taking actions that undermine the very interests of the people who elected them in such places? The moral panic of gay marriage established the emotional and cultural scripts and the political momentum to effectively push the election into the Republican and sexual conservatives' laps.

Of course, there are many factors that contribute to the elections of presidents, and we must be wary of reductive analyses that would place too much emphasis on a single factor. The Iraq War, if we are to believe the remarkable analysis of Frank Rich's book, *The Greatest Story Ever Sold*[134] (I, for one, am persuaded by its arguments), was decisive in Bush defeating his Democratic challenger and in carrying many marginal states for the Republicans. The winning of the election despite narrow margins in many places established in a new way the rhetoric of the blue (liberal) and red (conservative) states. We must think long and hard, however, on the role that the prior historical formation played in the moral panic of gay marriage in the election. And we must be respectful as well of the material and power bases of this panic, which formed part of a larger and more prevalent reaction to the direction of the country in the post–Cold War period: a sense of profound unease greatly exaggerated by the 9/11 attack on New York, which further eroded middle-class confidence in the safety and security of their homes and lives. This perceived fear in relation to "household security," as noted, for example, in stories about the suburban WASP mothers known as "security moms," must surely count as a critical force in the reelection of President Bush. These folks were opting for "household security" in the midst of a terrible and growing crisis in the long-term decline in health insurance, education, and job security in the United States. Surely it mattered to them that their intimate and sexual relationships were claimed by the president to be threatened by gay marriage as well.

Whatever the case, the White House political stratagem was successful; sexual conservatives turned out the vote for Bush—some of them, it is said, incited to do so by their own ministers on the Sunday immediately preceding the Tuesday election on November 5. The president was reelected handily, with margins in some states that suggest that "gay marriage" was the wedge issue that drove larger numbers of independents, middle- and working-class people to vote against the marriage rights for lesbians and gays. Two additional years enabled further gains by the Bush Administration—with many states around the country having now passed constitutional amendments or awaiting pending votes on amendments to ban gay marriage. Gay marriage stopped being a moral panic the moment that Bush was reelected. It is surprising how much the media attention has died down. But then, the attention to the Iraq War has increased steadily. This other issue, masked by the moral panic of gay marriage, would come back to haunt the Bush Administration.

Clearly, the recent spate of judicial decisions to reject the right of marriage or to thwart further legal contestation are signs that this relatively short but bitter period of moral panic has a long way to go before we see its end. In particular, the New York Supreme Court's decision to forbid gay marriage was a great shock to many LGBT advocates and their heterosexual allies—the logic of the opinion suggesting that the old sin and disease stereotypy of homosexuality has been helped by the recent moral panic on gay marriage. (In 2008, by executive decree, Governor Paterson of New York, however, directed all state officers to recognize the legality of gay marriages within New York.) Whatever the case, it is clear that same-sex marriage rights remain fragile. In particular, I want to draw attention to the fact that marriage denial continues to reproduce the fear of homosexuality as a dreaded form of otherness in the United States. It does this through a variety of mechanisms that result in perpetuation of what I called above the vicious cycle of discrimination and homophobia that are laced into perceptions of why gays should not be allowed to marry and why their denial of this right justifies the same conclusion.

Fast-forwarding toward the present day, the 2006 congressional elections have been viewed by many as a repudiation of the Bush Administration's policies, particularly in Iraq. For the first time in over a decade, the Democrats have returned to power in both houses of Congress. They have promised to end the Iraq War. One suspects that the great moral panic of gay marriage from the prior election was also reflected in election of a more powerful opposition to the Bush Administration. The fact that Arizona rejected a constitutional amendment banning same-sex marriage in spite of its endorsement by leading politicians, including Republican presidential candidate Senator John McCain, is a sign of some change in the air—and perhaps of hope for inclusion of the right to marry for gay men and lesbians. For a brief period, three-times married, prochoice and gay-friendly former New York Mayor Rudolph Giuliani emerged in March 2007 as the clear front-runner of the Republican Party, a blow to its moral brigade. Untarnished by the terrible disaster of the Iraq War and a hero of 9/11, Giuliani's moral views were less relevant to a nation in search of political leadership. Meanwhile, Hillary Clinton and Barak Obama emerged as the front-runners in the Democratic presidential race, and ultimately Obama received the nomination. McCain and Obama both support an end to Don't Ask, Don't Tell policies and both oppose gay marriage, although the contrast with 2004 was striking: no moral panic.

On May 15, 2008, the California Supreme Court ruled that gays and lesbians have the right to marry—a landmark decision that departs from past cases in significant ways—and initiated legal marriages in the state. The court ruled that gays and lesbians have the right to form an officially recognized family, with respect and dignity, which they argued was fundamental to equal treatment under the law as a part of inalienable civil rights. The court based some of its opinion on *Perez v. Sharp*, (1948), another landmark decision in which the California Supreme Court struck down miscegenation law as unconstitutional, noting that such statutes may have existed for long periods of time and, in that sense, were a part of cultural history, but nevertheless, that did not make them lawful or just. Furthermore the court rejected the reasoning of prior court cases, including the argument that marriage between men and women is historic, traditional, and customary, and that marriage is only for procreation. The court further applied a new standard, "strict scrutiny," which suggests that sexual orientation is a fundamental attribute of the individual, as much as race and gender, and therefore this area of equal treatment impels careful consideration in upholding rights. A challenge to the ruling is on the ballot for November, when a constitutional amendment would attempt to overturn the decision and invalidate the marriages. Both sides are in battle at this time and the outcome is uncertain. However, this is for sure: the California Supreme Court ruling has paved the way for new thinking about sexual and gender rights that will not be easy to undermine through moral panics.

Summing Up

The controversy surrounding whether gays and lesbians should have the right to marry has very old roots that ought to be telescoped since the Cold War and its image of homosexuality as thoroughly un-American and unmasculine—the antithesis of marriage and the family. The seeds of the Cold War planted the earlier panic surrounding homosexuality and the HIV pandemic and fed into a series of key court decisions on gay rights, waves of antihomosexual campaigns, and the moral panic of gays in the military during the 1990s. Republican political strategists observed the fall in public support for marriage rights soon after the *Lawrence v. Texas* decision, which led them to conclude that this was going to be a defining wedge issue against the Democrats.[135] In fact, through President

Bush's anointing of marriage as "the pillar of civilization" it may well be argued that marriage has become "the holy grail of gay politics."[136] These events took on sharper form with the reelection of President Bush, and they realized their final cultural logic in the moral sexual panic of gay marriage in the election of 2004.

The antigay marriage position may thus be seen as a cultural script or master narrative that articulates antigay rhetoric, antitolerance and diversity politics, and the stratagems of sexual conservatives and religious fundamentalists, with cultural values extremists, who have successfully deployed the use of the moral and sexual panic—as evidenced by the 2004 election, in which it appears that the antimarriage issue turned out these constituencies of voters to reelect President Bush. Frank Rich however has chided this result by asking, "Did the country really vote against *Will and Grace?*" Controversies over homosexuality, long the great stalwart of morality that helped defeat or elect politicians, reached their peak in the 2004 presidential campaign rhetoric surrounding marriage equality and the fear that marriage would be destroyed by extension of its rights to gay and lesbian couples.[137] Powerful and well-scripted rhetorical mechanisms have been put in place to massage public opinion regarding this issue on both sides of the political aisle. What caused these changes in the United States and how shall we understand their implications in arenas of policy formation?

The vignette from *USA Today* revealed several major scripts that now enable us to see the practice of a panic put into place to deny rights; the cultural scripts that emerged from this vignette express the fundamental marginalization of gay men and lesbians. In practice, these scripts are variants of ideas that have been around for decades—though they are more enlightened than before. Looking more deeply into the rhetoric of the Kansas community reveals some surprising indications about the direction of American politics. I mean that these narratives reveal how at the grassroots level sexual conservatives are gradually losing the battle against LGBT rights. The moral panic surrounding gay marriage in 2004 was part of a very significant transformation in American culture that is currently underway in the homes and schools and workplaces of this country, in which lesbian and gay rights are becoming increasingly part of the national dialogue about tolerance, diversity, and inclusion. In media in general, but especially in the province of the young—cyber space—the battle goes on, as an explosion of Web sites and blogs on the Internet support marriage rights all over the world, suggesting a movement that is gaining support and will not go away. Students, political groups, marriage and religious groups from every state have formed to normalize gay marriage in order to avert a future moral panic. In turn they are opposed by large numbers of significant Web sites, including religious and media and women's organizations, some promoting the Bible or biblical sources to fight gay marriage that demonize gay marriage.

Here I believe that history is on the side of the progressives: the closer the country moves toward the practice of secular marriage, as now embraced by many Western European countries—the policies of which recognize full marriage rights as basic to citizenship to an increasing extent—the greater is the threat to sexual conservatives' traditional worldview, steeped in fire and brimstone. Ironically, this panic is occurring at a time in which the number of homosexuals living together and number of heterosexuals living together without marriage has never been higher.[138] Indeed, one wonders if these strange social facts are not coincidental but rather politically interconnected.[139] Both trends—the visibility of gay and lesbian couples partnered and living together in arrangements previously designated "common law marriage" and heterosexual couples living together increasingly without being marriage—are grave threats to the Bible-based, fundamentalist, rhetorical images of the world as Jerry Falwell and followers know it and promote on television and in the media.[140] The attitude of Western Europeans today, that marriage is a right, a form of citizenship that everyone should have but that only some will chose as is their right, may be growing among younger Americans.

Traditionally, as noted previously, homosexuality was viewed as morally bad or pathologically diseased. This tragic history[141] gives salient context for the claims of psychological harm caused by the denial of marriage to lesbians and gay men. That a moral panic erupted around the rush of lesbian and gay marriages so dramatically staged in the early part of 2004 is not a surprise. Nor is the reaction in falling public opinion of gay marriage that greeted these events a surprise in view of the long and troubled history of homosexuality in this country. The United States is caught in a vicious cycle: stereotypes attribute abnormality and immorality to gay men and lesbians, which in turn fuels the sense that they are immoral and abnormal because they are sexually active without being married; concomitantly this reaction then further reinforces the stereotypes that deny the fitness of lesbians and gay men to marry or be parents. Sexual and religious conservatives then play on the slippery-slope analogy in the public discourse to infuse further fear and loathing that is disproportionate to either the claims or controversy at hand. As reviewed briefly,[142] there is no scientific basis to these cultural stereotypes. Indeed, current research generally supports the notion that marriage enhances mental and physical health, and the denial of marriage rights to gay men and lesbians compromises not only their well-being and the well-being of future generations, but also ultimately undermines the citizenship of these individuals.

Not surprisingly, given the changes in attitudes and values surrounding sexuality and gender, it is the different generations that broadly reflect a true cultural split on the issue of gay marriage in the United States. Average citizens have been influenced by the negative media campaigns and slippery-slope rhetoric that sexual conservatives used to create the moral panic of 2004. But there are many fence sitters.[143] Moreover, evidence from polls suggests that younger people also have developed meanings and feelings not entirely in sync with these positions, and the newest generation of younger people, in particular, seem more supportive of gay marriage—resisting the moral panic.[144] As previously noted, polls suggest that young people typically accept the right of marriage for gays and lesbians and do not see the moral, political, and economic threat that their parents and grandparents do in this regard. The gender, health, and reproductive changes transforming the lives of these young people are also at odds with the traditional cultural common sense appeals of neoconservatives to marriage as a sacred institution. Ultimately, I suspect that the baby boomers are going to decide the fate of this issue in coming elections.[145] Goldstein and Kenney[146] argue that 90 percent of all boomers will eventually marry. Higher numbers of women will marry and continue to work, in part linking marriage with security. *Newsweek* magazine has recently suggested that marriage "is becoming disproportionately reserved for better-educated, middle and upper class elites."[147] The class differences are significant, but more important is the fact that as they age and contemplate the challenges of household security and the maintenance of the quality of life, straight couples will identify with gay and lesbian peers struggling to uphold their own love and commitments.

The marriage rights movement has also evoked controversy and conflict within LGBT communities, which is also part of the story of this climatic period of change that was traced from the Reagan presidency through the 2004 election. Because of the patriarchal nature of marriage as an institution, feminist and gay and lesbian critics of marriage were placed in a very difficult position in the moral panic of 2004. While wanting to support the movement, they also feared that a focus on marriage would re-essential-ize gender, reinvent heteronormativity, and of course amount to implicit en-dorsement of deplorable legislation, such as DOMA and the Marriage Act of 2004. Their quandary was understandable. Some sympathetic critics, such as Duggan, have registered opposition to the LGBT movement focus on mar-riage rights: "Some gay groups are producing rhetoric that insults and mar-ginalizes unmarried people, whilst promoting marriage in much the same terms as the welfare reformers use to stigmatize single parent household, di-vorce and 'out of wedlock' births."[148] This will undermine justice and diver-sity, she argues. It is not "an impossibly utopian leap" to expand and change the nature of civil marriage.[149] Michael Warner has argued similarly.[150] How-ever, as Adam Goodheart wrote in the New York Times, "Gays and lesbians may have felt that the Massachusetts decision was premature, yet I suspect that there are very few who do not inwardly believe that in being forbidden marriage they have been denied a basic human right."[151]

I opened this chapter by noting that Foucault himself was famously opposed to marriage conformity—making his remark about homosex-ual marriage enigmatic and puzzling. We must remember that Foucault was writing during the time of the political change from advanced wel-fare capitalism at its peak in the 1960s to the beginning of the AIDS epi-demic and the rise of neoconservatism in the 1980s. As David Halperin notes, Foucault was interested in liberation of the self and the effective-ness of mobilizing people to resist conformity and provoke change.[152] He is sympathetic to critics, especially feminists,[153] and queer critics, such as Warner,[154] who complain about the amnesia of gays who worked hard for twenty years to resist "hierarchies of abjection," and the indignities of het-eronormativity, only to embrace marriage as a regulatory system. How-ever, Halperin also suggests that some opponents of marriage rights in the LGBT community may not have given due credit to the role that the marriage movement has played in galvanizing new forms of support and volunteers to aid in support of LGBT rights through this effort.

There is, of course, a great contradiction in the moral panic of 2004 surrounding gay marriage as advocated through the fear-based campaigns of sexual conservatives: if marriage is such a great support for individu-als and society, then why deny its benefits to all members of society, in-cluding LGBT people? The silence around this contradiction is gaping, although not surprising. All through the discussions of the passage of DOMA in 1996, and the Marriage Promotion Act of 2004, and the huge rhetoric in reaction to the court decisions,[155] the question of why not to

support gay marriage remains suspended in animation. There is no logical answer to this question in the rhetoric of the antihomosexual rights
and antigay marriage movement, of course, because their aim is not to
educate but to promote panic and confusion, thus shutting off debate. We
cannot have democracy in that way;[156] down that road lays fascism. Moral
panics that have such profound effects often court the end games and
tragedy of fascism, but in the great fear and moral panic of gay marriage
in 2004, it didn't go that far. An election was enough to satisfy the fear
mongers. They must fear that next time the pillar of civilization formed
by heteronormative marriage will be architecturally restructured to allow
gay marriage. However that plays itself out—and it shall, in good time—
we must hope that the American people on the way will not give into the
temptations to scapegoat the rights of gay men and lesbians again.

NOTES

1. The author wishes to thank Dr. Niels Teunis, Dr. Robert Kertzner, and Dr.
Judith Stacey for conversations that helped to frame this chapter and its analysis
of the research literature.

2. Frank Rich, *The Greatest Story Ever Sold* (New York: Penguin, 2006).

3. Thomas Frank, *What's the Matter with Kansas?* (New York: Metropolitan
Books, 2004).

4. Lisa Duggan, "Holy Matrimony!" *The Nation*, March (2004), 15.

5. Frank Rich, "On 'Moral Values': It's Blue in a Landslide," *New York Times*,
November 14, 2004: 8.

6. David Halperin, *Saint Foucault* (New York: Oxford, 1995).

7. Hazel Rowley, *Tête-à-Tête* (New York: HarperCollins, 2005).

8. Tanya Erzen, *Straight to Jesus: Sexual and Christian Conversions in the Ex-
Gay Movement* (Berkeley: University of California Press, 2006), 200–205. Rich,
Greatest Story Ever Sold.

9. G. M. Herek, "Beyond 'Homophobia': Thinking about Sexual Stigma and
Prejudice in the Twenty-First Century," *Sexuality Research and Social Policy* 1 (2004).

10. Frank, *What's the Matter with Kansas*, 9.

11. Glenda M. Russell, *Voted Out: The Psychological Consequences of Anti-Gay
Politics* (New York: NYU Press, 2000).

12. Michael Warner, "Normal and Normaller: Beyond Gay Marriage," *Gay Lesbian Quarterly* 5 (1999).

13. Amanda Paulson, "Debate on Gay Unions Splits along Generations," *Christian Science Monitor*, July (2003).

14. Warner, "Normal and Normaller," 123.

15. Gilbert Herdt and Robert Kertzner, "I Do, But I Can't: The Impact of Marriage Denial on the Mental Health and Sexual Citizenship of Lesbians and Gay Men in the United States," *Sexuality Research and Social Policy: Journal of the NSRC*, 3 (2006).

16. George Chauncey, "The Postwar Sex Crime Panic," in *True Stories from the American Past* (New York: McGraw-Hill, 1993). Lisa Duggan, *The Twilight of Equality* (Boston: Beacon, 2003). Cynthia Enloe, *The Morning After: Sexual Politics at the End of the Cold War* (Berkeley: University of California Press, 1993).

17. François Girard, "Global Implications of U.S. Domestic and International Policies on Sexuality," Working Paper No. 1, International Working Group on Sexuality and Social Policy, Sociomedical Sciences Department, Mailman School of Public Health, Columbia University, New York, 2004.

18. John D. D'Emilio, *Sexual Politics, Sexual Communities* (Chicago: University of Chicago Press, 1981).

19. Rich, *Greatest Story Ever Sold.*

20. Robert J. Corber, *Homosexuality in Cold War America* (Durham: Duke University Press, 1997); Didi Herman, *The Antigay Agenda: Orthodox Vision and the Christian Right* (Chicago: University of Chicago Press, 1997). Gayle Rubin, "Thinking Sex: Notes for a Radical Theory of the Politics of Sexuality," in *Pleasure and Danger: Exploring Female Sexuality*. C. S. Vance, ed. (New York: Routledge and Kegan Paul, 1984). Simon Watney, *Policing Desire: Pornography, AIDS and the Media* (Minnepolis: University of Minnesota Press, 1987).

21. James H. Jones, *Alfred Kinsey: A Public/Private Life* (New York: Norton, 1996), 628ff.

22. Herman, *The Antigay Agenda,* 29.

23. Marjorie Garber, *Vested Interests: Cross-Dressing and Cultural Anxiety* (New York: Routledge, 1992).

24. Paul Robinson, *The Modernization of Sex* (New York: Harper and Row, 1976).

25. Rich, *Greatest Story Ever Sold.*

26. Herman, *The Antigay Agenda.*

27. Lisa Duggan and Nan Hunter, *Sex Wars: Sexual Dissent and Political Culture* (New York: Routledge, 1995), 160.

28. Girard, *Global Implications.*

29. Frank, *What's the Matter with Kansas.*

30. Janice Irvine, *Talk about Sex* (Berkeley: University of California Press, 2002).

31. Duggan, *The Twilight of Equality.*

32. John Gagnon, *An Interpretation of Desire* (Chicago: University of Chicago Press, 2004).

33. Ed Laumann et al., *The Social Organization of Sexuality: Sexual Practices in the United States* (Chicago: University of Chicago Press, 1994).

34. Erzen, *Straight to Jesus.*

35. Duggan, *The Twilight of Equality.*

36. Steven Epstein, "Gay and Lesbian Movements in the United States: Dilemmas of Identity, Diversity and Political Strategy," in *The Global Emergence of Gay and Lesbian Politics*. B. D. Adam et al., eds. (Philadelphia: Temple University Press, 1999). Steven Epstein, "The New Attack on Sexuality Research: Moral Panic and the Politics of Knowledge Production," *Sexuality Research and Social Policy* 3 (2006).

37. DiMauro and Joffe, chapter 2.

38. Rubin, "Thinking Sex."

39. DiMauro and Joffe, chapter 2.

40. Frank, *What's the Matter with Kansas*.

41. David L. Kirp and Ronald Bayer, eds., *AIDS in the Industrialized Democracies* (New Brunswick, NJ: Rutgers University Press, 1992); Eric Rofes, *Dry Bones Breathe: Gay Men Creating Post-AIDS Identities and Cultures* (New York: Harrington Press, 1998). Rubin, "Thinking Sex."

42. Epstein, "Gay and Lesbian Movements."

43. Paul Farmer, *AIDS and Accusation* (Berkeley: University of California Press, 1992).

44. Randy Shilts, *And the Band Played On* (New York: St Martin's, 1987).

45. Michael Brown, *Replacing Citizenship: AIDS Activism and Radical Democracy* (New York: Guilford Press, 1997).

46. Rofes, *Dry Bones Breathe*.

47. Irvine, *Talk about Sex*.

48. Duggan, *The Twilight of Equality*.

49. The neoconservative Thatcher government is examined in detail on HIV and moral panics by Watney, *Policing Desire*.

50. Girard, *Global Implications*.

51. See also Cohen, chapter 3.

52. Farmer, *AIDS and Accusation*. John Gagnon, "Disease and Desire," *Daedalus* 118 (1989). Gilbert Herdt, "Representations of Homosexuality in Traditional Societies: An Essay on Cultural Ontology and Historical Comparison," *Journal of the History of Sexuality* 1 (1991).

53. Gagnon, *An Interpretation of Desire*.

54. Irvine, *Talk about Sex*.

55. Duggan, *The Twilight of Equality*.

56. Frank, *What's the Matter with Kansas*.

57. John D. D'Emilio and Estelle B. Freedman, *Intimate Matters: A History of Sexuality in America* (New York: Harper and Row, 1988).

58. I am referring to the symbolism of the city of San Francisco pioneering LGBT rights that dates from that period; the 2004 gay marriages performed at city hall harkened back to it.

59. Eve Sedgwick, "How to Bring Your Kids Up Gay," *Social Text* 29 (1991).

60. Clyde Wilcox, *God's Warriors* (Baltimore: Johns Hopkins University Press, 1992).

61. D'Emilio and Freedman, *Intimate Matters*, 363–64.

62. Rich, *Greatest Story Ever Sold*.

63. Enloe, *The Morning After*, 90.

64. Enloe, *The Morning After*, 91.

65. Enloe, *The Morning After*, 93.

66. Aaron Belkin and Geoffrey Bateman, *Don't Ask, Don't Tell* (Boulder: Lynne Rienner, 2003). Gregory Herek et al., eds. *Out in Force: Sexual Orientation and the Military* (Chicago: University of Chicago Press, 1996).

67. In 2006 the Vatican released a teaching that concerned "men with homosexual tendencies and the priesthood" (dated November 4, but issued only on November 29); it states that the church "cannot admit to the seminary or to holy orders those who practice homosexuality, present deep-seated homosexual tendencies, or support the so-called 'gay culture.'"

68. Boy Scouts of America, "News Release, "BSA Sustained by U.S. Supreme Court," June 28, 2000, Irving, Texas.

69. Boy Scouts of America Oath (1911).

70. William Donahue, "Culture Wars against the Boy Scouts," *Society* 31 (1994), 64.

71. Donahue, "Culture Wars," 64.

72. Alan Hunt, "Great Masturbation Panic and the Discourses of Moral Regulation in Nineteenth- and Early Twentieth-Century Britain," *Journal of the History of Sexuality* 8 (1998), 612.

73. Nancy Cott, *Public Vows: A History of Marriage and the Nation* (Cambridge: Harvard University Press, 2000), 216–17.

74. Geoffrey Bateman and Sameera Dalvi, "Multinational Military Units and Homosexual Personnel," Report commissioned by the Center for the Study of Sexual Minorities in the Military, University of California, Santa Barbara, 2004.

75. This is Rosalind Pertchesky's term and is cited in Carole Joffe, "Abortion as Moral Panic," *American Sexuality Magazine*, 2006.

76. Daniel Pinello, *America's Struggle for Same-Sex Marriage* (New York: Cambridge University Press, 2006), 28.

77. Led by Lambda Legal, ACLU, the Human Rights Campaign and NGLTF, see Evan Wolfson, *Why Marriage Matters* (New York: Simon & Schuster, 2004). Pinello, *America's Struggle*.

78. Jocelyn Elders, "Preface." In *Harmful to Minors*. Judith Levine, ed. (Minneapolis: University of Minnesota Press, 2002).

79. Susan Harding, *The Book of Jerry Falwell* (Princeton: Princeton University Press, 2000). Wilcox, *God's Warriors*.

80. Anna Smith, "The Politicization of Marriage in Contemporary American Public Policy: The Defense of Marriage Act and the Personal Responsibility Act," *Citizenship Studies* 5 (2001).

81. Cott, *Public Vows*.

82. H. Horowitz, *Rereading Sex: Battles over Sexual Knowledge and Suppression in Nineteenth-Century America* (New York: Knopf, 2002).

83. For more in the late 19th and early 20th centuries, see D'Emilio and Freedman, *Intimate Matters.*

84. She wrote, "Marriage is the antithesis of love, and will necessarily destroy it." Gust Yep, Karen Lovaas, and John Elia, "A Critical Appraisal of Assimilationist and Radical Ideologies Underlying Same-Sex Marriage in LGBT Communities in the United States," *Journal of Homosexuality* 45 (2003), 54.

85. Jyl Josephson, "Citizenship, Same-Sex Marriage, and Feminist Critiques of Marriage," *Perspectives on Politics* 3(2005), 275.

86. Horowitz, *Rereading Sex.*

87. Yep et al., "A Critical Appraisal."

88. Rubin, "Thinking Sex." Warner, "Normal and Normaller."

89. Erzen, *Straight to Jesus.* Wilcox, *God's Warriors.*

90. Yep et al., "A Critical Appraisal," 54.

91. Linda Waite and Maggie Gallagher, *The Case for Marriage: Why Married People Are Happier, Healthier, and Better Off Financially* (New York: Doubleday, 2000).

92. Herdt and Kertzner, "I Do, but I Can't."

93. See Catherine E. Ross, John Mirowsky, and Karen Goldsteen, "The Impact of Family on Health: The Decade in Review," *Journal of Marriage and the Family* 52 (1990). Debra Umberson and Kristi Williams, "Family Status and Mental Health," in *Handbook of the Sociology of Mental Health.* Carol Aneshensel and Jo Phelan, eds. (New York: Klewer Academic/Plenum, 1999). And Waite and Gallagher, *The Case for Marriage.*

94. Additionally, a large debate has centered on the value of using science or mental health data in defense of the marriage rights of sexual minorities, rather than appealing directly to human and sexual rights as the defense of their citizenship, see Celia Kitzinger and Sue Wilkinson, "Social Advocacy for Equal Marriage: The Politics of 'Rights' and the Psychology of 'Mental Health,'" *Analyses of Social Issues and Public Policy,* 4 (2004).

95. Edward Laumann et al., *The Sexual Organization of the City* (Chicago: University of Chicago Press, 2004).

96. M. V. Lee Badgett, "Will Providing Marriage Rights to Same-Sex Couples Undermine Heterosexual Marriage? Evidence From Scandinavia and the Netherlands," *Journal of Sexuality Research and Social Policy* 1 (2004).

97. Duggan, *The Twilight of Equality.*

98. Warner, "Normal and Normaller."

99. Michel Foucault, *The History of Sexuality,* Hurley, trans. (New York: Viking, 1980); Jeffrey Weeks, *Sexuality and Its Discontents* (London: Routledge and Kegan Paul, 1985).

100. Ronald Bayer, *Homosexuality and American Psychiatry* (Princeton: Princeton University Press, 1987).

101. "Doctor Who Helped Gay-Rights Movement Dies," ObituaryPlanetOut. com, December 22, 2003.

102. Herek, "Beyond 'Homophobia.'"

103. Paulson, "Debate on Gay Unions Splits along Generations," *Christian Science Monitor*, July 7, 2003.

104. Irvine, *Talk about Sex*. Rich, *Greatest Story Ever Sold*.

105. Herek, "Beyond 'Homophobia.'" Erzen, *Straight to Jesus*.

106. Erzen, *Straight to Jesus*, 200.

107. Doug Ireland, "Republicans Relaunch the Antigay Culture Wars," *The Nation*, October (2003), 22.

108. Cathy Cohen, *The Boundaries of Blackness: AIDS and the Breakdown of Black Politics* (Chicago: University of Chicago Press, 1998), 285.

109. Girard, *Global Implications*.

110. Frank, *What's the Matter with Kansas*.

111. *USA Today*/CNN/Gallup poll in January 2004 reported that 41 percent of Americans favored civil unions, while 53 percent opposed gay marriage. One in four people had no opinion.

112. "Quiet Division in the Heartland," *USA Today*, February 24, 2004, Life Section D: 1–2D.

113. Frank, *What's the Matter with Kansas*, 47–50ff.

114. Frank, *What's the Matter with Kansas*, 100.

115. Naomi Quinn, "'Commitment' in American Marriage: A Cultural Analysis." *American Ethnologist* 9 (1982).

116. Quinn, "'Commitment' in American Marriage," 793.

117. David Schneider, *American Kinship: A Cultural Analysis* (Chicago: University of Chicago Press, 1968).

118. Quinn, "'Commitment' in American Marriage," 795.

119. Quinn, "'Commitment' in American Marriage," 795.

120. Robert N. Bellah et al., *Habits of the Heart: Individualism and Commitment in American Life* (Berkeley: University of California Press, 1985).

121. Rich, *Greatest Story Ever Sold*, 68.

122. Cott, *Public Vows*. Pinello, *America's Struggle*.

123. Reviewed in Sonia Katyal, "Exporting Identity." *Yale Journal of Law and Feminism* 14 (2002).

124. Ireland, "Republicans Relaunch," 18.

125. Ireland, "Republicans Relaunch," 22.

126. Reviewed in Wolfson, *Why Marriage Matters*.

127. See Irvine, chapter 7.

128. Kitzinger and Wilkinson, "Social Advocacy."

129. C. Geertz, *Local Knowledge* (New York: Basic, 1984).

130. Duggan, "Holy Matrimony!" 15.

131. Rich, *Greatest Story Ever Sold.*

132. Rich, "On 'Moral Values.'"

133. Frank, *What's the Matter with Kansas.*

134. Rich, *Greatest Story Ever Sold.*

135. Ireland, "Republicans Relaunch."

136. Josephson, "Citizenship."

137. Rich, "On 'Moral Values.'"

138. Laumann et al., *The Sexual Organization.*

139. It appears that the social value of marriage declined in Western Europe as a function of advanced welfare capitalism, which provided a safety net of resources for parenting that circumvented marriage (Badgett 2004). In the United States, though, the number of people and especially younger people living together in civil marriage arrangements has increased sufficiently to ask whether the value of marriage has not also declined for elite Americans, which would then engender the kind of cultural anger from red states that Thomas Frank (2004) has mentioned as typifying the backlash against arrogance of latte liberals.

140. Harding, *The Book of Jerry Falwell.*

141. Kenneth Lewes, *The Psychoanalytic Theory of Male Homosexuality* (New York: Simon and Schuster, 1988). Vernon Rosario, ed. *Science and Homosexualities* (New York: Routledge, 1996).

142. For additional reviews of the literature revealing the nature of these stereotypes and the harm inflicted on LGBT communities, see Herdt and Kertzner, "I Do, but I Can't" and Judith Barker et al., "Social Support in the Lives of Gay Men and Lesbians at Mid-Life and Beyond," *Sexuality Research and Social Policy* 3 (2006).

143. Herek, "Beyond 'Homophobia.'"

144. Pew Center poll data reveal this tendency; see Pew Research Center, "Less Opposition to Gay Marriage, Adoption and Military Service," March 22, 2006.

145. Herdt and Kertzner, "I Do, but I Can't."

146. Joshua R. Goldstein and Catherine T. Kenney, "Marriage Delayed or Marriage Foregone? New Cohort Forecasts of First Marriage for U.S. Women," *American Sociological Review* 66 (2001): 506–19.

147. "Rethinking the Marriage Crunch," *Newsweek*, June 2006, 45.

148. Duggan, "Holy Matrimony!" 18.

149. Duggan, "Holy Matrimony!" 18.

150. Warner, "Normal and Normaller."

151. Adam Goodheart, "Small-Town Gay America," *New York Times*, November (2003).

152. David Halperin, *How To Do the History of Homosexuality* (Chicago: University of Chicago Press, 2004).

153. Josephson, "Citizenship."

154. Warner, "Normal and Normaller," 123.

155. *Lawrence v. Texas* (2003); Massachusetts Supreme Court decisions in 2003 and 2004.

156. Deborah Barrington, "The Public Square and Citizen Queer," *Polity* 31 (1998): 107–31.

REFERENCES

Badgett, M. V. Lee. 2004. "Will Providing Marriage Rights to Same-Sex Couples Undermine Heterosexual Marriage? Evidence from Scandinavia and the Netherlands." *Journal of Sexuality Research and Social Policy* 1: 1–10.

Barrington, Deborah. 1998. "The Public Square and Citizen Queer: Toward a New Political Geography." *Polity* 31: 107–31.

Bateman, Geoffrey and Sameera Dalvi. 2004. "Multinational Military Units and Homosexual Personnel." Report commissioned by the Center for the Study of Sexual Minorities in the Military, University of California, Santa Barbara.

Barker, Judith, Gilbert Herdt, and Brian DeVries. 2006. "Social Support in the Lives of Gay Men and Lesbians at Mid-Life and Beyond." *Sexuality Research and Social Policy* 3(2).

Bayer, Ronald. 1987. *Homosexuality and American Psychiatry.* Princeton: Princeton University Press.

Bech, Henning. 1997. *When Men Meet.* Chicago: University of Chicago Press.

Belkin, Aaron and Geoffrey Bateman. 2003. *Don't Ask, Don't Tell.* Boulder: Lynne Rienner.

Bell, David and Jon Binnie. 2000. *Sexual Citizen: Queer Politics and Beyond.* Malden, MA: Polity.

Bellah, Robert N., Richard Madsen, William M. Sullivan, Ann Swidler, and Steven M. Tipton. 1985. *Habits of the Heart: Individualism and Commitment in American Life.* Berkeley: University of California Press.

Boy Scouts of America. 2000. "News Release: BSA Sustained by U.S. Supreme Court." June 28. Irving, Texas.

Brown, Michael P. 1997. *Replacing Citizenship: AIDS Activism and Radical Democracy.* New York: Guilford Press.

Center for Disease Control. 2005. "HIV Prevalence, Unrecognized Infection, and HIV Testing among Men Who Have Sex with Men– Five U.S. Cities, June 2004–April 2005." *Morbidity and Mortality Weekly Report.* June 24. 54(24): 597–601.

Chauncey, George. 1993. "The Postwar Sex Crime Panic." In *True Stories from the American Past.* Edited by William Graeber. New York: McGraw-Hill.

Cohen, Cathy. 1998. *The Boundaries of Blackness: AIDS and the Breakdown of Black Politics.* Chicago: University of Chicago Press.

Corber, Robert J. 1997. *Homosexuality in Cold War America*. Durham: Duke University Press.

Cott, Nancy F. 2000. *Public Vows: A History of Marriage and the Nation*. Cambridge: Harvard University Press.

D'Emilio, D. John. 1981. *Sexual Politics, Sexual Communities*. Chicago: University of Chicago Press.

D'Emilio, John D. and Estelle B. Freedman. 1988. *Intimate Matters: A History of Sexuality in America*. New York: Harper and Row.

"Doctor Who Helped Gay-Rights Movement Dies." 2003. ObituaryPlanetOut. com. December 22.

Donahue, William A. 1994. "Culture Wars against the Boy Scouts." *Society* 31(4): 59–68.

Duggan, Lisa. 2004. "Holy Matrimony!" *The Nation*, March 15: 14–19.

———. 2003. *The Twilight of Equality*. Boston: Beacon.

Duggan, Lisa and Nan D. Hunter. 1995. *Sex Wars: Sexual Dissent and Political Culture*. New York: Routledge.

Duggan, Lisa and Richard Kim. 2005. "Beyond Gay Marriage." *The Nation*, July 25(1): 24–27.

Elders, Jocelyn M. 2002. "Preface." In *Harmful to Minors*. Edited by Judith Levine. Minneapolis: University Of Minnesota Press.

Enloe, Cynthia. 1993. *The Morning After: Sexual Politics at the End of the Cold War*. Berkeley: University of California Press.

Epstein, Steven. 2006. "The New Attack on Sexuality Research: Morality and the Politics of Knowledge Production." *Sexuality Research and Social Policy: Journal of the NSRC* 3:1–12.

———. 1999. "Gay and Lesbian Movements in the United States: Dilemmas of Identity, Diversity and Political Strategy. In *The Global Emergence of Gay and Lesbian Politics*. Edited by B. D. Adam et al. Philadelphia: Temple University Press.

Erzen, Tanya. 2006. *Straight to Jesus: Sexual and Christian Conversions in the Ex-Gay Movement*. Berkeley: University of California Press.

Farmer, Paul. 1992. *AIDS and Accusation*. Berkeley: University of California Press.

Foucault, Michel. 1980. *The History of Sexuality*. Translated by R. Hurley. New York: Viking.

Frank, Thomas. 2004. *What's the Matter with Kansas?* New York: Metropolitan Books.

Gagnon, John H. 2004. *An Interpretation of Desire*. Chicago: University of Chicago Press.

———. 1989. "Disease and Desire." *Daedalus* 118: 47–77.

Garber, Marjorie. 1992. *Vested Interests: Cross-Dressing and Cultural Anxiety*. New York: Routledge.

Geertz, Clifford. 1984. *Local Knowledge*. New York: Basic.

Giddens, Anthony. 1992. *The Transformation of Intimacy: Sexuality, Love & Eroticism in Modern Societies*. Stanford: Stanford University Press.

Girard, François. 2004. "Global Implications of U.S. Domestic and International Policies on Sexuality." Working Paper, No. 1, International Working Group on Sexuality and Social Policy, Sociomedical Sciences Department, Mailman School of Public Health. Columbia University, New York.

Goldstein, Joshua and Catherine Kenney. 2001. "Marriage Delayed or Foregone? New Cohort Forecasts of First Marriage for U.S. Women." *American Sociological Review* 66: 506–19.

Goodheart, Adam. 2003. "Small-Town Gay America." *New York Times*, November 23: 11.

Harding, Susan F. 2000. *The Book of Jerry Falwell*. Princeton: Princeton University Press.

Halperin, David. 2004. *How to Do the History of Homosexuality*. Chicago: University of Chicago Press.

———. 1995. *Saint Foucault*. New York: Oxford.

Herdt, Gilbert. 1991. "Representations of Homosexuality in Traditional Societies: An Essay on Cultural Ontology and Historical Comparison." *Journal of the History of Sexuality* 1(1): 481–504.

Herdt, Gilbert and Robert Kertzner. 2006. "I Do, but I Can't: Marriage Denial and Mental Health for Gay Men and Lesbians in the United States." *Sexuality Research and Social Policy* 3(1): 33–49.

Herek, Gregory M. 2004. "Beyond 'Homophobia': Thinking about Sexual Stigma and Prejudice in the Twenty-first Century." *Sexuality Research and Social Policy* 1(2): 6–24.

Herek, Gregory, Jared Jobe, and Ralph Carney, eds. (1996) *Out in Force: Sexual Orientation and the Military*. Chicago: University of Chicago Press.

Herman, Didi. 1997. *The Antigay Agenda: Orthodox Vision and the Christian Right*. Chicago: University of Chicago Press.

Horowitz, Helen L. 2002. *Rereading Sex: Battles over Sexual Knowledge and Suppression in Nineteenth-Century America*. New York: Knopf.

Hunt, Alan. 1998. "Great Masturbation Panic and the Discourses of Moral Regulation in Nineteenth- and Early Twentieth-Century Britain." *Journal of the History of Sexuality* 8(4): 575–616.

Ireland, Doug. 2003. "Republicans Relaunch the Antigay Culture Wars." *The Nation*, October 20: 18–23.

Irvine, Janice. 2002. *Talk about Sex*. Berkeley: University of California Press.

Joffe, Carole. 2006. "Abortion as Moral Panic." *American Sexuality Magazine*.

Jones, James H. 1997. *Alfred C. Kinsey: A Public/Private Life*. New York: Norton.

Josephson, Jyl. 2005. "Citizenship, Same-Sex Marriage, and Feminist Critiques of Marriage." *Perspectives on Politics*. 3(2): 269–84.

Katyal, Sonia. 2002. "Exporting Identity." *Yale Journal of Law and Feminism* 14:97–176.

Kinsey, Alfred, Wardell B. Pomeroy, Clyde Martin, and Paul Gerhard. 1953. *Sexual Behavior in the Human Female*. Philadelphia: W. B. Saunders.

Kinsey, Alfred, Wardell B. Pomeroy, and Clyde E. Martin. 1948. *Sexual Behaviors and the Human Male*. Philadelphia: W. B. Saunders.

Kirp, David L. and Ronald Bayer, eds. 1990. *AIDS in the Industrialized Democracies: Passions, Politics and Policies*. Rutgers, NJ: Rutgers University Press.

Kitzinger, Celia and Sue Wilkinson. 2004. "Social Advocacy for Equal Marriage: The Politics of 'Rights' and the Psychology of 'Mental Health.'" *Analyses of Social Issues and Public Policy* 4: 173–94.

Laumann, Edward O., et al. 2004. *The Sexual Organization of the City*. Chicago: University of Chicago Press.

Laumann, Edward O., John H. Gagnon, Robert T. Michael, and Stuart Michaels. 1994. *The Social Organization of Sexuality: Sexual Practices in the United States*. Chicago: University of Chicago Press.

Lawrence v. Texas. 2003. 539 U.S. 588.

Lawrence, J. G. and T. Garner. 2003. Petitioners v. Texas. U.S. Supreme Court Decision. June 26.

Lewes, Kenneth. 1988. *The Psychoanalytic Theory of Male Homosexuality*. New York: Simon and Schuster.

Levine, Martin, Peter M. Nardi, and John H. Gagnon, eds. 1997. *In Changing Times: Gay Men and Lesbians Encounter HIV/AIDS*. Chicago: University of Chicago Press.

Massachusetts Supreme Court. 2004. Opinions of Justices to State Senate. February 6.

McGerr, Michael. 2003. *A Fierce Discontent: The Rise and Fall of the Progressive Movement in America, 1870–1920*. New York: Free Press.

Paulson, Amanda. 2003. "Debate on Gay Unions Splits Along Generations." *Christian Science Monitor*, July 7.

Pew Research Center. 2006. "Less Opposition to Gay Marriage, Adoption and Military Service." March 22.

Pinello, Daniel R. 2006. *America's Struggle for Same-Sex Marriage*. New York: Cambridge University Press.

"Quiet Division in the Heartland." 2004. *USA Today*. February 24. Life Section. D: 1–2.

Quinn, Naomi. 1982. "'Commitment' in American Marriage: A Cultural Analysis." *American Ethnologist* 9(4): 775–98.

"Rethinking the Marriage Crunch." 2006. *Newsweek*. June 5.

Rich, Frank. 2006. *The Greatest Story Ever Sold*. New York: Penguin.

———. 2004. "On 'Moral Values,' It's Blue in a Landslide." *New York Times*. November 14: Arts & Leisure, 1, 8.

Robinson, Paul. 1976. *The Modernization of Sex*. New York: Harper & Row.

Rofes, Eric. 1998. *Dry Bones Breathe: Gay Men Creating Post-AIDS Identities and Cultures*. New York: Harrington.

Rosario, Vernon, ed. 1996. *Science and Homosexualities*. New York: Routledge.

Ross, Catherine E., John Mirowsky, and Karen Goldsteen. 1990. "The Impact of Family on Health: The Decade in Review." *Journal of Marriage and the Family* 52: 1059–78.

Rowley, Hazel. 2005. *Tête-à-Tête*. New York: HarperCollins.

Rubin, Gayle. 1984. "Thinking Sex: Notes for a Radical Theory of the Politics of Sexuality." In *Pleasure and Danger: Exploring Female Sexuality*. Edited by C. S. Vance. New York: Routledge and Kegan Paul.

Russell, Glenda M. 2000. *Voted Out: The Psychological Consequences of Anti-Gay Politics*. New York: NYU Press.

Schneider, David. 1968. *American Kinship: A Cultural Analysis*. Chicago: University of Chicago Press.

Sedgwick, Eve. 1991. *Epistemology of the Closet*. Berkeley: University of California Press.

———. 1991. "How To Bring Your Kids Up Gay." *Social Text* 29: 18–27.

Shilts, Randy. 1987. *And The Band Played On*. New York: St Martin's.

Smith, Anna M. 2001. "The Politicization of Marriage in Contemporary American Public Policy: The Defense of Marriage Act and the Personal Responsibility Act." *Citizenship Studies* 5(3): 303–20.

Umberson, Debra and Kristi Williams. 1999. "Family Status and Mental Health." In *Handbook of the Sociology of Mental Health*. Edited by Carol Aneshensel and Jo Phelan. New York: Klewer Academic/Plenum.

Vaid, Urvashi. 1995. *Virtual Equality*. New York: Anchor Books.

Waite, Linda J. and Maggie Gallagher. 2000. *The Case for Marriage: Why Married People Are Happier, Healthier, and Better Off Financially*. New York: Doubleday.

Warner, Michael. 1999. "Normal and Normaller: Beyond Gay Marriage." *Gay Lesbian Quarterly* 5(2): 119–72.

Watney, Simon. 1987. *Policing Desire: Pornography, AIDS and the Media*. Minneapolis: University of Minnesota Press.

Weeks, Jeffrey. 1985. *Sexuality and Its Discontents*. London: Routledge and Kegan Paul.

Wilcox, Clyde. 1992. *God's Warriors*. Baltimore: Johns Hopkins University Press.

Wolfson, Evan. 2004. *Why Marriage Matters*. New York: Simon & Schuster.

Yep, Gust A., Karen E. Lovaas, and John P. Elia. 2003. "A Critical Appraisal of Assimilationist and Radical Ideologies Underlying Same-Sex Marriage in LGBT Communities in the United States." *Journal of Homosexuality* 45(1): 45–64.

6

Postcolonial Amnesia

Sexual Moral Panics, Memory, and Imperial Power[1]

Saskia Eleonora Wieringa

Introduction

Sexual moral panics were an important motor for the establishment of imperial power in the late 18th, the 19th, and the early 20th centuries. Likewise, such panics have been used to establish or uphold dictatorial postcolonial regimes, such as "new order" Indonesia or present-day Zimbabwe. Postcolonial states have drawn on the memories of these colonial and postcolonial panics, as they have been etched into the collective unconsciousness of their subjects. In the process, the memories of certain sexual practices, cultures, or norms, specifically related to women's sexual agency and same-sex practices got lost, leading to a postcolonial amnesia on these topics. This amnesia in its turn could fuel present-day moral panics that are built on the manipulation of the fear of women's agency and same-sex practices. The relationship then between postcolonial amnesia and moral sexual panics is complex.

This chapter explores how present-day postcolonial amnesia around issues of sexuality can be traced back to certain colonial and postcolonial sexual moral panics. In some cases the erasure of the memory of women's sexual agency and same-sex practices also went more gradually. Sexuality, moral panics, and amnesia alike will be explored as deeply political constructions.

The imagination of the postcolonial states discussed here is partly drawn on their sexualized histories. Imagination being based on selectively memorizing, amnesia of certain sexual practices or customs plays an important role. The continuation of certain tropes in the examples of sexual panics and amnesia from mainly Indonesia and Southern Africa on which I base this discussion demonstrates their political motivations, though the core of that impulse has shifted. The focus of this chapter is on women's sexual autonomy and same-sex practices, which, I argue, are intimately linked. I will discuss how the motivation of such panics shifted from imposing a racialized and class-based colonial hegemony to the establishment of a nationalist and, again, class-based rule. The continuing process of women's subordination, through the "othering" of nonpatriarchal sexual practices is a constant factor in this process.

I suggest that the form some contemporary panics takes is fomented by two overlapping, seemingly paradoxical processes. On the one hand this concerns a postcolonial amnesia of particular sexual practices, politics, and relations, specifically those related to women's sexual autonomy and same-sex practices in general. This amnesia has critical consequences, not only in relation to the hate crimes committed on individuals who live lives that challenge or destabilize the unstable borders of the heteronormative gender regimes to which various postcolonial leaders engineer and cling, but also on women and men that live such normalized lives (their "normality" being dictated by the supposed abjection of the "others"). On the other hand, we witness striking continuities in the sexual politics of postcolonial rules compared to their colonial predecessors. So far, research has mainly focused on the racialization of society that sexualized colonial practices produced.[2] In postcolonial societies these moral sexual strategies are no longer used to mark racial boundaries but to demarcate the powers of the ruling national elites. Thus, class stratification (though no longer based on race), women's subordination, and heteronormativity are the lines of convergence. The differences between colonial and postcolonial regimes in the area of sexual politics are more of degree than of substance: the tropes are similar. If "tradition" was seen (and constructed as) the site of "moral decay" in colonial days, now "'tradition" is invested with nostalgia and reconfigured as a site of heteronormative "normalcy," while the West is seen as the site of perverse desires. Paradoxically, that same West, such as my country, the Netherlands, prides itself on its adherence to freedom, human rights, and tolerance, and its own misogynous, homophobic, and racist past is conveniently ignored in the interest of defending "Fortress Europe."

In the process of inventing itself as a viable nation-state patriarchal, heterosexual reproductive relations are (re)inscribed as normative, while women's autonomous sexual practices (whether heterosexual or same-sex) and same-sex practices in general are (re)constructed as marginal. Political and religious leaders join in mobilizing emotions to naturalize this fiction of the "always-already" patriarchal, heterosexual nation. I will discuss here some of these persuasive fictions, such as the demonization of same-sex practices in Southern Africa. Another example is Indonesian women's *kodrat* (moral code of conduct) that invokes women to be sexually passive and heterosexual, following a long process of the denial of women's sexual agency, which culminated in the campaign of sexual slander in 1965 and 1996.[3]

In the process, I will underline how the sexual is manipulated to underlie the (ever shifting) social contracts postcolonial leaders impose on their subjects. In doing so I will stress that the past should not be essentialized or romanticized. Here I am only interested in demonstrating that the sexual is not only a moral but also a political battlefield in which colonial and postcolonial policies are played out along remarkably similar lines and that the postcolonial amnesia on earlier forms of women's sexual agency, including women's same-sex relations is a major strategy to subjugate women.

I will not address all waves of sexual hysteria that swept over Indonesia and Southern Africa, but I will highlight some particularly striking examples with which I have become familiar through my research and discuss some underlying mechanisms. In the last part of this chapter I will describe some efforts that I have witnessed to overcome this amnesia. Both in Indonesia and in Southern Africa I have been involved in projects to dig up historical evidence of women's autonomous sexual practices. Women's groups are using this material to strengthen their own self-esteem and to remind their governments and the wider societies of practices and relations they so far conveniently ignored or demonized. Hopefully this subversive reading of history can serve as way of opening debates to counter the process of naturalizing a heteronormativity that is so oppressive to those who are "othered," that is, don't conform to this model, and who thus fall outside the narrowly defined boundaries of a hegemonic femininity and masculinity. The focus of discussion throughout this chapter is on the effects the processes described have on female-bodied persons. In many ways, the effects on men are different; they have been the subject of several other studies, such as those by Ronald Hyam and Mrinalini Sinha.[4]

Amnesia and Moral or Sexual Panics

A central concept in this discussion is amnesia. I use it here not just in its dictionary meaning as "loss of memory."[5] I extend its use to incorporate connotations of political convenience. The amnesia I am discussing here refers to a process of selectively memorizing certain aspects of a past while ignoring such aspects as are politically inconvenient to those who control the mechanisms to create a hegemonic vision of society. In this chapter, the focus of discussion is on the construction of patriarchal heteronormativity based on women's (sexual) subservience and the ignoring of aspects of women's autonomy and gender diversity. Amnesia and the construction of moral, sexual panics are major means to establish hegemonic thinking in any society.

Not every moral panic is also a sexual panic, that is, a moral panic around issues of sexuality. In a moral panic emotions are mobilized in order to stigmatize certain behaviors, either of individuals or of groups and frame them as posing a threat to social stability. The mass hysteria created by General Suharto in 1965 and 1966 is a major example of a sexual panic.[6] The media, whether the print media, radio, TV, or Internet, usually play an important role in mobilizing mass sentiments. In 1965 and 1966, in Indonesia the murder squads were trained and armed by the military, but the army press and the radio provided the fuel to unleash one of the largest genocides in modern history. The monument that was constructed on the site where the generals were murdered was an important tool for the campaign of slander and mystification of the "new order," until the fall of Suharto in 1998; it invokes women to be meek and sexually passive. The media, however, don't act on their own; there are usually other powers behind them. Such moral panics are generally not spontaneous, though they may be triggered by a particular incident (in Indonesia the abduction and murder of the country's top brass by rebellious army units, more details below). Generally they are built up gradually as fear is being mobilized. The creation of the myth of the "black peril" in British colonial Africa, also discussed below, is one such example.

The usual pattern of a panic is that a threat is constructed, feelings of fear are generated, and a particular group is demonized (communist women, black men). The exorcism of the scapegoats that are thus constructed is then felt as a process of ritual cleansing after which it is expected stability, harmony, or just simply the hegemony of a particular group will be established. Sexuality is one of the most intoxicating elements with which to whip up social hysteria, and when it is mixed with religion and/or race, a particularly potent explosive mix is created. In Indonesia, a myth of the castration of the abducted generals was created, reinforced with stories of sexual orgies and a tinge of lesbianism in which communists were said to be engaged.[7] So the means used in this process include distortion, lies, or various forms of exaggeration.[8] When a sexual moral panic is in full force, rational explanations are no longer heard as the floodgates are opened for ostracism, hate crimes, stigmatization, and violence.

After such a violent episode, when a new hegemony is established, either that of an imperial order or that of a postcolonial dictatorial regime, a political amnesia may set in, in which certain elements of the past may be conveniently ignored. I will discuss some examples of this process and focus on the continuity of the tropes used in the interest of normalizing heterosexuality as a basis of political power. Postcolonial amnesia on issues of sexuality may also come about more gradually and not spurred on by the shockwaves of an acute sexual moral panic, for instance, via the imposition of bourgeois morality, a process I will touch on only lightly. Though pointing out cultural and historical differences where they are relevant, I will not dwell on them here. My interest in this chapter is more on transcultural continuity, discussing the ways in which a colonial and postcolonial amnesia of aspects of women's sexual autonomy and particularly same-sex relations is deployed as a major means of establishing racial, class-based, heteronormative boundaries. This deployment may involve sexual moral panics.

Colonial and Postcolonial "Othering" as an Embodied Process

Before I embark on a discussion of sexual panics in relation to establishing postcolonial patriarchal heteronormativity, I want to give some examples that demonstrate the sexualized and embodied nature of the process of establishing colonial control. Ever since Jeffrey Weeks and Michel Foucault wrote their landmark studies on the historicity of Western sexuality, a wealth of scholarly publications appeared on the relation between imperialism and sexual domination.[9] Most of these scholars note the marking of racial boundaries as a deeply sexual process through which both misogyny and homophobia were strengthened and imperial social and political control established.

Whipping up some form of sexual hysteria has been one of the most powerful ways that colonial administrators and, in their wake, some post-colonial leaders, have found to maintain a bloody, militarized form of domination. In Africa, two examples immediately spring to mind. The myth of the "black peril" was constructed in the British colonies; an aggressive, potent African male sexuality was seen to create grave dangers for white women.[10] This paved the way for the British domination of areas such as (former) Rhodesia. In German southwest Africa (now Namibia), sexual hysteria took a slightly different form. Black housemaids were portrayed as possessing particular poisonous powers by which white male settlers might be sexually seduced and whole white settler families might be poisoned.[11] These myths came to inform the genocide of the Herero and Nama populations in the Namibian wars of 1904 to 1907. They justified the atrocities committed by German troops at the home front. A version of the "black peril" myth was created when wild stories began to appear in the German media about white women who were allegedly raped when taken prisoner by the Hereros.[12] Yet in reality the Hereros treated their prisoners much better than the Germans did.

Of a slightly different nature but similarly directed to institutionalize colonial control was the treatment of same-sex relations in Africa. On the one hand, there were those writers who invented a "pure" innocent continent in which those "vices" were absent. This was perceived as investing the whites with the moral duty to rule these "childlike natives." On the other hand, there were those who pointed out the depravity of the black population by dwelling on the same-sex practices they documented. This again was seen as "proof" of the way blacks were close to nature and needed the culturalizing strong hand of their colonial masters.[13] The latter discussions were mostly held in circles of missionaries and colonial administrators. In the process the meanings and forms of the various ways same-sex relations were lived got lost. In the case of women for instance women's same-sex relations could take the form of institutionalized bond friendships that might include erotic or sexual aspects and that existed beside heterosexual marriages. Or mighty and rich women could formally engage in marriages with other women, by paying the customary bride price and performing the usual rites. In some cases, these marriages were "dependent" on heterosexual relations, for instance, the ghost marriages widows might contract to ensure male heirs for their dead husbands. In other cases this involved autonomous women marriages, where rich or powerful women married other women for motivations of their own (offspring, establishment of an independent compound). In some cases, traditional healers, who were possessed by male ancestor spirits took ancestral wives. These women marriages have been recorded for over forty societies of the more than 200 that have been described in Africa. Women marriages thus can be seen to be fully culturally institutionalized in various parts of Africa and they were in many cases religiously sanctioned.[14]

Colonial rule meant the denigration of these practices, as well as the denial of the sexual components of their relationship. New marriage and inheritance regulations replaced customary rules, denying the women partners and their children the rights they used to enjoy. In many countries, women marriages and bond friendships have almost disappeared or they have become invisible. To such an extent that present-day postcolonial leaders such as President Mugabe of Zimbabwe, former President Nujoma of Namibia and former President Moi of Kenya claim that "homosexuality is un-African" and an import from the West.[15] The antigay and lesbian campaigns of these presidents can be seen as present day moral sexual panics.

Otherization via the imposition of racial/sexual boundaries took different forms in Indonesia, though it had some similar effects. Before the Java war (1825 to 1830) that marked the imposition of colonial rule over the whole Indonesian archipelago, women were important mediators between the races; Asian or Eurasian women who were married to Dutch merchants and soldiers provided their husbands with useful political and material connections. Asian or Eurasian widows, who inherited all of their husbands' wealth, were sought-after marriage partners.[16] After 1830 however, the relative autonomy and importance of "indigenous" partners of European men changed.[17] Dutch women were imported in large numbers and interracial sexual contacts were limited. Dutch men might take "indigenous" housekeepers, *nyai*, with whom they might father children, before they officially married a European wife. The status of these *nyai* was much lower than that of their earlier officially married counterparts. Fear of embittered *nyai*, they and their children deserted by their Dutch partners, permeated Dutch colonial society and is powerfully expressed in many novels of the period.[18]

In this process, the domestic realm became separated from the public realm of trade, politics, and the military, much as in bourgeois Dutch society of the time. Dutch women were considered responsible for preserving the unpolluted whiteness of the European community.[19] This is in stark contrast to the power and visibility of not only Eurasian women in early colonial society but also of the women in the Javanese courts who, as Peter Carey and Vincent Houben documented, held important commercial, military, and political positions.[20] The concomitant subordination of women's sexual autonomy is also played out in the arena of the Javanese courts themselves. Florida researched into the "sex wars in the 19th-century Javanese courts in which Javanese wives were strongly advised to be meek and obedient sexual partners to their Javanese husbands.[21] Nancy Florida suggests that this is related to the failed quest of the Javanese ruler Pakubuwana IX. His beloved, Princess Sekar Kedhaton refused to surrender to him and instead rose to great spiritual and intellectual heights.

Particularly during the so-called ethical period around the turn of the 19th and into the 20th century, education into wifehood became a central concern.[22] The ethical policy was introduced to mitigate the detrimental effects of Dutch colonial greed on the Indonesian population but strengthened Dutch bourgeois values on gender and racial superiority. The creation of subordinate, Dutch-styled housewives did much to wipe out or deflect the memories of powerful Indonesian women. One example is the transformation of the brilliant, rebellious regent's daughter Kartini, one of the most important precursors of the Indonesian women's movement, into an example of what the paternal colonial power might do: educate Javanese girls. Suharto's new order regime went even further, recasting her as a model housewife.[23] Many more examples can be cited.[24]

This brief exposition of the different ways sexual colonial politics worked on these two continents demonstrates that though the actual historical processes are complex and differ considerably, their effects show some marked similarities. In both cases we see a creation and/or strengthening of sexual/racial boundaries in order to support the fiction of the white heterosexual male as the legitimate hero of imperial rule. Misogyny and the breakdown of women's sexual autonomy were not only the means by which these campaigns were accompanied but also produced its results. In Africa, one of the central topics was the denigration and invisibilization of women's same-sex relations and gender transgression in general. Although this also played a role in Indonesia, the weakening of women's heterosexual power seems to be more visible.[25] In Indonesia, male transgender and same-sex behavior has always been more visible than that of female-bodied persons. The sexual panic and resulting wave of arrests of homosexual men in 1938 (possibly triggered by growing political anxiety leading up to World War II) mainly targeted Western men.

Homosexuality was seen as common for Indonesian men in many parts of the archipelago.[26] Women's same-sex relations were only targeted around 1965.[27] Just as in Southern African countries, apart from South Africa itself, present-day gay and lesbian groups have a hard time in Indonesia to convince law makers, politicians, and the general public that same-sex relations are not a novelty imported from the West, despite the visibility of particularly transgendered men.

Contemporary Panics

On October 29, 2005, three schoolgirls were beheaded by masked men with machetes in the religiously-divided town of Poso, Central Sulawesi, Indonesia. Their heads were later delivered to a local church with a letter indicating that the heads of 100 more girls were needed to avenge the misdeeds of the "Christian homos".[28] This incident followed in the wake of religious clashes that some years earlier cost thousands of lives in this area alone (at the time there were other clashes in the Malukus, for instance). This example indicates the fault lines in Indonesian society along which deeper laying power struggles are fought out: religion, gender, and homosexuality.[29] In this section I will discuss some contemporary sexual panics, namely on homosexuality, women's dress codes, the debates on polygyny and pornography in Indonesia, and the fear of sexually depraved women underlying the mass murders in 1965 and 1966 in Indonesia. My focus here is on demonstrating the linkages between postcolonial power struggles and these panics and the convenient clouds of amnesia related to (pre)colonial forms of women's sexual agency and same-sex practices.

The association of Christianity with homosexuality in the Poso murders is not only an indication of perverse and murderous fantasies but is also ahistorical. As is the case in Africa, colonial administrators and missionaries are rather the ones who introduced homophobia into these countries (I have discussed that elsewhere).[30] Similar examples can be cited for Asia as well.[31] The confrontations between West and East didn't have to be in the form of colonial impositions. Countries that didn't fall under direct colonial rule also adopted elements of the sexual ideologies that they noted underlay the perceived superiority of the "modern" Western powers.[32] Timon Screech provides an interesting example for Japan, which had a tradition of *nanshoku*, male same-sex relations, that were often depicted in the popular *shunga*, pornographic woodblock printings.

There were also some, much more rare, *shunga* that showed female same-sex relations.[33] In the course of the 19th century, *nanshoku* declined and was gradually being replaced by the heteronormative model along which present day Japanese society is structured. The ways of the West were diligently studied, and as one observer noted:

> In their countries nanshoku is ferociously prohibited. They say it is counter to human ethics. There was someone found guilty of it then who was burned at the stake, and the youth was drowned in the sea. Apparently this is still done. My source is this year's scribe, Rikarudo.[34]

This observation, as Screech noted, related to the encounter of the author with a Mr. Ricard, who visited Japan in the late 18th century. The same source, according to Screech, later wrote that "nanshoku prohibitions extended to the Western colonies too."[35]

If it was clear to an astute 18th-century Japanese observer that the West was curtailing expressions of same-sex relations where they found them, what kind of relations did they actually encounter? Here I will present some illustrations of the forms same-sex practices and relations have taken from both Africa and Indonesia. In spite of President Mugabe's protestations that homosexuality is un-African, one of the oldest pictures of male same-sex behavior is found close to his capital city of Harare. It concerns a Stone Age homoerotic cave painting, dating from at least two thousand years ago.[36] Other sources, such as Kurt Falk, indicate that same-sex practices were not uncommon.[37] Provided by Parcival Kirby from research in 1941, an example that I think is particularly interesting is the description of the use of a secret musical instrument among the Ovambo of Northern Namibia. Kirby discovered that this instrument, the *ekola*, was used by the shamans of certain villages to call the "sodomites" of the village together and that the instrument was played by the sodomites themselves. If the medicine doctors were known to use it, the existence of "sodomites" must have been a not uncommon phenomenon in the area.[38] The *ekola* only became a secret instrument due to the colonial authorities.[39]

Murray and Roscoe brought together a collection of articles on many more aspects of same-sex relations in Africa, including female marriages.[40] In spite of colonial obstacles, the custom of female traditional healers taking "ancestral wives" is still very much alive in South Africa, as we discovered doing fieldwork on contemporary women's same-sex practices in Southern Africa.[41] In most other African countries the custom is on the decline, and present-day women engaged in relations with other women are denounced; in Tanzania, for instance, they are described as "satanic."

In modern Indonesia the picture is more complex, as the acceptance of male-bodied *banci* (cross-dressing men who engage in sex with other men) has persisted over time.[42] This happened in spite of occasional outbursts such as the one in 1938, described above. The history of women's same-sex relations, however, has mostly been lost, and middle-class self-identified lesbian women as well as lower-class women who are engaged in femme/butch relations live either in fear or in secrecy.[43] Yet Indonesia does have a tradition of same-sex relations and gender inversion, also of female-bodied persons, as has been amply documented by scholars such as Evelyn Blackwood and Sharyn Graham.[44]

An interesting example of how in earlier times male-bodied and female-bodied cross-dressing and transgender practices were more common and called by the same name, *banci* (which is mostly reserved for males now), is found in a painting on the roof of the Kertha Gosa (the palace court building of the Balinese kingdom of Klungkung). The painting contains the Balinese version of Dante's Hell. The Mahabharata warrior-hero, Bhima, is sent by his siblings on a quest to rescue their parents from Hell, into which they have been thrown after violating a curse.[45] While there, he encounters numerous sinners who are severely punished for their misdeeds, such as violating the laws of the village, committing adultery or abortion, stealing rice, or remaining childless. He also comes across a pair of *banci*. On his request for an explanation as to who these "enigmatic-looking" people were and what crime they had committed, he received the answer that they had not committed a sin: "It's a kind of imperfection. And that's why a *banci*, however good his [or her] life has been still has to spend some time in Hell before he can be admitted to the highest spheres."[46] It is telling that the guides in the Kertha Gosa hall do not admit to knowing this story, while the book that contains it is sold on the premises.

The association of same-sex practices and gender reversal with Christianity or the West in general, as is common parlance now among conservative and fundamentalist Islamic circles, is clearly a gross distortion of history. Political motivations, particularly centering on the recent move toward more regional autonomy, as I will discuss below, add to a climate of growing homophobia—a homohobia that was introduced by colonial leaders.

Dress codes, particularly those of Muslim women, are the subject of a contemporary panic in the West. Paradoxically, if Muslim women are seen nowadays to cover too much of their bodies, colonialists were concerned with women who covered themselves with too little cloth. Colonial literature is rife with references to the amorality or childlike purity of the so-called primitive, nude peoples. In Indonesia, for instance, the patriarchal colonial hand was extended to clothe the bare buttocks and/ or breasts of these "pagans." The outrage at the presumed "depravity" of particularly native women did not prevent the colonial voyeuristic gaze to dwell with satisfaction on the breasts of young women of various Indonesian groups and to photograph young women with attractive breasts. These pictures are interesting because as early as 2005, the present Indonesian president, Susilo Bambang Yudhoyono (or SBY, as he is commonly called), hit the press with alarmed remarks about the dangers to Indonesian morality of copying the "Western" custom of showing bare navels on TV. Many Indonesians reacted with ridicule. Some remembered that in Madura, for instance, women's traditional dress was similar to the Indian sari, so a large part of the belly was exposed. This type of dress is hardly used any more.[47]

In Indonesia, the debate on women's belly buttons may have been subdued, but a new controversy has arisen that will have a longer-standing impact. In 2004, a draft law on pornography and pornoaction was prepared. In it, "porno acts," defined, for instance, as masturbation, are penalized, and women's clothing must be regulated in a trade off between local politicians and the dress-making industry. The introduction of this law is related to the controversy around the spectacular success of Inul Daratista, an East Javanese singer and dancer, who designed the so-called drilling dance that is considered shockingly erotic to her more conservative audience. The controversy was fuelled by her much older musical rival, the male *dangdut* singer, Rhoma Irama.[48] In the ensuing sexual moral panic it was ignored that Indonesia has a tradition of female singers who perform in erotic ways.

This outburst of postcolonial decency, as encoded in this new draft law, is linked to the growth of a conservative Muslim movement, spearheaded by the influential Ulama Council. In the process, not only particular sexual regimes are naturalized and others denaturalized (such as same-sex relations) but also the present ways of decency, sexual relations, and even dress codes are retroactively fossilized. In Indonesia, for instance, the Muslim head cover (*jilbab*) for women is presented by various Muslim groups as having always belonged to a (invented) pure Muslim past that is now suddenly being threatened by loose, decadent, Western styles of dressing. However, studying precolonial pictures of women in the Minangkabau, one of the most staunchly Islamic regions in Indonesia, one is struck by the fact that women generally wore loose scarves draped around their heads, exposing large parts of their hair. Until recently this was also the case in many other parts of Indonesia, such as East Java. In Bali and some other islands, dress codes and sexual morality have always been different from that of Islamized Java.

Today, Indonesian Muslim women are wearing the *jilbab* in large numbers. When I did my first fieldwork in Java at the end of the 1970s, I hardly saw women wearing the full headscarf; now the streets are full of headscarves and, in Aceh, for instance, they are obligatory. This movement set in during the reign of President Suharto. Islamization occurred during this new order period both as an expression of resistance to his dictatorial, secular, regime and, to counter this movement, stimulated by Muslim intellectuals around the president himself.

The anti-pornography bill has been the center of a major controversy. Artists, such as painters and performers of traditional forms of puppet theatre and dance, as well as feminist lawyers and women and human rights activists have fiercely protested the attack on freedom of expression and the curtailing of women's autonomy they fear will be the result of this law. At the moment of writing this chapter (the end of 2006), the debates are still raging on.

The contemporary political debate in Indonesia in which the anti-pornography and pornoaction laws must be seen is that of a movement toward greater regional autonomy. President Habibie, who, in 1998 succeeded President Suharto, paved the way for this shift in policy. Several regions, eager to free themselves from the military, political, and economic yoke of Jakarta, declared themselves autonomous in the following years. Noerdin and others who studied the gender effects of this process for ten different regions, note that the major consequences are an increased emphasis on women wearing a *jilbab* and the public separation of women and men.[49] In some regions women are not allowed to go out at night without a male relative accompanying them. If they do, they are classified as prostitutes and are liable to be arrested. In general, women's morality is coming under attack, as is common in other projects of nationalist identity formation. Another serious concern in Indonesia is that women's traditional rights are eroded, for instance, their access to forest products, so their economic dependency on men is strengthened.

Thus, paradoxically women are both seen to be the keepers of religion and tradition, but at the same time their traditional rights in both these systems are eroded. This is a similar to what happened under colonial rule, when the growing political colonial control was accompanied by increasing separation of the sexes as part of a racist policy of separating the colonial powers from the subjugated populations. In the present case in Indonesia, a regional identity must be rediscovered. It is found to lie in women's behavior, particularly their sexual conduct and dress. This revivalism of traditional customs vis à vis the unitary national state is built on misogyny, increasing heteronormativity, and an amnesia regarding the power women used to have as guardians of *adat*, traditional custom.[50]

A concomitant effect is the increasingly patriarchal interpretation of Islam. Feminist readings, such as those by Fatima Mernissi, Leila Ahmed, and Riffat Hassan, are known in Indonesia but they are ignored by the male leaders of the major Islamic parties and of the Ulama Council.[51] In general, conservative Islam is growing more confident. Ratna Batara Munti gives a striking example of this increasing influence, the case of the polygamy (read polygyny) award by businessman Puspowardoyo.[52] This was a direct slap in the face of the women's movement, a major part of which has been fighting against polygyny since the days of Kartini. Though women protested, the event took place and generated enormous publicity as well as wide support among conservative circles. The award cannot be disconnected to the growing controversy between Muslims and Christians in the country and the rising tide of resistance against what is seen as the West's attempt to humiliate Islam, both in Palestine and Iraq.

However, the women's movement had already been dealt a devastating blow a few decades earlier in late 1965 to mid-1966 in the "creeping coup" of General Suharto.[53] The campaign of sexual slander that brought him to power is one of the most wide-ranging moral panics and waves of sexual hysteria in history. After a putsch of leftist colonels on September 30 and October 1, 1965, in which the six senior generals of the country were murdered at a nationalist training site for socialist girls, General Suharto was the only surviving general of his generation. Yet, he was not promoted to chief-of-staff by President Sukarno. Enraged, General Suharto oversaw the creation of a mass media campaign in which the girls were said to have seduced (with the help of the erotic "Flower Dance"), castrated, and murdered the generals. "Proof" of these allegations appeared in the army press, as indicated above, based on "testimonies" elicited after heavy torture and a film shot in prison.[54] Following this campaign, the army trained and armed youth groups, mainly of Ansor, the youth wing of the Muslim mass organization Nahdlatul Ulema (NU), and of the

Hindu nationalist right in Bali. The gangs murdered between 1 million (according to Amnesty International) and 3 million (according to colonel Sarwo Edhie, the organizer of the campaign) socialist people. No one was ever brought to trial for this genocide, and the mass graves remain unopened.[55]

This campaign not only terrorized the Indonesian population into obedience, but it also discredited the women's mass organization Gerwani (Gerakan Wanita Indonesia, an Indonesian women's organization) and, in general, associated women's political agency with sexual depravity, including lesbianism. Indonesian women still have to fight that image. Since the campaign, the only "good" woman is someone who obeys her husband, attends to his sexual needs, looks after his children, and cooks his food. Gone are the days when women were honored for helping build the nation and shape its future. Now, in the reformation era (after 1998 and the fall of Suharto), women's organizations are still fighting that ideology, and one of the most difficult topics for them to address is sexual empowerment.

Fabricating Identities

Above I sketched two overlapping processes that work toward fabricating gendered ethnic and national identities. First is the convenient amnesia of identities and sexual practices by postcolonial leaders in an effort to construct the nation as an "always-already" patriarchal and heterosexual entity. And second is the continuity of certain colonial policies and practices that denied women's power and gender and sexual diversity. In this process, critical modifications appeared. First of all, the composition of the ruling elite changed. It was no longer white colonial men who dominated the scene, so race became a less useful a vehicle of differentiation. Ethnicity might remain, though. Both in Africa and in Indonesia, certain ethnicities managed to get the upper hand. Instead, wealth and power became the critical axes around which gender and sexual politics were played out. The fictional heroes in the political theatre changed color but not tactics. During the protracted and bloody shift of power, they might even use the same discourse and metaphors–usually that of a patriarchal, omnipotent father who knows best for his subalterns.[56] These parental metaphors are used to this day. In Indonesia, for instance, President Suharto used to call himself the "Father of Development." His communist adversaries had deployed the same terminology before him. The party saw itself as the masculine head of the socialist family, while the women's organization was shoved into the role of the "mother," albeit a militant one.[57] The Dutch had introduced education into wifehood as part of their "Ethical Policy;" the new order Indonesian elite only slightly modified the model and propagated it through the women's organizations they set up and/or controlled.[58] The only disruptions in this transition were the war of independence (from 1945 to 1949), in which many women joined the guerrilla and the above-mentioned militant mothers of Gerwani. The potential power of the women liberation fighters was quickly deflected into a reference to their motherly capacities as giving birth to the nation. It took a campaign of sexual slander and a genocide to wipe out the memory of Gerwani's subversive women.

If race and, with it, Christianity, has lost some of its defining power in this discourse, Islam has gained importance. It is one of the major mechanisms of identity formation in the process of regional autonomy in Indonesia, as discussed above. In Southern Africa, with its large Christian populations, Christianity keeps playing a political role.

Thus beside sexuality, for many people, religion is one of the defining aspects of one's identity—the privileged, "central" part of one's being. Religions have increasingly become major political factors, and in the misogynous and homophobic interpretation favored by most religious and political leaders, lead to widespread suffering. Both in my research in Jakarta and in the oral history project in Southern Africa the same-sex identified women interviewed often told about their pain that their lives were not accepted by the religions to which they adhered. To them, their spiritual and sexual inspirations were similarly located in their souls. It hurt them deeply to find that influential clerics and in their wake the population at large declared these two crucial aspects of their being as incompatible. In the Southern Africa oral history project, only a few women managed to reconcile these aspects of themselves.[59]

What other mechanisms fuel the production of these national/regional fictions or interact with them? As in any production of fantasy the choice of protagonist is vital. For instance, out of the possible female role models in Indonesia, which present day heroines are selected and how are they presented? Kartini's rebelliousness was tamed during Suharto's New Order regime and that hasn't changed much since then, although the women's movement has gotten stronger. Other possible heroines are either ignored, such as Sekar Kedhaton, sidelined or, as in Kartini's case, presented in their simpering, dependent forms. The warrior wife of Mahabharata, hero prince Arjuna, princess Srikandhi, for instance, a role model for Gerwani, is at present seldom portrayed in her autonomous form but usually in association with her male consort. In a move to reserve spiritual, ascetic power to men, the spiritual sides of another popular heroine of the Mahabharata cycle, princess Sumbadra, Srikandhi's cowife, are downplayed.[60] She has become increasingly popular, particular during the Suharto era, portrayed as the ideal wife/mother figure, devout, and meek.

Policies and Practices To Address Postcolonial Amnesia

How to make a dent into the continuing invisibilization of nonhegemonic sexualities, which is enacted through both ignoring their historical presence and emphasizing repressive policies and practices started by the colonial regime? I will give two examples from my own research and policy-oriented work that are intended to do that. They are both oral history projects, one in Jakarta and the other one in Southern Africa. The first project was carried out with the help of staff from the Koalisi Perempuan Indonesia (KPI), the Indonesian Women's Coalition. The second was initiated and implemented together with Ruth Morgan from the Johannesburg-based Gay and Lesbian Archives (GALA). In the first project I held the interviews myself, in the second project Ruth Morgan and I trained nine researchers who all held interviews in their own (seven) countries and communities.

Both projects were designed to get to know the daily lives of female-bodied persons in same-sex relations, to establish their presence politically ("we also want to share in the building of a new democratic Indonesia," as one of my Jakartan interviewees said) and to give their lives a historical, cultural, and religious context. The background of both projects was that the women live lives of secrecy, which, though it may afford some of them (particularly in Indonesia and South Africa) some freedoms, ultimately also circumscribes those freedoms.

I maintain that historical research is relevant; the memories of past nonheteronormative practices and relations can remind ourselves that the present is just the most recent form of history and that its particular way of regulating sexuality and in general surveying social and political norms serves the interests of particular groups. It definitely demonstrates that same-sex practices and relations are not a recent or un-African or un-Asian phenomenon and may thus help to prevent the panics described here. Historical research should not serve to construct a romanticized past that should be emulated.

But finding traces of women's same-sex relations, however differently lived from present forms, can also be stimulating to the participants in such a research project themselves; it can give them the kind of affirmation they are looking for in vain in their present context. In Jakarta, for instance, I went with a group of butch-femme lesbians to the national museum to show them statues of proud Durga, of sexually assertive goddesses such as Parvati, and of the Ardhanary figure, half-male-half-female, which connotes a superior spiritual consciousness and (for instance in the figure of Ken Dhedhes) an awe-inspiring sexuality.[61] They all liked the Durga; the femmes were happy with Parvati, as they felt the free way in which the extremely feminine goddess expressed her sexual desire vindicated their own sexual initiatives (frowned upon in a society that imposes modesty on women), and the butches were thrilled with Ardhanary ("that's me!" one exclaimed). In October 2005, this group formed a new lesbian organization called Ardhanary, which will cooperate with the KPI to fight for lesbian rights. Similarly, the researchers in the GALA project were delighted to learn of the various historical forms women's same-sex relations in some African countries. They related to these "foremothers" and were stimulated to find out more. After this research project they have set up the Coalition of African Lesbians (CAL). One of the planned activities of CAL is another research project that will incorporate more countries than the first project did.

Conclusion

Postcolonial leaders suffer from amnesia on the existence of particular forms of nonheteronormative practices and relations. This amnesia is partly based on moral panics created by the earlier colonial regimes. To a certain extent, these moral panics are also created and maintained by these leaders themselves. As I have noted, glaring examples are General Suharto and President Mugabe. Researchers, activists, and policymakers should collaborate to expose these moral panics for what they are—instruments in the service of particular power constellations—and to fight for gender, racial, and sexual justice and equality.

Historical research into various forms of nonhegemonic sexualities can widen the rights discourse. It may incorporate people with a broad range of identities and with different desires and practices. It should also dispel the myth that homosexuality is un-African or un-Asian. It might even disrupt Westerners' arrogance as the keepers of a tradition of rights. The Netherlands, for instance, prides itself on its adherence to human right and paints Islam as a barbaric force incapable of such tolerance. Its leaders suffer from acute amnesia as well, in this case on the country's colonial past with its racial arrogance, its intolerance, and its oppression. If Holland is tolerant now, it once stifled traditional women's rights in its own colony and exported its virulent homophobia to other continents.

NOTES

1. This chapter was originally presented as the opening address of the IASSCS 5th International Conference, "Sexual Rights and Moral Panics," San Francisco State University, June 21–24, 2005.

2. See Mrinalini Sinha, *Colonial Masculinity: The "Manly Englishman" and the "Effeminate Bengali in the Late Nineteenth Century* (Manchester: Manchester University Press, 1995) and Ann Stoler, *Race and the Education of Desire: Foucault's History of Sexuality and the Colonial Order of Things* (Durham: Duke University Press, 1995).

3. Saskia E. Wieringa, *Sexual Politics in Indonesia* (Houndmills: Palgrave Macmillan, 2000).

4. Ronald Hyam, *Empire and Sexuality: The British Experience* (Manchester: Manchester University Press, 1991); and Mrinalini Sinha, *Colonial Masculinity.*

5. See, for instance, the *Shorter Oxford English Dictionary.*

6. Saskia E. Wieringa, *Sexual Politics,* and Saskia E. Wieringa, "The Birth of the New Order State in Indonesia," *Journal of Women's History* 15:1 (Spring 2003): 70–92.

7. Saskia E. Wieringa, "Communism and Women's Same-Sex Practices in Post-Suharto Indonesia," *Culture, Health and Sexuality* 2:4 (2000): 441–57.

8. In the case of Indonesia, a film was shot of naked girls huddled together in prison. This was then portrayed as "proof" the girls had raped and castrated generals approximately one month earlier.

9. Antoinette Burton, *Burden of History: British Feminists, Indian Women and Imperial Culture, 1865–1915* (Chapel Hill: University of North Carolina Press, 1994); Michel Foucault, *History of Sexuality, Volume 1: An Introduction* (New York: Pantheon 1978); Ronald Hyam, *Empire and Sexuality*; Sinha, *Colonial Masculinity*; Ann Stoler, *Race and the Education of Desire*; Jeffrey Weeks, *Sex, Politics, and Society: The Regulation of Sexuality since 1800* (London: Longman, 1981).

10. Gareth Cornwell, "George Webb Hardy's *The Black Peril* and the Social

Meaning of "Black Peril" in Early Twentieth-Century South Africa," *Journal of Southern African Studies* 22:3 (1996): 441–53; Diana Jeater, *Marriage, Perversion and Power: The Construction of Moral Discourse in Southern Rhodesia 894–1930* (Oxford: Clarendon Press, 1993); John Pape, "Black and White: The Perils of Sex in Colonial Zimbabwe," *Journal of Southern African Studies* 16:4 (1990): 699–720.

11. Krista O'Donnell, "Poisonous Women: Sexual Danger, Illicit Violence and Domestic Work in German Southern Africa, 1904–1915," *Journal of Women's History* 11:3 (1999): 31–54.

12. Johannes Lukas de Vries, *Mission and Colonialism in Namibia* (Johannesburg: Raven, 1978).

13. Rudi Bleys, *The Geography of Desire: Male-to-Male Sexual Behavior outside the West and the Ethnographic Imagination, 1750–1918* (New York: NYU Press 1995); Ferdinand Karsch-Haack, *Das Gleichgeschlechtliche Leben der Naturvölker* (München: Reinhardt, 1911; reprint New York: Arno, 1975).

14. Elisabeth Tietmeyer, *Frauen Heiraten Frauen: Studien zur Gynaegamie in Afrika*/Women Marrying Women: Studies on Gynaegamie in Africa (Höhenschäftlarn: Renner 1985); Saskia E. Wieringa, "Women Marriages and Other Same-Sex Practices: Historical Reflections on African Women's Same-Sex Relations," in *Tommy Boys, Lesbian Men and Ancestral Wives*, Ruth Morgan and Saskia E. Wieringa, eds. (Johannesburg: Jacana, 2005).

15. Margrete Aarmo, "How Homosexuality Became "Un-African": The Case of Zimbabwe," in *Female Desires: Same-Sex Relations and Transgender Practices across Cultures*, Evelyn Blackwood and Saskia Wieringa, eds. (New York: Columbia University Press 1999); Chris Dunton and Mai Palmberg, "Human Rights and Homosexuality in Southern Africa," *Current African Issues* 19 (1996): 48: "We haven't fought for an independent Namibia that gives criminals, gays and lesbians the right to do bad things," Nujoma fulminated in 2004 (NRC04/04). Earlier, President Mugabe had famously said that gays and lesbians were "worse than dogs and pigs" (see Aarmo, "How Homosexuality Became 'Un-African"). It comes as no surprise that the International Gay and Lesbian Human Rights Commission (IGLHRC) 2003 report, "More Than a Name: State-Sponsored Homophobia and Its Consequences in Southern Africa," lists many incidences of police harassment and community violence against gays and lesbians.

16. Jean Gelman Taylor, "Women as Mediators in VOC Batavia," in *Women and Mediation in Indonesia*, Sita van Bemmelen, Madelon Djajadiningrat-Nieuwenhuis, Elsbeth Locher-Scholten and Elly- Touwen-Bouwsma, eds. (Leiden: KITLV, 1992).

17. Though England and Holland share a similar history of colonization, and "apartheid" is a Dutch term, the pre-1825 and even post-1830 Dutch East Indies society was much more tolerant of hybridization than the British colonial empire. Eurasian women and their offspring could rise to important positions

in Batavia (Taylor, "Women as Mediators"; Gouda, *Dutch Culture Overseas*). In British India, Eurasians were practically barred from all social spaces. William Dalrymple, in his novel *White Mughals,* brilliantly evokes the effects of this sudden shift in British policy from a trade-based relation, in which Indian traditions were respected, to imperial control, in which British arrogance insisted on racial purity. The early British so-called White Mughals—administrators, who to such an extent adopted Hindu or Muslim Indian ways that they spoke the various languages fluently—were able to exchange views and ideas with the local rulers on a more or less equal footing and honored their own Indian wives, were deliberately undermined by the beginning of the 18th century. They were replaced by arrogant English colonial servants, who maintained a great distance from the Indian people, didn't speak any other languages than English or French, and married English or other European wives. In this way colonial rule became racialized and multicultural relations were frowned upon (William Dalrymple, *White Mughals: Love and Betrayal in Eighteenth-Century India* (New Delhi: Penguin, 2002). The book is a well-researched account of the life of a high-class Indian lady. In fact, Penguin lists it under its "history" series. See also Mrinalini Sinha, *Colonial Masculinity*.

18. See, for instance, Thérèse Hoven, "Vrouwen Lief en Leed onder de Tropen" (Utrecht, Holland: Utrecht, 1892). See, also, Pamela Pattynama "Secrets and Danger: Interracial Sexuality in Louis Couperus's *The Hidden Force* and Dutch Colonial Literature around 1900" in *Domesticating the Empire: Race, Gender and Family Life in French and Dutch Colonialism,* Julia Clancy-Smith and Frances Gouda, eds. (Charlottesville: University Press of Virginia, 1998); and Frances Gouda, "Good Mothers, Medeas and Jezebels: Feminine Imagery in Colonial and Anticolonial Rhetoric in the Dutch East Indies, 1900–1942" in Clancy-Smith and Gouda, *Domesticating the Empire.* The famous Indonesian writer Pramoedya Ananta Toer created the formidable Nyai Ontosoroh, who lost the fight for the rights of her daughter to the son of her partner's white wife. She is the female protagonist in his novel *This Earth of Mankind.*

19. Gouda, *Dutch Culture Overseas*; Stoler, *Race and the Education of Desire*; For India, see, Burton, *Burden of History.*

20. Peter Carey and Vincent Houben, "Spirited Srikandhis and Sly Sumbadras: The Social, Political and Economic Role of Women and the Central Javanese Courts in the 18th and early 19th Centuries," in *Indonesian Women in Focus*, Elsbeth Locher-Scholten and Anke Niehof, eds. (Dordrecht: Foris, 1987).

21. Nancy Florida, "Sex Wars, Writing Gender Relations in Nineteenth-Century Java," in *Fantasizing the Feminine in Indonesia*, Laurie J. Sears ed. (Durham: Duke University Press, 1996).

22. Gouda, *Dutch Culture Overseas*; Elsbeth Locher-Scholten, *Women and the Colonial State: Essays on Gender and Modernity in the Netherlands Indies 1900–1942* (Amsterdam: Amsterdam University Press, 2000); and Sylvia Tiwon,

"Models and Maniacs: Articulating the Female in Indonesia," in Sears, ed., *Fantasizing the Feminine*.

23. Raden Adjeng Kartini, who died in childbirth in 1904, wrote a series of brilliant letters to Dutch feminist friends in which she critiqued colonial policy as well as Javanese court culture, polygyny, and patriarchal religion. The new order is the period from 1966 to 1998 in which President Suharto ruled. Kartini's letters were published posthumously and received wide international attention. A selection was translated into English in 1920 (as *Letters of a Javanese Princess*). See Joost Coté, *On Feminism and Nationalism: Kartini's Letters to Stella Zeehandelaar 1899–1903* (Clayton, Australia: Monash University Press, 1995) and Wieringa, *Sexual Politics* for a discussion of the reception of her letters. See also Tiwon, "Models and Maniacs."

24. For instance, painting Sumbadra, one of Arjuna's wives, as a whimpering coward, ignoring her ascetic and spiritual powers, or the neglect of powerful mythical goddesses such as Durga and the warrior wife of Arjuna, Srikandhi (see Carey and Houben, *Spirited Srikandhis*; Tiwon, "Models and Maniacs"). Arjuna is one of the Korawa from the Hindu epic of the Mahabharata. It would also be interesting to trace the various versions of the awesome mythical figure of Ken Dhedes, with her fire-spewing vagina, but there is hardly any literature available on her in a Western language. Along with her second husband, Ken Arok (who murdered her first husband), Dhedes is the founder of the East Javanese Hindu realm of Singosari.

25. See, for instance, Evelyn Blackwood, "Gender Transgression in Colonial and Post-Colonial Indonesia," *Journal of Asian Studies* 64:4 (2005): 849–79.

26. Tom Boellstorff, *The Gay Archipelago: Sexuality and Nation in Indonesia* (Princeton: Princeton University Press, 2004); see, also, Gouda *Dutch Culture Overseas*.

27. Wieringa, "Communism and Women's Same-Sex Practices."

28. *Jakarta Post*, 2 November 2005.

29. The perpetrators of these and similar crimes in Indonesia, such as those in Ambon, are hardly ever captured. It is whispered that powerful factions in the armed forces are involved alongside jihadist Muslim groups, such as the Jema'ah Islamiyah. Only after the 2002 bombings in Bali, when it could be denied no longer that hard-line Muslim groups were also active in Indonesia, have some perpetrators been brought to trial.

30. Saskia E. Wieringa, "Gender, Tradition, Sexual Diversity and AIDS in Postcolonial Southern Africa: Some Suggestions for Research," in *Challenges for Anthropology in the "African Renaissance,"* Debie LeBeau and Robert J. Gordon, eds. (Windhoek: University of Namibia Press, 2002); Morgan and Wieringa, *Tommy Boys, Lesbian Men*. See, also, Marc Epprecht, *Hungochani: The History of a Dissident Sexuality in Southern Africa* (Montreal: McGill-Queen's University Press, 2004).

31. Evelyn Blackwood, *Gender Transgression*; Tom Boelstorff, *Gay Archipelago*; Saskia E. Wieringa, "Globalisation and Shifts in Sexual Cultures in Asia: Are the Discourses Adequate?" Paper presented at ESSH Conference, Amsterdam, March 2006.

32. See Wieringa, *"Globalisation,"* and Saskia E. Wieringa, "Silence, Sex and the System: Women's Same-Sex Practices in Japan" in *Women's Sexualities and Masculinities in a Globalizing Asia,* Saskia E. Wieringa, Evelyn Blackwood, and Abha Bhaiya, eds. (New York: Palgrave/MacMillan, 2007).

33. Wieringa, "Silence, Sex and the System."

34. Timon Screech, *Sex and the Floating World: Erotic Images in Japan, 1700– 1820* (Honolulu: University of Hawai'i Press,1999).

35. Screech, *Sex and the Floating World,* 288.

36. Marc Epprecht, in *Hungochani,* imputes the decline of such homoerotic practices initially to the migration of Bantu-speaking groups into the region, who, though their sedentary economy, were more concerned with fertility and heterosexuality than the preceding San, who were a society of gatherers and hunters. The picture is on page xv.

37. Kurt Falk, "Homosexuality among the Natives of Southwest Africa," in *Boy-Wives and Female Husbands, Studies of African Homosexualities*, Stephen Murray and William Roscoe, eds. (New York: St. Martin's, 1998 (original published 1925–1926).

38. Wieringa, "Gender, Tradition, Sexual Diversity."

39. Kirby describes the *ekola* as a "ritual musical instrument of considerable antiquity," the "use of which has, in spite of the march of civilization lingered on to the present time." Parcival Kirby, "A Secret Musical Instrument: The Ekola of the Ovakunayama of Ovamboland," *South African Journal of Science* 38 (January 1942): 345–51.

40. Murray and Roscoe, eds. *Boy-Wives and Female Husbands.* Ferdinand Karsch-Haack, *Gleichgeschlächtlige Leben* (Naturvolker Munchen: Reinhardt, 1911); Elisabeth Tietmeyer, *Frauen Heiraten Frauen*; Morgan and Wieringa, *Tommy Boys.*

41. Morgan and Wieringa, *Tommy Boys.*

42. Dede Oetomo, "Gender and Sexual Orientation in Indonesia," *Fantasizing the Feminine in Indonesia,* Laurie J. Sears, ed. Durham: Duke University Press 1996); and Dede Oetomo, *Memberi Suara pada yang Bisu*/Giving a Voice to the Mute (Yogyakarta: Galang, 2001), and see, also, Boelstorff, *Gay Archipelago.*

43. See Saskia E. Wieringa, *Globalisation, Love, Intimacy and Silence in a Working-Class Butch/Fem Community in Jakarta,* Amsterdam, Amsterdam University, ASSR Working Paper, 2005. After a 2004 television appearance of the coordinator of the sexual minorities group of the Indonesian KPI (Koalisi Perempuan Indonesia, Coalition of Indonesian Women) that deals with sexual

minorities, the organization received hate mail, stating that it was "allowed according to Islam to drink their blood."

44. Blackwood, "Gender Transgression"; and Sharyn Graham, "It's Like One of Those Puzzles: Conceptualising Gender among Bugis," *Journal of Gender Studies* 13:2 (2004): 107–16.

45. The Mahabharata is one of the great Hindu epics, the other being the Ramayana, which are very popular in Indonesia. The Mahabharata tells the story of the struggle between the five Pandawa brothers and their numerous Kurawa cousins. Bhima is the strongest, Pandava, renowned for his courage. Ardjuna is the most ascetic and revered Pandava brother. He is known for his inner strength and sexual prowess.

46. Adriana Pucci, *Bhima Swarga: The Balinese Journey of the Soul.* (Boston: Bulfinch, 1992): 59.

47. See the *Jakarta Post,* March 29, 2005. The information on Madura was communicated to me personally by Nursyahbani Katjasungkana. Around the same time, however, a similar panic in Delhi arose around a series of violent rapes. Female students were advised "to replace skimpy dresses with the more modest folds of a salwar-kameez trouser suit." The motto was clear: "no thigh flesh, no cleavage and certainly no belly buttons" (*International Herald Tribune,* June 16, 2005). Men's violent behavior was thus reduced to concern over women's clothes, ignoring the fact that traditionally worn saris expose much more bare flesh than modern Western clothing.

48. Dangdut is a popular mix of traditional Indonesian music style with elements of pop and Hindu music.

49. Endriana Noerdin, Lisabona Rahman, Ratna Laelasari Y., and Sita Aripurnami, *Representasi Perempuan dalam Kebijakan Publik di Era Otonomi Daerah/* The Representation of Women in Public Policy in the Ear of Regional Autonomy (Jakarta: Women Research Institute, 2005).

50. See, for instance, Carey and Houben, *Spirited Srikandhis,* and Tiwon, "Models and Maniacs."

51. Leila Ahmed, *Women and Gender in Islam: Historical Roots of a Modern Debate* (New Haven: Yale University Press, 1992); Riffat Hassan, *Women's Rights and Islam: From the I.C.P.D. to Beijing* (Louisville:, KY NISA, 1995), and Fatima Mernissi, *Beyond the Veil: Male-Female Dynamics in a Modern Muslim Society* (New York: John Wiley and Sons 1975).

52. Ratna Batara Munti, *Demokrasi Keintiman: Seksualitas di Era Global/*The Democracy of Intimacy: Sexuality in the Global Era) (Yogyakarta, Indonesia: LKIS, 2005).

53. Wieringa, *Sexual Politics,* and Wieringa, "The Birth of the New Order State."

54. The girls were arrested and released again several times, until they were definitely detained by the end of October 1965. Around that time they were forced to undress in prison. These shots were later used to "prove" that naked

girls had seduced the generals a month earlier. Watching this propaganda film was obligatory for school children.

55. A few years ago, graves in East Java were opened by relatives of the victims. However the state has never made any attempt to locate and open the mass graves systematically. As many bodies were thrown in the rivers the exact number of those slaughtered will probably never be known.

56. See, also, Julia Clancy-Smith and Frances Gouda, eds., "Introduction," in Clancy-Smith and Gouda, *Domesticating the Empire*.

57. See Wieringa, *Sexual Politics*, and Wieringa, "The Birth of the New Order State." After the putsch, Suharto branded them as "whores," the other model available for women in the binary framework Indonesia inherited from colonial days. He portrayed himself as the defender of "good Indonesian mothers" and thus capable of restoring social stability–as that rests on domesticating women. In both cases, as wife/mother or as whore, women are portrayed in relation to a dominant male sexuality.

58. See Wieringa, *Sexual Politics*; and Julia Suryakusuma, "The State and Sexuality in New Order Indonesia," in *Fantasizing the Feminine in Indonesia*, Laurie J. Sears, ed. (Durham: Duke University Press 1996).

59. Morgan and Wieringa, *Tommy Boys*.

60. See, also, Carey and Houben, "Spirited Srikandhis"; and Tiwon, "Models and Maniacs."

61. Durga is the Hindu goddess who combines female and male powers to slay a demon that the male gods on their on could not defeat. Parvati is the consort of Shiva who is initially the sexually most active partner of the two. Ken Dhedhes is the legendary East Javanese queen of the Singosari realm. She is said to be extraordinarily attractive and sexually potent. The Jakarta Museum has a stature of her that is labeled the "Indonesian Mona Lisa."

REFERENCES

Aarmo, Margrete. "How Homosexuality Became "Un-African": The Case of Zimbabwe." In *Female Desires: Same-Sex Relations and Transgender Practices across Cultures*. Edited by Evelyn Blackwood and Saskia E. Wieringa. New York: Columbia University Press, 1999.

Ahmed, Leila, *Women and Gender in Islam: Historical Roots of a Modern Debate*. New Haven: Yale University Press, 1992.

Blackwood, Evelyn. "Gender Transgression in Colonial and Post-Colonial Indonesia," *Journal of Asian Studies* 64:4 (2005): 849–79.

Blackwood, Evelyn and Saskia. E. Wieringa, eds. *Female Desires: Same-Sex Relations and Transgender Practices across Cultures*. New York: Columbia University Press, 1999.

Bleys, Rudi. *The Geography of Desire: Male-to-Male Sexual Behavior outside the West and the Ethnographic Imagination 1750–1918*. New York: NYU Press, 1995.

Boellstorff, Tom. *The Gay Archipelago: Sexuality and Nation in Indonesia* (Princeton: Princeton University Press, 2004).

Burton, Antoinette. *Burden of History: British Feminists, Indian Women and Imperial Culture, 1865–1915* (Chapel Hill: University of North Carolina Press, 1994).

Carey, Peter and Vincent Houben, "Spirited Srikandhis and Sly Sumbadras: The Social, Political and Economic Role of Women and the Central Javanese Courts in the 18th and early 19th Centuries." In *Indonesian Women in Focus*. Edited by Elsbeth Locher-Scholten and Anke Niehof. Dordrecht: Foris, 1987.

Clancy-Smith, Julia and Frances Gouda, eds. "Introduction." In *Domesticating the Empire; Race, Gender and Family Life in French and Dutch Colonialism*. Edited by Julia Clancy-Smith and Frances Gouda. Charlottesville: University Press of Virginia, 1998.

Cornwell, Gareth. "George Webb Hardy's *The Black Peril* and the Social Meaning of "Black Peril" in Early Twentieth-Century South Africa." *Journal of Southern African Studies* 22:3 (1996): 441–53.

Coté, Joost. *On Feminism and Nationalism: Kartini's Letters to Stella Zeehandelaar 1899–1903*. Clayton, Australia: Monash University, 1995.

Dalrymple, William. *White Mughals: Love and Betrayal in Eighteenth-Century India*. New Delhi: Penguin, 2002.

De Vries, Johannes Lukas. *Mission and Colonialism in Namibia*. Johannesburg: Raven, 1978.

Dunton, Chris and Mai Palmberg. "Human Rights and Homosexuality in Southern Africa." *Current African Issues* 19 (1996): 48.

Epprecht, Marc. *Hungochani: The History of a Dissident Sexuality in Southern Africa*. Montreal: McGill-Queen's University Press, 2004.

Falk, Kurt. "Homosexuality among the Natives of Southwest Africa." In *Boy-Wives and Female Husbands, Studies of African Homosexualities*. Edited by Stephen Murray and William Roscoe. New York: St. Martin's, 1998 (originally published 1925–1926).

Florida, Nancy. "Sex Wars, Writing Gender Relations in Nineteenth-Century Java." In *Fantasizing the Feminine in Indonesia*. Edited by Laurie J. Sears. Durham: Duke University Press, 1996.

Foucault, Michel. *History of Sexuality, Volume 1: An Introduction*. New York: Pantheon, 1978.

Gouda Frances. "Good Mothers, Medeas and Jezebels: Feminine Imagery in Colonial and Anticolonial Rhetoric in the Dutch East Indies, 1900–1942." In *Domesticating the Empire: Race, Gender and Family Life in French and Dutch Colonialism*. Edited by Julia Clancy-Smith and Frances Gouda. Charlottesville: University Press of Virginia, 1998.

————. *Dutch Culture Overseas: Colonial Practice in the Netherlands Indies 1900–1942*. Amsterdam: Amsterdam University Press, 1995.

Graham, Sharyn. "It's Like One of Those Puzzles: Conceptualising Gender among Bugis." *Journal of Gender Studies* 13:2 (2004): 107–16.

Hassan, Riffat. *Women's Rights and Islam: From the I.C.P.D. to Beijing* Louisville, KY: NISA, 1995.

Hyam, Ronald. *Empire and Sexuality: The British Experience.* Manchester: Manchester University Press, 1991.

Jeater, Diana. *Marriage, Perversion and Power: The Construction of Moral Discourse in Southern Rhodesia 894–1930*. Oxford: Clarendon, 1993.

Karsch-Haack, Ferdinand. *Das Gleichgeschlechtliche Leben der Naturvölker*. München: Reinhardt, 1911. Reprint, New York: Arno, 1975.

Kirby, Parcival R. "A Secret Musical Instrument: The Ekola of the Ovakunayama of Ovamboland." *South African Journal of Science* 38 (1942): 345–51.

Locher-Scholten, Elsbeth. *Women and the Colonial State: Essays on Gender and Modernity in the Netherlands Indies 1900–1942*. Amsterdam: Amsterdam University Press, 2000.

Mernissi, Fatima. *Beyond the Veil: Male-Female Dynamics in a Modern Muslim Society.* New York: John Wiley, 1975.

Morgan, Ruth and Saskia E. Wieringa. *Tommy Boys, Lesbian Men and Ancestral Wives.* Johannesburg: Jacana, 2005.

Munti, Ratna Batara. *Demokrasi Keintiman: Seksualitas di Era Global/*The Democracy of Intimacy: Sexuality in the Global Era. Yogyakarta, Indonesia: LKIS, 2005.

Murray, Stephen O. and William Roscoe, eds. *Boy-Wives and Female Husbands: Studies of African Homosexualities.* New York: St. Martin's, 1998.

Noerdin, Endriana, Lisabona Rahman, Ratna Laelasari, and Sita Aripurnami. *Representasi Perempuan dalam Kebijakan Publik di Era Otonomi Daerah/*The Representation of Women in Public Policy in the Era of Regional Autonomy. Jakarta: Women Research Institute, 2005.

O'Donnell, Krista. "Poisonous Women: Sexual Danger, Illicit Violence and Domestic Work in German Southern Africa, 1904–1915." *Journal of Women's History* 11:3 (1999): 31–54.

Oetomo, Dede. "Gender and Sexual Orientation in Indonesia." In *Fantasizing the Feminine in Indonesia.* Edited by Laurie J. Sears. Durham: Duke University Press, 1996.

————. *Memberi Suara pada yang Bisu/*Giving a Voice to the Mute. Yogyakarta, Indonesia: Galang, 2001.

Pape, John. "Black and White: The Perils of Sex in Colonial Zimbabwe." *Journal of Southern African Studies* 16:4 (1990): 699–720.

Pattynama, Pamela. "Secrets and Danger: Interracial Sexuality in Louis Couperus's *The Hidden Force* and Dutch Colonial Literature around 1900." In

Domesticating the Empire: Race, Gender and Family Life in French and Dutch Colonialism. Edited by Julia Clancy-Smith and Frances Gouda. Charlottesville: University Press of Virginia, 1998.

Pucci, Adriana. *Bhima Swarga: The Balinese Journey of the Soul.* Boston: Bulfinch, 1992.

Screech, Timon. *Sex and the Floating World: Erotic Images in Japan 1700–1820.* Honolulu: University of Hawai'i Press, 1999.

Sinha, Mrinalini. *Colonial Masculinity: The "Manly Englishman" and the "Effeminate Bengali" in the Late Nineteenth Century.* Manchester: Manchester University Press, 1995.

Stoler, Ann. *Race and the Education of Desire: Foucault's History of Sexuality and the Colonial Order of Things.* Durham: Duke University Press, 1995.

Suryakusuma, Julia. "The State and Sexuality in New Order Indonesia." In *Fantasizing the Feminine in Indonesia.* Edited by Laurie J. Sears. Durham: Duke University Press, 1996.

Taylor, Jean Gelman. "Women as Mediators in VOC Batavia." In *Women and Mediation in Indonesia.* Edited by Sita van Bemmelen, Madelon Djajadiningrat-Nieuwenhuis, Elsbeth Locher-Scholten, and Elly- Touwen-Bouwsma. Leiden: KITLV, 1992.

Tietmeyer, Elisabeth. *Frauen Heiraten Frauen: Studien zur Gynaegamie in Afrika/ Women Marrying Women: Studies on Gynaegamie in Africa.* Höhenschäftlarn: Renner, 1985.

Tiwon, Sylvia. "Models and Maniacs: Articulating the Female in Indonesia." In *Fantasizing the Feminine in Indonesia.* Edited by Laurie J. Sears ed. Durham: Duke University Press, 1996.

Toer, Pramodedya Ananta. *This Earth of Mankind.* New York: Penguin, 1996.

Weeks, Jeffrey. *Sex, Politics and Society: The Regulation of Sexuality since 1800.* London: Longman, 1981.

Wieringa, Saskia E. "Communism and Women's Same-Sex Practices in Post-Suharto Indonesia." *Culture, Health and Sexuality* 2:4 (2000): 441–57.

———. *Sexual Politics in Indonesia.* Houndmills, England: Palgrave Macmillan, 2000.

———. "Gender, Tradition, Sexual Diversity and AIDS in Postcolonial Southern Africa: Some Suggestions for Research." In *Challenges for Anthropology in the "African Renaissance."* Edited by Debie LeBeau and Robert J. Gordon eds. Windhoek: University of Namibia Press, 2002.

———. "The Birth of the New Order State in Indonesia." *Journal of Women's History* 15:1 (2003): 70–92.

———. *Globalisation, Love, Intimacy and Silence in a Working-Class Butch/Fem Community in Jakarta.* Amsterdam: Amsterdam University, ASSR Working Paper, 2005.

————. "Women Marriages and Other Same-Sex Practices: Historical Reflections on African Women's Same-Sex Relations." In *Tommy Boys, Lesbian Men and Ancestral Wives.* Edited by Ruth Morgan and Saskia E. Wieringa. Johannesburg: Jacana, 2005.

————. "Globalisation and Shifts in Sexual Cultures in Asia: Are the Discourses Adequate?" Paper presented at ESSH Conference, Amsterdam, March 2006.

————. "Silence, Sex and the System, Women's Same-Sex Practices in Japan." In *Women's Sexualities and Masculinities in a Globalizing Asia.* Edited by Saskia E. Wieringa, Evelyn Blackwood, and Abha Bhaiya. New York: Palgrave Mac-Millan, 2007.

7

Transient Feelings

Sex Panics and the Politics of Emotions[1]

Janice M. Irvine

Throughout the 1990s, during my field research into conflicts over sexuality education, I was initially riveted by what I found—public discussions that flared into furious arguments. Neighbors hurled epithets such as "fascist" and "McCarthyite" at each other, while school board meetings went from sleepy affairs to late-night shouting matches involving hundreds of residents. Adrenaline buzzed throughout public meetings, all of us alert to the next outburst. School board members told me about receiving death threats, being spit on, and having tires slashed. After explosive meetings they received police escorts to their cars. One prominent sex education foe collapsed from an anxiety attack during his speech at an especially rancorous meeting, while those of us left waiting in the school auditorium worried in hushed whispers that he had died of a heart attack. Sex education conflicts escalated rapidly through the 1990s and spread to nearby cities as though contagious. Sensational media coverage heightened these public battles, while officials scrambled for solutions. These were the feelings of community controversies, local dramas played out in the shadow of national politics.

To paraphrase the British sociologist Stanley Cohen, societies appear to be subject, every now and then, to periods of sex panic.[2] A derivative of Cohen's concept "moral panic," the term "sex panic" was coined in 1984 by the anthropologist Carole Vance to explain volatile battles over sexuality.[3] Both moral panic and sex panic have been used by activists and the media and have been adopted and revised by sociologists, historians, and cultural studies scholars. Prominent researchers, among them

Estelle Freedman, Gayle Rubin, Jeffrey Weeks, and Lisa Duggan, deployed the panic metaphor—moral panic, sex-crime panic, AIDS panic, or sex panic—to explore political conflict, sexual regulation, and public volatility about sex.[4]

A vivid analytic term, moral panic bespeaks the mobilization of intense affect in the service of moral politics. Cohen's moral panic, which described the 1960s reaction to rioting by youth groups (the mods and the rockers) in the vacation town of Brighton, featured angry crowds milling at British seacoast towns and hyperbolic media coverage. Likewise, sex panic aptly captured the hostile political climate during late-twentieth-century controversies over gay rights, censorship, and sex education.

Sex panics are significant because they are "the political moment of sex," which Jeffrey Weeks and Gayle Rubin both describe as the transmogrification of moral values into political action.[5] I extend their important claim by suggesting that public emotion is a powerful catalyst in effecting this political moment. In this article, I suggest that we can enhance the analytic power of the moral/sex panic framework by integrating social theories of emotion. As I discuss below, the sex panic literature tends to focus on structural elements, in particular the expansion of state power through institutional mechanisms of regulation. Public feeling, although acknowledged in passing by most sex panic scholars, is often represented as anarchic, moblike, and hysterical, all descriptions that recall late-nineteenth-century critiques of the irrational crowd. Lack of attention to public sentiment in the sex panic literature is likely intended to minimize its importance, in contrast to moral conservatives who exaggerate the significance of collective outrage to legitimate social control. As Cohen noted in the recent thirtieth-anniversary edition of *Folk Devils and Moral Panics*, political progressives tend to use the term moral panic to expose collective volatility as "tendentious."[6] Unfortunately, however, this strategy places the panic of a sex panic outside social and political reach. I am suggesting that we broaden our analysis of sex panics to include their deep emotional dimensions, including how emotions braid through and legitimize structures of domination.

Overt emotion is not only increasingly acceptable but seemingly required in contemporary politics, where it conveys righteous solidarity and demands state intervention. Contemporary Western societies consider feelings the core of the self; they are constructed as a site of truth and ethics. Hence feelings, as Michel Foucault has argued, are "the main field of morality," and indeed of the moral panic.[7] In contrast to scholars who view the emotions of sex panics as irrational, moral conservatives cast them as authentic moral outrage. Because of its cultural authority, public emotion can pressure politicians, police, media, and other regulatory agents to respond to fierce community battles. As a result, laws and policies that restrict sexual rights may be hastily enacted yet exert a pernicious influence for decades. Moreover, the legitimating power of emotions naturalizes sexual hierarchies, establishing some sexualities as normal and others as disgusting or unspeakable. Affective conventions of sexuality—in particular, sexual shame, stigma, fear, disgust—enforce and reinforce this regulatory system and are therefore political. In its wake, the panic of moral panics legitimizes enhanced state power through fostering the illusion of a singular public mobilized in support of traditional values.

Rather than see the public feelings of sex panics as either irrational or as deeply authentic outrage, my analysis resolutely sticks to the surface. Indeed, it problematizes a popular notion of authenticity that casts feelings as expressive of a core, moral self. It does not take the psychoanalytic path to the unconscious, nor does it deny its possible influence. I posit emotion as deeply social, constructed from the outside in. Likewise, this article explores the public feelings of sex panics as produced through dynamic flows of encounters and interactions, scripts, and political spaces. I argue for the political significance of emotions and emotional publics, and suggest theoretical possibilities for analyzing what I call the transient feelings of moral panics and sex panics.

This concept is informed by Ian Hacking's "transient mental illness," his term for a historically and culturally specific malady that "appears at a time, in a place, and later fades away."[8] In his case study of fugue and other disorders in the late nineteenth century, Hacking argues that it is unproductive to debate whether such illnesses are real. Rather, these illnesses occupy an ecological niche created by specific historical circumstances. They are incomprehensible outside their niche.

Whether individual, collective, cultural, or structural, sex panic feelings are transient because they are the product of a specific context; in its absence, they recede. Like Hacking's transient mental illnesses, moral panics emerge in a particular space and time. The seemingly irrational and contagious expression of emotion during these panics is instead social and discursive. That is, transient feelings can be usefully understood as dramaturgically produced and performed in local settings.

It is no coincidence that a metaphor of illness should resonate with the study of moral panics. Disease tropes have long abounded in accounts of moral panic: contagion, epidemics of fear, mass hysteria, fevered atmosphere. Moreover, both moral panics and the syndromes Hacking calls transient mental illnesses are outbreaks of a sort, subject to debates about whether they are real or constructed, valid, or disproportional. Hacking historicizes his disorders, showing how they emerge and thrive in specific structural and cultural contexts. The transience is not a characteristic of the afflicted individual but expresses the historical evanescence of these maladies. However, the analytic significance of transient mental illnesses and what I am calling transient feelings is not that they come and go. It is that their comings and goings must be explained, lest they be naturalized as a form of universal irrationality (or morality).

The concept of transient feelings encourages the mapping of specific features of the historical moment, institutional agents and practices, cultural and discursive strategies, media representations, dynamics of specific political movements and their activists as a way to understand the eruption of feeling at public events along with the complex processes by which individual citizens embody or refuse this feeling. As I explore how emotional demands and public feelings are produced and suppressed by these myriad historical and situational factors, I use transient feelings as a concept with which to analyze the crucial nodes of connection among the state, political interest groups, social movements, media representations, and individual citizens who themselves constitute multiple, intersecting emotional publics.

I make the following arguments about moral/sex panic, as both political event and analytic term. First, moral/sex panic concepts are stronger when they attend to how emotion weaves through structural, cultural, and political processes, as well as to how public settings produce collective feelings. Second, collective activity is an important level of analysis in sex panics, although an emphasis on structural factors has obscured its significance. Moreover, this collectivity more closely resembles a public, or more accurately multiple publics, than the anomic crowd. The sex panic public, miscast as singular, is often internally fractured. Third, public feelings matter in politics. These public emotions are neither eruptions of irrationality, as they are depicted in some academic research, nor authentic expressions of moral outrage, as depicted by religious conservatives and the media.

Local moral/sex panics are paradoxical events, unpredictable outbreaks that are highly scripted. Seemingly timeless, they both rupture and reinforce ordinary political life. They are discrete, episodic uprisings within a generalized climate of social regulation.[9] The moral/sex panic framework must be agile enough to embrace and explore these paradoxes of continuity and change, spontaneity and performativity.

Elsewhere I have written about the volatile emotions of sex education panics. Since the late 1960s, Americans have fought bitterly over sex education. In my book *Talk about Sex*, I demonstrated a national dimension to these local panics.[10] Starting in the 1960s, leaders of the early Christian right wing recognized that sexuality could be exploited to agitate citizens, recruit constituents, raise money, and ultimately consolidate political power. They captured the terms of debate about sex education through emotionally powerful rhetoric used nationally and also locally at school board sessions and town meetings. Rather than epiphenomenal, intense emotional reactions were strategically produced through a discourse of sexual danger and depravity that shaped how citizens throughout the United States spoke and felt about sex education. Thus local confusion about sex education programs morphed into sex panics. In what follows, I use examples from these conflicts to speculate about the transient feelings of moral/sex panics. Intended as a series of theoretical reflections on moral/sex panics, this article is written in the spirit of ongoing conversation about public feelings in politics.

These conversations are occurring—somewhat separately—in both sociology and cultural studies, two fields that have been cotravelers in the past.[11] Indeed, the moral panic concept—as developed in Stuart Hall's *Policing the Crisis* and Cohen's *Folk Devils and Moral Panics*—has early roots in the unruly inter- and extradisciplinary mix at the Department of Cultural Studies and Sociology (the Birmingham School).[12] Since then, social scientists, historians, and cultural studies scholars in both the United Kingdom and the United States have deployed the moral panic concept across disciplines, although with somewhat different emphases. Unfortunately, the scholarship on emotions enjoys less cross-disciplinary vibrancy. Sociologists and cultural studies theorists often explore the affective dimension of political culture with little productive engagement.[13] This article acknowledges but does not pretend, or aspire, to bridge this gap. Instead of conducting exhaustive literature reviews of moral panic theory, sex panics, or sociological and cultural studies work on emotions, I use some of the representative literature in these areas to imagine new possibilities for research on the role of emotions in politics.

In its substantive reflections, this article focuses on sex panics. I use the term sex panic as a form of moral panic to designate sites of public

conflict over sexuality and sexual morality. I use this term when referring to my own research or specifically to controversies related to sexuality. However, my theoretical suggestions about public feelings apply to the
concept of moral panics in general and its uses in controversies such as
those over drug use, youth violence, or satanic rituals. When I am making
an analytic or theoretical point, I sometimes use the terms "moral panic"
and "sex panic" interchangeably or fuse them into "moral/sex panic."

Panics: Moral and Sex

In Cohen's enduring book *Folk Devils and Moral Panics,* the moral panic
has a natural history. In the first stage, a group, person, or issue emerges
as a social threat. The media frame this "threat" in a simplistic and
stereotypical way, fueling intense public concern. In the second stage,
moral crusaders devise coping mechanisms and solutions. Moral panics
are significant in their potential to enhance state power by triggering
repressive changes in law or social policy. In the third stage, the perceived threat diminishes, and the panic recedes. Conflicts over sexuality
have followed this condensed cycle of putative threat, collective outrage,
demonization, and state repression, and so the moral panic begat the
sex panic.

The "panic," as Cohen stresses, is social reaction operating as social
control and is therefore ideological and political. Conflicts over pornography, public funding of art with sexual themes, gay rights, sexuality in
media, and sexuality and AIDS education lend themselves to a moral/sex
panic framework, because of the volatility of sexual politics.[14] As I review
below, the concept has enabled researchers to make powerful analytic
moves in three areas: sexual demonization; institutional mechanisms of
sexual regulation and social control; and the residual of repressive laws
and policies.

Informed by the reconceptualization of deviance in U.S. sociology in
the 1960s, moral panic foregrounds how moral crusaders turn a controversial issue or marginal cohort into a "folk devil." The concept locates the
origins of deviance in the proliferation of social rules rather than in the
inherent characteristics either of certain behaviors or of individuals who
engage in those behaviors. Deviance, in other words, is socially produced.
The panic framework is highly productive for analyzing sexual politics,
where the folk devil metaphor is so resonant. In addition, the panic

framework has been applied to the scapegoating of sexual minorities such as lesbians and gay men, as well as alleged sex offenders.[15]

Moral panic highlights the relationship between the "deviant" act and the reactions of institutions and agents of social control. Sex panic scholars have focused on state sexual regulation, exploring interconnections among courts, law enforcement agents and agencies, and legislators. For example, the historian David Johnson argues that a "moral panic within mainstream American culture" in the 1950s justified a vast expansion of the U.S. security state.[16] Johnson examines how congressional hearings, presidential executive orders, and state security bureaucracy operated during this panic. In her study of antiobscenity moral panics in the first half of the twentieth century, the historian Andrea Friedman explores the roles of government officials, religious organizations, censorship boards, and interest groups such as the Woman's Christian Temperance Union.[17] The journalist Neil Miller exposes how the institution of psychiatry and its mental hospitals reinforced the harsh punitive measures of the state against gay men swept up in sex-crime panics of the 1950s.[18]

Media representation is the institutional unit of analysis for many moral panic theorists.[19] Likewise, many sex panic studies examine how the media operate to establish legitimacy for state control. Miller, for example, shows how newspaper editorials, letters to the editor, and editorial cartoons all helped produce a volatile climate for the enactment of sexual psychopath laws. Newspapers, he notes, "tried to stir up as much public feeling as possible" in their sensational coverage of child murders. One cartoon depicted a rat walking away from an overflowing garbage can with the caption: "A Bad Smell—In Sioux City . . . the Morals Problem."[20] The hyperbolic media coverage that both reflects and produces sex panics has been a theme in many other studies.[21]

Finally, moral/sex panics may leave repressive measures of sweeping scope. The historian James Morone writes that even "passing panics" lead to enhanced state powers in the form of new legislation, reinterpretations of the Constitution, and the establishment of public regulatory agencies.[22] The sexual psychopath laws, obscenity crackdowns, and restrictions on public AIDS and sexuality information are compelling examples of this. Additionally, in separate studies, Duggan and Vance have mapped the restrictive measures enacted by conservatives in the wake of sex panics sparked, paradoxically, by feminists. Duggan shows how antipornography feminists fostered and reinforced a climate supportive of conservative initiatives to eliminate public funding of erotic art and ban information on childhood sexuality.[23] In her discussion of sex panic at the Barnard sexuality conference, Vance not only describes the sexual scapegoating of conference speakers by antiporn feminist protesters, but also shows how the university administration mobilized to increase surveillance of the women's center and seized and attempted to censor the conference diary.[24] In addition to provoking punitive measures, sex panics can generate enough fear to exert a widespread chilling effect on art, academic scholarship, political activism, and journalism.

Although sex panic literature has accomplished significant theoretical and historical work with a structural analysis that exposes moral actors along with their regulatory activities, two crucial aspects of sex panics have yet to be studied: the specific role of the public and the nature of collective emotion. Most sex panic scholars suggest that volatile public reaction prompts state response in debates over pornography or sex offenders. These studies describe "public opinion," "public pressure," "public outrage," "public clamor," and "public anger."[25] However, it is unclear who this public is and what exactly it is up to in exerting pressure or producing a clamor. The public's feelings are often similarly glossed. As I discuss later, one close reading of emotional politics and a climate of sexual shame appears in Vance's work on the Attorney General's Commission on Pornography, which operated in the 1980s.[26] Largely, however, the emotional dynamics of sex panics appear only through hyperbolic metaphors (even panic itself!). Although some scholars mention public meetings or letters to the editor, we read about "moral fever," "fevered atmosphere," and "cultural fears" without much specific discussion of the heightened emotional climate. Despite thoroughgoing feminist critiques of the nineteenth-century medical use of the term *hysteria*, it remains a popular metaphor for the collective emotion of sex panics, as in "national hysteria" and "public hysteria."[27] We find "completely unhinged hysterics" engaged in "irrational panic and hate-filled attack."[28]

Inattention to the emotions of sex panics has several possible sources. As I discussed earlier, downplaying public feelings seemingly offsets the moral and cultural authority that conservatives give to them. In addition, emotions have only fairly recently garnered academic attention. And, given the tendency toward insularity in academic subfields, moral/sex panic studies have not drawn on the contemporary social movements and cultural studies literatures on politics and emotions. Moreover, the false binaries of cognition versus feeling and macro versus micro politics plague the study of politics. Many scholars relegate emotions to the realm of individual or social psychology, ignoring the structural, cultural, and political realms of feelings. Public feelings—clamor, outrage, hysteria— occupy a seemingly inconsequential status compared with enduring regulatory structures.

While this theoretical inattention might seem to diminish the significance of public reaction in a sex panic, it has some unfortunate analytic consequences. For one, the broad terms "public anger" or "public outrage" give the erroneous impression of a public united in moral fury or possessed by a wave of outrage that is largely uncontested.[29] In the earliest edition of *Folk Devils and Moral Panics*, Cohen noted that there was, in fact, heterogeneity to public responses in the moral panic at Brighton.[30] Indeed, there is often fierce contestation in moral politics. Cohen called for future research to emphasize the plurality of public positions, interests, and values, but one finds scant mention in sex panic literature of internal conflict and resistance, thus making a fractured public appear unified. Failure to theorize the public feelings of sex panics makes "the hysterical public" seem not only unified but also anonymous and inscrutable. Its feelings are allegedly irrational and easily manipulated, residing outside social influence. This renders public feeling itself seemingly impervious to social analysis. As I discuss later, this approach harks back to early social theories that cast overt collective emotion as evidence of a crowd or herd mind-set.

Public Feelings and Feeling Publics

Sex panics are locally situated in arenas of discursive interaction and debate, such as school board meetings, legislative hearings, and town-hall events—the hypothetical public sphere of rational discourse. In my own research on local sex panics over sexuality education, I found that they were provoked by only a very small minority of citizens.[31] These religious conservatives—with their own sophisticated discursive infrastructure— can be considered a subaltern counterpublic, substantiating Nancy Fraser's suggestion that subaltern counterpublics may well be "antidemocratic and antiegalitarian."[32] Moreover, religious conservatives' success in sex education battles underscores how public emotion can make a fractured public appear unified and a weak public appear dominant. Conservative religious activists on the national level came to dominate the public conversation on sex education through discursive strategies that triggered the fierce emotions of local political debates.

This article also argues that the rational public sphere is, indeed, also emotional. Sex panics belie an easy distinction between a rational, deliberative public and an irrationally emotional crowd. Further, they challenge the rational/emotional binary itself. If, as the cultural theorist Michael Warner suggests, the public in modern society involves us in "speaking, writing, and thinking," the public is also an emotional field; affect suffuses these various forms of civic engagement.[33] Discursive strategies designed to evoke intense public affect through provocative and stigmatizing sexual rhetoric have played an important role in igniting community battles. Individuals engage in emotional deliberation in emotional settings, having been drawn into civic debate through emotional scripts.

While both popular media and academic accounts may mistake intense emotion as the spontaneous outrage of a singular dominant public, the alleged spontaneous outrage of panics is similarly misrepresented as a singular affect. Yet like the "phobia" of homophobia, the "panic" of moral panic and sex panic is metaphoric. References to hysterical mobs and stampedes in the sex panic literature are likely intended merely to conjure a climate of public volatility. Our research might productively disaggregate the many highly condensed emotions that constitute particular sex panics.

What, then, are the emotions of a sex panic? Broadly, the diverse emotions of a sex panic draw their affective power from historically specific conventions in the broader emotional culture of sex. Sex, for Western cultures, is a paradoxical domain of desire and dread, excitement and fear. It is taboo yet considered the core essence of the modern self, simultaneously repulsive and attractive, disgusting and vital to our happiness. This is an affectively dense mix, escalating through social interaction and varying contextually in any given sex panic.

The term "sex panic," of course, highlights aversive feelings such as fear, anxiety, anger, hatred, and disgust. Indeed, these emotions may inhere in what the sociologist James Jasper calls the "moral shock," a powerful impetus for social activism and, we might infer, moral/sex panics.[34] The galvanizing outrage of a moral shock occurs either from a sudden incident or from news perceived as threatening. For example, sex education panics commonly erupt when one or two parents begin to describe a program with inflammatory terms such as "sodomy curriculum." Although fear and anger are highly mobilizing emotions, in order for protest to arise from moral shock, there must be a target of blame. Demonization of an enemy is crucial in moral protests such as sex panics, in part because this strategy triggers strong feelings of hatred that may temporarily bind together activists in opposition to a folk devil who is cast as a legitimate and deserving target.

Disgust is another powerful emotion in moral politics. It evokes sensory images so deeply unpleasant that, as the cultural theorist William Miller says, "no other emotion, not even hatred, paints its object so unflatteringly."[35] In sex panics related to issues such as AIDS education, sexual disgust can be particularly powerful for mobilizing parents. Antigay materials have been used to link gay sexuality to fetishes such as boot licking and sadomasochism in order to conjure public disgust.

Meanwhile, a palpable frisson of pleasure may accompany the moral politics of sex panics. This emotional energy may be the dynamic Foucault had in mind when he referred to "the pleasure of the pleasure of surveillance."[36] Emotions not only attract individuals to moral conflicts such as sex panics, they may perpetuate them through what the sociologist Jeff Goodwin and colleagues call "the pleasures of protest."[37] These pleasures might involve enhanced sociality; they can also include the enhanced energy of passionate emotional arousal.[38] Moral sentiment, however, often promotes a sense of righteousness that easily turns to rage.[39] We would do well to explore the degree to which a thrill of collective rage and scapegoating underpins particular sex panics.

Who panics in a sex panic? As I showed above, regulatory institutions mobilize against sexual folk devils, inflamed by sensationalist media representation. However, the sex panic climate does not simply exist institutionally or discursively, most notably in media space. It also depends on public dynamics. Sex panics thrive in the energy generated by embodied emotional battle in public settings. Fighting and shouting erupts at public meetings, derailing community debate. Emotional conflicts may escalate rapidly and spread to nearby cities as though contagious.

Media coverage heightens such public arguments, prompting regulatory efforts by politicians and other officials. It is this public volatility to which sex panic scholars refer with metaphors such as "outraged stampede" and "rabid mob." For more than a century, social scientists have examined the political significance of crowds versus publics; their emotionality or rationality; and the role of discourse in constructing a public. This early social theory anticipates these concerns about collective fervor that are evoked in the sex panic literature.

In a necessarily brief discussion of this extensive body of work, I focus on the varied ways that earlier theorists used to explain collective feelings and the rapid escalation of emotional intensity and display, and then draw on cultural sociology and cultural studies to argue that the seemingly irrational expression of feeling during sex panics is deeply social. In a sex panic, emotional publics temporarily engage in moral politics. Collective emotion, evoked discursively, can bring publics into being, organizing diffuse, sometimes inchoate beliefs and moralities into political action.

Crowds and Publics

Early European social theorists viewed overt emotion as evidence of a crowd or herd mind-set. They condemned the crowd as a powerful, potentially disruptive, and easily manipulated unit. Writing in the late nineteenth century, the French social psychologist Gustave Le Bon lamented that the masses were reshaping society, displacing old power structures that had favored the divine right of kings. Le Bon argued that crowds form a collective mind resembling "inferior forms of evolution" such as women, savages, and children.[40] This crowd mind, he suggested, is irrational, prone to sentiment and hallucination. Antidemocratic theorists such as Le Bon saw the putative irrationality of the milling masses as a threat to social order and elite dominance. He advocated social control measures to govern the masses, whose alleged suggestibility rendered them unfit to govern themselves.

Sociological theorists of collective behavior challenged this antidemocratic view of crowds. In perhaps the earliest of this work, Robert Ezra Park (who launched the collective behavior field) argued in his doctoral dissertation that the crowd (as well as the public) served to "bring individuals out of old ties and into new ones."[41] Crowds, Park noted appreciatively, could be a vehicle for social change, dealing the deathblow to existing institutions and introducing a new social or political spirit.

Despite the significance of emotions in early- to mid-twentieth-century social psychology, most writers simply assumed the spontaneous irrationality of mass sentiment. Le Bon compared the emotionally reactive crowd to leaves swirled and scattered by tempests, a dynamic that the social psychologist Wilfred Trotter later likened to the "herd instinct."[42] Many theorists used the metaphor of contagion to describe how the emotion of each individual pervaded the entire group.

Emotional contagion in crowds, for theorists like Le Bon and Trotter, was a primitive, instinctual process. In contrast, sociologists eventually brought the notion of emotional contagion into a social framework. Park viewed emotions as extremely contagious, especially in gatherings like political meetings, yet he understood collective emotions as socially interactive. Emotional contagion, for Park, occurred when everyone's attention was collectively focused. Suggestibility—that herdlike quality derided by other critics—was, he argued, a form of "collective attention."[43] While Park's student Herbert Blumer viewed contagion as a common mood that rapidly intensifies and can "spread like wildfire," eventually contagion theory fell from favor as too mechanistic.[44]

Although many early social theorists disagreed on the particulars, they distinguished between the emotionally irrational crowd and the discursively engaged, rational public. Early-twentieth-century social theorists such as the French scholar Gabriel de Tarde viewed "the public" as the new social form of modernity brought into being by an expanding mass media.[45] Unlike the physical crowds of the older marketplaces, the modern public was dispersed and fragmented, brought together through the shared experience of newspaper reading. The public, for Park, was a "universe of discourse," a notion that reached its apotheosis in the theater of rational discourse known as the bourgeois public sphere.[46]

In contrast to the deliberative style of political engagement idealized in the concept of the public sphere, crowds were seen as anomic. Their individuals lacked an enduring social tie that would seemingly protect them from being swept up into emotional fervor. It was visceral emotion rather than deliberative reason that characterized a crowd, discrediting the crowd as irrational. Implicit in this distinction between a crowd and a public, of course, is the problematic assumption that emotion itself is irrational, constituted outside social influence, and devoid of power to forge bonds among crowd members.

Still, even some early theorists worried that the boundary between the emotional crowd and the rational public is clearly porous. The same burgeoning media that, however partially and imperfectly, brought a public into being could also create news events to cultivate mass emotion and manipulate public opinion. The social psychologist Edward Ross, for example, saw the press as effecting mass suggestion among a public that no longer had to be physically present as a crowd in order to "share the same rage, alarm, enthusiasm, or horror."[47] Mass media of the twentieth century, in Ross's view, thus constituted a "space-annihilating" apparatus, a conclusion shared by the political theorist Graham Wallas, who dubbed this development "organized thought."[48]

As I suggest later, discourse has the power to bring into being publics produced through what might instead be called organized feeling. The term "transient feelings," however, more accurately captures this powerful but fleeting coalescence of emotion. Hostilities temporarily bind citizens together in explosive public events whose fury is captured in, and further cultivated by, media coverage. These hostilities are not the instinctual and irrational reflexes of the milling crowd, as imagined by earlier theorists, nor are they the rabid mobs described by contemporary scholars. These are emotional publics, produced through specific historical and social conditions, engaged in moral politics.

The "Panic" of Moral Panic

The *panic* had a long lineage by the time Cohen adopted the term. Blumer had referred to panics as a form of primitive grouping, like the stampede and the riot, while the sociologist Neil Smelser defined panic as collective flight based on "hysterical beliefs."[49] Panics represented extreme, disorganized fear and flight, such as that seen on the battlefield, in burning buildings, or during natural disasters.

Cohen's moral panic was a different conceptual animal; it afforded the panic logic and cyclic structure, while the term itself acknowledged the affective component of these episodic dramas. Cohen himself shifted perspective on the nature of the actual "panic," variously describing it as concern, outrage, or "a splutter of rage."[50] The first edition of *Folk Devils and Moral Panics* in 1972, in which Cohen compared the moral panic with mass reaction to, for example, natural disasters, drew criticism that the moral panic was yet another version of the irrational crowd or herd mentality.[51] In the thirtieth-anniversary edition of his book, Cohen wrote that he had once downgraded the panic to "mere metaphor" after criticism of his use of the term.[52] He later insisted on the usefulness of "panic" as an idiom for a particular emotional outburst—the "microphysics of outrage" (xxxi). His moral panic was a step away from the herd of early-twentieth-century social theorists and toward situating collective emotional expression in a social and political context.

Still, discussions of moral panic have lacked a theory of the emotional dimension that *panic* so viscerally evokes. In this sense, the term was a product of its historical moment, the "rational turn" in 1970s social sciences. Inspired by radical protests of the 1960s, social theorists of the 1970s de-emotionalized theories of collective action. They stressed the strategic rationality of activists to counter classical notions of the irrationally emotional actor[53] The cognitive practices of the allegedly rational actor moved to the foreground of psychology, political science, and sociology.

The current renaissance in the study of emotion across the disciplines now allows us to view moral/sex panics not as reflexes of the milling crowd but as social and political practices that produce public feelings. Although a complete review of this literature exceeds the scope of the present article, I briefly mention scholarship on the politics of emotions in sociological theories of social movements and in humanities research, particularly history and cultural studies.

In the introduction to their influential collection on emotions and social movements, *Passionate Politics*, the sociologists Jeff Goodwin, James Jasper, and Francesca Polletta observe that in these last several decades of backlash against earlier notions of the irrational crowd, "emotions have led a shadow existence" in the study of politics.[54] Recently, however, sociologists have drawn from symbolic interactionism, social constructionism, and the cultural sociology of emotions to examine myriad connections among social movements, politics, and public feelings.

For example, social movement theorists, particularly feminists, have demonstrated how feelings such as love and anger play a significant part in both the strategic actions and internal dynamics of movements.[55] In his call for a more comprehensive examination of feelings in protest movements, Jasper has shown how social movement concepts such as identity and frames have significant emotional dimensions.[56] A proliferation of edited volumes, case studies, and special journal issues have articulated new theoretical perspectives and added to our empirical evidence of the operations of emotions in politics.[57]

Research on emotion and politics burgeons in the humanities as well. Informed by social constructionist theory that posits emotion as variable across eras and cultures, historians are exploring how dynamics of emotional expression vary during specific periods. For example, in *American Cool*, Peter Stearns argues that emotional conventions in this country have evolved from a late-nineteenth century valorization of emotional intensity into a contemporary ethos of emotional restraint (my own research belies this view). Meanwhile, literary theorists examine emotions in cultural politics as, for example, in Eve Kosofsky Sedgwick's rich explorations of shame, and Lauren Berlant's analysis of rhetorics of affective persuasion in the intimate public sphere.[58] (Berlant is also a cofounder of Feel Tank

Chicago, a group of activists, academics, and artists in creative and critical engagement with the public feelings of the U.S. political sphere.) Linda Kintz shows how the Right creates "resonance" for its politics among a diverse public through the skillful use of intimate emotions, and Ann Cvetkovich explores how affective experience shapes public culture.[59] The cultural theorist Sara Ahmed takes up many of the subjects in this article from the perspective of philosophy and cultural studies, while poststructuralist analysis has suggested how emotions could be deployed in the governance of the self, a notion with clear significance for moral/sex panics.[60] This work is significant for its attention to the affective dimension of political culture.

Social theory on emotions has advanced significantly since Le Bon wrote that the feelings of an individual in a crowd "are atavistic residuum of the instincts of the primitive man."[61] However, early theorists' convictions that collective feelings were irrational, residing outside the social, have had lingering influence, including in the moral/sex panic literatures. What follows draws on diverse social and cultural theories to propose alternative strategies for examining emotions, politics, and moral/sex panics. Unbraiding the twists of emotion in specific sex panics helps us ground transient feelings in local social contexts and recognize them as products of specific political strategies. We can explore how public feelings are evoked, in what ways they are expressed, whether and how resistance emerges in a competing public, how collective emotions fade, and under what circumstances they might backfire against those who seek to provoke them.

Dramaturgical Production of Transient Feelings

If it can be pleasurable to engage in moral panics, it can also be pleasurable to study them. I was, for several contented years, "the sociologist as voyeur"—a term Laud Humphreys coined in his enduring book *Tearoom Trade* to convey the passionate pleasures of social research.[62] Yet one morning when I picked up the newspaper and saw that yet another nasty conflict over sex education was raging in a city to the north of me, I paused before packing the car. I couldn't bear the idea of visiting one more virulent school board meeting. What's this about? I wondered.

Sex panics were thrilling—all that fighting, shoving, and screaming was at least as compelling as those tabloid television shows that were proliferating at that very mid-1990s moment. And yet, oddly, I realized I was bored. Initially I had viewed the fighting and vitriol as spontaneous eruptions of community disagreement. Then I began to discern striking similarities in both the form and content of local sex panics. It was as if there was a national script, rendering every unhappy city unhappy in precisely the same way. I had anticipated, and found, an eerie uniformity in activists' accounts of their beliefs and motivations.[63] Both seasoned activists and newcomers repeated rhetoric right down to the exact same stories, sentences, and even phrases. Moreover, activists "borrowed" freely from each other, and many anti–sex education documents read like carbon copies. Often I recognized material as verbatim quotes from the documents of national Christian right-wing groups. At times, reading the local documents from widely diverse communities was like grading papers from a course in which every student had plagiarized from the same text, right down to the typos and bad grammar. I had been less alert to the affective dynamics of communities in conflict, with citizens expressing the same feelings in precisely the same ways. I began to feel as if I were in my very own Groundhog Day of field research, each emotional conflict seemingly repeating the one before it.

Part of the cultural power of sex panics is that they are read as unmediated public expressions of the attitudes and feelings of individual Americans in response to controversial issues. But if, as I am arguing, sex panics are not simply indigenous uprisings, how can we interpret disagreements among citizens that become hostile, even violent, sex panics? There are different analytic approaches to the emotional intensity of moral/sex panics. As I discussed earlier, many sex panic researchers simply avoid the problem of collective volatility, presuming it to be irrational outrage. Others view emotions as perhaps the deepest, most natural expression of our core selves. "The public is outraged!" Headlines of this sort demand regulatory action.

The sociologists Erich Goode and Nachman Ben-Yehuda suggest that we can empirically measure the proportionality or disproportionality of public anxiety.[64] Collective uprisings can be considered moral panics, they argue, only when public fears far exceed the putative actual harm posed by the condition or group. Social scientists, they argue, could empirically evaluate the (dis)proportionality of public feelings by measuring the degree of threat posed by erstwhile folk devils in any collective outburst.[65] Such evidence, supposedly, could reveal whether intense public feelings are justifiable. This approach has many problems. In addition to the ahistorical reification of emotion, it lands us in the quagmire of debating the reality or unreality of public feeling.

Rather than ignore public feelings, study them as static entities subject to empirical verification, or afford them the moral power of collective outrage, I suggest that they are transient social practices that are dramaturgically produced in a specific historical context. In this section, I foreground the transient feelings of sex panics as they appear in such local contexts as town meetings, school board sessions, legislative hearings, and public protests. I suggest that emotional actors in local sex panics are not acting irrationally, outside the social. Nor are they merely expressing authentic outrage. I have shown elsewhere that these debates are often scripted; virtually identical dialogue is often employed not only in different communities but across decades.[66] The emotional arc of sex panics can be similarly routinized, as outrage, anger, and disgust are dramatized in public arenas.

As a sociological paradigm, dramaturgy explores the creation of meaning, emphasizing the situational context rather than the causes of individual and social behavior.[67] Dramaturgy posits social life as a series of performances, deploying metaphors of the theater—settings, cast, audience, staging, masks—to explain human action. Erving Goffman, who is considered the "godfather of dramaturgy" within sociology, concentrated on surfaces, appearances, and impressions rather than a fundamental, core self.[68] The self, he argued, is a performed character, "a dramatic effect arising diffusely from a scene that is presented."[69] Dramaturgy underscores that the self and identity are not stable and autonomous but inherently social, accomplished through interactive performance rather than preceding it.

By extension, I suggest that emotions are similarly dramaturgical. Although intense feelings appear seemingly "contagious" in mass settings, they are best viewed as scripted and situationally produced rather than instinctively aroused, authentic sentiments.[70] This perspective on emotions as social does not mean they are not "real." The dichotomy between real and scripted is a false one in its implication that there is emotion/thought/behavior that is original and outside culture. As I show below, a dramaturgical approach to the transient feelings of politics underscores the importance of space, discursive scripts, situational events, and social actors engaged in strategic performances.

The Scripts of Sex Panics

As early social theorists recognized, discourse brings a public into being. Sex panics can be understood as an emotional public brought into being by the feeling rules and expression norms of particular sexual discourses. Coined by the sociologist Arlie Hochschild, the term "feeling rules" denotes social guidelines for how individuals will produce and manage affect.[71] Like feeling rules, which govern the content of daily emotional life, expression or display norms govern emotional behavior.[72] These norms cue us to the appropriate range and intensity by which to communicate (and interpret) feelings. There is, for example, a palpable difference in tone, gesture, and volume between showing irritation and expressing rage. Feeling and expression norms constitute an important way in which emotions are not outside the social. Emotion is not an unmediated response but an arena of social performance entailing systems of meanings, norms, motivation, and social reaction.

Moreover, these social norms deeply affect the individual in the ways that they shape embodied feelings. Sex panic discourses authorize and legitimate particular ways of thinking and talking about sex in public.[73] In addition, feeling rules, Hochschild notes, are the "underside of ideology."[74] Likewise, I argue that both feeling and expression rules, the norms that define emotional tone and expectations of a situation, are interwoven through the language and symbols of discourses such as those of religious conservatives. Discourse not only authorizes and legitimates particular ways of thinking and talking but ways of feeling as well. This is, as the cultural theorist Raymond Williams said, "not feeling against thought, but thought as felt and feeling as thought."[75]

Discourse, rhetoric, and language have received widespread attention in the mainstream media since the 2004 presidential election. Linguists such as George Lakoff in his influential book *Don't Think of an Elephant!* and Geoffrey Nunberg in *Talking Right* argue that Republicans have captured the terms of public debate through powerful political frames and resonant language.[76] Social movement theorists have long defined frames as interpretive schemata that code issues and events into common understandings.

However, many sociologists have argued that the framing approach is limited in several ways, including its failure to encompass a theory of power in its analysis of different framing strategies employed by conservatives as compared with liberals. Framing theory, as many linguists and social movement theorists use it, is largely cognitive; it ignores the important emotional dimension in the success or failure of frames. Finally, the framing concept is fairly static, failing to account for the instability of discourses and language.[77] As I discuss later (and as is also implicit in the term "transient feelings"), this instability applies to the emotional dimensions of frames (and scripts) as well.

I use the term "sex panic scripts" to denote affectively rich ways of talking. Intended to evoke intense emotional responses, the scripts themselves are emotional. When they are successful, scripts represent, to paraphrase Williams, speech as felt. I am not suggesting a mechanistic or deterministic process, however. Discourse is unpredictable, and the plurality of discourses in operation during any particular conflict may trigger unexpected reactions and counterreactions. The notion of sex panic scripts is meant to suggest merely one way in which social factors can create emotional publics as part of panics.

Sex panic scripts stress danger and disease. They employ provocative language and symbols, scapegoating, and depravity narratives. Their striking similarity in both form and content, even across decades, is an important indication of how national organizations can authorize specific ways of thinking and talking through their broader discourses. These national scripts are exported to the local level through printed resources, prominent speakers, and media such as evangelical television, radio, and now the Internet. In Goffmanesque fashion, scripts (along with the staging of public space) encourage the production of feelings such as outrage and fear in community debates. By the end of the century, conservative religious activists came to dominate the public conversation on sex education through discourse that triggered fierce, albeit transient, emotions. Sex panic scripts rely heavily on tales about sexual groups or issues that use distortion, hyperbole, or outright fabrication. Two prominent depravity narratives circulated in the late 1960s in sex education battles. The first story was that a sex education teacher had had intercourse in front of the class as a pedagogical strategy. The second was that male students raped a teacher after they watched a sex-ed film in class. Other tales circulated to the effect that children were being encouraged to fondle each other, sexual intercourse would be taught in kindergarten, schools would install coed bathrooms with no partitions between stalls, and youth were being told about bestiality with donkeys and sheep.

A crucial element of sex panic scripts is evocative sexual language and imagery. Conservatives use strategic vocabularies and images to outrage and thereby mobilize a diverse constituency. For example, critics of a first-grade teacher's guide in New York City that mentioned lesbian and gay families dubbed it "homosexual/lesbian propaganda" that was "teaching sodomy to first graders."

The allegation of "sodomy curriculum" conjured up images of six-year-olds learning about oral and anal sex. Some conservatives insisted on calling gay individuals "sodomites," characterized gay reform initiatives as "sex clubs" or "sodomy curricula," and described homosexuality as "sodomy," "anal sex," "deviant sex practices," "sodomythology," and "homosexology." In other sex education conflicts, opponents described curricular materials as "pornography."

Sex panic scripts operate as what Ahmed calls "sticky signs," or words that accumulate affective value.[78] Ahmed stresses that emotions do not reside within texts; rather, texts "work" emotionally through the "sticking" of signs to bodies. The language and images in sex panic scripts are cultural and historical, interacting with negative affects in the broader sexual culture. Sex panic scripts employ frank sexual language in a context intended to be emotionally evocative, in order to prompt fears of sexual transgression and perversion.

The emotions of sex education conflicts are intensified by conventions in the broader emotional culture, such as those concerning children and sexuality. Our modern ideal of an asexual, pure childhood requires shielding young people from all sexual knowledge.[79] Since the earliest calls for sex education in the public schools at the turn of the twentieth century, the phantasm of the innocent child corrupted by sexual information has provoked controversy. Embedded in the iconic image of the sexually innocent child is the emotional expectation to feel uneasy, at best, when sexual speech in any way connects to childhood. Sex education opponents hope to produce anger, fear, and disgust among parents by tapping those affective expectations inherent in our cultural narrative about violating childhood innocence. Provocative speech about sexuality is used to scare parents with threats to their children and to mobilize parents into overt emotional displays opposing comprehensive sex education. Rather than being an instinctual reaction, the public expression of anger and intolerance is cultivated in sex education debates.

Scapegoating

Moral/sex panics depend on a folk devil, an issue or minority group that is scapegoated. Hence sex panic scripts demonize sexual groups or issues through association with highly stigmatized forms of sexuality. Warner notes that despite the contemporary public visibility of sexuality, "anyone who is associated with actual sex can be spectacularly demonized."[80] Indeed, strong language in sex panics is intended to scapegoat its folk devils. While these folk devils are often members of sexual minorities, sometimes they are simply individuals who have acquired a "courtesy stigma" through employment or political involvement with sexual issues.[81]

Sex educators have been vulnerable to such stigma for decades, through scripts that depict them as sexually troubled, out of control, or perverted. In the 1960s, hate mail flooded the office of a prominent sex education advocate, calling her "Mistress of the Devil" and "Misfit Prostitute of Hell."[82] More recently, conservatives have described sex educators as "the pornographers in the public school system."[83] In the 1990s, the national right-wing activist Judith Riesman claimed that sex educators tend to be pedophiles seeking access to young people.[84]

A scapegoating script usually entails lengthy lists of sexual terms, many of which are unfamiliar or denote uncommon sexual practices. As a political strategy, sexual demonization deploys deeply unpleasant sensory images in what William Miller calls "the idiom of disgust," a powerful tool in moral politics.[85] Disgust reinforces social boundaries over which citizens are worthy and acceptable and which are not. For example, Pat Robertson, founder of the Christian Coalition, said about Planned Parenthood, "It is teaching kids to fornicate, teaching people to have adultery, teaching people to get involved in every kind of bestiality, homosexuality, lesbianism—everything that the Bible condemns."[86] These are the sorts of terms, or "sticky signs," that Ahmed suggests operate in an economy of disgust, sticking to certain bodies such that they become disgusting.[87]

Opponents of gay rights link gay sexuality to historically stigmatized sexual activities. Antigay videos, such as *The Gay Agenda* (released by a group called "The Report" in 1992), associated gay sexuality with eating and smearing feces, drinking and bathing in urine, and other fetishes. High-profile religious conservatives made heavy use of a sexual scapegoating script in response to landmark gay rights rulings. After the Supreme Court nullified sodomy laws in *Lawrence v. Texas* (2003), Justice Antonin Scalia warned that without such laws it would be impossible to uphold "state laws against bigamy, same-sex marriage, adult incest, prostitution, masturbation, adultery, fornication, bestiality, and obscenity."

Admonitions about bestiality proliferated after the Massachusetts Supreme Judicial Court legalized gay marriage in that state. This rhetoric prompted the *Village Voice* journalist Richard Goldstein's article about "petaphilia" and the "man-dog marriage panic."[88] Goldstein claimed that a LexisNexis search turned up over a thousand citations of this rhetoric, a clear example of the proliferation of this sex panic script.

Emotional Space

Setting matters. Against the grain of a therapeutic culture of individualism, sociology argues for the power of context and situation. The emotions of sex panics do not primarily and originally reside within the individuals who constitute a public but are brought into being by the situation. Certain settings are more densely configured than others to produce emotions through particular webs of scripts, staging, actors. (Think, for example, of a funeral home.) Space itself is emotionally saturated, and, in turn, spatial elements transmit the feeling and expression rules that fuel sex panics. A buzz can be produced through spatial features such as police presence; the visibility of reporters or other media; picketers protesting inside or outside the event; a domineering, provocative chairperson; and arguments erupting in hallways or lobbies. Some of these elements, such as warning signs posted in a meeting place, might be thought of as props, in Goffman's dramaturgical sense. In this section, I discuss the emotional geography of local sex panics such as those unfolding in public meetings and legislative hearing rooms.[89]

Situational norms for emotional expression can be transmitted formally through institutional mechanisms. In her research on the Meese Commission, Vance exposed the shrewd tactics by which antipornography officials in the Reagan Administration created an emotional climate of shame and intimidation during the commission's public hearings. Commissioners humiliated witnesses who did not hew to an antipornography ideology and frequently projected sexually charged images of stigmatized behavior in the federal courthouse chambers, thereby fostering an atmosphere of anxious arousal. These strategies, Vance noted, produced "the ritual airing and affirmation of sexual shame in a public setting."[90] Individual resistance to these institutional mechanisms of shaming can be almost impossible, since any objection to the proceedings is itself stigmatized and dismissed.

Known for her work on the power of pleasure for feminist politics, Vance correctly anticipated that the emotional atmosphere produced by right-wing "pleasures of looking" would become a political force with which to reckon.[91] In other contexts, media and word of mouth can establish permission, even expectations for, conspicuous display of feelings. These might include attempts to dominate meetings, shouting, and shoving matches. Newspaper headlines and articles emphasize feelings of rage and hatred, often framed in the language of battle: "A Fight Rages . . ."; "Battlelines Drawn . . ."; "Amid the Uproar . . ."

They not only sell newspapers but coach citizens in the emotional possibilities of town meetings: "Parents: Emotion Is Running High," "Parents Clash . . . ," "Outcry Grows. . . ." These articles spread the message that public meetings are polarized in irreconcilable hostilities. Nearby towns that have not even had conflicts often take preventive measures such as assembling a police presence. At one town meeting I attended, written warnings circled the auditorium: ALLOW SPEAKERS TO FINISH THEIR PRESENTATIONS; THIS MEETING IS NOT A DEBATE!; RAISE YOUR HAND AND STAY IN YOUR SEAT. The very presence of these structural deterrents sets an emotional tone. Telling people what is prohibited instructs them in what is possible.

Physical proximity facilitates the escalation of emotional intensity. Large numbers of people can establish the expectation of unrestrained emotional displays and demonstrations of fury. One school board president in Brooklyn said, "In the early meetings people were yelling 'Faggots out!' and stuff like that. We stopped that and tried to create a tone that didn't let any of that happen. But every once in a while people just went off the rails, and publicly—a thousand people in the audience."[92] In these large public settings, emotional acts and outbursts can seem like obligatory forms of civic engagement. He continued, "The thing I did understand is that you needed a mass to do that. The same people who were passionately and wildly furious in large group settings were different in smaller group settings." A school board member in another town concurred that people reacted very differently in mass settings. She said, "People that I trusted and had good relationships with would at least engage me in dialogue and they never came out and verbally abused me except at public meetings where everybody was yelling and you couldn't figure out what they were calling you."[93] This is not the primitive contagion described by early-twentieth-century social theorists but a manifestation of transient feelings. Because emotions are interactive, different settings establish different affective norms.

Sex panic scripts, seemingly static when out of context, come alive in public settings. When conservatives at public demonstrations called a curriculum that mentions gay families "the sodomy curriculum," they recuperated historical meanings about the perversion of homosexuality while also tapping emotional expectations of fear or anger on the part of concerned parents. Speakers can use fiery rhetoric to inspire public performances of feeling, an important element of sex panic emotion work. The spectacle of a crowd in action, leaping to its collective feet, acts as a further emotional accelerant. One parent later told me how she was galvanized by a speaker: "I see this woman up there, and she gets up and in the middle of this just flips out. I mean, the woman, I don't think she went crazy but she was slamming her fists down and—do you remember how she was? She was 'Stand up if you would die for your children!' Wow, this is heavy. You know, I just thought, do we want to teach this or don't we?"[94] Never before involved with sex education, this mother became an activist right after the forum, showing how emotion can draw us into civic and political engagement.

Sex panics depend on repetition for their power. This feature makes them not simply performances (which might or might not be unique) but performative, that is, governed by the repetition of a prior set of authorizing norms while appearing to be eruptions outside the social.[95] The performativity of sex panic emotion underscores the productive power in repeating regulatory norms. The reproduction of highly charged sexual speech by critics who wish to censor it is a familiar tactic in sex-related political contests.[96] Sex education opponents commonly read explicit sexual materials aloud at public venues. One activist from the 1960s told me how, undaunted by imposed three-minute time limits, people would line up at the microphone and simply hand off the material to the next person like a baton in a relay race.[97] In the 1990s, one community school board chair told me she privately warned a sex education opponent four times that he couldn't read explicit sections of a book at school board meetings, so he called various media and read the text over the phone. Finally, at a public meeting he read a section on sexual foreplay and oral sex.[98]

The tactic of repeating the unspeakable is intended to produce public feelings. Local sex panics depend on iterative public dramatizations deploying these scripts.[99] Sexual language and images are strategically repeated in order to trigger intense emotional displays of anger, fear, and disgust, even if an audience is skeptical. Regardless of whether the activists themselves or their audience believed these provocative scripts, they encourage citizens to express sexual fears for political purposes. This can foster the social process that earlier theorists described as "contagion." It should not be surprising that, indeed, scary rhetoric often scares, or hateful images evoke hatred through the stickiness of such signs. Alternatively, as I explain below, individuals perform the emotion work necessary to produce such feelings, however briefly. Moreover, sexually charged language and the screening of taboo images in an anomalous public setting create an atmosphere that Vance described as "excited repression," further heightening and complicating the collective mood.[100] This electricity can transmit and escalate affect in settings such as school board meetings.

I have argued that sex panics are temporal and spatial events in which intense feelings are evoked, produced, and homogenized into a seemingly unified public emotional reaction. Although they depend on situated conflict, however, they are not simply confined to physical space. Heightened media coverage that is characteristic of sex panics, and the "space-annihilating" feature of mass media, generate a broader sex panic climate. This generalized emotional combustibility, in circular fashion, may well then prompt situated conflicts such as demonstrations, informal arguments, even violence. And out of this hostile emotional climate arise police action, legislative hearings, and policy implementation.

The Affective Citizens of a Panic

Sex panics, such as those over sex education, are a form of citizenship politics. These struggles determine which sexualities will be recognized and valued, what will be spoken, and what remains excluded and silenced. Sex panics may buttress state regulatory power by implementing policy or legislation that restricts sexual rights. This has certainly been the case with comprehensive sexuality education, for which the space is shrinking in U.S. public schools.[101] Advocacy groups now argue that access to sexual knowledge is not simply an individual privilege or health concern but a fundamental element of citizenship. In 2001, for example, the National Coalition against Censorship opposed reauthorizing federal funding for abstinence-only programs, saying that they exercise government control over what students were allowed to "read, see, hear, think, and say."[102] These programs not only constrain teachers from speaking but also determine acceptable and legitimate boundaries of speech. Sex panics are public arguments about sexual citizenship.

I have shown how the affective discourse of religious conservatives can amplify local debate into a sex panic. But how, specifically, is the individual drawn into this realm of citizenship politics? How does affective discourse bring into being the affective citizens of an emotional public? I have earlier noted a tendency in the sex panic literature to view heightened emotions as hysterical or irrational. This perspective would suggest that individuals are simply manipulated or dupes of the crowd mind. Conversely, when religious conservatives insist on the moral authenticity of collective outrage, it suggests that individuals respond to sex panic scripts because of deep religious and political predispositions. Unlike either of these perspectives, a dramaturgical approach allows us to see how historically specific and situational factors can produce outbursts of public feelings.

In the theater of a local moral/sex panic, we observe one specific formation of affective citizenship. I would suggest that some citizens at explosive public events produce affect that they decide is called for by the situation. They read the feeling and expression rules, and they temporarily produce public displays of emotion. They do so partly to conform to the feeling rules in discursive scripts and partly to conform to norms of emergent expression. At times, the emotions of moral/sex panics may have a cultural logic, serving as a form of social communication among multiple publics.

Individuals may escalate public emotion as a response to the feeling rules and expression rules that both circulate in the broader culture and are implicit in political discourses. When political activists evoke feelings, they do not tap into essences that are outside discourse and culture. Rather, they engage in strategic practices that will motivate individuals to engage in what Hochschild calls "emotion work"—the effort to produce "a desired feeling which is initially absent."[103] We engage in "emotion work," or emotion management, to produce feelings suitable to the situation.

This is not merely a mechanistic process in which feelings are faked. On the contrary, Hochschild identifies two levels of emotion management. "Surface acting" is the Goffmanesque monitoring of outward appearance such as gestures and facial expression. Additionally, Hochschild argues that adults have considerable capacity to manage their emotions, and in a complex process of microaction that she calls "deep acting," individuals can evoke or suppress internal feelings in order to correspond with emotional norms and conventions. Deep acting entails actively working to produce a normatively appropriate feeling or banish an errant one. Individuals tap their knowledge about the feeling and expression rules in the broader emotional culture in order to accomplish the emotion work required in both surface and deep acting, and both entail some level of emotional embodiment.

The production and display of intense affect can serve as social communication in its own right. Emotional displays may become signifiers of identity, status, and beliefs. Moreover, individuals may engage in emotion work to communicate very different messages, reminding us that despite the power of norms, participants do not necessarily have identical experiences of the event. Whether through "surface" or "deep" acting, citizens who express fear or anger may be doing so in order to communicate political beliefs, sexual orientation, degree of religiosity, or even parental protectiveness. For example, one parent told me she began shouting at a public event in order to signal concern for her children, while an official who failed to protest publicly the inclusion of masturbation in a school curriculum told me that she had been made to "feel dirty" and neglectful as a parent.

This notion of emotion work for social communication is further evidence that the public feelings of sex panic are neither irrational nor core authentic expression. It suggests, rather, that audiences are themselves strategic actors, sometimes deploying emotional displays for their own purposes. The use of such displays for a specific presentation of self is another way in which feeling, both individual and collective, is profoundly social. This sort of emotion work bridges the personal and the political, and the public sphere of conflict and everyday citizenship.

I found surface acting to be prevalent in local sex education conflicts, during which citizens at times hewed to particular emotional norms solely for communication, regardless of whether they actually believed in the rhetoric. At one town meeting I attended, a speaker exhorted audience members to leap to their feet if they would be willing to die for their children. Virtually the entire audience immediately arose. Most were clapping, although a strong undercurrent of grumbling suggested surface acting on the part of some who were on their feet. By calling for the performance of public feeling to demonstrate parental caring, this speaker made it difficult for parents to remain seated. On these occasions, individuals, as social agents, produce and display feelings for social communication. Still, the situational pressures underscore a coercive dimension of these social and political demands to produce suitable feelings.

Indeed, Hochschild aptly notes that in emotion work, especially deep acting, we can grasp the reach of the social into the individual psyche.

In both surface and deep acting, response to social norms may produce affect. In this sense, Hochschild challenges characterizations of moral/sex panic emotion as hysterical, moblike behavior. If anything, Hochschild's concept of emotion work tends toward the cognitive, where individuals produce emotion in response to their reading of social norms.

So, what about the "vibe" of public feelings—the energy of collective affect and the physical sensations of the emotional body? In moral panics, how might we understand the corporeality of emotion, how emotional experience transforms "the embodied vehicle of conduct" and likewise permeates a broader emotional climate?[104] With some interesting intersections, scholars in both sociology and cultural studies are troubling the familiar boundaries between the biological and social, and natural and cultural, dimensions of emotion.[105] This work explores how emotion works on the body and how it seems to be transmitted among individuals in a group situation, reworking late-nineteenth-century ideas of the crowd mind and contagion.[106]

Ahmed argues that emotions like hate and disgust operate to reorganize or "re-form" both social and bodily space. The language of hate, as manifested, for example, through hate crime, transforms surfaces of bodies and their alignment with each other in physical space, as "the hated" is expelled from social proximity. Likewise, disgust operates through a relationship between bodies, or "the intercorporeality of the disgust encounter."[107] In her intriguing book *The Transmission of Affect*, the feminist theorist and humanities professor Teresa Brennan asks who has not, at least once, "walked into a room and 'felt the atmosphere'?"[108] Brennan uses the term "transmission of affect" to describe a process that is social in origin but biological and physical in effect. Socially induced affect changes our bodies and in turn is transmitted in social groups. The emotions of a person or crowd can enter the body of another, either enhancing or depressing that individual's emotional energy.

Inverting Hochschild, Brennan argues that affects evoke thoughts; individuals may become emotionally attuned, or "entrained," even though the particular meanings one attaches to those affects will vary. Much more specific than Ahmed in theorizing the mechanism of transmission, Brennan combines diverse social theories with neuroendocrinology to suggest that affective energy moves among humans through palpable chemical and electrical exchanges. In particular, she believes we "feel the atmosphere" through unconscious olfaction. Brennan applies this idea to conditions such as chronic fatigue syndrome and attention deficit disorder.

Like Brennan, the sociologist Randall Collins explores embodied emotion and its entrainment in collectivities.[109] Collins argues, following Émile Durkheim and Goffman, that when human bodies share space, the result is body synchronization and rhythmic alignment. The energy of bodies attunes to the energy of other bodies. Occasions with a high degree of emotional entrainment, along with a mutual focus of attention, constitute what he calls "interaction rituals." Although it is impossible here to capture adequately Collins's expansive concept of interaction ritual, several aspects of his research suggest further areas of inquiry concerning moral panics. He argues, for example, that interaction rituals pump up emotional energy in individuals, which becomes a gratifying experience that individuals seek to replicate. These group experiences leave them with a heightened sense of the group's moral rightness and its need to adhere to its symbols and defend them. Collins's arguments place intense emotional embodiment at the heart of moral politics and panics.

These social and cultural theories help us consider the charged vibe of moral panics—the energetic and embodied quality of the escalation and spread of public feelings. While it might seem to evoke the organicity of Le Bon's swirling leaves and Trotter's herd instinct, contagion is rather a social process and a physical experience for Brennan and Collins. The transmission and escalation of emotional energy depend on a shared focus of attention and physical proximity. (Collins argues that powerful symbols keep individuals emotionally engaged in the absence of the social group, and I would suggest the same is true of discursive scripts.) Ahmed, however, rejects the contagion or transmission model embraced by Brennan. You might enter a room and feel the atmosphere, but you may readily discover that others in fact do *not* share those feelings. Emotion is not a property passed along to others, she argues. Despite their disagreements, these theorists expand the possibilities for social and cultural research on the emotional spark of sex panic and its embodiments. Moreover, they may help us think through the ways that sex panics fade.

Denouement

In one town I visited, the emotional strategies deployed by conservative activists intent on provoking a sex panic ultimately backfired on them. Religious conservatives on the school board enacted the most restrictive public school antigay speech initiative in the nation. It banned any instructional or counseling activity that had "the effect of encouraging or supporting homosexuality as a positive lifestyle alternative."[110] Suddenly, the town was galvanized by discussion of homosexuality.

One newspaper proclaimed, "Homosexuality remained foremost on the minds of residents on Tuesday's raucous School Board meeting, the first since the board approved a landmark policy last month banning any mention of homosexuality in a positive light."[111] Visibility and support for gay issues further increased on the night of the school board vote, when protesters held the city's first-ever gay rights rally in the school's parking lot. About 150 participants stood in peaceful protest outside the school, where speakers addressed them from the back of a pickup truck adorned with American flags.[112] A local newspaper covering the rally concluded that "the angry debate over a policy that seeks to limit discussion of homosexuality will have the opposite effect, making students more interested than ever before in talking about it in school."[113] One teacher said the conservative Christian majority on the school board "took out the smoking gun, which is homosexuality, and it backfired on them because it enraged the town."[114] In the end, the anger that conservatives mobilized was directed back toward themselves.

The sociologist Philip Jenkins wondered in his book *Moral Panic*, "Why has the public been so fickle with its fear?"[115] Although his question concerns the characteristically cyclical nature of moral panics, it might just as easily speak to the unpredictability of emotional politics. Moral panics end. And when people aren't provoked by emotional scripts, conservatives risk encountering ambivalence and indifference or even fostering the circumstances for public resistance wherein provocative speech casts suspicion on the speakers rather than the targets.

The concept of transient feelings situates public emotionality in social, temporal, and spatial contexts rather than in the irrationality or false consciousness of participants, suggesting that the same shifting mix of historical and situational factors that ignite a panic—scripts, setting, normative demands—can also extinguish it or enable resistance. Shifts in the broader emotional culture of sex—such as growing public acceptance of lesbian and gay rights and culture—may exhaust certain scripts. Like crying wolf, the same repetition that escalates affect in certain settings can also deaden the metaphors, images, and symbols of provocative discourse. Or, as Judith Butler suggests, with the repetition of injurious speech may come an erosion of prior associations, allowing for the possibility of reworking and resistance.[116] It remains to be seen, for example, how long it will be strategically effective for religious conservatives to employ their "petaphilia" script. Their long lists of allegedly frightening perversions may collapse through sheer banality, failing to bring into being an emotional public. Likewise, vagaries of physical setting shape moral panic. Speakers may be flat, the attention of the group wanders, a buzz never builds. Media coverage may diminish or, through lack of sensationalism, fail to outrage. Finally, citizens may simply move on, out of fatigue or when reassured that officials have vanquished the folk devil through new repressive policies.

I have discussed the role of political discourse in sex panics. Yet political discourse is unpredictable and may, as the sociologist Marc Steinberg points out, take "a wolfish turn on the activists who rely upon it."[117] Likewise, the feeling rules bound up in discourse are similarly unruly. Ultimately, emotional appeals are no more under the control of activists than is the language of their scripts. This is not because emotions are irrational but because, like language and symbols, they are overdetermined. When the emotional demands of a political situation call for people to produce strong negative emotions, they may comply. But the target of those emotions is beyond the control of strategists.

The sociologist Josh Gamson found striking emotional fluidity in his analysis of sexual nonconformity and tabloid talk shows. When episodes featured virulently antigay, right-wing experts, the audiences turned their wrath on them and not the lesbian, gay, or bisexual guests. Such experts served as "hateful embodiments of intolerance."[118] However, in the experts' absence, the audiences direct hatred and anger toward sexual minorities. This dynamic is not unlike that of moral/sex panics; it shows that a collective emotional response is not a fixed expression of the aggregate of individual beliefs but is more situationally produced. This instability underscores that the emotions of moral/sex panics—hatred, anger, disgust—are not immutable mental states or discrete essences residing within individual bodies. Instead, hatred and fear might well be viewed as transient feelings—interactional processes and community events that are either mobilized or assuaged in specific historical and situated contexts.

The terms moral panic and sex panic ought not simply reference the volatility of certain political conflicts. If the terms are to be analytically and conceptually useful, they must be good to think with in ways other than the merely structural. Through social and cultural theories of emotion, moral/sex panic concepts can be strengthened. Without theorizing public feelings, we cannot fully understand the volatile cycle of panics, the tenacity of media coverage and its impacts, the pressures brought to bear on various institutional agents such as legislators or psychiatrists, or the putatively contradictory actions of individuals in collective situations.

I have argued that the concept of transient feelings encourages analytic questions about the production and operation of emotion under specific historical, social, and political conditions. Discursive scripts, scapegoating, and spatial features can be important elements in creating emotional publics in opposition to a putatively threatening folk devil. In these instances, discourse temporarily unites publics by transmitting scripts that guide the production of emotion. Emotion, transmitted through these affective elements of discourse, captures attention, focuses mutual engagement, and fosters a sense of intense moral righteousness.

The local moral/sex panic—with its settings, performances, scripts, and transient feelings—is a dramaturgical event with significant political impact. Sex panics and moral panics are only one form of affective politics in the early twenty-first century. For example, political fear—what the political scientist Corey Robin calls "Fear, American Style"—has been a rationale for many policies in the United States after the 9/11 attacks.[119] The Bush Administration uses color-coded "terror alerts" and emotionally provocative rhetoric to enlist individuals into affective citizenship, encouraging national performances of hatred, outrage, or fear. A view of the public as a hysterical mob, or constructions of these intense feelings as expressions of either irrationality or a core moral essence, masks political strategies and diverts attention from those who both foster and benefit from panics. The recognition that sex panics and other political emotions reside within social and discursive realms affords us considerably more space for social theory than a perspective that locates public feelings outside the social. Mapping transient feelings in space and time reveals the "panic" as contestation among emotional publics. We may see resistance, reversals, and backlashes by citizens both locally and nationally, suggesting that while moral regulation through panics is formidable, it is not inevitable or irrevocable. As such, sex panics are potentially open spaces for progressive political intervention.

NOTES

I am grateful for the comments from three readers of an early draft of this article: Barbara Cruikshank, Regina Kunzel, and Francesca Polletta. Discussions at several public presentations helped me clarify these ideas. My thanks to Advocates for Youth in Washington, DC; the Gender and Women's Studies Program at the University of Illinois; Judith Halberstam for hosting a talk at the Center for Feminist Research at the University of Southern California; and Judith Levine and Ann Snitow for inviting me to present at the Third Thursday series in New York City. This article has been vastly improved by suggestions from four anonymous GLQ reviewers. Finally, Sarah Babb continues to inspire with her methodological strategies for research on emotions and politics!

1. This essay was previously published as Janice Irvine, "Transient Feelings: Sex Panics and the Politics of Emotions," in *GLQ: A Journal of Lesiban and Gay Studies* 14:1 (2008): 1–40. Copyright 2008, Duke University Press. All rights reserved. Used by permission of publisher.

2. Stanley Cohen, *Folk Devils and Moral Panics: The Creation of the Mods and Rockers* (London: MacGibbon and Kee, 1972). The well-known first sentence reads, "Societies appear to be subject, every now and then, to periods of moral panic."

3. Carole S. Vance, ed., *Pleasure and Danger: Exploring Female Sexuality* (Boston: Routledge and Kegan Paul, 1984), 434.

4. See Estelle Freedman, "'Uncontrolled Desires': The Response to the Sexual Psychopath, 1920–1960," *Journal of American History* 74 (1987): 83–106; Gayle Rubin, "Thinking Sex: Notes for a Radical Theory of the Politics of Sexuality," in Vance, *Pleasure and Danger*; Jeffrey Weeks, *Sexuality and Its Discontents: Meanings, Myths, and Modern Sexualities* (London: Routledge and Kegan Paul, 1985); Lisa Duggan and Nan D. Hunter, *Sex Wars: Sexual Dissent and Political Culture* (New York: Routledge, 1995).

5. Jeffrey Weeks, *Sex, Politics, and Society: The Regulation of Sexuality since 1800* (London: Longman, 1981), 297; Rubin, "Thinking Sex," 14–15.

6. Stanley Cohen, *Folk Devils and Moral Panics: The Creation of the Mods and Rockers*, 3rd ed. (London: Routledge, 2002), xxxi.

7. Michel Foucault, "On the Genealogy of Ethics," in *Michel Foucault, beyond Structuralism and Hermeneutics*, Hubert L. Dreyfus and Paul Rabinow, eds. (Chicago: University of Chicago Press, 1983), 238.

8. Ian Hacking, *Mad Travelers: Reflections on the Reality of Transient Mental Illnesses* (Cambridge: Harvard University Press, 1998), 1.

9. Stuart M. Hall, *Policing the Crisis: Mugging, the State, and Law and Order* (London: Macmillan, 1978). Hall approached moral panics as discrete but interconnected eruptions in which the media operate to secure consensus and establish legitimacy for punitive state control. Simon Watney rejected the moral panic concept, however, arguing that it is unable to account for the generalized climate of sexual policing that comprises the "overhead narrative" of each distinct controversy about AIDS. Moreover, he argued that media representation is an

ongoing rather than episodic location of ideological struggle and suggested that "we do not in fact witness the unfolding of discontinuous and discrete 'moral panics,' but rather the mobility of ideological confrontation across the entire field of public representations, and in particular those handling and evaluating the meanings of the human body, where rival and incompatible forces and values are involved in a ceaseless struggle to define supposedly universal 'human' truths." See Simon Watney, *Policing Desire: Pornography, AIDS, and the Media* (Minneapolis: University of Minnesota Press, 1987), 41–42.

10. Janice M. Irvine, *Talk about Sex: The Battles over Sex Education in the United States* (Berkeley: University of California Press, 2002).

11. Sociology and cultural studies were likely more comingled in the United Kingdom than in the United States. While sociology is far too capacious a discipline for making generalizations, I would venture that some contemporary points of difference among certain scholars in sociology and cultural studies might concern methodologies, the nature and quality of evidence, and the bases for making claims about the social world. Still, there are many points of overlap between cultural sociologists and cultural studies scholars. For example, there are many sociologists, myself included, who resonate with the cultural theorist Judith Halberstam's notion of a scavenger methodology that refuses strict disciplinary confines. Halbertram, *Female Masculinities* (Durham: Duke University Press, 1998), 13.

12. I largely discuss moral panic and sex panic work done by historians and social scientists. For key examples of a cultural studies approach, see Angela McRobbie and Sarah L. Thornton, "Rethinking 'Moral Panic' for Multi-Mediated Social Worlds," *British Journal of Sociology* 46 (1995): 559–74; Arnold Hunt, "'Moral Panic' and Moral Language in the Media," *British Journal of Sociology* 48 (1997): 629–47 (note the UK sociology–cultural studies crossover in terms of publication venue); and Joanna Zylinsak, "Ethics and 'Moral Panics,'" in *The Ethics of Cultural Studies* (London: Continuum, 2005), 41–61.

13. Sara Ahmed's book *The Cultural Politics of Emotion* (New York: Routledge, 2004) is an exception. Ahmed references the work of sociologists such as Émile Durkheim, Arlie Hochschild, and Jack Katz, along with anthropologists such as Catherine Lutz and Lila Abu-Lughod. Still, her book resides largely in cultural studies. Conversely, the present article draws on cultural studies while residing mainly in sociological theory.

14. Andrea Friedman, *Prurient Interests: Gender, Democracy, and Obscenity in New York City, 1909–1945* (New York: Columbia University Press, 2000); Weeks, *Sexuality and Its Discontents*; Rubin, "Thinking Sex"; Duggan and Hunter, *Sex Wars*; Janice M. Irvine, "Emotional Scripts of Sex Panics," *Sexuality Research and Social Policy: Journal of NSRC* 3 (2006): 82–94.

15. David K. Johnson, *The Lavender Scare: The Cold War Persecution of Gays and Lesbians in the Federal Government* (Chicago: University of Chicago Press, 2004); Neil Miller, *Sex-Crime Panic: A Journey to the Paranoid Heart of the 1950s*

(Los Angeles: Alyson Publications, 2002); Freedman, "Uncontrolled Desires"; Philip Jenkins, *Moral Panic: Changing Concepts of the Child Molester in Modern America* (New Haven: Yale University Press, 1998).

16. Johnson, *Lavender Scare*, 9.

17. Friedman, *Prurient Interests*.

18. Miller, *Sex-Crime Panic*.

19. Stuart M. Hall, *Policing the Crisis: Mugging, the State, and Law and Order* (London: Macmillan, 1978); McRobbie and Thornton, "Rethinking 'Moral Panic'"; Hunt, "'Moral Panic' and Moral Language in the Media."

20. Miller, *Sex-Crime Panic*, 85.

21. Freedman, "Uncontrolled Desires"; Weeks, *Sexuality and Its Discontents*; Jenkins, *Moral Panic*; Irvine, "Emotional Scripts of Sex Panics."

22. James A. Morone, *Hellfire Nation: The Politics of Sin in American History* (New Haven: Yale University Press, 2003), 11.

23. Lisa Duggan, "Censorship in the Name of Feminism" and "Sex Panics," in Duggan and Hunter, *Sex Wars*, 30–42, 74–78.

24. Vance, *Pleasure and Danger*. Also, *Diary of a Conference on Sexuality* (New York: Barnard College Women's Center, 1982), 431–39.

25. See the following sources for the quotations in this sentence: Friedman, *Prurient Interests*, 32; Miller, *Sex-Crime Panic*, 191; Duggan and Hunter, *Sex Wars*, 78; Miller, *Sex-Crime Panic*, 87; Jenkins, *Moral Panic*, 185.

26. Vance does not use the sex panic framework in this discussion, but it remains an influential analysis of emotional strategies in volatile political conflicts. See Carole S. Vance, "Negotiating Sex and Gender in the Attorney General's Commission on Pornography," in *Uncertain Terms: Negotiating Gender in American Culture*, ed. Faye Ginsburg and Anna Lowenhaupt Tsing (Boston: Beacon, 1990), 118–34.

27. One notable exception is Elaine Showalter, who writes about "hysterical epidemics," of which her examples include chronic fatigue syndrome and Gulf war syndrome, and "hysterical movements," of which her examples include witch hunts and the recovered memory movement. Showalter sees hysterical epidemics and movements as universal and transhistorical. Contrary to my own argument, she largely situates hysteria as a psychological process through which "human beings convert feelings into symptoms when we are unable to speak," and she concludes that "if we can begin to understand, accept, pity, and forgive ourselves for the psychological dynamics of hysteria, perhaps we can begin to work together to break the crucible and avoid the coming hysterical plague." See Elaine Showalter, *Hystories: Hysterical Epidemics and Modern Media* (New York: Columbia University Press, 1997), 207.

28. See the following sources for the quotations in this paragraph: Rubin, "Thinking Sex," 297; Eric Rofes, "The Emerging Sex Panic Targeting Gay Men" (speech given at the Creating Change Conference, National Gay and Lesbian

Task Force, San Diego, November 16, 1997); Morone, *Hellfire Nation*, 3; Jenkins, *Moral Panic*, 62; Freedman, "Uncontrolled Desires," 206; Jenkins, *Moral Panic*, 62.

29. Erich Goode and Nachman Ben-Yehuda argue that although there may be disagreement, a moral panic is marked by consensus about folk devils. They note that "while there is often—usually—disagreement concerning definitions of a condition as a threat, a substantial segment of the public must see threat in that condition for the concern to qualify as a moral panic." See Erich Goode and Nachman Ben-Yehuda, *Moral Panics: The Social Construction of Deviance* (Cambridge: Blackwell, 1994), 35.

30. See Cohen, *Folk Devils*, 49–58.

31. For example, the degree of consensus that citizens publicly report about their attitudes toward sex education is striking, even in embattled communities. Public opinion polls since the sixties have consistently shown widespread support for sex education. A 2000 poll sponsored by the Kaiser Family Foundation indicated that by a large majority, parents want their children to have *more* classroom hours of sex education that covers "sensitive topics" than such programs currently do.

32. Nancy Fraser, "Rethinking the Public Sphere: A Contribution to the Critique of Actually Existing Democracy," in *The Phantom Public Sphere*, ed. Bruce Robbins (Minneapolis: University of Minnesota Press, 1993), 15. For discussion of counterpublics, see Michael Warner, *Publics and Counterpublics* (New York: Zone Books, 2002).

33. Michael Warner, "Publics and Counterpublics," *Public Culture* 14 (2002): 52.

34. James M. Jasper, "The Emotions of Protest: Affective and Reactive Emotions in and around Social Movements," *Sociological Forum* 13 (1998): 397–424; Jasper, *The Art of Moral Protest: Culture, Biography, and Creativity in Social Movements* (Chicago: University of Chicago Press, 1997).

35. William Ian Miller, *The Anatomy of Disgust* (Cambridge: Harvard University Press, 1997), 9.

36. Michel Foucault, "The History of Sexuality," interview with Lucette Finas, in *Power/Knowledge: Selected Interviews and Other Writings, 1972–1977*, ed. Colin Gordon (New York: Pantheon, 1980), 186.

37. Jeff Goodwin, James M. Jasper, and Francesca Polletta, *Passionate Politics: Emotions and Social Movements* (Chicago: University of Chicago Press, 2001), 20.

38. Randall Collins, *Interaction Ritual Chains* (Princeton: Princeton University Press, 2004); Teresa Brennan, *The Transmission of Affect* (Ithaca: Cornell University Press, 2004).

39. Émile Durkheim, *The Elementary Forms of the Religious Life, a Study in Religious Sociology* (London: Allen and Unwin, 1915); Collins, *Interaction Ritual Chains*.

40. Gustave Le Bon, *The Crowd: A Study of the Popular Mind* (London: Unwin, 1896), 10.

41. Robert Ezra Park, *The Crowd and the Public, and Other Essays* (Chicago: University of Chicago Press, 1972), 76.

42. Wilfred Trotter, *The Instincts of the Herd in Peace and War* (London: Unwin, 1916).

43. Park, *Crowd and the Public*, 49.

44. Herbert Blumer, "Collective Behavior," in *Principles of Sociology*, ed. A. M. Lee (New York: Barnes and Noble, 1951), 176.

45. Gabriel de Tarde, *The Laws of Imitation*, trans. Elsie Worthington Clews Parson (New York: Holt, 1903).

46. Jürgen Habermas, *The Structural Transformation of the Public Sphere: An Inquiry into a Category of Bourgeois Society* (Cambridge: MIT Press, 1989).

47. Quoted in Stuart Ewen, *PR! A Social History of Spin* (New York: Basic Books, 1996), 72.

48. Quoted in Ewen, *PR!* 72.

49. Blumer, "Collective Behavior"; Neil J. Smelser, *Theory of Collective Behavior* (New York: Free Press of Glencoe, 1963), 153.

50. Cohen, *Folk Devils*, 3rd ed., xxx.

51. Cohen does discuss crowds in *Folk Devils*, but his crowds are the milling youth and their audience. This is distinct from the social reaction, which is the "panic." Still, like most theorists of collective behavior, Cohen had harked back to Le Bon in his examination of the crowds at Brighton. In contrast to Le Bon, however, Cohen saw emotional crowd behavior as meaningful and interactive. Whereas Le Bon had compared crowd sentiment to windswept grains of sand, Cohen described the affective "air of expectancy" as "a process of communication" in which the members of a crowd send and decode social cues (*Folk Devils*, 129). "A common emotional tone develops," he argued, through a collective process of interpretation (129). This happens not through the organic reaction whereby flowers turn en masse to seek the sun, the metaphor described by Park early in the century.

52. Cohen, *Folk Devils*, xxx.

53. Mayer Zald and John McCarthy, *Dynamics of Social Movements* (Cambridge: Winthrop Publishing, 1979); Charles Tilly, *From Mobilization to Revolution* (Reading, MA: Addison-Wesley, 1978).

54. Jeff Goodwin, James Jasper, and Francesca Polletta, "Why Emotions Matter," in Goodwin, Jasper, and Polletta, *Passionate Politics*, 1.

55. V. Taylor, "Watching for Vibes: Bringing Emotions into the Study of Feminist Organizations," in *Feminist Organizations: Harvest of the New Women's Movement*, ed. Myra Marx Ferree and Patricia Yancey Martin (Philadelphia: Temple University Press, 1995), 223–33.

56. James Jasper, "The Emotions of Protest: Affective and Reactive Emotions in and around Social Movements," *Sociological Forum* 13 (1998): 397–424.

57. Helena Flam and Debra King, *Emotions and Social Movements* (London: Routledge, 2005). See also the special issue on emotions and contentious politics in *Mobilization* 7, no. 2 (2002), guest edited by Ronald Aminzade and Doug McAdam.

58. Peter N. Stearns, *American Cool: Constructing a Twentieth-Century Emotional Style* (New York: NYU Press, 1994); Eve Kosofsky Sedgwick, *Touching Feeling: Affect, Pedagogy, Performativity* (Durham: Duke University Press, 2003); Lauren G. Berlant, *The Queen of America Goes to Washington City: Essays on Sex and Citizenship* (Durham, NC: Duke University Press, 1997).

59. Linda Kintz, *Between Jesus and the Market: The Emotions That Matter in Right-Wing America* (Durham: Duke University Press, 1997); Ann Cvetkovich, *An Archive of Feelings: Trauma, Sexuality, and Lesbian Public Cultures* (Durham: Duke University Press, 2003).

60. Ahmed, *Cultural Politics of Emotion*; Deborah Lupton, *The Emotional Self: A Sociocultural Exploration* (London: SAGE, 1998).

61. Le Bon, *Crowd*, 22.

62. Laud Humphreys, *Tearoom Trade: Impersonal Sex in Public Places* (Chicago: Aldine, 1970).

63. This experience is not uncommon for field research with social movements, and Kathleen Blee has also discussed this phenomenon in relation to her work with organized racist groups in the United States (*Inside Organized Racism: Women in the Hate Movement* [Berkeley: University of California Press, 2002]). Such homogenization of discussion about sexuality education is an important indication of how national organizations can authorize particular ways of thinking and talking through discourses. Additionally, I argue that these national discourses can also evoke routinized feelings and emotional expressions in local community debates.

64. Goode and Ben-Yehuda, *Moral Panics*.

65. Their four indices of measurement are exaggerated figures, fabricated figures, comparison to other harmful conditions, and changes over time.

66. Irvine, *Talk about Sex*.

67. I use the term "dramaturgy" in this article in its sociological sense, as a form of symbolic interactionism, rather than in its theatrical meaning as a term related to writing and representation of drama. I use the terms "performance" and "performativity" in ways that draw from both sociology and queer theory, perspectives that actually overlap in significant ways. In the 1990s, feminist and queer theorists posited the performative aspects of both gender and sexuality. The concept of performativity drew on diverse intellectual influences such as philosophy, psychoanalysis, and performance studies, while as Eve Sedgwick noted, it carried "the authority of two quite different discourses, that of theater

on the one hand, of speech-act theory and deconstruction on the other." Theorists deployed the concept of performativity in myriad ways, for example, to challenge stable notions of identity, to examine how gender performativity produces (hetero)sexuality, and to interrogate the power and practices of speech acts such as coming out. While interpretive sociology of the 1960s and 1970s lacked this sophisticated theoretical power, the Meadian concept of the interactive self, along with dramaturgy and ethnomethodology, did support a body of sociological work that prefigured at least one dimension of the concept of performativity that emerged in the 1990s—it used metaphors of the theater to challenge both gender and sexual essentialism. Using the language of their time period, sociologists in the 1960s and 1970s argued that sexuality and gender were dialogic performances, dramatic roles, scripted dramas, displays, and accomplishments. Judith Butler rightly emphasizes that *performance* (a bounded act) cannot be conflated with *performativity* (a coercive and productive reiteration of norms). However, the work of sociologists such as Harold Garfinkel, Erving Goffman, and William Simon and John Gagnon much anticipates this later notion of performativity without using the term itself. See Eve Kosofsky Sedgwick, "Queer Performativity: Henry James's 'The Art of the Novel,'" *GLQ* 1 (1993): 1–16; Judith Butler, "Critically Queer," *GLQ* 1 (1993): 17–32; George H. Mead, *Mind, Self, and Society* (Chicago: University of Chicago Press, 1934); Harold Garfinkel, *Studies in Ethnomethodology* (Cambridge: Polity, 1967); Erving Goffman, *The Presentation of Self in Everyday Life* (Garden City, NY: Doubleday, 1959).

68. Dennis Brissett and Charles Edgley, eds., "The Dramaturgical Perspective," in *Life as Theatre* (New York: Aldine, 1990), 1.

69. Goffman, *Presentation of Self in Everyday Life*, 24.

70. No one comes to sex education debates devoid of prior experiences that might shape an emotional response. Nor, conversely, is the particular reaction of anyone involved in a community dialogue fixed or determined. Individual predispositions interact with contextual dynamics in a person's response to the emotional triggers that abound in local sex education debates. Predispositions might include factors such as strong political inclinations, personal experiences with sexual diversity, and openness toward sexual pluralism. Religious commitments can mediate emotional responses in important ways. Values can predispose an individual toward specific feelings, while the display of intense emotions can also be a means by which one demonstrates religious or political affiliation. Still, many people come to community debates without extreme predispositions. I am suggesting that the polarization of debates over the last decades stems from practices purposely intended to evoke passionate feelings.

71. Arlie R. Hochschild, "Emotion Work, Feeling Rules, and Social Structure," *American Journal of Sociology* 85 (1979): 551–75.

72. Peggy Thoits, "The Sociology of Emotions," *Annual Review of Sociology* 15 (1989): 317–42.

73. Irvine, *Talk about Sex*; Irvine, "Emotional Scripts of Sex Panics."

74. Hochschild, *Emotion Work, Feeling Rules, and Social Structure*, 557.

75. Raymond Williams, *Marxism and Literature* (New York: Oxford University Press, 1977), 132.

76. George Lakoff, *Don't Think of an Elephant!* (White River Junction, VT: Chelsea Green, 2004); Geoffrey Nunberg, *Talking Right: How Conservatives Turned Liberalism into a Tax-Raising, Latte-Drinking, Sushi-Eating, Volvo-Driving, New York Times–Reading, Body-Piercing, Hollywood-Loving, Left-Wing Freak Show* (New York: PublicAffairs, 2006).

77. Marc Steinberg, "Tilting the Frame: Considerations on Collective Action Framing from a Discursive Turn," *Theory and Society* 27, no. 6 (1988): 845–72.

78. Ahmed, *Cultural Politics of Emotion*, 92.

79. Rubin, *Thinking Sex*; Berlant, *Queen of America Goes to Washington City*; Anne Higonnet, *Pictures of Innocence: The History and Crisis of Ideal Childhood* (New York: Thames and Hudson, 1998).

80. Michael Warner, *The Trouble with Normal: Sex, Politics, and the Ethics of Queer Life* (New York: Free Press, 1999), 23.

81. Erving Goffman, *Stigma: Notes on the Management of Spoiled Identity* (Englewood Cliffs, NJ: Prentice-Hall, 1963), 147.

82. Gary Clabaugh, *Thunder on the Right: The Protestant Fundamentalists* (Chicago: Nelson-Hall, 1974), 43.

83. Don Feder, "What's Wrong with Sex Education Anyway?" public forum sponsored by Newton Citizens for Public Education, Newton, MA, March 31, 1993.

84. Judith Riesman, "What's Wrong with Sex Education Anyway?"

85. Miller, *Anatomy of Disgust*, 9.

86. Robert Boston, *The Most Dangerous Man in America? Pat Robertson and the Rise of the Christian Coalition* (Amherst, NY: Prometheus Books, 1996).

87. Ahmed, *Cultural Politics of Emotion*, 82–100.

88. Richard Goldstein, "Petaphilia: The Great American Man-Dog Marriage Panic," *Village Voice*, March 23, 2004.

89. For new work in this area of space and emotion, see Joyce Davidson, Liz Bondi, and Mick Smith, eds., *Emotional Geographies* (Hampshire, UK: Ashgate, 2005).

90. Vance, "Negotiating Sex and Gender," 129.

91. Vance does not use the sex panic framework in this discussion, but it remains an influential analysis of emotional strategies in volatile political conflicts. See Vance, "Negotiating Sex and Gender."

92. Local activist, interview with author, 1994.

93. Local activist, 1994.

94. Local activist, interview with author, 1993.

95. See Judith Butler, *Gender Trouble: Feminism and the Subversion of Identity* (New York: Routledge, 1990); Sedgwick, "Queer Performativity"; Butler, "Critically Queer"; Butler, *Excitable Speech: A Politics of the Performative* (New York: Routledge, 1997).

96. Marjorie Heins, *Sex, Sin, and Blasphemy: A Guide to America's Censorship Wars* (New York: New Press, 1993); Nadine Strossen, *Defending Pornography: Free Speech, Sex, and the Fight for Women's Rights* (New York: NYU Press, 2000).

97. Local activist, interview with author, 1994.

98. Local activist, interview with author, 1990.

99. As Ahmed notes, signs become more affective the more they circulate (*Cultural Politics of Emotion*, 45).

100. Vance, "Negotiating Sex and Gender," 126.

101. While in 1988 only 2 percent of teachers taught abstinence as the *sole* means of pregnancy and disease prevention, 23 percent did so in 1999. A poll of schools in September 2000 indicated a sharp increase to 30 percent among instructors who taught abstinence only and did not provide information about condoms and other contraceptives. A study of public schools revealed that among all districts in the United States, 10 percent had a comprehensive sexuality education policy, 34 percent promoted abstinence as the preferred option for teenagers but allowed for discussion of contraception, and 23 percent required the sole promotion of abstinence. The researchers concluded that of all U.S. students who attended a public school including grades six and higher, only 9 percent were in districts with a comprehensive sexuality education policy. See Tina Hoff and Liberty Greene, *Sex Education in America: A Series of National Surveys of Students, Parents, Teachers, and Principals* (Menlo Park, CA: Kaiser Family Foundation, 2000).

102. National Coalition against Censorship, "Abstinence-Only Education: A Joint Statement," NCAC, New York, Winter 2000–2001. See also Gary Simson and Erika Sussman, "Keeping the Sex in Sex Education: The First Amendment's Religion Clauses and the Sex Education Debate," *Southern California Review of Law and Women's Studies* 9 (2000): 265–97. Thanks to Joan Bertin for a discussion of these issues.

103. Hochschild, *Emotion Work, Feeling Rules, and Social Structure*, 561.

104. Jack Katz, *How Emotions Work* (Chicago: University of Chicago Press, 1999), 407.

105. Collins, *Interaction Ritual Chains*, 2004; Thomas Scheff and Suzanne Retzinger, *Emotions and Violence: Shame and Rage in Destructive Conflicts* (Lexington, MA: Lexington Books, 1991); Katz, *How Emotions Work*; Eve Kosofsky Sedgwick and Adam Frank, eds., *Shame and Its Sisters: A Silvan Tompkins Reader* (Durham: Duke University Press, 1995); Brennan, *Transmission of Affect*. Sedgwick and Frank criticize the approach to emotions in much of contemporary

cultural studies as an antiessentialism that morphs into a highly moralistic, antibiologism. They criticize a simplistic binarization of concepts such as internal/external, natural/cultural, biological/social.

106. Although not directly relevant to this article, in *Mass Hysteria: Critical Psychology and Media Studies* (London: Palgrave, 2001), Lisa Blackman and Valerie Walkderdine challenge Le Bon and early notions of the crowd mind through analysis of media coverage of events such as the mourning following the death of Diana, Princess of Wales.

107. Ahmed, *Cultural Politics of Emotion*, 85.

108. Brennan, *Transmission of Affect*, 1.

109. Collins, *Interaction Ritual Chains*.

110. Merrimack School District, "Prohibition of Alternative Lifestyle Instruction," policy 6540, August 1995, New Hampshire.

111. Jeffrey Merritt, "Opponents of Gay Policy Plead with Board to Rescind Vote," *Nashua Telegraph*, September 6, 1995.

112. See Don Botsch, "Meanwhile in the Parking Lot," *Merrimack Village Crier*, August 22, 1995; and Jeffrey Merritt, "Enforcement of Gay Policy Stirs Concern," *Nashua Telegraph*, August 16, 1995.

113. Merritt, "Enforcement."

114. Local activist, interview with author, New Hampshire, July 29, 1996.

115. Jenkins, *Moral Panic*, 216.

116. Butler, *Excitable Speech*.

117. Steinberg, *Tilting the Frame*, 17.

118. Joshua Gamson, *Freaks Talk Back: Tabloid Talk Shows and Sexual Nonconformity* (Chicago: University of Chicago Press, 1998), 126.

119. Corey Robin, *Fear: The History of a Political Idea* (New York: Oxford University Press, 2004), 316.

About the Contributors

CATHY J. COHEN is the David and Mary Winton Green Professor of Political Science at the University of Chicago and author of *The Boundaries of Blackness: AIDS and the Breakdown of Black Politics.*

DIANE DIMAURO is Assistant Professor of Clinical Sociomedical Sciences at Columbia University Mailman School of Public Health and Program Director of the MAC AIDS Fund Leadership Initiative at Columbia University and the University of California, Los Angeles. She is author of *Sexuality Research in the United States: An Assessment of the Social and Behavioral Sciences.*

GARY W. DOWSETT is Professor, Deputy Director, and VicHealth Senior Research Fellow at the Australian Research Centre in Sex, Health, and Society at LaTrobe University. He is coauthor of *Individualization and the Delivery of Welfare Services: Contestation and Complexity.*

GILBERT HERDT is Professor of Sexuality Studies and Anthropology and Director of the National Sexuality Resource Center at San Francisco State University and author of many books, including *The Sambia: Ritual, Sexuality, and Change in Papua New Guinea.*

JANICE M. IRVINE is Professor of Sociology at the University of Massachusetts and author of *Disorders of Desire: Sex and Gender in Modern American Sexology.*

CAROLE JOFFE is Professor of Sociology at the University of California, Davis, and author of *Doctors of Conscience: The Struggle to Provide Abortion before and after* Roe v. Wade.

SASKIA ELEONORA WIERINGA holds the chair of Gender and Women's Same-Sex Relations Crossculturally at the University of Amsterdam and is Director of the Amsterdam International Women's Library and Archives. She is author of *Sexual Politics in Indonesia*.

Index